ERASMUS AND LUTHER

The Battle over Free Will

Edited, with notes, by
Clarence H. Miller

Translated by
Clarence H. Miller and Peter Macardle

Introduction by James D. Tracy

Hackett Publishing Company, Inc.
Indianapolis/Cambridge

15   14   13   12   1   2   3   4   5   6   7

For further information, please address
 Hackett Publishing Company, Inc.
 P.O. Box 44937
 Indianapolis, Indiana 46244-0937

 www.hackettpublishing.com

Cover design by Listenberger & Associates
Interior design by Elizabeth L. Wilson
Composition by Innodata-Isogen, Inc.
Printed at Sheridan Books, Inc.

Library of Congress Cataloging-in-Publication Data

Erasmus and Luther : the battle over free will / edited, with notes, by Clarence
H. Miller ; translated by Clarence H. Miller and Peter Macardle ; introduction
by James D. Tracy.
         p. cm.
   Includes bibliographical references and index.
   Selections translated into English from Latin originals.
   ISBN 978-1-60384-548-9 (cloth) — ISBN 978-1-60384-547-2 (pbk.)
   1. Free will and determinism—Religious aspects—Christianity—History
of doctrines—16th century—Sources. I. Miller, Clarence H.   II. Macardle,
Peter.   III. Erasmus, Desiderius, d. 1536. Selections. English.   IV. Luther,
Martin, 1483–1546. Selections. English.
   BT809.E73 2012
   233'.7—dc23   2011042581

The paper used in this publication meets the minimum requirements of
American National Standard for Information Sciences—Permanence of Paper
for Printed Library Materials, ANSI Z39.48–1984.

CONTENTS

Preface   vii

Introduction   ix

An Outline of All Three Works   xxix

Erasmus: *A Discussion or Discourse concerning Free Will* (1524)   1

Luther: *The Enslaved Will* (1525)   32

Erasmus: *The Shield-Bearer Defending A Discussion*, Part 1 (1526)   127

Erasmus: *The Shield-Bearer Defending A Discussion*, Part 2 (1527)   217

Bibliography and Abbreviations   347

Index   351

PREFACE

We are grateful to the University of Toronto Press for permission to reprint portions of Erasmus' original 1524 treatise on free will (Διατριβή *sive collatio de libero arbitrio* [*A Discussion or Discourse concerning Free Will*], 1524), shortened here to *De libero arbitrio,* and of his reply to Luther's attack against it (*Hyperaspistes* 1 and 2 [*The Shield-Bearer Defending A Discussion*, Parts 1 and 2], 1525–1526), which appeared in volumes 76 and 77 (1999–2000) of *Collected Works of Erasmus* (abbreviated in this volume as CWE; see the list of Abbreviations in the Bibliography).

In those volumes and in our selections from them, *De libero arbitrio* was translated by Peter Macardle. Passages from *De libero arbitrio* not included among our selections but cited in the Introduction or text are cited as they appear in *Collected Works of Erasmus.*

The selections from *The Shield-Bearer* 1 and 2 were translated by Clarence H. Miller.

The selection offered here from Luther's *De servo arbitrio* (*The Enslaved Will, 1525*), his counterblast to *De libero arbitrio,* was translated by Clarence H. Miller, who also provided the commentary to all three works included in this volume. Passages from *De servo arbitrio* not included among our selections but cited in the Introduction are cited as they appear in Philip S. Watson's translation of Luther's *De servo arbitrio* (called *The Bondage of the Will;* see the Bibliography s.v. "Luther").

Erasmus' Latin has been translated from texts derived directly from the earliest editions. The Latin text from which our selection of Luther is derived is that given in the authoritative *Gesamtausgabe* (noted as WA in the Bibliography). Scriptural passages have been translated directly from the Latin texts given by Erasmus and Luther, which are generally taken from the Vulgate.

The boldface headings in our outline and in the selections by both Erasmus and Luther are editorial additions. So too, the verse numbers for biblical citations have been silently added; such numbers were not standardized or available in printed volumes in the mid-1520s, when Erasmus and Luther were writing these works. The paragraphing in this edition is also editorial.

INTRODUCTION

In the history of the European Reformation,[1] few issues were as important as the one debated by Erasmus and Luther: Are human beings capable of contributing to their own salvation by what they choose to do or not to do? Or is the unmerited grace of God the sole and sufficient reason why some sinners but not others are reckoned as righteous by God? To understand how and why Erasmus and Luther disagreed about grace and free will, one must also take into account three related issues.

1) How is Scripture to be interpreted? Erasmus and Luther were masters of the biblical languages[2] and pioneers in the new Renaissance philology.[3] Yet while Erasmus believed that the "consensus" of the Church down through the centuries was the only sure guide for understanding a sacred text whose meaning is at times ambiguous,[4] Luther insisted that for those in whom the Holy Spirit has instilled faith in Christ, the meaning of Scripture is on essential points "clear," requiring interpretation neither by the Church nor by the Fathers of the Church.

2) How is one to understand the purpose of God's revelation? Here too Erasmus represented the traditional view: Scripture was the repository of all the truths that God had deemed useful for man's instruction. By contrast, Scripture for Luther conveyed the answer to the one question that mattered: how was it possible for sinners to escape God's wrath? This way of reading the Bible reflected Luther's life story—his passage from the depths of despair to a joyful confidence in God's mercy. Erasmus grasped Luther's meaning, but not fully; that

---

1. For religious life and theological controversy, the best and most comprehensive survey is Diarmaid MacCulloch, *The Reformation* (New York, 2004). My own *Europe's Reformations, 1450–1650,* 2nd ed. (Lanham, MD, 2002) puts the religious history of the era into its political and social contexts.

2. Erasmus was a superb Greek scholar, but Luther knew Hebrew as well as Greek.

3. For Lorenzo Valla (d. 1455), the Italian humanist whose critical edition of the Latin Vulgate New Testament was particularly important in Erasmus' intellectual development, see Brian P. Copenhaver, "Valla Our Contemporary: Philosophy and Philology," *Journal of the History of Ideas* 66 (2005), 507–25.

4. James K. McConica, "Erasmus and the Grammar of Consent," in *Scrinium Erasmianum,* vol. 2, ed. J. Coppens, (Leiden, 1969), 77–99.

one man's experience should become the norm for belief was to him incomprehensible.[5]

3) To what extent has the human capacity for knowing and doing what is right been vitiated by the sin of Adam? And how ought Christians to think about those who had the light of reason but not that of faith—particularly the pagan authors (e.g., Aristotle, Virgil) whose writings had been a mainstay of Christian education for more than a thousand years? Although it was an accepted maxim that outside the Church there is no salvation, Erasmus held to a minority view: God's mercy must somehow extend to righteous men and women having no knowledge of Christ.[6] He believed that the human conscience was dimmed by Adam's fall, not wholly corrupted,[7] and in debate with Luther he kept open the possibility that "virtuous pagans" might live in such a way as to be deemed worthy of God's mercy.[8] Luther for his part had no intention of throwing pagan authors out of the schools.[9] But for him "Since we are all under sin and damnation" by Adam's sin, "how can we attempt anything that is not sinful and damnable?"[10] Any claim to virtue apart from divine grace was sheer human arrogance.

On all of these issues—exegesis, divine grace, and original sin—both sides looked for authoritative answers in the Epistles of St. Paul. But what exactly had St. Paul said? By way of showing how Erasmus and Luther came to the positions they took in debate with each other, this essay will touch briefly on the careers of both men, with special reference to how they interpreted the New Testament book that figures as the leitmotif of their confrontation: St. Paul's *Epistle to the Romans*.

5. *Hyperaspistes* 2 (CWE 77 pp. 704–5).

6. See the comments of editor Craig R. Thompson on Erasmus' "An Examination concerning the Faith," (CWE 39 pp. 444–45).

7. *Hyperaspistes* 2 (CWE 77 p. 592).

8. In an argument that Erasmus accepted, John Duns Scotus (d. 1308) distinguished between "condign merit" (*meritum de condigno,* referring to a human act intrinsically worthy of being rewarded by God) and "congruous merit" (*meritum de congruo,* referring to an act that God in his mercy might choose to reward). See *A Discussion of Free Will* (CWE 76 p. 28 n. 103). This distinction applied to virtuous pagans as well as to Christians.

9. See his "To the Councilmen of All Cities That They Establish and Maintain Christian Schools" (1524), in *Luther's Works* (hereafter abbreviated LW), vol. 45 (Philadelphia, 1962), 347–78.

10. *The Enslaved Will,* p. 107.

Erasmus: The Epistle to the Romans *as read by a student of Origen*

Erasmus claimed that he entered the monastery because, having but a slender legacy from his parents, he saw no other way to pursue his studies.[11] This account glosses over evidence for his initial contentment with monastic life,[12] but the young Erasmus certainly did have a passion for classical Latin authors. The first major work from his pen, *The Book against the Barbarians*,[13] excoriates unnamed monks who, incapable of appreciating the elegance of ancient Latin,[14] alleged religious scruples to spare themselves the trouble of reading pagan texts. Erasmus at this time had yet to study scholastic theology, but he had little good to say for exponents of Scripture who wrote in barbarous (that is, medieval) Latin, and followed the rules of Aristotle's logic. Instead, he championed not merely a revival of classical Latin, but also a new, or rather an "ancient," theology, modeled on the Fathers, who drank from the wellsprings of Latin and Greek eloquence, and could speak to the heart.

By this time Erasmus had "escaped" his cloister by joining the entourage of the prince-bishop of Cambrai. Not fond of court life either, he persuaded his patron to let him study theology at the University of Paris. Here he lived at the Collège de Montaigu, where followers of Duns Scotus represented the dominant school of thought.[15] Erasmus would later defend Scotus against Luther, but at the time he was scornful of lectures that left a "primitive theologian" like himself "with wrinkled brow and glazed eyes."[16]

On a visit to England (1499), Erasmus met John Colet (d. 1519) who encouraged his enthusiasm for St. Paul and prodded him to take up the

---

11. *Compendium Vitae Erasmi* (CWE 4 pp. 404–6, lines 40–104). At Steyn (near Gouda, in his native province of Holland), Erasmus entered a priory of the Canons Regular of St. Augustine, not to be confused with Luther's order, the Augustinian Friars.

12. Cf. his early treatise *De Contemptu Mundi,* ed. S. Dresden, ASD, vol. 1, pp. 1–87.

13. For the text and a good introduction, see CWE 23.

14. For what classical Latin meant to humanists of Erasmus' generation, see Josef Ijsewijn, "Erasmus ex Poeta Theologus," in Coppens, vol. 2, 375–89.

15. Charles Trinkaus, Introduction to CWE 76 p. lxxxii n. 169.

16. Allen 1, 192, Letter 64:74–76, (my translation).

study of Greek.[17] Upon leaving Paris to stay with patrons in Artois (1501), he met Jean Vitrier (d. 1521?), guardian of the Franciscan house in St. Omer. Vitrier induced Erasmus to use his Greek to study Origen.[18] This Christian thinker (d. 254) represented a synthesis between biblical faith and the Neoplatonic school in Alexandria, where he had been a student. Origen had idiosyncratic ideas that left him under a cloud (he was never counted among the Fathers of the Church), but he had been the greatest biblical scholar of the early Christian centuries,[19] and this was what mattered to Erasmus. Early in 1504 Erasmus reported to Colet on his progress. He had planned to "do something on St. Paul's Epistle to the Romans," but after completing "four volumes" he was "distracted" by the need to know Greek better. Meanwhile he had "gone through a good part of Origen's works; under his guidance I think I have achieved worthwhile results."[20]

With this letter Erasmus sent Colet a copy of his *Handbook of the Christian Knight (Enchiridion Militis Christiani)*,[21] a manifesto of the "ancient" theology. The *Enchiridion* attacked what Erasmus called the "superstition of ceremonies": because of a sluggish contentment in the outward observance of ritual, Christian piety languished. This was especially true for monks, whom lay people took as models. Yet "monkhood is not the same as piety." True piety meant penetrating beyond the "flesh" to the "spiritual" meaning, not just in the rites of the Church, but also in Scripture. For "it is the spirit that gives life; the flesh is useless" (John 6:64); or, as St. Paul says, "we know that the law is spiritual" (Romans 7:14). André Godin has shown in detail how Erasmus appropriated the theology and the exegesis of Origen. For example, Erasmus borrowed from Origen, and ultimately from Plato,[22] a tripartite anthropology or doctrine of human nature, according to which man's reason (*to hegemonikon*, "the ruling part") is aided by "spirit" (the noble passions) in its struggle against the base passions of the flesh. According to the *Enchiridion*, "perfect piety is the attempt to progress always from the visible . . . to invisible things." [23]

17. For Colet, see John B. Gleason, *John Colet* (Berkeley, 1989).

18. André Godin, *Érasme, lecteur d'Origène* (Geneva, 1982), 21–33.

19. Joseph Trigg, *Origen* (New York, 1998).

20. Letter 181:35–46 (CWE 2).

21. The *Enchiridion* was, with some minor works, included in a collection titled *Lucubratiunculae* (Antwerp: Hillen, February 1503).

22. See in particular Book 4 of Plato's *Republic*.

23. Godin, 33–75.

In 1505 Erasmus published the first edition of a text that would give his work on the New Testament a new direction: the *Annotations on the New Testament* by the Italian humanist Lorenzo Valla (d. 1457). Valla had identified discrepancies between the Latin Vulgate version and Greek manuscripts of the New Testament. Erasmus, following the same philological principles, set out to produce a critical edition of the Greek text. Over the next decade, even as other books that made him a prince among humanists appeared one after another,[24] he pored over Greek New Testament manuscripts he found at Cambridge and in Basel, and combed through the writings of the Fathers, looking for variant readings attested in the early centuries. His *Novum Instrumentum* (*New Testament*, Basel, 1516) was followed by new and expanded editions of the *Novum Testamentum* in 1519, 1522, 1527, and 1532.

The *Novum Testamentum* offered Erasmus' Greek text on one page, his new Latin translation[25] on the facing page, and, below, the footnotes that justified his choices among possible readings.[26] (His *Annotations on Romans* may reflect the "something on St. Paul's *Epistle to the Romans*" he had begun years previously).[27] For those who had Latin but were not scholars, Erasmus wrote *Paraphrases*, intended to preserve the "sense" while making it possible to read the New Testament "without stumbling."[28] Instead of starting with the gospels, in keeping with the traditional order of New Testament books, he began his *Paraphrases* with the *Epistle to the Romans* (1517).

The paraphrast's role, to "bring . . . simplicity out of complication,"[29] was particularly appropriate for *Romans,* which Origen and other ancient commentators had seen as an especially difficult text. If Origen and Jerome can be seen to stand behind many of Erasmus'

---

24. E.g., *The Praise of Folly,* published in 1511 (CWE 27), and the *Adages* (CWE 31–36), of which the most important edition was published in 1515.

25. For the 1516 *Novum Instrumentum* Erasmus used the Vulgate Latin text. His Latin translation was first published with the 1519 *Novum Testamentum*.

26. Jerry H. Bentley, "Erasmus, Jean Le Clerc, and the Principle of the Harder Reading," *Renaissance Quarterly* 31 (1978): 309–21.

27. CWE 56, *Annotations on Romans*. The notes for chapter 1 (pp. 3–69) are fuller than for any other chapter.

28. For this quotation and for Erasmus' understanding of the function of a paraphrase, see CWE 42 p. xv.

29. CWE 42 p. xv–xvii.

interpretations, the influence of Augustine is "notable by its absence."[30] For example, Augustine regarded Romans 5:12 as a proof-text for the doctrine of original sin: sin entered the world through one man "in whom all sinned." Erasmus preferred the reading of Pseudo-Jerome (actually Pelagius): "in this, that we have all sinned."[31] At Romans 7:14–17 ("sin resides in me"), Augustine took Paul as speaking for himself: not even he was without sin. By contrast, Erasmus followed other ancient commentators who took Paul as speaking here in the person of a sinner.[32] At Romans 9:14–16, "it is not a question of man's willing or doing, but of God's mercy," Augustine understood Paul as proclaiming the doctrine of predestination. Erasmus followed Origen in taking Paul's words as spoken by an imaginary opponent.[33]

As Erasmus read him, "our great hero Paul" was "toiling to defend Christ against Judaism,"[34] that is, against "the superstition of ceremonies." Erasmus envisioned a Christian world transformed by the gospel, conveyed to the faithful in vernacular translations[35] and by

30. John B. Payne, Albert Rabil Jr., and Warren S. Smith Jr., "The *Paraphrases* of Erasmus: Origin and Character," (CWE 42 p. xi–xix); this quote is from xviii.

31. From Erasmus' translation: CWE 56 p. 139–41 and 151 nn. 1 and 2; in his paraphrase of *The Epistle to the Romans* he wrote: "the evil originated by the first of the race spread through posterity, since no one fails to imitate the first parent" (CWE 42 p. 34). The argument turns on whether the Greek pronoun Paul uses is better translated "in whom" or "in that." Erasmus' view is favored by modern exegetes; Calvin Roetzel in *The Letters of Paul: Conversations in Context* (4th ed., Louisville, Kentucky, 2009), 173 says Augustine was "apparently unfamiliar with the Greek text." In Roetzel's opinion the Greek pronoun "would have required reading the Latin *in quo* as neuter, giving the passage a completely different meaning more consonant with the typical Jewish view: 'death came to all *because* all had sinned.'" Erasmus did not reject the doctrine of original sin, but it is hard to find in his writings any sign of enthusiasm for it.

32. Erasmus, *Paraphrases* (CWE 42 pp. xviii, 43–44, and 149–50 nn. 7 and 8). Cf. Roetzel, 116: despite indications "that Paul may be speaking autobiographically," it is "more likely" that he "used the first person singular to refer not just to his personal experience but representatively to all human experience."

33. Erasmus, *Paraphrases* (CWE 42 p. xviii, 55, and 153 n. 13).

34. Erasmus, Letter 541:164–65 (CWE 4 pp. 267–68).

35. Between the Gutenberg Latin Bible of 1453 (the Latin Vulgate) and the year of Luther's *Ninety-Five Theses* (1517) there were multiple full or partial printed translations of the Bible in German, but the German lands were an exception in this respect. England had only the manuscript translation of John Wyclif (d. 1384), condemned as heretical by the Church; see Paul Arblaster, Gergely Juhász, Guido

sound preaching.[36] Early in 1517 he wrote a German humanist friend a letter filled with hope. The "elegant literature" that had so long been obscured by barbarism was now "studied and absorbed by Scots and Danes and Irishmen;" and even in theology, "hitherto taught as a rule by obstinate opponents of the humanities," the study of the biblical languages was gaining "public recognition in the universities." "I should almost be willing to grow young again," said Erasmus, for "I perceive we may shortly behold the rise of a new golden age."[37] Something new was indeed about to happen, but not along the lines Erasmus expected.

In December 1516 Martin Luther prevailed on his humanist friend, Georg Spalatin, to convey to Erasmus the objection of a certain "Augustinian priest" to his interpretation of Romans 5:12: "you would not have the Apostle in his *Epistle to the Romans* to be speaking at all about original sin. He thinks therefore that you should read Augustine in his treatises against the Pelagians."[38] No response to Spalatin's letter is known, and Erasmus probably did not receive it. We do not know when Erasmus first became aware of Luther, but there is in his correspondence an echo of the great and growing excitement evoked by the *Ninety-Five Theses*, published at the end of 1517. In March 1518, he sent his English friend Thomas More "the Conclusions on Papal pardons . . . as I suspect they may not yet have reached your part of the world."[39]

Erasmus had now been accepted as a member of the theology faculty at Louvain, despite the fact that several of his colleagues had grave misgivings about a mere "grammarian" meddling in Scripture.[40] But when the Louvain faculty formally condemned certain of Luther's teachings as heretical (October 1519), Erasmus suspected a hidden

Latré, eds., *Tyndale's Testament* (Brepols, 2002). For Erasmus on translating Scripture into the vernacular, see the *Paraclesis,* in Hajo Holborn, Annemarie Holborn, eds., *Desiderius Erasmus Roterodamus ausgewähte Werke* (Munich, 1933), 139–49, p. 142., one of the prefatory writings to his 1516 New Testament.

36. In 1535 Erasmus published an extensive manual for preachers, the *Ecclesiastes*.

37. Erasmus, Letter 541: 58–60, 66–75, 111–13 (CWE 4 p. 261–64).

38. Erasmus, Letter 501:49–64 (CWE 4 pp. 167–68). Luther (through Spalatin) also contended that the law by which no man is justified (Romans 3:21) should be taken as referring to the Ten Commandments and the whole law, not just (as Erasmus had said) to the Jewish ceremonial law.

39. Erasmus, Letter 785:39–41 (CWE 5 p. 327).

40. Erika Rummel, *Erasmus and his Catholic Critics* (2 vols., Nieuwkoop, 1989).

agenda: the Saxon reformer's most vehement Catholic opponents blamed him for what Luther did, and had him in mind as their next target. In his first letter to Luther (May 1519), he spoke of how hard it was "to root out from men's minds the most groundless suspicion that your work is written with assistance from me."[41] Meanwhile, many of Erasmus' humanist friends assumed that he too supported Luther, and they tried in various ways to pressure him into declaring himself.[42] The publication in June 1520 of *Exsurge, Domine*, the papal bull threatening Luther with excommunication, prompted an attempt by Erasmus to forestall an open breach in Christendom. Together with a Dominican friend, he published an anonymous treatise contending that this ferocious bull could not possibly have been written by the learned Pope Leo X; Europe's princes ought to intervene by convoking a meeting of compromise-minded theologians from both sides.[43]

This proposal came to naught. But as Europe became enveloped in the controversies of the Reformation and as Erasmus continued with his *Paraphrases* and his *Novum Testamentum*, he issued from time to time works that conveyed his middle-ground position. For example, in a colloquy entitled "An Examination concerning the Faith," written in 1523 and published early in 1524, he has a Catholic speaker interrogate a Lutheran on the Apostle's Creed; much to the former's surprise, there is no difference between the two on the fundamental articles of belief.[44] Erasmus was no supporter of Luther's, but neither would he give aid and comfort to the "mendicant tyrants"[45] whose aim was to bring down not just Luther and all he stood for but also Erasmus and all he stood for.

---

41. Erasmus, Letter 980 (CWE 6 p. 391); this letter responds to a flattering letter from Luther, his Letter 939.

42. See CWE 7 p. 108–109, introduction to Letter 1033 (October 1519), addressed to Albert of Brandenburg, Archbishop of Mainz, a letter in which Erasmus expresses guarded support for Luther (lines 73–74, "if he is innocent, I should be sorry to see him overwhelmed by some villainous faction"). Erasmus sent the letter by way of Ulrich von Hutten, then at Albert's court, but instead of giving it to his patron, Hutten had the letter published.

43. *Minute Composed by a Certain Person Who Seriously Wishes Provisions to Be Made for the Reputation of the Roman Pontiff and the Peace of the Church:* CWE 71 pp. xl–xlvi and 106–12.

44. CWE 39 pp. 419–47.

45. For this phrase, see the index of my *Erasmus of the Low Countries* (Berkeley, California, 1996).

Luther: The Epistle to the Romans *as read by a student of Augustine*

At the University of Erfurt in Saxony, where he matriculated in 1501, Martin Luther followed the traditional scholastic curriculum. After receiving his MA in 1505 he enrolled in the faculty of law. That summer, passing through a terrible storm, he vowed to St. Ann[46] that if he were delivered from danger, he would become a monk. Having made an irrevocable promise, he seems to have chosen his congregation carefully: the Augustinian Friars of Erfurt had a reputation for learning and good discipline. Luther also took his monastic duties seriously, to the point of being scrupulous.[47] He confessed his sins frequently but could not be assured of God's forgiveness; for (as many theologians taught) a penitent must be truly sorry for having offended God, and how could one be certain that one was not feeling sorrow for one's sins merely because one feared the pains of hell? [48]

Luther's superior at Erfurt, Johann Staupitz, also held the chair in theology allotted to their order at the new University of Wittenberg. Sensing Luther's talent, Staupitz singled him out to take over his university chair. When Brother Martin proffered a list of reasons why he was unworthy to become a doctor of theology, Staupitz commanded him, under his monastic vow of obedience, to go to Wittenberg. Luther soon had his degree and his professorship; he was also the preacher at the castle church[49] and the superior of the Augustinian house in Wittenberg.[50]

Neither his studies nor his busy life as a professor stilled Luther's inner doubts. In the nominalist[51] school of thought that prevailed at

46. St. Ann was the patroness of miners; Luther's father was a miner.

47. Martin Brecht, *Martin Luther,* tr. James Schaaf, 3 vols. (Philadelphia: 1985–1993), vol. 1, 27–70.

48. On the distinction between "contrition" (sorrow for having offended God) and "attrition" (sorrow because one feared the pains of hell), see Tracy, *Europe's Reformations,* 48–49.

49. Wittenberg was the capital of Frederick the Wise, Elector of Saxony (d. 1525). He was one of the seven princes by whose votes the Holy Roman Emperor was elected.

50. Brecht, 19–27 and 150–61.

51. Like Duns Scotus, St. Thomas Aquinas was a realist in the sense that he believed that abstract terms denoting a class of things (e.g., "man," or "human nature") had an existence outside the mind of the knower, as constituent components of the individuals that were members of the class. William of Ockham (d. 1348) and

Wittenberg, the human will was deemed to play an important part in the process of salvation. If the pious Christian merely did what lay within his power, God's grace would make up for what was lacking. In his *Lectures on the Psalms* (1513–1514), Doctor Luther came to a very different conclusion: the pious Christian always fell short of God's demands, and the worst of sins was to deem one's own actions righteous in the sight of God. Consulted by Luther, Staupitz confirmed his misgivings about the modern[52] school of theology in vogue at Wittenberg: for a true theology, one must take up the writings of St. Augustine, the holy founder of their order.[53]

The *Lectures on Romans* (1515–1516) reflect a deeper study of Augustine but also a deeper dilemma for Luther himself. Augustine's treatises against the Pelagians, written late in his life,[54] depicted all of humanity as worthy of condemnation to hell in consequence of Adam's sin; from the "mass of damnation" that was the human race, God predestined for grace those it pleased him to choose, with no regard to any human action. Knowing the duplicity of the human heart, and of his own heart in particular, Luther could not believe that God had chosen for glory such a sinner as himself. Hence he adopted the view that the true Christian resigns himself to damnation in hell, and still praises God's justice.[55]

Even as Luther's *Anfechtungen* (temptations to despair) continued,[56] Rome reached into his corner of Germany. Those who contributed to a fund for rebuilding St. Peter's Basilica were to receive letters of indulgence, promising remission of the time their souls would spend

---

his followers were nominalists in the sense that they believed that such abstract terms were mere names that existed only in the mind of the knower. See Claude Panaccio, *Ockham on Concepts* (Aldershot, UK, 2004).

52. The nominalist "way" in philosophy and theology was also called the modern way, *via moderna;* the "way" of Thomas Aquinas or Duns Scotus was called the *via antiqua.*

53. For the "Augustinian renaissance" of the fourteenth and fifteenth centuries, see Heiko A. Oberman, *The Dawn of the Reformation* (Grand Rapids, MI, 1992), 8–12.

54. James Wetzel, "Predestination, Pelagianism, and Foreknowledge," in *The Cambridge Companion to Augustine,* ed. Eleanor Stump and Norman Kretzmann, (Cambridge, 2001), 49–58.

55. Brecht, 76–82.

56. Luther also uses (even in his Latin writings) the German term *Angst,* a word that is etymologically related to, but not fully conveyed by, the English word "anxiety."

in purgatory.[57] Luther's *Ninety-Five Theses* rejected the whole idea that the pope had power to remit the pains of purgatory by drawing for this purpose on a "treasury of merit" accumulated by the prayers and good deeds of saints through the ages. As if overnight, the *Nine-Five Theses* were in every bookseller's shop, and printers clamored for more works by Doctor Luther. Humanists turned *Lutherus* into *Eleutherius*, a Greek word that can mean "liberator": here was the man to free Germany from Roman oppression.[58]

In May of 1518 Luther was summoned to Augsburg for an interview with Cardinal Cajetan, a leading official at the Vatican and also a leading theologian. Cajetan found in Luther's writings two and only two propositions that caused concern. The first has already been noted: Luther had denied the pope's authority over the treasury of merits. The second troublesome point was Luther's assertion that a penitent who receives absolution in the sacrament of confession must be certain of being in a state of grace; as Cajetan explained, certitude of this kind was not a part of the Catholic tradition. The cardinal demanded a recantation, but on both points Luther stood his ground.[59] As he left a cheering crowd behind in Augsburg, Luther knew that he must appeal to an authority higher than the pope. In fact, many theologians believed there was such an authority: a universal council of the Church.[60]

In late 1518 or early 1519 Luther had a transforming experience. In recollections of the event, he connects it to his wrestling with Romans 1:17: "In the gospel is revealed the righteousness of God from faith unto faith; as Scripture says, 'The just man shall live by faith'." This expression, the "righteousness of God," was hateful

57. The Catholic doctrine of purgatory is immortalized in the middle section of Dante's *Divine Comedy*, the *Purgatorio*. For the souls of those who upon the point of death are not found worthy either of admission to God's presence or of condemnation to an eternity of punishment in hell, there is an intermediate state of purgation where souls are cleansed of the dross of sin and so prepared for admission to paradise.

58. For antipapalism in Germany, based in part on a reading of German history made popular by German humanists, see Kurt W. Stadtwald, *Roman Popes and German Patriots: Antipapalism in the Politics of the German Humanist Movement* (Geneva, 1996).

59. Scott H. Hendrix, *Luther and the Papacy* (Philadelphia, 1981).

60. For conciliarism—the doctrine that the highest authority in the Church rests not with the pope but with a universal council—see Francis Oakley, *The Conciliarist Tradition* (Oxford, 2003).

to him, for he took it as referring to the justice by which sinners stand condemned. But a different meaning suddenly dawned on him: God's righteousness was "His mercy through which he regards us and keeps us as just." For this new understanding of Paul, Luther found confirmation (albeit with some differences) in Augustine. Once he came to believe that God "imputes" to sinners a righteousness that is entirely "passive," this "passage from Paul" became for Luther "truly the gate to Paradise."[61]

At about this time, one of Luther's Catholic critics, Johann Eck, a professor of theology at the University of Ingolstadt in Bavaria, issued a challenge he knew Luther would accept, calling for a public debate at Leipzig, at the court of the Duke of Saxony.[62] Eck planned to embarrass Luther by showing how his teaching agreed with that of Jan Huss of Bohemia, who was condemned as a heretic by the Council of Constance (1415), and who had gotten some of his ideas from another reputed heretic, England's John Wyclif (d. 1384).[63] Having asked for a few days' time to examine Huss' writings, Luther returned with an unequivocal answer: Constance was wrong, Huss had been condemned unjustly. Thus councils of the Church were not free from error. By implication, the only sure source of religious authority was Scripture itself—*sola scriptura*.[64]

Events now moved rapidly toward schism. The papal bull threatening Luther with excommunication—unless he recanted on a list of propositions that had now grown to forty-one—was issued in June 1520. Luther's *Babylonian Captivity of the Church*—rejecting five of the seven sacraments long accepted as such by the Church[65]—appeared in October. In December, or perhaps in January 1521, he published his *Assertio Omnium Articulorum*, a defense of all the propositions condemned by Rome, in which he sharpened his position on several

---

61. Heiko A. Oberman, "The Reformation Breakthrough," in *Luther: Man between God and the Devil* (New Haven, CT, 1989), 151–74; quotes are from p. 154.

62. Duke George (d. 1539), a cousin of Elector Frederick the Wise (see n. 39), was an ardent Catholic.

63. Huss' aggrieved followers in Bohemia provoked a series of wars that were still remembered in ducal Saxony; see Howard Kaminsky, *A History of the Hussite Revolution* (Berkeley, 1967).

64. Brecht, 299–323.

65. Luther accepted only baptism and the eucharist as rituals through which God's grace was conveyed. Other practices—for example, marriage and confession of one's sins to a clergyman—he accepted as proper Christian rites but not as sacraments.

issues, including the doctrine of predestination.[66] In April 1521 he was summoned to the Diet of Worms, to appear before Emperor Charles V (r.1519–1555) and the assembled estates, or Diet of the Holy Roman Empire. Luther again refused to recant, and his defiance was again widely hailed. Though the Edict of Worms placed Luther beyond the protection of the law, many people, including Luther's prince, the elector of Saxony, did not believe he had received a fair hearing. Hence Luther had his prince's permission to live in disguise at the Wartburg, one of the elector's castles, where he began work on his epoch-making German translation of the Bible from Hebrew and Greek. He emerged from hiding (March 1522) to find a world in which the new "evangelical" teaching was vigorously promoted, albeit not always in ways that Luther himself approved.[67]

Erasmus versus Luther

Erasmus and Luther were as different in personality as they were in theology. Erasmus wrote for those who could read Latin and only for them. He envisioned a process of reform working by persuasion and from the top: as the study of biblical languages and the Church Fathers made headway in faculties of theology, newly graduated clergy would begin teaching "the philosophy of Christ" from their pulpits. Always circumspect,[68] he thought about the consequences of the words he published,[69] and tried to avoid giving offense to men in positions of power and authority. Luther wrote in German as well as in Latin, and his movement was carried forward by popular demonstrations of a kind that Erasmus feared. Believing himself to be both

66. For an English translation of Article 36, a text particularly targeted by Erasmus, see CWE 76 pp. 299–309.

67. The term "Protestant," stemming from a 1529 protest by the evangelical estates that were a minority in the imperial diet, was not commonly used until later. The title "evangelical" was claimed both by Luther and his followers and by adherents of what historians call the Reformed Reformation, led initially by Huldrych Zwingli (d. 1531) in Zurich and subsequently by John Calvin (d. 1564) in Geneva; see Bruce Gordon, *The Swiss Reformation* (Manchester, UK, 2002). Erasmus was more sharply critical of this version of the evangelical movement than he was of Lutheranism; his writings against Reformed Protestant foes are contained in volume 78 of CWE.

68. Tracy, *Erasmus of the Low Countries,* Chapter 13, "Circumspect Reformer."

69. For his own editing of letters he published, see L. E. Halkin, *Erasmus ex Erasmo: Érasme, éditeur de sa correspondance* (Aubel, Belgium, 1983).

sustained by the Holy Spirit and opposed at every turn by the devil himself, Luther let God worry about consequences. He proclaimed what he saw as the truth and relished opportunities to lash out at enemies of truth. Erasmus wrote with finesse, balancing conflicting points of view (on, for example, exegesis) in a way that after five hundred years still commands respect.[70] Luther wrote with power, and with a vehemence by which Erasmus was instinctively repelled, but Luther's words could also touch the heart and change a reader's whole understanding of the Christian life.[71]

That two such men would come to blows may seem inevitable, and in a sense it was. Erasmus had moved from the Low Countries to Basel (in the fall of 1522) specifically to avoid writing against Luther; had he stayed, he feared a personal request from Emperor Charles V, a request that no loyal subject of his majesty could have refused. Luther for his part did nothing to provoke Erasmus, with whom Luther's friend and collaborator Philip Melanchthon kept up a mutually respectful correspondence.[72] But as the religious controversy and the bitterness attending it continued to grow, it became more and more difficult for a neutral Erasmus to maintain his credibility with important Catholic patrons, including (at the time) England's King Henry VIII.

Having made his decision, possibly as early as the fall of 1523,[73] Erasmus likely consulted Catholic friends in Basel[74] about how to approach his task. As for a theme on which to attack Luther, free will may have seemed a natural choice for anyone who believed, as Erasmus did, that the moral teachings of the ancient pagans had a proper place in Christian life. He particularly objected to the passage in the *Assertion of All the Articles* in which Luther (citing Isaiah 40:6,

---

70. Bentley, see above, note 26.

71. For example, Johann Bugenhagen, a Cistercian prior in north Germany, took up Luther's works in order to refute younger brethren who were sympathetic to Luther. Instead, Bugenhagen went to Wittenberg, studied with Luther, and became an important reformer in his own right. See Peter B. Bietenholz and Thomas B. Deutscher *Contemporaries of Erasmus*, 3 vols. (Toronto, 1985–1987), vol. 1, 217–19.

72. See Timothy J. Wengert, *Human Freedom, Christian Righteousness: Philip Melanchthon's Exegetical Dispute with Erasmus of Rotterdam* (New York, 1998)

73. See his letter of September 4, 1523 to Huldrych Zwingli, Letter 1384: 50–52 in CWE 10 p. 83: "And yet I am resolved either not to write [against Luther] or to write in such a strain that my writing will not satisfy the Pharisees."

74. E.g., Ludwig Baer, a member of the university theology faculty, who advised Erasmus on certain of the arguments he made in *De Libero Arbitrio*.

"All flesh is grass") contended that human nature is irretrievably corrupt: Was Luther not aware of the distinction between base or fleshly desires and that noble striving for virtue so often praised by the Greek and Roman philosophers? Augustine was known to be skeptical of the claims of the philosophers in this regard, but while Luther had always admired Augustine, Erasmus found him excessively dogmatic, not least in his polemics against Pelagius.[75] Yet there was also reason for caution, because Luther's emphasis on placing all one's trust in God's mercy had struck a chord with Erasmus. This point may seem surprising to readers, but it was clear to contemporaries, especially to papal censors who marked up Erasmus' works in the 1550s, calling for deletion of frequent Lutheran-sounding phrases like *sola fide*, "by faith alone."[76]

Accordingly, *A Discussion or Discourse concerning Free Will* (September 1524) threads a path between conflicting priorities. In the preface Erasmus presents himself as one who weighs competing arguments.[77] For unlike Luther, in his *Assertion of All the Articles*, Erasmus is not fond of making assertions: indeed, he "will gladly seek refuge in Skepticism wherever this is allowed by the inviolable authority of Holy Scripture and the Church's decrees."[78] Scripture is often difficult—"there are some secret places into which God did not intend us to penetrate very far"—and some of the questions that theologians take pleasure in debating are simply not suitable for public discussion: "Supposing that what Wyclif taught and Luther defends is in some sense true—that whatever we do happens not by free will but by absolute necessity—what could be more useless than to spread this paradox abroad?"[79] In his Introduction, Erasmus proposes to consider only arguments from Scripture, since Luther will recognize neither the councils of the Church nor the writings of the Fathers as having any authority. Even so, Erasmus jabs at Luther's contention that Scripture is clear, for interpretation is needed and who is to interpret? "It is more probable

75. Cf. Erasmus, Letter 1334:516–18 in CWE 9 p. 261: "St. Augustine, in combating Pelagius with all his energy, somewhere attributes less to free will than those who now reign in the theological schools think ought to be attributed."

76. Greta Grace Kroker, *Erasmus in the Footsteps of Paul: A Pauline Theologian* (Toronto, 2011).

77. On the diatribe as a rhetorical form, see Marjorie O'Rourke Boyle, *Rhetoric and Reform: Erasmus' Civil Dispute with Luther* (Cambridge, MA, 1983).

78. *A Discussion of Free Will*, tr. Peter Macardle (CWE 76 pp. 6–7).

79. Erasmus, ibid., p. 12.

to presume that God has infused his Spirit into those whom he has ordained, just as we believe it is more probable that grace has been given to someone who is baptized than to someone who is not."[80]

In the main body of his work Erasmus weighs various biblical passages. Those that seem to support free will include the many exhortations to virtue in the gospels and elsewhere—would the Lord command what is not possible? Those that seem to negate free will include Exodus 9:12, "The Lord hardened Pharaoh's heart," and the ninth chapter of Romans, where, at verses 19–21, Paul compares the relation between God and his creatures to that between a potter and the clay he fashions into pots. What right has the clay to complain if the potter makes of it "vessels fit for wrath" rather than "vessels . . . prepared for glory"? For Erasmus, the passage refers to the contrast between Jews and gentiles: "The potter here makes a vessel for menial use, but because it has previously deserved it, as God rejected certain Jews, but on account of their lack of faith. On the other hand, he has made an honorable vessel out of the gentiles, on account of their faith."[81]

In the course of this discussion Erasmus develops his own position. One gets the sense that he did not wish to commit himself to a choice between two alternatives that were both permissible. On one hand, his words suggest a preference for opinions that attribute a great deal to free will, such as those opinions Erasmus had learned from his Scotist professors in Paris many years earlier. On the other hand, what he calls "probable" is the very different opinion that he credits to Augustine, one that accepts free will but attributes to it almost nothing in the process of salvation. In this light, orthodoxy is not so much a defined position as a field of discussion moving through time, allowing for many, but not all, points of view.[82] Instead of labeling Luther a heretic, Erasmus argues that Luther's extreme assertions—especially in his *Assertion of All the Articles*—put him beyond the pale of the theological tradition.

Having been attacked for being too assertive, Luther prefaces his *Bondage of the Will* (December 1525) with a fusillade of assertions responding to the opening sections of *A Discussion or Discourse*

80. Ibid., p. 17.

81. Ibid. pp. 46–55 (the quotation is from page 55).

82. For a suggestion that Erasmus' views on Church history are at times reminiscent of the modern idea of the development of doctrine, see Tracy, "Erasmus and the Arians: Remarks on the *Consensus Ecclesiae*," *Catholic Historical Review* 67 (1981): 1–10.

concerning Free Will.[83] Making assertions, Luther says, is precisely what
is proper to a Christian. Erasmus, by contrast, is accused of being more
of a skeptic than he lets on: "you only succeed in showing that you
foster in your heart a Lucian, or some other pig from Epicurus' sty
who, having no belief in God himself, secretly ridicules all who have
a belief and confess it."[84] As for alleged obscurity of Scripture, "this is
an idea put about by the ungodly sophists."[85] For Luther Scripture has
both an "internal clarity" and an "external clarity." The former means
"the inner judgment, through which someone enlightened by the
Holy Spirit or by the unique gift of God . . . distinguishes and judges
with complete certainty the dogmas and opinions of everyone."
The latter means that "nothing at all is left obscure or ambiguous,
but everything there is in the Scriptures has been brought out by
the Word into the most definite light." But the "external clarity"
of Scripture also involves a judgment that "belongs to the external
ministry of the word and to public office and pertains above all to the
leaders and heralds of the word."[86] As for absolute necessity, a topic
that Erasmus called unsuitable for public discussion, Luther asserts that
it is "fundamentally necessary and salutary for a Christian to know
that God foreknows nothing contingently, but that he foresees and
purposes and does all things by his immutable, eternal, and infallible
will. Here is a thunderbolt by which free choice is completely
prostrated and shattered."[87]

Luther, like Erasmus, devotes the main body of his treatise to
scriptural texts, following Erasmus point by point, but always with
a different interpretation. Righteous living is indeed commanded in
the gospels and elsewhere, but Erasmus has altogether missed what
Luther considers the fundamental distinction between command
and promise: God commands what we cannot accomplish, to lead
us to despair in ourselves and thus prepare us for the promise of his
gratuitous forgiveness.[88] Luther dwells at length on the hardening of

---

83. Luther's comments on Erasmus' introduction are included in this volume on
pp. 32–45; cf. *De Servo Arbitrio* (LW 33 71–102). Luther's comments on Erasmus'
preface (LW 33 19–70) are not included here.

84. Luther, *De Servo Arbitrio* (LW 33 24).

85. Ibid, 25.

86. Luther, *The Enslaved Will*, pp. 45–58; *De Servo Arbitrio* (LW 33 28); *The
Enslaved Will*, pp. 46–47.

87. Luther, *De Servo Arbitrio* (LW 33 37).

88. Luther, *The Enslaved Will*, pp. 75–81.

Pharaoh's heart[89]and on the simile of the potter and the clay: "Diatribe is baffled and beaten by that simile of the potter, and all she does is to try to get away from it."[90]

In a concluding summary of his position,[91] Luther relies heavily on St. Paul. When the apostle speaks of the "wickedness and injustice of mankind" (Romans 1:18), Luther asserts that Paul means all mankind, without distinction; thus virtue, even in "extremely remarkable men," is "nevertheless wicked, unjust, and deserving of the wrath of God." At Romans 3:19–20, Paul is clearly speaking about "the best and most virtuous" among men, for he says "that the mouths of all may be stopped and the whole world may be liable to God, because from the works of the law no flesh is justified in his eyes." These words Erasmus took as referring to Jewish ceremonial law, not the moral law. But "this is the ignorant error of Jerome, though Augustine strongly resisted it." In sum, Luther says, "If I wished to recount all the arguments against free will in Paul alone, I could do nothing better than to compose a continuous commentary on him."[92]

To the insults and assertions contained in the introductory sections of *The Bondage of the Will* Erasmus responded quickly. *Hyperaspistes* 1 (February 1526) concentrates on what is perhaps Erasmus' fundamental assertion, namely, Scripture does not speak for itself, it is of necessity interpreted.[93] Why, he asks of Luther, "should one believe that you and your few adherents teach the truth, while so many Doctors of the Church, so many universities, councils and popes etc. were blind, even though both sides have Scripture in common?" Luther rejects the Church's claim to interpret Scripture, yet he accepts the decisions of the early ecumenical councils: "How, then, are you sure that Wyclif was a holy man and that the Arians were heretics?" There was also the fact that Zurich's Huldrych Zwingli and others who claimed the title of evangelicals sharply disagreed with Luther on important points of doctrine: "If Holy Scripture is perfectly clear in all respects, where does this darkness among you come from, whence arise such fights to the death about the meaning of Holy Scripture?"[94]

89. Luther, *De servo arbitrio* (LW 33 164–74).

90. Luther, *De servo arbitrio* (LW 33 206–10); the quotation is from p. 210.

91. Luther, *The Enslaved Will*, pp. 86–126.

92. Luther, *The Enslaved Will*, pp. 86, 91–92, 95.

93. CWE 76 pp. 197–260.

94. CWE 76 pp. 197, 210, 222.

Hyperaspistes 2 (August 1527) was a long time in coming, and the delay raised questions among Erasmus' Catholic friends. When Thomas More pointedly inquired as to why Erasmus had not yet completed his response to Luther, Erasmus responded that he was having trouble in squaring his authorities—Paul and Augustine— with the point of view he preferred to defend: "If I follow Paul and Augustine, very little is left to free will."[95] *Hyperaspistes* 2 shows that Erasmus had been reading Augustine more carefully, though at certain points he uses Bernard of Clairvaux (also admired by Luther) as a surrogate for Augustine. Erasmus acknowledges the ambiguity of his own stance: "My *Discussion* sets out various opinions which are not rejected by the Church. And in the course of that debate I have not merely one [opinion] in mind."[96] He acknowledges too that Luther's interpretation of the simile of the potter and the clay (Romans 9:19–21) cannot be ruled out. Erasmus thinks that in the context of the epistle, Paul was explaining in Chapter 9 "why the Jews . . . were rejected . . . and why the gentiles were suddenly accepted." But if one construes the context differently, so that Paul was "teaching that no influence at all is inherent in our will for good or bad, Luther is right to cite this passage" in favor of his views.[97] On other points Erasmus stands his ground, sometimes against Augustine as well as Luther. At Romans 7:11–14 ("sin resides in me"), Erasmus writes that although Augustine strove " mightily" in one of his later works "to make this whole passage fit Paul," he distorts it in such a way that "the more zealously he tries to persuade me the less I agree with him." For "that Paul is speaking in the persona of someone else is clear from what follows [i.e., Romans 8:1–2], where he speaks once more in his own person."[98]

★★★

On the whole, Luther was the better debater. For example, he skillfully exploited the ambiguities of Erasmus' deliberately ambiguous definition of free will and he also showed how Erasmus was attributing to Augustine positions that this great Church Father recanted later in

95. Allen VII, 8, Letter 1804:75–95, Erasmus to More, May 30, 1527.
96. CWE 77 p. 391.
97. CWE 77 pp. 423–24.
98. CWE 77 pp. 699–703; cf. note 31, above.

life.[99] But while Erasmus cannot match Luther's grasp of the Hebrew Bible, he comes off as the better New Testament and patristic scholar, not entirely sure where he wants to take a dogmatic stand but willing, as it were, to argue with himself before the public eye. Luther's words carried his readers along with a force that was rare even in an age in which the reading public devoured theological works. In what was also an age of ferocious polemics, conducted by men brimming with certitude, the honest hesitation of Erasmus was perhaps even more rare.

James D. Tracy
2011

99. Notably, the idea that the human will is free to accept or reject God's grace; on this point see Eleanore Stump, "Augustine on Free Will," in Stump and Kretzmann, *The Cambridge Companion to Augustine*, 125–47.

AN OUTLINE OF ALL THREE WORKS

(Sections presented in this volume appear in **boldface** type.)

ERASMUS

A Discussion or Discourse concerning Free Will

Preface

A temperate debate is better than extreme dogmatism and assertion.

Scripture is sometimes obscure, but it is clear enough for ordinary Christians.

Some theological topics are too abstract and difficult for public discussion.

Introduction

Scripture is primary, but tradition is also important.

If Scripture is clear to those who have the Spirit, how do we know who has the Spirit?

Passages from the Old Testament Supporting Free Will

A brief definition of free will

Ecclesiasticus 15:14–18: free will in Adam and Eve

Reason, will, and law in postlapsarian mankind

Ancient and modern views of free will and grace

Other Old Testament passages supporting free will

Scriptural exhortations are meaningless if we have no power to comply.

God's figurative changes from wrath to mercy imply that our will can change.

Passages from the New Testament Supporting Free Will

Gospel exhortation are meaningless if we have no power to comply.

Passages from Paul supporting free will

Passages from Scripture Seeming to
Oppose Free Will

The hardening of Pharaoh's heart in Exodus and Chapter 9 of Romans
Divine foreknowledge and necessity: the case of the Pharaoh
Jacob and Esau: the Jews and the gentiles
The potter and the clay
The workman and the axe
Other scriptural examples of divine power and human will

Passages Cited by Luther to Deny
the Existence of Free Will

The limited application of Genesis 6:3 and 8:21 and of Isaiah 40:2–5
"All flesh is grass" (Isaiah 40:6–8) does not mean that all human
  inclination and abilities are flesh.
Jeremiah 10:23, Proverbs 16:1–6 and 16:21: divine providence does
  not preclude free will.
John 15:5—"Without me you can do nothing"—is not to be taken
  literally.

Additional Passages That Seem to
Oppose Free Will

Some Gospel passages only seem to undermine free will.
Pauline passages do not preclude free will if they are correctly
  interpreted.
Gospel parables do not deny free will if they are interpreted according
  to their context.
The very fact of God's help implies some action by the human will.

Judgments concerning Free Will And Grace

Motives for overstressing grace or free will
**To assert necessity to the exclusion of free will makes God cruel
  and unjust.**
**Faith must not be exalted to the exclusion of free will: free will
  cooperates with grace.**
Illustrations of the cooperation of grace and free will
**Absolute necessity makes God unjust: he would punish people
  who are not responsible for their sins.**
**Luther and Karlstadt overreacted against abuses associated with
  free will.**
**Reasons why we must attribute something (however little) to free
  will**

LUTHER

The Enslaved Will

Review of Erasmus' Preface

Luther's delay in writing

Christianity requires assertions; Christians are not skeptics.

The clarity of Scripture; it is vital to know the truth about free will and God's foreknowledge.

Should divine truth be kept from common ears and God's necessitating will be suppressed?

Divine necessity and the human will

Comments on Erasmus' Introduction

The evidence of tradition: the true church is hidden.

Internal and external clarity of Scripture is the test of who has the Spirit.

Refutation of Erasmus' Passages from the Old Testament Supporting Free Will

Erasmus' definition of free will

Three views of grace and free will—or rather three statements of one view

Ecclesiasticus 15:14–18: the foolishness of reason

Other Old Testament passages: the imperative and indicative moods

Erasmus fails to distinguish between Law and gospel.

God preached, God hidden; God's will revealed, God's will secret

New Testament Passages

Man must not pry into the secret will of God.

Precepts and rewards in the New Testament: the question of merit

Erasmus undermines his own case.

Defense of Passages which Seem to Oppose Free Will

Erasmus' use of tropes in interpreting Scripture

The hardening of Pharaoh's heart (Exodus 4:21)

How God's omnipotence can be said to work evil

How God's foreknowledge imposes necessity

Two kinds of necessity: the case of Judas
Jacob and Esau
The potter and the clay
Erasmus' way of reasoning does not allow God to be God.

Rebuttal Of Erasmus' Critique
Of *The Enslaved Will*

Genesis 6:3 and the biblical meaning of "flesh"
Other Old Testament passages—the universal sinfulness and impotence
  of man under the Law
The whole man—body, soul, and "spirit"—is "flesh."
Erasmus persistently evades the issue.
John 15:5 etc.: free will is "nothing" *coram deo*.
Divine grace and human cooperation
Erasmus' "middle way" leads nowhere.

A Display of Forces on Luther's Side

St. Paul: universal sinfulness nullifies free will.
Free will may do the works of the Law but not fulfill the Law.
Congruous merit and condign merit
The righteousness of works and of faith, and a summary of St.
  Paul's testimony against free will
St. John: free will is of the world and the flesh; grace is of Christ,
  by faith. The two are opposites.
The two kingdoms of Christ and of Satan. The assurance of faith
The mercy and justice of God in the light of nature, grace, and
  glory
Conclusion: the case against free will is unanswerable; Erasmus
  must yield.

ERASMUS

The Shield-Bearer Defending A Discussion, Part 1

Circumstances of Composition and Motivations for Writing
Erasmus' temperate discussion vs. Luther's inconsistent insults

Erasmus' Response to Luther's Review
of the Preface to A Discussion

The obscurity of Scripture
Erasmus' formulation of a Christian outlook for ordinary persons

"Sailing between Scylla and Charybdis": Erasmus' alleged neutrality
Theological topics that are unsuitable for public discussion, such as
   God's foreknowledge, or contingency and necessity, or the question
   whether God knows things contingently
Other unsuitable topics
The imperative of expedience
The human will is not completely passive but cooperates with grace.
A summary of why not all topics are suitable for all audiences

Erasmus' Response to Luther's Review of Erasmus' Introduction

The centrality of Scripture in the debate must also include its interpreters.
Not all of Scripture is fully clear.
Who has the Spirit that understands Scripture?
Erasmus' definition of free will
Luther's distortion of some minor points; his malevolence and Erasmus'
   sincerity

ERASMUS

The Shield-Bearer Defending A Discussion, Part 2

Introduction and Recapitulation of Book 1

Erasmus' Response to Luther's Critique of Erasmus' Arguments Supporting Free Will

Old Testament passages
The interpretation of Ecclesiasticus 15:11–22
The use of conditional assertions
The value of ordinary human speech in theology
Are divine precepts issued to show they cannot be observed?
The meaning of Romans 3:20: "Through the Law comes knowledge
   of sin"
God as teacher: the spiritual progression of mankind from Law to grace
Return to interpretation of Ecclesiasticus 15:11–22
The parting of the ways
Imperative and indicative moods
The position of man in the presence of grace
**Does Erasmus attribute good works to free will alone and fail to
   include grace?**

On the distinction between Law and gospel
The secret and revealed wills of God
New Testament passages
Necessity and the hidden will of God
Keeping the precepts, and the question of merit and reward in the
    Gospels
Does Erasmus subvert his own position?

Erasmus' Response to Luther's Defense of Scriptural Passages Opposing Free Will

The use of figures of speech in Scripture
Is the hardening of Pharaoh's heart a figure of speech?
Does God's omnipotence produce evil?
Paul's explanation of why God rejected the Jews and received the
    gentiles
Does divine foreknowledge impose necessity?
Judas: the necessity of immutability
The meaning of the story of Jacob and Esau (Genesis 25:23, Romans
    9:11–13)
The meaning of the potter and the clay
Does free will violate God's power and freedom?

Erasmus' Response to Luther's Defense of His *Assertio*

On spirit and flesh: Genesis 6:3
Other Old Testament passages: Genesis 6:5, Isaiah 40:2, Isaiah 40:6
Reason, spirit, and flesh: τὸ ἡγεμόνικον and the virtue of the pagans
Does divine providence remove free will?
Jeremiah 10:23
Proverbs 16:1, 22:1
John 15:5 and similar passages
How free will and grace work together
Luther's diverse charges against free will in his *Assertio* and *The Enslaved
    Will*
Luther and St. Paul: a contrast

Erasmus' Response to Luther's Presentation of His Case

Is mankind universally sinful and lacking free will?
Can free will fulfill the Law?
Congruous and condign merit
The true relation of faith and works; final assessments of Paul

The testimony of John the Evangelist: Is free will of the world and of the flesh?

The kingdoms of Christ and of Satan: the conflict between spirit and flesh

God's justice and mercy seen through nature, grace, and glory

On Luther's epilogue

Erasmus' Conclusions

The terms of the controversy and their history

Grace and the process of conversion

Augustine's stance on the human will

The virtues of the pagans and of the Old Testament Jews

Augustine and congruous merit

Erasmus' peroration: admonitions to all parties

ERASMUS

A Discussion or Discourse concerning Free Will (1524)

Introduction

Scripture is primary, but tradition is also important

Now, Luther admits the authority of no writer, however approved he may be, but accepts only the canonical Scriptures—and how gladly I welcome this opportunity of lessening my work! Since there are innumerable authors, among both the Greeks and the Latins, who treat free will either as their principal theme or incidentally, it would have been no mean task to assemble from all of them what each had said for or against free will, and to embark on the long, tedious business of explaining the meanings of their individual statements, or of refuting or confirming their arguments: yet this would have been wasted on Luther and his friends, especially since they contradict not only one another, but also often themselves.

Nonetheless I would remind readers that if Luther and I seem to be evenly matched on the basis of scriptural testimonies and sound arguments, they should then take into consideration the long list of highly learned men approved by the consensus of very many centuries, all the way up to our own day, most of them commended by their exemplary lives as well as by their admirable learning in the Scriptures. Some even gave their testimony in blood to the teaching of Christ, which they had defended in their writings. Such are, amongst the Greeks, Origen, Basil, John Chrysostom, Cyril, John Damascene, and Theophylact;[1] and amongst the Latins Tertullian, Cyprian, Arnobius, Hilary, Ambrose, Jerome, and Augustine.[2] I say nothing of those such

---

1. These fathers and theologians lived between the second and the eleventh centuries.

2. These fathers and theologians lived between the second and the fifth centuries. St. Augustine (354–430) was a pagan rhetorician and then a Neoplatonic philosopher before his conversion to Christianity. He became the bishop of Hippo and the most influential theologian among the Latin church fathers during

as Thomas, Scotus, Durandus, Capreolus, Gabriel, Giles, Gregory, or Alexander,[3] whose force and adroitness in argument I feel no one should entirely disdain; not to mention the authority of the many universities, councils, and popes. From the apostles' times to this day, there has not been a single writer who has completely denied the power of free will (excepting only Manichaeus[4] and John Wyclif[5]), for the authority of Lorenzo Valla,[6] who seems virtually to agree with them, carries little weight amongst theologians.

Although the Manichaean dogma has long since been utterly rejected and laughed out of court by universal consensus, yet I would hardly think that it is less conducive to true religion than Wyclif's. For Manichaeus refers good and evil deeds to two natures in man, yet in such a way that our good deeds are owed to God as our creator. And in addition he leaves us grounds for imploring the creator's aid against the powers of darkness, and this helps us to sin less gravely and to do good more easily. But by referring everything to absolute necessity, what scope does Wyclif leave to our prayers or our endeavors?

And so to return to my actual theme. If the reader sees that my argument proves a match for that of my opponents, then he should consider whether more weight ought to be given to the judgments already made by very many learned and orthodox men, many saints and martyrs, many ancient and modern theologians, many universities, councils, bishops, and popes, or to the private judgment of one individual or another. Not that I would gauge the worth of my opinion by the number of votes or the eminence of the speakers, as in human assemblies. I know it often happens that the more numerous side defeats the better one. I know that what the majority approves

---

the Middle Ages and the Reformation. Both Luther and Erasmus were admirers of Augustine but for different doctrines and different writings.

3. These scholastic theologians lived between the twelfth and the fifteenth centuries. Erasmus made it clear on many occasions that they were not his favorite theologians. On this point he could agree with Luther. St. Gregory the Great (c. 540–604) was pope and one of the four major Latin fathers of the church.

4. Mani (216–277), founder of the Manichaean religion and a dualistic determinist.

5. John Wyclif (c. 1330–1387) was an Oxford theologian and reformer. His doctrine of the absolute necessity of all events was condemned by the Council of Constance.

6. Valla (1407–1457), an Italian humanist and moralist, was an important influence on Erasmus, especially through his *In Novum Testamentum* (published by Erasmus in 1505). But Erasmus shows little respect for Valla's dialogue on free will (1482).

is not always the best. I know that in inquiry into the truth there will always be something to add to our predecessors' achievements. I concede that it is right for the authority of Holy Scripture alone to outweigh all the decisions of all mortals. But the debate here is not about Scripture itself. Both sides gladly accept and venerate the same Scripture: the quarrel is over its meaning. And if any weight is given to intelligence and learning in scriptural interpretation, whose minds are sharper and more perceptive than those of the Greeks? Who is more versed in the Scriptures? The Latins, too, lacked neither intelligence nor knowledge of Holy Writ; though their natural ability was less than that of the Greeks, with the help of the writings the Greeks left they were well able to equal their diligence. And if in this inquiry holiness of life is more regarded than learning, then the quality of those in the party that affirms free will is obvious. But no "odious comparison," as the lawyers call it, here—I should not care to compare some of the heralds of this new gospel with those men of old.

If Scripture is clear to those who have the Spirit, how do we know who has the Spirit?

But now comes the objection, "What need of an interpreter, when Scripture is perfectly clear?" If it is so clear, why have such distinguished men throughout so many centuries been blind, precisely in a matter of such importance, as Luther and his adherents want us to see it? If there is nothing obscure in Scripture, what need was there for prophecy in the apostles' time?[7] It was a gift of the Spirit, but I suspect that this charism has ceased, just like those of healing and speaking in tongues; and if it has not ceased, the question is, to whom has it been handed on? If it has come to anyone and everyone, then every interpretation is uncertain; if to no one (seeing that many obscurities torment scholars even today) then no interpretation is sure. If it has come to the successors of the apostles, my opponents will claim that many men entirely lacking the apostolic spirit have, for many centuries now, succeeded the apostles. [And yet, other things being equal, it is more probable to presume that God has infused his Spirit into those whom he has ordained, just as we believe it is more probable that grace has been given to someone who is baptized than to someone who is not.]

But let us grant, as indeed we must, the possibility that the Spirit may reveal to some humble, unlearned individual what he has not revealed to many learned men, seeing that Christ gives thanks to

7. See 1 Cor. 13:2.

the Father for having concealed from the wise and the learned (that is, Scribes, Pharisees and philosophers) what he had revealed to little children (that is, the simple and foolish by the standards of the world).[8] And perhaps Dominic and Francis might have been such fools, had they been allowed to follow their own spirit. Yet if Paul, in his own age, when this gift of the Spirit was flourishing, orders spirits to be tested whether they are of God,[9] what ought we to do in this carnal age?

And so, how shall we test the spirits? By learning? There are scholars on both sides. By behavior? On both sides there are sinners. On one side there is a whole choir of saints who defend the freedom of the will. My opponents may object that they were only human: yet I am comparing humans with humans here, not with God.[10] "What help in knowing the Spirit are a great number of men?" my opponents ask. "What help are a very few?" I reply. "How does a miter help us to comprehend the Holy Scriptures?" they ask. "How does a coarse robe help," I reply, "or a cowl?"[11] "What use is an understanding of philosophy in understanding the Scriptures?" they ask. "What use is ignorance?" I reply. They ask, "In understanding the Scriptures, what use is an assembled synod, in which it may happen that no one has the Spirit?" I reply, "What use are small private assemblies, where it is more probable that there is no one who has the Spirit?"

Paul cries, "Do you seek for proof of Christ who dwells in me?" (2 Cor. 13:3). People would not have believed the apostles if miracles had not strengthened belief in their teaching. Nowadays anyone and everyone demands to be believed because he asserts that he has the evangelical spirit. The apostles were at last believed for shaking off vipers, curing the sick, raising the dead, and bestowing the gift of tongues by the laying on of hands; and that belief did not come easily, for their teachings were paradoxical. Yet now, though some assert what in the general view are hyperparadoxes,[12] so far not one of them is to be found who could even cure a lame horse! And miracles apart, I wish that some of them would show the uprightness and simplicity

8. Cf Matt 11:25 and 1 Cor 1:27.

9. 1 Cor 12:3; cf 1 John 4:1.

10. Erasmus implies that Luther and his associates are claiming near divine perfection in insisting that they alone are right.

11. Erasmus refers to the coarse robe and monastic cowl Luther wore as an Augustinian friar and was probably still wearing when Erasmus wrote this.

12. Luther's views were often extremely paradoxical.

of the apostles' way of life, which would do instead of miracles for us spiritually backward mortals.

I do not intend this as a specific reference to Luther, whom I do not know personally and whose writings produce a mixed impression on me when I read them; I refer to others whom I know better. If, in the event of some disagreement over the meaning of Scripture, we quote the interpretation of the ancient orthodox authorities, they immediately sing out, "But they were only men." If asked by what means we can know what the true interpretation of Scripture is, seeing that there are "only men" on both sides, they reply, "By a sign from the Spirit." If you ask why the Spirit should be absent from those men—some of whom have been world-famous for their miracles—rather than from themselves, they reply as though there had been no gospel in the world these thirteen hundred years. If you demand of them a life worthy of the Spirit, they reply that they are justified by faith, not works. If you ask for miracles, they say that miracles have long ceased and that there is no need of them now that the Scriptures are so clear. And if you then say that Scripture is not clear on this point, on which so many eminent men have apparently been blind, the circle is complete.

Now, admitting that whoever has the Spirit is certain of the meaning of Scripture, how can I know if the claims he makes for himself are true? What am I to do if many people assert different opinions, every one of them swearing that he has the Spirit? And, since the Spirit does not reveal everything to every single person, even someone who has the Spirit may occasionally be mistaken. So much for those who so readily reject the ancient theologians' interpretation of the Bible and set up their own against us as if it had been spoken by an oracle. And even granting that the Spirit of Christ had allowed his people to err in matters of little importance, on which human salvation does not particularly depend, how credible is it that he should have overlooked his church's error for more than thirteen hundred years and have found not a single one of all those saintly people worthy of being inspired with what my opponents claim is the most important teaching of the entire gospel?

But to conclude this argument: let others decide what claim they will make for themselves. For myself I claim neither learning nor holiness, nor do I trust in my own spirit. I will simply and diligently expound what is on my mind. If anyone attempts to instruct me, I will not knowingly resist the truth; but if they prefer to hurl insults at me, though I discuss rather than dispute the matter politely and without abuse, will not anyone judge them lacking in the evangelical spirit of which they constantly speak?

Paul proclaims, "Receive the one who is weak in faith" (Rom. 14:1). Christ "does not quench the smoldering wick."[13] And the apostle Peter tells us to be "always ready to satisfy all those who require you to give an account of the hope that is in you, yet with gentleness and respect" (1 Pet. 3:15–16). If my opponents retort that Erasmus is like an old skin, and cannot contain the new wine of the Spirit (Matt. 9:17) which they are dispensing to the world, then if they are so sure of themselves they should at least treat us as Christ treated Nicodemus (John 3:1–21), and as the apostles treated Gamaliel (Acts 5:34–39). Nicodemus was ignorant, yet eager to learn, and so the Lord did not reject him; the disciples showed no aversion to Gamaliel, because he suspended his judgment about them till the outcome of the affair should show in what spirit it was being directed.

Passages from the Old Testament Supporting Free Will

I have now completed the first part of this book. If in it I have persuaded my readers of what I undertook, namely that it is preferable not to dispute matters of this kind too pedantically, especially in front of the masses, there will be no need for the argument for which I now gird myself, in the hope that truth may everywhere prevail, shining forth, it may be, from this discussion of the Scriptures like fire from the percussion of flints. [First of all, it cannot be denied that there are many passages in Holy Scripture which clearly seem to support the freedom of the human will and, on the other hand, some which seem to deny it completely. Yet it is certain that Scripture cannot contradict itself, since it all proceeds from the same Spirit.] And so we shall first review those which confirm our opinion; then we shall attempt to explain those which seem to oppose it.

A brief definition of free will

[By "free will" here we understand a power of the human will by which man may be able to direct himself towards or turn away from what leads to eternal salvation.][14]

---

13. Matt. 12:20, quoting Isa. 42:3.

14. This is Erasmus' deliberately general definition of free will, which will be attacked by Luther and defended at length by Erasmus.

Ancient and modern views of free will and grace

But as concerns the power of free will in us after sin and before the infusion of grace, the opinions of ancient and modern commentators vary to a remarkable degree, for each is concerned with a different aspect of the question. Those who wished to avoid despair and complacency, and to spur men on to hope and moral endeavor, attributed much to free will. Pelagius taught that once the human will has been freed and cured by the grace of God, there is no further need of grace, but that eternal salvation can be attained by dint of free will;[15] yet humans owe their salvation to God, without whose grace the human will would not be effectively free to do good; and this power of the soul, by which man recognizes good and chooses it, turning away from its opposite, is a gift of the creator, who might have created a frog instead of a human being.[16] Those who follow Scotus' opinions[17] are even more favorable to free will,[18] for they believe its power to be such that even though man has not received the grace that destroys sin, he can, by his natural powers, perform what they call

15. Pelagius, an ascetic British monk who died after 419, was the leader of a heretical movement fully and frequently attacked by St. Augustine and condemned by the Council of Carthage in 417/18. For Pelagius a sinner, either before or after baptism, by freely choosing to do good, merits the grace which has become generally available through Christ's redemption; no preceding or particular grace is necessary, and the beginning and continuation or reinitiation of the process consists merely in the will's acceptance of grace.

16. Apparently an echo of the position of late medieval scholastics, who distinguished God's absolute power (totally unconstrained) and his ordained power (constrained by the particular choices made by his absolute power). Thus by his absolute power God could have made man with no more ability to choose than a frog has; but his absolute power actually chose or ordained to make man with fully human powers (and thus, in a sense, limited itself).

17. It is clear that many followers of John Duns Scotus (1265/66–1308), such as William of Ockham, Pierre d'Ailly, and Gabriel Biel, held the view Erasmus describes here. But it is not entirely clear that Scotus himself held precisely such views, though he did discuss *meritum condignum* and *meritum congruum*. See note 20, below.

18. Erasmus exaggerates here in order to place the views of Scotus' followers as far as possible from the next category (those who believe that even "morally good" acts before grace are evil). In fact Pelagius apparently believed that the good actions of the will before grace actually merit grace not merely *ex congruo* but *ex condigno* (though those terms were not used in Pelagius' time)—a position which Scotus did not accept.

"morally good works"[19] which merit sanctifying grace not *ex condigno* but *ex congruo*—such are the terms they use.[20]

"At the opposite pole," as they say, are those who assert that all works, however morally good, are no less detestable to God than villainous deeds such as adultery and murder, since they do not proceed out of faith in and love for God. Their view seems too severe, especially given that some philosophers had a certain knowledge of God, and so may well have had some trust in and love for him too, and have not always acted for vainglorious motives, but out of a love of goodness and virtue, which they teach should be embraced simply because it is virtuous. (For someone who endangers his life for the good of his country out of vainglorious motives performs a work that is good in general,[21] but whether it is "morally good" is doubtful.)

St. Augustine and his followers, considering how harmful to true godliness it is for people to trust in their own abilities, are more inclined to favor grace, which is constantly stressed by Paul. And so Augustine teaches that man, in thrall to sin, cannot change his ways so as to amend his life, or do anything that contributes to salvation, unless he is divinely impelled by the freely given grace of God to desire what leads to eternal life. Some call this grace "prevenient"; Augustine calls it "operating," for even faith, the doorway to salvation, is itself a freely given gift of God. The charity added to faith by an even more generous gift of the Holy Spirit he calls cooperating grace,[22] for it unceasingly helps those who are making an effort until

19. "Morally good works" are performed by natural powers, without the aid of grace.

20. By *meritum de congruo* the natural disposition and acts of man can solicit (but not strictly earn) grace because its bestowal is "fitting"; *meritum de condigno,* on the other hand, is the merit of a good act performed in the state of grace. Such an act meets the standard of God's justice and earns salvation as a reward, but only because God has committed himself to accepting it as fully meritorious.

21. Translating *ex genere bonum;* that is, the deed itself is generically good, entirely apart from the motives of the doer.

22. In *De gratia et libero arbitrio (Grace and Free Will)* 17.33 Augustine distinguished between operating grace (*gratia operans*), through which man's good will is initially stimulated, and cooperating grace (*gratia cooperans*) through which God cooperates with man's free will in good acts. Operating grace is sometimes called particular (*peculiaris,* as distinct from grace in general, not applied to a particular person), prevenient (*preveniens*), stimulating (*exstimulans*), impelling (*pulsans*) and grace given gratuitously (*gratia gratis data*). This initial grace when accepted is fulfilled by justifying grace,

they achieve their goal; but although free will and grace cooperate in the same task, grace is the leader, not merely a partner. Some theologians, however, make a distinction here saying that if you consider an action according to its nature, the more important cause is human will; but if you consider it according to the merit involved, the more important is grace.[23] And yet faith, the reason that we desire what leads to salvation, and charity, the reason that we do not desire it in vain, are distinguished not so much in time as in nature (though they can both increase with time).]

And so, since "grace" means a "favor freely bestowed," it is possible to posit three or indeed even four kinds of grace.[24]

One is the grace naturally present in us, vitiated, as we said, but not destroyed, by sin; some call it a "natural influence."[25] Common to all humans, it remains even in those who persevere in sin; for they are free to speak or be silent; to sit or stand up; to help the needy, read the Scriptures, or listen to a sermon, though according to the opinion of some, none of these things leads to eternal life.] There is however a considerable body of opinion that, given the immense benevolence of God, man can progress so far by performing such good works as to prepare himself for grace, and to move God to have mercy on him; though there are some who deny that even this can happen without particular grace. Since this natural grace is

---

continued by cooperating grace and finalized by persevering grace. The perplexing variation in terminology is one sign of the perplexing character of the problem.

23. In the preceding pages Erasmus has listed many of the questions actually discussed by scholastic theologians from the twelfth to the sixteenth century. Scotus discusses the primary and secondary causality of a meritorious act, concluding: "I say therefore that these two coincide, will and grace, as a superior cause and an inferior one, and in this way the inferior cause, while it exists, always co-acts, while the superior, which is the principal cause, acts. But we can consider this act in itself or insofar as it is meritorious. In the first way will is the principal cause. In the second way grace is said to act principally, because it is more acceptable to God."

24. The three principal kinds are prevenient, sanctifying (or justifying), and persevering. Natural grace (or the *concursus generalis* by which God sustains creation, the first kind discussed by Erasmus) can be thought of as a gift or "grace" but is not strictly a supernatural grace like the others.]

25. Latin *influxum naturalem*: a technical term (also named *concursus* or *influxus generalis* or *influentia generalis*) which means "the cooperation of the first cause (God) with the second cause (creature) which is indispensable for any action of the second cause irrespective of the presence of grace."

common to all, it is not called grace, though in reality it is[26]—just as in creating, preserving, and governing the universe God daily performs greater miracles than if he were to cure a leper or exorcize a demoniac, yet they are not called miracles because they are performed for the benefit of all, without distinction, every day.

The second kind is particular grace:[27] through this, God in his mercy urges the sinner, still without merit, to repentance, but does not yet infuse the highest grace, which destroys sin and makes man acceptable to God.[28] So the sinner, aided by the second kind of grace which we called "operating" above, is dissatisfied with himself and, though he has not yet thrown off the attachment to sin, he can give alms, pray, perform pious exercises, listen to sermons, request the prayers of holy men for himself, and perform other works that are morally good, as they say: he can behave, as it were, as a candidate for the highest kind of grace. There is, further, the opinion that this second kind of grace which we have just mentioned is, through God's goodness, never lacking to any mortal being, because the divine beneficence supplies everyone with suitable occasions in this life to amend their ways if, as far as they are able, they bring the remainder of their will into harmony with the assistance of the Spirit who invites, but never compels, us to greater goodness.[29] It is even believed that we have the power to choose whether to turn our will towards or away from grace, just as it is in our power to open or close our eyes to the light that shines on them from without. Since God's great love for humanity does not suffer man to be deceived with false hopes even of the grace known as sanctifying grace, if he strives for it with all his might, it is true that no sinner should be presumptuous but that none should despair, either; and it is also true that no one perishes except through his own fault.

---

26. The *concursus generalis* (what Erasmus here calls natural grace) by which God creates and sustains all beings and actions is not a grace in the sense that it does not rise to the level of supernatural gifts, deeds, or rewards, but it is a grace in the general sense of a favor or gift.

27. See n. 22 above.

28. What is now usually called sanctifying grace; in Erasmus' time it was usually called *gratia justificans* (justifying grace) or *gratia gratum faciens* (grace that makes pleasing to God).

29. The doctrine of *facere quod in se est* (to do as much as you can) or *meritum de congruo* (congruous merit): that God will not withhold his grace from those who do their very best. See Oberman, *Harvest* 132–33, 468, and 471–72.

[And so there are natural grace; stimulating grace (admittedly imperfect); the grace that makes the will effective, which we referred to as cooperating grace and which carries on what we have begun; and there is the grace which brings it to completion.[30] These last three are thought to be the same grace, though they have different names from their different effects in us: the first stirring up, the second continuing, the third bringing to completion.]

And so those farthest from Pelagius' position attribute a great deal to grace and almost nothing to free will, though they do not deny it altogether. [They say that without particular grace man cannot desire good, can neither make a beginning, nor persevere, nor bring to completion without the perpetual help of God's grace from the very beginning. This opinion seems highly probable, for it permits man the opportunity for serious moral endeavor, but not for making any claims for his own powers.[31] [Harder is the opinion of those who assert that free will can do nothing but sin, and that grace alone works good in us, not *through* or *in cooperation* with, but *in* free will, so that our volition does no more in the process than wax does while it is being shaped by the sculptor's hand into whatever shape he, the craftsman, envisages.][32] I feel that these people are so anxious to escape reliance on human works and merits that they "run beyond the pale," as the saying goes.

[Hardest of all, apparently, is the opinion of those who say that free will is an empty term, that it has not, and never has had, any power, either in the angels or in Adam or in us, before or after the infusion of grace, but that God works evil as well as good deeds in us, and that everything happens out of absolute necessity.][33] And so I will take issue particularly with these last two positions.

I have gone into this at slightly excessive length so as to enable the less expert reader to grasp the rest of the argument—for I write as non-expert for non-experts, and for this reason I first quoted the passage in Ecclesiasticus (15:14–18), which seems to offer the clearest description of the origin and power of free will. Now I will review the other scriptural testimonies with more dispatch. Before doing so, I should

---

30. This grace is usually called *gratia perseverans* (the grace of perseverance).

31. This is the position of Augustine and Thomas Aquinas. Although Erasmus calls it "highly probable," he does not definitively endorse it.

32. Erasmus holds this to be the position of Karlstadt. See *The Shield-Bearer* 1, n. 165.

33. Erasmus identifies this as the opinion of Wyclif and Luther.

point out that this passage is different in the Aldine edition than in the version used in the Latin church today. The Greek version does not add "and they will keep you"; nor does Augustine in his occasional quotations of this text. Also, in my opinion ποιῆται should read ποιῆσαι.

Other Old Testament passages supporting free will

And so, just as God had offered the choice of life or death in paradise—"If you obey my commandments you will live; if you do not, you will die. Avoid evil and choose what is good"[34]—in the same way he talks to Cain in Genesis (4:6–7): "Why are you angry, and why has your face fallen? If you do good, will you not receive? And if you do evil, your sin will immediately be at your door. But the desire for it will be within your control, and you will master it." God offers a reward if man will choose what is right and threatens punishment should he prefer to follow the opposite path. And he shows that evil thoughts and desires can be overcome and do not compel us to sin.

In agreement with these passages are the Lord's words to Moses: "I have placed before you the way of life and the way of death. Choose what is good, and walk in it" (Deut. 30:15, 19). What could be more clearly expressed? God shows us what is good and what is bad, and shows the two different consequences for each—life and death; the freedom to choose he leaves to man. It would be ridiculous to tell someone to choose if it were not in his power to turn this way or the other, as though someone standing at a crossroads were to be told, "you see the two roads—take whichever you want," if only one were open.

Again, in Deuteronomy 30:15–19:

> See, this day I have placed before you life and goodness, and on the other hand death and evil, so that you shall love the Lord your God, and walk in his ways, and keep his commandments and his ordinances and his laws, and you may live, and he will multiply you and bless you in the land which you are entering to possess. But if your heart turns away, and you will not hear, and you are deceived by falsehood into worshipping false gods and serving them, I tell you today that you will perish, and you will not live long in the land that you will cross the Jordan to enter and possess. Today I call

---

34. Cf. Gen. 2:17 and Deut. 30:19.

upon heaven and earth as witnesses that I have placed before you life and death, blessings and curses. And so choose life, so that you and your descendants may live.

Here again we hear the terms "place before you," "choose," and "turn away"—terms which would be inappropriate if human will were not free to choose good, but only evil.[35] Otherwise it would be exactly as if someone tied up in such a way that he could only stretch out his arm to the left were to be told, "There is some excellent wine to your right and poison to your left. Reach out and take whichever you want."

Consistent with this are the words of the same Lord in Isaiah (1:19–20): "If you are willing and obey me, you will eat the good things of the earth; but if you are not willing and will not obey me, the sword will devour you." If the human will were in no sense free to do good, or even, as some assert, not free to do either good or evil,[36] what is the meaning of the words "if you are willing" and "if you are not willing"? It would have been more suitable to have said, "if I am willing" or "I am unwilling." And since many similar words are addressed to sinners, I do not see how we can avoid attributing to them a will which is in some sense free to choose good, unless we prefer to call it a thought or a desire rather than a will, since will is decisive and is the result of judgment. Yet in chapter 21:12 of the same prophet we read, "Ask if you will; turn and come back." What point would there be in urging people to "turn and come back" if they do not in the least have it in their power to do so? Would it not be exactly like saying to a man in shackles, whom one was not prepared to free, "Bestir yourself, come and follow me"? And in chapter 45:20 of the same prophet we find, "Gather yourselves and come!" and "Turn to me and you will be saved, all you ends of the earth!" (Isa. 45:22) And again in chapter 52:1–2: "Arise, arise, shake off the dust, loose the halter from your neck!" The same in Jeremiah, chapter 15:19: "If you change your ways, I will change you, and if you distinguish the precious from the base, you will be as my mouth." The use of "distinguish" indicates the freedom to choose. Zechariah demonstrates more clearly still the exercise of free will and the grace in store for whoever exercises it: "Turn back to me, says the Lord of Hosts, and I will turn back to you, says the Lord" (Zech. 1:3). In Ezekiel chapter 18:21–22 God speaks thus: "If the sinner does penance for all the sins he has

35. An allusion to Karlstadt's position.
36. Allusions to the view of Karlstadt and then of Luther.

committed, and does what is right, etc." and immediately afterwards "I will not remember all the wicked deeds he has done"; likewise: "But if a righteous man turns away from his righteousness, and does what is wrong" (Ezek. 18:24). In this chapter the terms "turn away," "do," "perform," constantly recur, in both a good and a bad sense.

And where are those who claim that man does nothing but is only worked upon by operating grace?[37] ["Cast off all your iniquities," says the Lord, "and why do you wish to die, house of Israel? I do not desire the sinner's death; turn back and come to me!" (Ezek. 18:31–32) Would the good Lord lament the death of his people which he himself brought about in them? If he does not desire our death, we must indeed ascribe it to our own will if we perish; but what can you ascribe to someone who can do nothing, good or bad?[38] It would be futile for the mystic psalmist to sing "Depart from evil and do good; seek out peace and pursue it" (Ps 33:15) to people who had absolutely no control over their will.

Scriptural exhortations are meaningless if we have no power to comply

But what point is there in quoting a few passages of this kind when all Holy Scripture is full of exhortations like this: "Turn back to me with all your heart" (Joel 2:12); "Let every man turn from his evil way" (John 3:8); "Come back to your senses, you transgressors" (Isa. 46:8); "Let everyone turn from his evil way, and I will repent the ill that I have thought to do them on account of the evil of their endeavors"; and "If you will not listen to me, to walk in my law" (Jer. 26:3–4). Nearly the whole of Scripture speaks of nothing but conversion, endeavor, and striving to improve. All this would become meaningless once it is accepted that doing good or evil is a matter of necessity; and so too would all the promises, threats, complaints, reproaches, entreaties, blessings, and curses directed towards those who have amended their ways, or those who have refused to change:] "As soon as a sinner groans at his sin";[39] "I have seen that this is a stubborn people" (Exod. 32:9);

37. Such as Karlstadt.

38. Luther's position.

39. The precise language of this text is not biblical, but it is quoted in the form Erasmus gives (and as if it were biblical) by Peter Lombard, Abelard, Bernard of Clairvaux, and several minor writers. Editors generally refer to Ezek. 18:21, 33:12, 16, 19, and Isa. 30:15. It is possible that Erasmus' form of the verse comes from the liturgy, where biblical quotations sometimes differ somewhat from the Vulgate.

"Oh my people, what have I done to you?" (Mic. 6:3); and "They have rejected my laws" (Ezek. 20:13); "Oh, that my people had listened to me, that Israel had walked in my ways!" (Ps. 80:14); "He who wishes to see good days, let him keep his tongue from evil (Ps 33:13–14). The phrase "he who wishes to see" speaks of free will.[40]

Since such phrases are frequently encountered, does it not immediately occur to the reader to ask, "Why promise conditionally what is entirely dependent on your will? Why complain of my behavior, when all my actions, good or bad, are performed by you in me regardless of my will? Why reproach me, when I have no power to preserve the good you have given me, or keep out the evil you put into me? Why entreat me, when everything depends on you and happens as it pleases you? Why bless me, as though I had done my duty, when whatever happens is your work? Why curse me, when I sinned through necessity?" What is the purpose of such a vast number of commandments if not a single person has it at all in his power to do what is commanded? [For there are some who believe that man, albeit justified by the gift of faith and charity, cannot fulfill any of God's commandments, but rather that all good works, because they are done "in the flesh," would lead to damnation were not God in his mercy to pardon them on account of the merit of our faith.][41]

Yet the word spoken by God through Moses in Deuteronomy, chapter 30:11–14, shows that what he commands is not merely within our power, but that it demands little effort. He says: "The commandment that I lay upon you this day is not beyond you, nor is it far away. It is not in heaven, that you might say, 'Which one of us is strong enough to go up to heaven and bring it back to us, that we may hear and fulfill it?' Neither is it beyond the sea, that you should make excuses, and say, 'Who among us can cross the sea and bring it back to us, that we may hear what is commanded?' No, the word is very near to you, on your lips and in your heart, that you may do it."

Yet here he is speaking of the greatest commandment of all: "that you turn back to the Lord your God with all your heart and with all

---

40. Augustine gives a similar list of scriptural commands in support of free will in *De gratia et libero arbitrio (Grace and Free Will)* 2.3.

41. An allusion to Luther's doctrine of *simul justus et peccator* (justified and a sinner at the same time). See his *Assertio,* article 36 (CWE 76 p. 301): "*In omni opere bono iustus peccat mortaliter*" (When a just man does a good deed, he sins mortally). [The phrase "on account of the merit of our faith" is a misunderstanding of Luther, who did not believe that we merit anything because of our faith.]

your soul."[42] And what is the meaning of "but if you will listen," "if you will keep the commandments," "if you will turn back" (Deut. 30:10), if none of this is in our power at all? I will not attempt to quote an extensive selection of such texts, for the books of both testaments are so full of them, wherever you look, that anyone attempting to search them out would simply be "looking for water in the sea," as the saying goes. And so, as I said, a considerable amount of Holy Scripture will obviously become meaningless if you accept the last opinion discussed above or the previous one.[43]

Judgments Concerning Free Will and Grace

Motives for overstressing grace or free will

Up to this point we have collected scriptural passages which establish the existence of free will and, on the other hand, passages which seem to deny it utterly. But since the Holy Spirit, the author who produced them, cannot contradict himself, we are forced, whether we like it or not, to seek a more moderate opinion.

Now, the reason that different scholars have reached different opinions working from the same Scripture is that they directed their attention to different things and interpreted what they read in the light of their individual aims. Some reflected on the great extent of human religious apathy and on the great evil of despairing of salvation; in the attempt to remedy these ills, they fell unawares into another evil and exaggerated the role of free will. Others, however, considered how destructive it is of true godliness for man to rely on his own strength and merits, and how intolerable is the arrogance of certain parties who display their own good deeds and even weigh and measure them out for sale to others like oil and soap. In their valiant efforts to avoid this evil, they have either taken half of free will away, to the extent that it plays no part at all in a good work, or they have destroyed it altogether by propounding the absolute necessity of all events.[44] Presumably they felt that it was highly conducive to the unreserved obedience proper to a Christian attitude that man should depend utterly on the will of God; that he should place all his hope

42. Deut. 6:5; see also Matt. 22:37, Mark 12:30.
43. Those of Luther and Karlstadt.
44. That is, it wills only evil works, not good ones (as Karlstadt taught) or it wills nothing at all because everything happens by absolute necessity (as Luther taught).

and trust in God's promises and, acknowledging how wretched he is in himself, should admire and love God's immense mercy, which freely lavishes so much on us. He should submit himself entirely to God's will, whether that will is to preserve or to destroy him; he should claim no praise for himself for his own good deeds, but ascribe all the glory to God's grace, bearing in mind that man is nothing but a living instrument of the Holy Spirit, who has cleansed and consecrated man to himself through his freely given benevolence and who guides and governs him in his unsearchable wisdom. He should also consider that in this process there is no claim that anyone can make for his own powers; yet he should hope with complete confidence for the reward of eternal life from God, not because he has merited it through his own good deeds but because God in his goodness has been pleased to promise it to those who trust in him. It is man's duty constantly to pray God to bestow his Spirit on us and increase it within us; to give him thanks if anything good has been done because of us; and in all things everywhere to worship his power, admire his wisdom, and love his goodness.

This formulation seems entirely praiseworthy to me, for it is consistent with Scripture and accords with the belief of those who, through baptism, have died to the world once and for all and have been buried with Christ, so that after this mortification of their flesh they should henceforth live and be guided by the Spirit of Jesus, onto whose body they have been grafted by faith.[45] Surely this is a godly, pleasing position, which does away with all our arrogance, gives all glory to Christ and places all our trust in him, casts out all our fear of men and demons, and makes us distrust our own powers and become strong and courageous in God; we will gladly give it our limitless approval.[46] But when I hear people maintain that all human merit is so worthless that all human works, even those of godly men, are sins; when they claim that our will does no more than clay in the potter's hands or attribute everything we do or will to absolute necessity, then I become exceedingly uneasy.

45. Rom. 6:4–10 and 11:17–18; Gal. 6:14; Col. 2:20.

46. The Latin for "limitless approval" (*usque ad hyperbolas*) translates a Greek idiom, "even to excess," as in Plato, (*Letters* 326d). Erasmus plays on the fact that he usually finds Luther's hyperboles quite unacceptable.

To assert necessity to the exclusion of free will makes God cruel and unjust.

First, how can you constantly read that holy people, full of good works, "did justice,"[47] "walked righteously in the sight of God,"[48] "turned neither to the left nor to the right,"[49] if everything that even the godliest do is a sin, and such a sin that without the intervention of God's mercy someone for whom Christ died would be cast into hell? How can you constantly read of a reward where there is absolutely no merit? How can the obedience of those who complied with God's commandments conceivably be praised, and the disobedience of those who did not, be condemned? Why is judgment constantly mentioned in the Scriptures if merits are not weighed at all? [Why are we made to appear before the judgment seat if we have done nothing through our own will but everything has been done in us by absolute necessity?]

There is the further objection: what need is there of the many admonitions, commands, threats, exhortations, and remonstrances in the Scriptures if we do nothing, but God works everything in us—the deed as well as the will[50]—in accordance with his immutable will? God requires us to pray without ceasing, to stay vigilant, to struggle, to contend for the prize of eternal life. Why does he want to be constantly asked for something which he has already decided whether or not to give, seeing that his decisions cannot be changed, since he himself is unchangeable? Why does he tell us to labor to obtain what he has decided to bestow on us as a free gift? We suffer affliction, rejection, ridicule, torture, and death; thus God's grace fights, wins, and triumphs in us. [A martyr undergoes such torments, yet no merit is credited to him for doing so—indeed he is said to have sinned in having exposed his body to suffering in the hope of heavenly life. But why did the all-merciful God wish to work in the martyrs in this way? A man would seem cruel if he had decided to make a friend a free gift of something but would not give it to him until he had been tortured to the point of despair.]

But when we come to this obscure aspect of the divine purpose, perhaps we will be told to worship what we are not permitted to understand, so that the human mind should say, "He is the Lord, he

47. 2 Kings 8:15; 1 Macc. 14:35; Ps. 105:3 (cf. Deut. 33:21).
48. 3 Kings 2:4, 3:6, 8:23 and 25; Isa. 38:3; 2 Chron. 6:14.
49. Deut. 5:32; Josh 1:7; 4 Kings 22:2; Prov. 4:27.
50. Cf. Phil 2:13.

can do whatever he wills, and since he is entirely good by nature, whatever he wills must be entirely good." It is also quite praiseworthy to say that God crowns his own gifts in us and wills his own good deeds to be our reward, and that in his freely given generosity he sees fit to credit what he has worked in us to those who believe in him as though it were a debt that he owed them, so that they may attain immortality. But I can see no consistency in those who exaggerate God's mercy in good men in such a way as to make him seem almost cruel towards others. [Believers' ears will readily accept the benevolence of a God who credits his good deeds to us; but it is difficult to explain how it can be just, let alone merciful, for him to condemn others—in whom he has not seen fit to work good deeds— to eternal torment, although they themselves can do nothing good; for either they have no free will, or, if they have, it has the power to do nothing except sin.]

If a certain king were to give a huge reward to the man who had done nothing in a war, while the rest, who had acted bravely, received nothing beyond their normal pay, he could perhaps reply to the soldiers' murmurings, "What injustice do you suffer if it is my pleasure to be gratuitously generous to this man?" But how could he possibly seem just and merciful if he equipped one general for war with an ample supply of siege-engines, troops, funds, and all kinds of supplies, then heaped him with honors for military success but sent another to war unarmed, without any supplies, then executed him for failure? Would the dying general not be entitled to say to the king, "Why punish me for a fault for which you are to blame? Had you equipped me in the same way, I would have been victorious too."

Again, if a master were to free a slave who did not deserve it, he might perhaps have an answer to the murmuring of the other slaves: "You are no worse off if I am kinder to this man. You have your due." But anyone would deem a master cruel and unjust if he were to flog a slave for being too short or having too long a nose or for some other physical imperfection. Would the slave not be justified in complaining to the master as he beat him, "Why am I being punished for what I cannot help?" And he would be the more justified in saying this if it were in the master's power to change the slave's bodily defects, as it is in God's power to change our will; or if the master had given the slave the very defect which offended him—had cut off his nose, or hideously scarred his face, just as God, in the opinion of some, works even all bad acts in us. Again, regarding God's commands, if a master were to issue many orders to a slave shackled in a treadmill, "Go there, do this, run, run back," threatening dire consequences if he disobeyed, but without unshackling him the while, and then prepared a rod for him because he had not obeyed, would the slave not seem correct in calling his master insane or cruel, flogging him for having failed to do what was not in his power?

Faith must not be exalted to the exclusion of free will: free will cooperates with grace.

We listen with equanimity, however, to our opponents' boundlessly exalting faith in and love of God, for we are of the opinion that the corruption of Christian life everywhere by so many sins has no other cause than the coldness and drowsiness of our faith, which gives us a merely verbal belief in God: a faith on the lips only, whereas according to Paul "man is justified by believing from the heart" (Rom. 10:10). Nor will I particularly take issue with those who refer all things to faith as their ultimate source, even though I believe that faith is born from and nurtured by charity, and charity in turn is born from and nurtured by faith. Charity certainly feeds faith, just as the light in a lantern is fed by oil, for we more readily trust the person we ardently love, and there is no dearth of people who contend that faith is the beginning rather than the completion of salvation. But our argument does not concern these matters.[51]

Yet here we should beware of being so absorbed in enlarging on the praises of faith that we subvert the freedom of the will; and once it has been denied I do not see how the problem of the justice and mercy of God can be resolved. When the ancient authors found they could not extricate themselves from these difficulties, some were forced to posit two Gods: one of the Old Testament who they argued was only just, not good; and one of the New Testament who they argued was only good, not just. Tertullian adequately refuted their wicked fabrication.[52] Manichaeus, as we said, dreamed up the notion of two natures in man, one which could not avoid sinning and one which could not avoid doing good.[53] Pelagius, concerned for God's justice, attributed too much to free will.[54] There is little difference between him and those

---

51. Tangentially and briefly Erasmus expresses his reservations about Luther's doctrine of salvation *ex fide sola* (by faith alone).

52. *Adversus Marcionem (Against Marcion)* 1.2–8.

53. See n. 4 above.

54. See n. 15 above.

who attribute so much to human will as to say that through our natural powers, by morally good works, it can merit the supreme grace by which we are justified.[55] They seem to me to have wanted to urge man to moral effort by holding out a good hope of obtaining salvation, just as Cornelius, because of his prayers and almsgiving, deserved to be taught by Peter (Acts 10:1–43) and the eunuch by Philip (Acts 8:26–38), and St. Augustine, who assiduously sought Christ in Paul's letters,[56] deserved to find him. Here we can placate those who believe that man cannot do any good deed which he does not owe to God, by saying that the whole work is no less due to God, without whom we could achieve nothing; that the contribution of free will is very tiny indeed; and that our very ability to direct our mind to the things that pertain to salvation or to cooperate with grace is itself a gift of God. As a result of the controversy with Pelagius, Augustine reached a less favorable view of free will than he had previously held.[57] In the opposite way, Luther, who previously attributed something to free will, has been carried so far by the heat of his defense as to remove it altogether.[58] Yet I believe that among the Greeks, Lycurgus is blamed for having had the vines cut down because he hated drunkenness, whereas by bringing the sources of water closer he could have prevented drunkenness without abolishing wine-drinking.[59]

In my opinion, free will could have been established in such a way as to avoid that trust in our own merits and the other harmful

55. Neither Pelagius nor theologians like Biel believed quite what Erasmus says here: that justifying grace (sanctifying, cooperating grace) could be merited in any fashion. Pelagius held that once justifying grace had been given (not merited), free will was sufficient on its own. Biel held only that prevenient grace (not justifying grace) could be merited ex congruo.

56. Augustine, Confessions 7.21[27].

57. For an account of Augustine's confrontation with Pelagius see Peter Brown, Augustine of Hippo (London, 1967) 340–75.

58. Erasmus claims that the change in Luther's view of free will in his Assertio arose as his response to the papal bull Exsurge Domine of June 15, 1520. Erasmus is undoubtedly right that the extremity of Luther's position was provoked by the papal condemnation, but he was also aware of how far Luther had already moved in this direction as part of his theological evolution from 1516 to 1520.

59. According to Suetonius (Lives of the Caesars and Domitian 7.2), Domitian, not Lycurgus, ordered the vines cut down; Suetonius' anecdote says nothing about water. Athenaeus (Deipnosophista 10.445e) mentions that Lycurgus lopped off the drinkers of Dionysus and cast horns and drinking cups out of doors. But Erasmus seems to be drawing on some other source.

consequences which Luther avoids, as well as those which we mentioned above, yet so as not to destroy the benefits which Luther admires. This I believe is achieved by the opinion of those who ascribe entirely to grace the impetus by which the mind is first aroused, and only in the succeeding process attribute something to human will in that it does not resist the grace of God. Since there are three parts to everything—beginning, continuation, and completion—they ascribe the first and last to grace and allow that free will has an effect only in the continuation, insofar as in a single, indivisible act there are two causes, divine grace and human will, working together. However, grace is the principal cause and will the secondary cause, unable to do anything without the principal cause, whereas the principal cause is sufficient in itself.[60] Just so the power inherent in fire burns, yet the principal cause is God acting at the same time through the fire, a cause which would be sufficient in itself, and without which fire would have no effect if that cause were to withdraw itself.[61]

[On this moderate view man must ascribe his salvation entirely to the grace of God; for what free will accomplishes in this is very insignificant indeed, and what it can accomplish is itself due to divine grace, which first created free will, then freed and healed it.] And this will appease (if they can be appeased) those who believe that there is no good in man which he does not owe to God. Owe it he does, but in a different way and for a different reason, as an inheritance falling to children in equal shares is not called benevolence, since it comes to them all in the ordinary course of law. (It is called liberality if one or other of them has been given something over and above his legal due.) Yet children are indebted to their parents even on account of an inheritance.[62]

Illustrations of the cooperation of grace and free will

We will also try to give metaphors to illustrate what we are saying. A human eye, however healthy, sees nothing in the dark, and a blind one sees nothing even in the light. Just so the will, however free, can do nothing if grace withdraws itself from it; and even if it is light, a man with healthy eyes can close them so as not to see and can turn

---

60. See n. 23 above.

61. The view expressed in this paragraph is that of Augustine in *De civitate Dei* (*The City of God*) 5.10 and Thomas Aquinas (*Summa theologiae* Ia–IIae q 109 a 6).

62. That is, an inheritance is a free gift (grace) whether it is directly given or legally inherited.

them away so as no longer to see what he had been able to see. A man whose eyes have been blinded by some disorder is even more indebted, first to the creator, then to the doctor. However healthy the eye was before sin, it is injured by sin. And so what can the man who sees claim for himself? He can, however, impute something to himself if he deliberately closes his eyes or turns them away.

Here is another illustration. A child who still cannot walk has fallen, however hard he tried to walk; his father sets him back on his feet and shows him an apple some distance away.[63] The boy very much wants to run towards it, but because his limbs are so helpless he would soon have fallen again if the father did not put out his hand to support him and did not guide his steps. So, with his father guiding him, he reaches the apple, which his father gladly gives him as a reward for having run. The child could not have stood up unless his father had supported him; he would not have seen the apple unless his father had shown it to him; he would not have been able to walk unless his father had constantly aided his tottering steps; he could not have reached the apple unless his father had placed it in his hands. What claim can the child make for himself in this? And still he has done something; yet he has no reason to glory in his own powers, for he is completely in his father's debt.

Let us suppose for the moment that this is true of God. What does the child do in this process? He leans as best he can on the one who picks him up and he adjusts his stumbling steps to the father's guidance as well as he is able. The father could have dragged him against his wishes, and the child's mind could have resisted by refusing the apple. The father could have given him the apple without making him run, but he preferred to give it to him in this way, because it was better for the boy. I will readily allow that in gaining eternal life somewhat less can be ascribed to our own efforts than to the efforts of the boy running along guided by his father's hand.

Although we see that this attributes very little indeed to free will, even that seems too much to some, for they claim that grace alone works in us and that in all things our will is entirely passive, like an instrument of the Spirit of God, so that a good act cannot be called ours at all save insofar as divine generosity freely imputes it to us: for grace works in us not so much *through,* as *in* free will, just as the potter works *in* clay, not *through* it. Why, then, speak of a crown and

63. Augustine, *In Ioannis evangelium tractatus* (*Treatise on the Gospel of John*) 124.26.5.

a reward? God, they say, crowns his own gifts in us, desires his own good deeds to be our reward, and is pleased to count what he has done as fitting us for the heavenly kingdom. I do not see how, on these grounds, they can posit the existence of a free will which achieves nothing. The explanation would be easier if they were to say that it is worked upon by grace in such a way that it acts even as it is acted on; just as our body, according to the natural philosophers, is set in motion by the soul and cannot move at all without the soul, yet it is not only moved itself but moves other things, and sharing as it were in the activity, is called to share in the glory. For if God works in us as the potter works in clay, what credit or what blame can be imputed to us?

It is distasteful to bring the soul of Jesus Christ, which was itself unquestionably the instrument of the Spirit of God, into this inquiry. Yet if the weakness of the flesh prevents man from having merit, well, Christ himself was terrified of death, but wished that his Father's will, not his own, should be done.[64] Yet those who deprive all the other saints of any merit based on good works say that Christ's will is the source of merits.

Absolute necessity makes God unjust: he would punish people who are not responsible for their sins.

Moreover, those who say that there is no such thing as free will but that everything happens by absolute necessity are saying that God works not only good deeds in everyone but bad ones too.[65] It seems to follow from this that just as man cannot on any account be called the author of good works he cannot in any sense be called the author of bad ones either. Although this view seems openly to attribute cruelty and injustice to God, a most abhorrent charge to Christian ears (for he would not be God if any vice or imperfection were found in him), they have a counterargument to support even such an implausible case: "He is God, and what he does cannot but be entirely good and glorious. Even things which are bad in themselves are good if you

---

64. Matt. 26:39. See Erasmus' *Disputatiuncula de taedio, pavore, tristicia Iesu (A Short Debate concerning the Distress, Alarm and Sorrow of Jesus)* CWE 70 pp. 9–67. This brief treatise is a report of a friendly debate between John Colet—who held that Christ's suffering sprang from grief over the defection of his apostles and the Jews—and Erasmus, who held that it was caused by his human fear of suffering and death.

65. Though Erasmus mentions only "those who say," he is clearly thinking of Luther in his *Assertio*, article 36 (CWE 76 p. 306).

consider what is fitting for the universe, and they show forth the glory of God. No creature has any right to judge the creator's plan; it must submit itself absolutely to him in all things, to the extent that if it pleases God to damn this or that man, he must not complain but must willingly accept whatever is God's pleasure, being convinced once and for all that he directs all things in the best possible manner and cannot direct them in any way but the best way. Otherwise who could tolerate a man if he were to ask God, 'Why did you not make me an angel?' Would God not be justified in replying, 'You impudent man! If I had made you a frog, what cause for complaint would you have?' And if a frog were to remonstrate with God, 'Why did you not make me a peacock with colorful, eye-catching plumage?' would God not be right to say, 'You ungrateful beast! I could have made you a mushroom, or an onion; as it stands you can jump, drink, and croak.' And again, if a basilisk or a viper were to ask, 'Why did you make me an animal loathsome and deadly to all, instead of a sheep?' what would God reply? He might perhaps say, 'So it pleased me, and so it accorded with the beauty and order of the universe. You have suffered no injustice, no more than have flies, gnats, and other insects, every one of which I fashioned so as to be very wonderful to those who behold them. The spider is no less beautiful and wondrous an animal for being different from the elephant; indeed there are more wonders in a spider than in an elephant. Are you not satisfied with being a perfect animal of your kind? And you were not given poison to kill, but as a weapon to protect yourself and your offspring, just as oxen were given horns, lions claws, wolves teeth, and horses hooves. Every single animal has its use: the horse carries burdens, the ox draws the plough, the ass and the dog are helpful working beasts, the sheep serves to feed and clothe humans, and you have your medicinal uses.'"[66]

But let us stop reasoning with these creatures devoid of reason.[67] The disputation we undertook was on the subject of man, made in the image and likeness of God (Gen. 1:26) and for whose sake God created everything. And yet when we see that some men are born with

---

66. This paragraph setting forth the divine necessity of all creatures in their predetermined modes of existence may echo a passage in Valla's *De libero arbitrio dialogus* (*A Dialogue on Free Will*), trans. Charles Trinkaus, in *The Renaissance Philosophy of Man*, ed. Ernst Cassirer, Paul Oscar Kristeller, and John Herman Randall (Chicago, 1948), 173–4.

67. There is a suggestion that the animals are not the only ones devoid of reason but also the opponents to whom Erasmus here returns.

well-formed bodies and with splendid characters which seem innately inclined to goodness, but that other men, by contrast, are born with monstrous bodies, some suffering from appalling diseases, some with wits so dull as to be scarcely different from brute beasts, some even more brutish than the beasts themselves, some with characters so prone to evildoing that they seem to be drawn to it by the power of fate, and some utterly demented and possessed by demons, how ever shall we solve the problem of the justice and mercy of God? Shall we say with Paul, "Oh the depth, etc."? (Rom. 11:33). I think this is better than passing judgment with sinful presumption on God's counsels, which are unfathomable to man.

Still, it is far more difficult to explain why in some people God crowns his own good deeds with eternal glory, and in others punishes his own wrongdoings with everlasting torment. In order to explain this paradox, Luther's adherents need many auxiliary paradoxes to hold the line against the opposite side. They vastly exaggerate original sin, by which they claim that even the highest powers of human nature have been corrupted, so that of himself man can only be ignorant of God and hate him and even when justified by grace through faith can perform no action which is not a sin. They maintain that the tendency to sinning left in us from our first parents' sin is itself a sin, and an invincible one, so that there is not a single one of God's commandments which man, albeit justified by faith, can fulfill; and that all God's commandments have the sole purpose of magnifying God's grace, which bestows salvation without regard to merits.[68]

Yet it seems to me that all the while they are diminishing God's mercy in one place in order to increase it in another, as though someone were to serve a miserable lunch to his guests in order to appear all the more splendid at dinner, or were to imitate the painters, who give the illusion of light in a picture by shading the adjacent areas. For a start they make God almost cruel, venting his wrath on the whole of mankind for someone else's sin, especially since the people who committed it amended their ways and were punished most severely for the rest of their lives. Then when they say that those who have been justified by faith do nothing but sin, so that by loving and trusting God we become worthy of his hatred, are they not making God's grace extremely miserly? Grace justifies man by faith in such a way that he is

---

68. Erasmus here protests against Luther's exaggerated view of original sin and the consequent doctrine of "justified and sinner at the same time" (*simul justus et peccator*).

still nothing but sin! Moreover, in saying that God burdens man with so many commandments which have no other purpose than to cause him to hate God more and so be more utterly condemned, are they not making him even more merciless than Dionysius, the tyrant of Sicily, who deliberately promulgated many laws which he suspected most people would break if no one were to enforce them? At first he turned a blind eye, but soon, when he saw that nearly everyone had offended in some respect, he began to prosecute them and so brought everyone under his domination; yet his laws were of a kind that could easily have been kept had anyone so desired.[69]

Luther and Karlstadt overreacted to abuses associated with free will.[70]

I will not discuss now the reasons for which they teach that all God's commandments are impossible for us, for that is not what we undertook to do. I wanted only to show in passing that by trying too hard to extend the role of grace in the process of salvation they obscure it in other areas. I do not see how certain of their propositions can be consistent: they destroy free will and say that man is already guided by the Spirit of Christ, whose nature cannot abide the company of sin, and yet the very same people say that man, even after receiving grace, does nothing except sin. Luther seems to delight in hyperboles of this kind in order to drive out the hyperboles of others, as one cracks a tough knot in wood with the proverbial tough wedge. In some quarters audacity had reached enormous proportions: people were selling not only their own merits, but those of all the saints as well. And what manner of works? Singing hymns, muttering psalms, eating fish, fasting, wearing habits, and bearing titles. Luther drove out this nail with another, to the extent of saying that the merits of the saints were nonexistent,[71] that all good men's deeds had been sins,[72] which

69. The legal trickery used by Dionysius I of Syracuse (c. 430–367 BCE) to bilk his people of money and property is recounted in Pseudo-Aristotle, *Oeconomica* 2.2.20 1349a–1350a, though this particular ruse is not mentioned there.

70. See *The Shield-Bearer* 1, n. 165.

71. Erasmus refers to Luther's thesis 58 in his *Ninety-Five Theses* of October 15, 1521, elaborated in his *Explanations of the Ninety-Five Theses*. Luther says not that the merits of the saints are nonexistent but that they do not constitute a treasury of merits which might be dispensed, or even sold, as indulgences.

72. See Luther, *Assertio,* article 31 (WA 7, 136:21), *"In omni opere bono iustus peccat"* *("In Every Good Deed the Righteous Man Sins"); and article 36 (CWE 76 p. 301).*

would have drawn eternal damnation down on them unless faith and God's mercy had come to their aid.

In the same way, one side was making a juicy profit from confession and satisfaction, in which they had wonderfully entangled human consciences, and from purgatory, about which they had handed down a number of paradoxes. The opposing faction corrects this error by calling confession an invention of Satan (the most moderate of them say only that it need not be required), that there is no need of any satisfaction for sins, since Christ has paid the price of the sins of all mankind, and finally that purgatory does not exist.

One side says that every little prior's regulations are binding on pain of eternal damnation, and unhesitatingly guarantee salvation to those who obey them; the opposing side counters this hyperbole by calling all papal, conciliar, and episcopal constitutions heretical and anti-Christian. Thus one side exalts the pontiff's power most hyperbolically; the other side speaks of the pope in a manner I dare not repeat. One side says that monastic and priestly vows bind men in perpetuity under pain of damnation; the other side says such vows are sacrilegious and should not be taken or, if already taken, not be kept. The clash of such hyperboles produces the thunder and lightning which are now battering the world. If both sides continue to defend their overstatements so savagely, I foresee a battle between them such as there was between Achilles and Hector, who, being equally fierce, could only be parted by death.[73]

There is a proverb that says you should straighten a bent stick by bending it in the opposite direction;[74] but though that may be advisable in correcting behavior, I am not sure that it is tolerable in doctrinal matters. I admit there is a certain role for overstatement when encouraging or discouraging. For instance, to boost a fearful person's confidence you might well say, "Don't be afraid, God will say and do all things in you"; to check someone's sinful insolence, you might helpfully say that man was nothing but sin; or to counter those

73. Cf. Horace, *Satires* 1.7.11–3. These two paragraphs summarize some of the basic issues that were at stake in the Reformation. Erasmus contrasts the exaggeration and abuses of the catholic clergy with the reformers' extreme rejection of the institutional bases of catholicism: sacramental confession, the authority of the priesthood, and the power of the papacy. The bloody battle Erasmus foresees was waged fiercely for more than a century.

74. Cf. Aristotle, *Nicomachean Ethics* 2.9 1009b5: "We must drag ourselves away to the opposite extreme, for we shall get into the intermediate state by drawing well away from error, as people do in straightening sticks that are bent."

who put their own teachings on a par with the canonical Scriptures, you might usefully say that man was nothing but deceit. But when propounding principles in an inquiry into the truth, I do not think that paradoxical formulas like these, not far removed from riddles, should be used: here I favor restraint.

Pelagius seemed to attribute too much to free will; Duns Scotus attributed an ample amount; at first Luther merely mutilated free will by cutting off its right arm, but soon, not content with this, he cut its throat and made away with it altogether. I favor the opinion of those who attribute something to free will but most to grace. For you must not give so wide a berth to the Scylla of arrogance that you are driven towards the Charybdis of despair or indolence.[75] In treating a dislocated limb you must set it in its proper position, not twist it in the opposite direction. You must not fight the enemy in front of you so incautiously that you are wounded from behind. This moderate view will recognize the existence of some good work, admittedly imperfect, on account of which man can claim nothing for himself; but still of a certain degree of merit, but such that its completion will be due to God. There is such a vast amount of weakness, vice, and villainy in human life that if anyone is prepared to examine himself he will soon hang his head in shame; but we do not assert that man, though justified, is nothing but sin, especially since Christ calls him "born again" (John 3:3–8) and Paul calls him a "new creation" (2 Cor. 5:17).

Reasons why we must attribute something (however little) to free will

Why, you may ask, attribute anything at all to free will? To allow the ungodly, who have deliberately fallen short of the grace of God (Heb. 12:15), to be deservedly condemned; to clear God of the false accusation of cruelty and injustice; to free us from despair, protect us from complacency, and spur us on to moral endeavor. For these reasons nearly everyone admits the existence of free will; but, lest we claim anything for ourselves, they assert that it can achieve nothing without the perpetual grace of God. "What good is free will," someone may ask, "if it can achieve nothing?" What good is the whole man, I reply, if God works in him as the potter works with clay, and as he could have worked with stone? And now, it may be, this subject has been

---

75. Scylla was a sea monster on the Italian side of the straits of Messina; Charybdis, a whirlpool on the Sicilian side (Homer, *Odyssey* 12.73–110).

adequately proven to be such that it is not conducive to godliness to examine it in more detail than necessary, especially in front of the unlearned. I believe it has been shown that this doctrine is supported by more (and plainer) scriptural testimonies than the opposite doctrine. It seems clear that in many places Holy Scripture is obscured by figures of speech, or seems at first sight to contradict itself, so that whether we like it or not we must depart from its literal meaning and guide our judgment by interpretation. Finally, it seems obvious how many disagreeable, not to say absurd, consequences follow once free will is denied; and it appears that if we accept the opinion which I have expounded, it does not invalidate Luther's godly, Christian assertions that we must love God above all else, that we must remove our trust from our own merits, deeds, and powers and put it all in God and his promises. If all this is so, I should like the reader to consider whether he thinks it right to condemn the opinion of so many Doctors of the church, approved by the consensus of so many ages and nations, and to accept a number of paradoxes which are causing the present uproar in Christendom.[76] If these paradoxes are true, then I will frankly admit that I am too dull to follow them. I certainly do not knowingly oppose the truth; I wholeheartedly support true evangelical freedom, and I detest anything contrary to the gospel. I do not play the part of a judge here but of a disputant, as I have said; and yet I can truly affirm that in disputing I have acted with the same scrupulousness once demanded of those sworn to judge capital cases. Nor, though an old man, will I be either ashamed or reluctant to learn from a young one, if there is anyone who can teach me more evident doctrines with evangelical mildness.

I know I shall hear the objection, "Erasmus should come to know Christ and bid farewell to human learning. No one understands these matters unless he has the spirit of God."[77] Well, if I still have no understanding of Christ, I have clearly been far off the mark till now!

76. The full-scale Peasants' Revolt (*Bauernkrieg*) of 1525 had not yet occurred when Erasmus wrote, but there was much ferment and unrest among the peasants in the autumn and winter months of 1524.

77. Erasmus has in mind such accusations as Luther made in a letter to Conradus Pelicanus dated October 1, 1523: "I grieve and fear when I am praised, but I joy when I am maligned and cursed. If this surprises Erasmus, I am not at all surprised. He should learn to know Christ and say farewell to human wisdom. May the Lord illuminate him and make a new man out of Erasmus . . . Give my regards to Erasmus, if he will permit it." *Briefwechsel* 3 160:32–161:2, n. 661 (my translation).

And yet I would be glad to learn what spirit all the Christian Doctors and people (for it is likely that the people agreed with the bishops' teaching) have had these last thirteen hundred years, since they too lacked that understanding.

I have discussed the issue.[78] Let others pass judgment.

End of *A Discourse or Discussion concerning Free Will*,
by Desiderius Erasmus of Rotterdam

---

78. Latin CONTULI (printed in capital letters), referring back to the words of his title "Διατριβή *sive collatio*" ("Discourse or Discussion"). The importance of the title and this conclusion is that Erasmus presents and discusses opposing arguments; this does not mean that one side is not favored, but the issue is treated as if it were a question open to debate. At the end of *De servo arbitrio (The Enslaved Will)*, Luther specifically rejected Erasmus' stance, also in capital letters: "*NON CONTULI, SED ASSERUI ET ASSERO*" (I have not discussed the issue but rather I have asserted and do assert). See *The Enslaved Will*, p. 126.

LUTHER

The Enslaved Will (1525)

Comments on Erasmus' Introduction

The evidence of tradition: the true church is hidden

And so, as you take up the argument, you promise that you will deal only with canonical Scripture because Luther is not bound by the authority of any other writer. Well and good, and I accept your promise, although you do not make it with the supposition that these same writers would be useless for your case but rather so as not to expend effort to no avail. For you do not really approve of my boldness or my intention, whatever you may call it. For you set a good deal of stock by the long list of learned men accepted and approved throughout the ages, among whom were many who were most learned in theological studies, and also very holy men, some of them martyrs, many of them famous for their miracles. Add to them modern theologians, so many universities, councils, bishops, and popes. In sum, you have on your side learning, talent, numbers, greatness, lofty rank, bravery, holiness, miracles, and whatever else. But on my side I have only Wyclif and then Lorenzo Valla[1] (although Augustine, whom you ignore, is completely mine).[2] But such allies have no weight compared to the others. Luther is left all alone, a private person, a newcomer, with his friends, who do not have enough learning or talent or numbers or greatness or holiness or miracles to be able to cure so much as a lame horse. They make a display of Scripture, even though they consider it inconclusive, just as the other side does. And then they boast of the Spirit (which they never show) and of all the other things "which you could recount at length."[3] But then to us that is nothing more than what the wolf said to the nightingale it had devoured: you are a voice

---

1. See *A Discussion,* nn. 5 and 6.

2. Luther does rely heavily on Augustine about matters concerning free will and grace, but they are not in absolutely total agreement, for however little Augustine seems finally to allow for it, he does not believe that free will is nonexistent.

3. Virgil, *Aeneid* 4.333–34.

and nothing more.[4] For they want whatever they say to be believed (according to you) just because they say it.

I grant, my dear Erasmus, that you are not wrong to be moved by all these considerations. For more than a decade I myself was taken by them, so much so that I think no one was more taken in by them. To me also it seemed incredible that this Troy of ours, unconquered for so long, throughout so many wars, could one day be captured. And by my soul I swear to God that I would have persevered and would still be taken in by them today if God had not driven me to a different position by the goading of conscience and the factual evidence. Surely you can imagine that my heart is not made of stone (or if it were, that it could have melted when stricken and struggling against such huge waves and surges) when I dared to do something which I saw would bring the authority of your whole list dashing and flooding down on my head.

But now is not the time to weave the historical fabric of my life and deeds; I have undertaken these things not to commend myself but to extol the grace of God. Who I am, and the Spirit and intention that has caught me up in these matters, I commend to him who knows that all these things were accomplished by his will, not by my free will, although the world itself should have known this long since. And clearly, in your exordium, you put me in the hateful position of having no easy way to extricate myself except by boasting about myself and vilifying so many church fathers. But I will put it briefly. I accept your judgment; I yield in learning, talent, number of supporters, authority, and all else. But as for showing what the Spirit is or what miracles are or what holiness is, if I should demand these three from you, so far as I know you from your writings and books you will be seen to be so unlearned and ignorant that you could not have a single syllable to show us. Or if I were to require and demand that you be able to demonstrate with certainty which of all those persons you boast about was or is holy or had the Spirit or performed true miracles, I think you would work away at it mightily but futilely. You talk about many things which are commonly accepted and ordinarily preached, but you do not realize how lacking they are in credibility and authority if they are called to the judgment of conscience. The proverb is true: many are believed to be saints on earth whose souls are in hell.[5]

---

4. Erasmus, *Apophthegmata* 2.13 (LB IV 136CD); Plutarch, *Moralia* 233A; Karl Friedrich Wilhelm Wander, *Deutsches Sprichwörter-lexikon,* 5 vols (Leipzig, 1867–1880; repr. Scientia Verlag Aalen, 1963), IV, 861, nr. 12.

5. Wander II, 465 nr. 54.

But let us grant, if you like, that they all were holy, that they all had the Spirit, that they all performed miracles (which in fact you do not insist upon). Tell me this: were any of them holy, did any receive the Spirit or perform miracles in the name of or by the power of free will or in order to confirm the dogma of free will? Not at all (you will say), but rather all these things were done in the name of and by the power of Jesus Christ and for the dogma of Christ. Why, then, do you cite their holiness, Spirit, and miracles in favor of the dogma of free will, for which they were neither granted nor performed? And so all their miracles, Spirit, and holiness are on our side because we preach Jesus Christ and not the power or works of men. Why is it surprising that men who were holy, spiritual, and marvelous should be hindered by the flesh so that they spoke and acted according to the flesh, since that happened more than once to the apostles themselves when they were with Christ himself? And in fact, you do not deny but rather assert that the business of free will does not belong to the Spirit or to Christ but rather is something human, so that the Spirit which according to the promise would glorify Christ (John 16:14) is totally incapable of proclaiming free will. Thus, if the fathers sometimes proclaimed free will, they certainly spoke out of the flesh (according to their humanity), not out of the Spirit of God—much less did they do any miracles to support it. Therefore your allegation concerning the holiness, Spirit, and miracles of the fathers is irrelevant because they do not prove free will but rather the dogma of Jesus Christ, contrary to the dogma of free will.

But come now, you proponents of free will who assert that this dogma is true (that is, that it came from the Spirit of God), come now, I say, show the Spirit, perform the miracles, display the holiness! Certainly you, who assert, owe this much to us, who deny free will. Spirit, holiness, and miracles should not be required of us, who deny, but rather from you, who assert. Since a negative proposition has no force, it is nothing; it is not considered to prove anything nor does it need to be proved.[6] An affirmative one needs to be proved. You claim that the force and fact of free will is human, but no miracle has ever been seen or heard of that was performed by God for any dogma about a human matter but only to support a dogma about something divine. And we have been commanded never to admit any dogma

---

6. He seems to mean that a negative proposition such as "there are no snakes in Ireland" says nothing positively about what is in fact in Ireland; it has no positive meaning. And it is very difficult to prove a universal negative.

whatever that was not proved by signs from God (Deut. 18:22). Indeed Scripture calls mankind "vanity" (Eccles. 1:2) and "a lie" (Rom. 3:4)—which is to say that all things human are vanities and lies. Come then, come (I say), prove that this dogma of yours about a human vanity and a lie is true.

On this point, where is the showing of the Spirit? Where is the holiness, where the miracles? I see talent, learning, authority, but God gave these even to the gentiles. And yet I will not force you to perform any great miracles, not even to heal a lame horse, lest you should offer as an excuse that the times are carnal—although God is accustomed to confirm his dogmas with miracles with no regard to carnal times; for he is not moved by the merits or demerits of carnal times but only by his mercy, grace, and love of confirming souls in his unshakeable truth for his own glory. You can choose to do any miracle at all, however small. Indeed I will provoke, I will challenge and taunt your Baal (3 Kings 18:25–27)—I call upon you to create even a single frog in the name of and by the power of free will, though the pagan and wicked magicians in Egypt were able to create many of them (Exod. 8:7). For I will not burden you with the task of creating lice, which even they could not bring forth (Exod. 8:18). I will say something easier: take just one flea or louse (since you tempt and taunt our God to heal a lame horse); concentrate all the force and focus all the endeavors both of your god and of all your adherents, and if you can kill it in the name of and by the power of free will, you will be the victors, your case will be won; we, too, will come at once to adore that marvelous god, the killer of the louse. Not that I would deny that you can move mountains (Matt. 17:19), but it is one thing to say that something has been done by the power of free will and another to prove it.

And concerning holiness, I say the same as I said about miracles: in such a succession of times, men, and of everything you mention, if you can show one work (even picking up a straw from the ground) or one word (even the syllable "my"[7]) or one thought springing from free will (even the slightest sigh) by which they applied themselves to grace or merited the Spirit or obtained forgiveness or accomplished anything at all together with God (even the least bit, to say nothing of actual sanctification), once more you can be the victors and we the vanquished—if this happens (I say) by the power and in the name of free will. For there is plenty of evidence in Scripture about

---

7. That is, the tiniest syllable.

what is accomplished among mankind by means of divine creation.[8] And certainly you ought to show such things if you do not want to seem like ridiculous teachers who bruit throughout the world, with such supercilious authority, dogmas for which you can bring forth no evidence. For they will be called merely inconsequential fantasies, which it would be quite shameful to attribute to so many extraordinarily learned, holy, and miraculous men throughout so many ages. In that case we will prefer Stoics over you: though they described a wise man beyond anything they had seen, they at least tried to give a partial picture of him.[9] You cannot give any picture at all, not even a shadow, of your dogma.

Concerning the Spirit I say this: if, out of all those who assert free will, you can show me even one who had even the tiniest strength of mind or heart so as to be able, in the name and by the power of free will, to despise even a single penny, or to do without the least tidbit, or to put up with a single insulting word or gesture (to say nothing of despising wealth, life, or fame), once more you may have the palm of victory, we will gladly submit to your sway. This is what you owe us, since you have such mouthfuls of words asserting the power of free will, or else you will seem once more to be handing down decisions about angels on a pinhead[10] or you will look like the man enjoying a play in an empty theater.[11] But for my part I can easily show the opposite: those holy men you boast about, whenever they approached God in prayer or action, they proceeded with total oblivion of free will, despairing of themselves, asking nothing for themselves but grace pure and simple, quite different from merits—as Augustine often did and as Bernard said on his deathbed, "I have wasted my life because I have lived as a wastrel."[12] I do not see here any claim to a power which could apply itself to grace but rather the repudiation of all power because it is nothing but deleterious. It is true that sometimes these same saints spoke of free will in argumentation, just as I see it usually happens that people are different when they are concentrating

---

8. That is, man's will does cooperate with God's power in that all human functions and actions depend on God's active creation and sustenance; but salvation is willed entirely by God, with no input from the human will.

9. Seneca, *Epistles* 71.27–28. See also Erasmus, *Praise of Folly*, tr. Miller, 45–46.

10. Literally "about goat's wool," proverbial for a trivial question such as whether goat's hair can be called wool. See *Adages* 1.3.53 and Horace, *Epistles* 1.18.15.

11. Horace, *Epistles* 2.2.128–40.

12. See *Shield-Bearer* 1, n. 93.

on words and argument than when they are focused on feelings and deeds. In the one case, they speak differently than they felt before; in the other, they feel differently than they spoke before. But everyone, both the pious and the wicked, should be judged by their feelings rather than their speech.

But we will grant you even more; we will not require miracles, the Spirit, holiness. Let us return to the dogma itself. We ask only this: point out to us what work, what word, what thought this power of free will causes or attempts or accomplishes in order to apply itself to grace. For it is not enough to say "there is a power, there is a power, there is some power of free will." Nothing could be easier than just to say it. And that is not what was said by very learned or holy men who have been commended through the ages.[13] Rather, the baby simply needs a name (as the German proverb has it);[14] we need a definition of what that power is, what it does, what it suffers, what happens to it. For example, to use rather simplistic terms, this is the question: should this power pray or fast or labor or wear out the body, or give alms, or any such action, or at least attempt to do these things? For if it is a power it will achieve some operation. But on this point you are as dumb as a doornail—not a peep out of you.[15] And how should you define it, since by your own testimony you are still uncertain about this very power, varying and disagreeing about it among yourselves? How can something be defined if there is no consistency about what is to be defined? But let it be so; after Platonic millennium upon millennium, let it happen that at some time you agree among yourselves about it, and that its action then be defined as prayer or fasting or something else which may still lie hidden among the Platonic ideas;[16] who can make us certain that this is true, that it pleases God, that we are safe by doing what is right? especially since you yourselves confess that it is a human thing which does not have the witness of the Spirit, such a thing as the philosophers boasted about, which was in the world before Christ came and before the Spirit was sent from heaven, so that it is quite certain that this dogma was not sent from heaven but was born from

13. That is, they did not simply repeat a formula.

14. Wander, II, 1321, nr. 1114: *Das Kind muss doch einen Namen haben.*

15. Luther refers to the Seriphian frogs described in Pliny's *Naturalis historia* 8.83.227, which were proverbial for silent persons (*Adages* 1.5.31). Fish were also proverbial for silence (*Adages* 1.5.29).

16. Plato argues that ideas (abstract, immaterial entities) are the beings partially realized in the material world—a point on which Aristotle disagrees with him.

the earth long before, and hence it is all the more necessary to have some substantial testimony to confirm that it is certain and true.

Granted, then, that we are private and few, while you are public[17] and numerous; we are ignorant, you most learned; we are crude, you most talented; we were born yesterday, you are older than Methusalah;[18] we never had any acceptance, you were approved for so many centuries; and in brief we are sinners, fleshly and stupid, you are formidable for your holiness, Spirit, and miracles, fearful to the very devils themselves—assume this is all true, grant us at least the right you allow to the Turks and Jews, that we ask a reason for your dogma, as your Peter commanded you to do.[19] We ask it most humbly, that is, we do not require you to prove it by holiness, Spirit, or miracles, as we would have every right to demand from you, since you demand it of others. Indeed we will not even require you to show us a single example of a deed or word or thought in your dogma, but rather we ask you to simply teach us what it is, to clarify the dogma itself, what you mean by it and how you formulate it; and at least let us try to provide an example if you cannot or will not do so yourselves. Imitate the pope himself and his adherents, who say "do what we say, not what we do." And so you, also, say what this power requires to be done; we will gird ourselves and leave you at your leisure. Can't we get even as much as this from you? Since there are more of you, since you are more ancient, more venerable, more powerful in all respects than we are, it is all the more shameful for you to give no explanations to us (who are nothing at all by comparison with you), not to be able to give a proof to us (who are willing to learn and act according to your dogma), not to be able to prove it even by the miracle of killing a louse or by the least movement of the Spirit or by the tiniest work of holiness, not to be able to give an example of any work or word, and then finally—what is completely beyond the pale—not to be able even to give a clear formulation or understanding of your dogma so that we may at least imitate it. O you merry masters of free will! What are you now but a voice and nothing more?[20]

17. The Latin has *publicani,* rather than the usual *publici,* so as to suggest "publicans," the detested tax-gatherers of the New Testament.

18. In the Latin, Deucalion, the progenitor of a new human race after the great flood sent by Jupiter (Ovid, *Metamorphoses* 1.318–415).

19. 1 Pet. 3:15. "Your Peter" is a gibe against the papacy's claim of direct descent from the apostle Peter.

20. See note 4 above.

Now, my dear Erasmus, who are those who boast of the Spirit
and show nothing, who merely speak and want to be immediately
believed? Is it not your adherents, so praised to the skies? you who
say nothing and yet boast of so much and demand so much? For
Christ's sake, my dear Erasmus, we beg you and your adherents
at least to allow us to live in fear and trembling at the danger to
our conscience, or at least to put off assent to a dogma which you
yourself see is nothing more than an empty phrase and a sounding
of syllables, "there is a power of free will, there is a power of free
will," even if you should reach your final goal and all your points
were consistent and proved. Then, too, it is still uncertain among
your adherents whether the phrase has existence or not, since they
vary and disagree among themselves. It is very unfair—indeed it is
very miserable—to trouble our consciences with a mere ghost of
a phrase, and that an uncertain one, the consciences which Christ
redeemed with his blood. And if we do not allow ourselves to be
troubled, we are convicted of inconceivable pride, because we scorn
the fathers of so many ages who have asserted free will, whereas in
fact, as you see from what has been said, they made no definition
whatever of free will and the dogma of free will is constructed under
the pretext of their names though they cannot show us either its
species or its name, and thus they deceive the world with a lying
little word.

And so here, my dear Erasmus, I invoke the advice which you
yourself gave earlier, that we should avoid all such questions and teach
only Christ crucified, together with whatever is sufficient for Christian
piety.[21] That is what I have aimed at and done for a long time. For
what do I strive for except that the simplicity and purity of Christian
doctrine should reign and that all human inventions and additions
should be discarded and neglected? But what you advise us to do, you
do not do yourself. Indeed you do the opposite: you write discussions,
you celebrate papal decrees, you boast of human authority, and you
do everything you can to whisk us into what is foreign and alien to
Holy Scripture and to involve us in nonessentials so as to corrupt the
simplicity and sincerity of Christian piety and confound it with human
additions. Hence it is easy for us to understand that your advice to us
was not sincere and that what you write is not to be taken seriously,
but rather that you are confident you can lead the world wherever
you want with your empty verbal bubbles.

---

21. 1 Cor. 2:2. See *A Discussion*, CWE 76 p. 13.

And yet you never do lead it, since everything you say is absolutely and totally inconsistent, so that the person who called you a perfect match for Proteus or Vertumnus[22] was absolutely right or, as Christ says, "Physician, cure thyself" (Luke 4:23). It is shameful for a teacher to fall victim to the very vice he rebukes.[23] And so until you prove your affirmative we will stand by our negative, and facing the judgment of that whole choir of saints you boast about, and indeed the whole world itself, we are bold, we glory in not having to accept that which is nothing (and what it is cannot be certainly shown), and we charge all of you with incredible presumption and insanity for demanding that we accept it for no more reason than that you and your numerous, great, and ancient writers are pleased to assert something that you yourselves confess does not exist, as if it were a worthy thing for Christian teachers, in a matter of piety, to mock their miserable flock by treating something that does not exist as if it were a matter of great importance to their salvation.

Now where is that depth of Grecian perception which, up to this point at least, has manufactured pretty-seeming lies but now tells lies openly and nakedly? Where is that Latin industry (on a par with the Greeks) which thus deludes and is deluded by an utterly empty little word? But this is what happens to unwise or malevolent readers of books: everything which is due to weakness in the fathers or the saints they make into matters of the highest authority—a fault which is due not to the authors but to the readers. It is as if someone relying on the holiness and authority of St. Peter should contend that everything St. Peter said is true, trying to persuade us that he spoke the truth when, in Matthew 16:22, out of carnal weakness, he urged Christ not to suffer or when he ordered Christ to depart from him out of the ship (Luke 5:8) and in many other places where he was reproached by Christ himself.

Such people are like those who make jokes by babbling about how not everything in the gospel is true, seizing upon that passage in chapter 8:48 of John where the Jews say to Christ, "Are we not right to say that you are a Samaritan and that you have a devil?" Or the text "He is guilty of death" (Matt. 26:66). Or the text "We have found that this man is subverting our nation and forbidding us to give tribute to Caesar" (Luke 23:2). The asserters of free will do

22. Both were proverbial for shape-shifting (*Adages* 2.2.74) See *Shield-Bearer* 1, n. 22.

23. Dionysius Cato, *Disticha moralia* 1.30.

the same thing for a different reason and not intentionally but out of blindness and ignorance: they take from the fathers something which, out of the weakness of the flesh, they have said in favor of free will so as to set it over against something which, in the strength of the Spirit, the same fathers have said elsewhere against free will, and then they immediately insist and demand that the better yield to the worse. Thus it happens that they attribute authority to the worse passage because it agrees with their carnal meaning and they deny it to the better passage because it disagrees with their carnal meaning. Why not choose the better instead? For there are many such places in the fathers. And, to give one example, what could be more carnal—nay, what more impious, sacrilegious, and blasphemous—than to repeat Jerome's familiar saying, "Virginity fills heaven; marriage, the earth,"[24] as if the earth, not heaven, were owed to the patriarchs and apostles and Christian spouses or as if heaven were owed to pagan vestal virgins without Christ? And yet the sophists collect these passages and the like from the fathers, striving to give them authority by numbers rather than by judgment, as was done by that witless Faber of Constance, who recently bestowed on the public that "pearl" [Margaritum] of his, or rather that Augean stable, so that the pious would have something to make them sick to their stomachs.[25]

This is my response to you when you say it is unbelievable that God should have paid no attention to an error in his church for so many centuries and not revealed to any of his saints what we contend is the principal teaching of the gospel. First, we do not say that this error was tolerated by God in his church or in any of his saints. For the church is directed by the Spirit of God; saints are led by the Spirit of God (Rom. 8:14). And Christ remains with his church even to the end of

24. *Epistola XXII Ad Eustochium de custodie virginitatis (Epistle to Eustochium on Safeguarding Virginity)* 19 (PL 22, 405–6).

25. Johann Faber (1478–1541), a theologian who was originally attracted by the efforts at reform by Melanchthon, Zwingli, and Oecolampadius, but when he saw the dogmatic and ecclesiastical extremes to which they went he broke with them. He became a lifelong friend of Erasmus. In 1518 he was the vicar-general of Constance; in 1524 he became the confessor and chaplain of Ferdinand I of Austria; and in 1530 he was appointed bishop of Vienna. Two of his early polemical works against Luther were published in 1522 and 1524. Here Luther calls one of these works a "pearl," perhaps in reference to a dissolved pearl as a medicament or emetic or (ironically) to the pearls not to be thrown before swine (Matt. 7:6). Cleansing the Augean stables was one of the heroic labors of Hercules (*Adages* 2.4.21).

the world (Matt. 28:20). And the church of God is the foundation and the pillar of truth (1 Tim. 3:15). These things, I say, we know. For the creed we all accept says "I believe in the holy, catholic church," so that it is impossible for it to err even in the smallest point. And even if we admit that some of the elect are detained in error throughout their lives, nevertheless before their death they must necessarily return to the right path, because Christ says in chapter 8 of John "No one will snatch them from my hand."[26] But here is the task, here the toil,[27]—to establish with certainty whether those whom you call the church are the church indeed or whether instead they wandered astray throughout their lives but were finally brought back before they died. For if God allowed all those very learned men whom you mention to err throughout the course of however many centuries, it does not immediately follow that therefore he allowed his church to err. Look at God's people, Israel, where not even one of so many kings, over such a long time, can be reckoned as never erring. And under the prophet Elijah, all the people and all their public institutions were so far gone in idolatry that he thought he was the only one left (3 Kings 18:22), whereas in fact, though the kings, leaders, priests, and prophets, and whatever could be said to constitute the people of God were going to perdition, God had reserved seven thousand for himself (3 Kings 19:18). But who saw them or knew that they were the people of God? And so who is bold enough even now to deny that under these leading figures of yours (for you do not list any but men of public standing and reputation) God preserved his church among the common people and let all the others perish, as he did in the kingdom of Israel, for it is characteristic of God to lay low the elite of Israel and to destroy their fat cats (Ps. 77:31) but to preserve the dregs and remnants of Israel, as Isaiah says (10:22).

What happened in Christ's own time, when the apostles were scandalized (Matt. 26:31, 56) and he himself was denied and condemned by the whole people (Matt. 27:22–23), when only a few, like Nicodemus and Joseph[28] or even the thief on the cross (Luke 23:40–43), were saved? Were they then called the people of God? Indeed, they were the remnant of the people of God, but they were not given that name, and the ones given that name were not in fact the people of God. Who

---

26. John 10:28. The reference to John 8 in the Latin is an error, made either by Luther or the early printers.

27. Virgil, *Aeneid* 6.126–29.

28. John 3:1, Matt. 27:57.

knows whether or not, in the whole history of the world from the very beginning, the condition of the church of God has not been such that those who were not in fact the people and the saints of God were said to be so and that those among them, the remnant who were the people and the saints, were not said to be so, as is shown in the story of Cain and Abel (Gen. 4:1–8), Ishmael and Isaac (Gen 16:15. 21:12–14), and Esau and Jacob (Gen. 27:1–41)? Look at the age of the Arians, when hardly five bishops in the whole world were preserved as orthodox, and even they were expelled from their sees while the Arians ruled everywhere as the recognized, official church; nevertheless, among these heretics, Christ preserved his church, but in such a way that it was far from being considered or held to be the church.[29] Show me a single bishop who fulfills his office under the reign of the pope, show me a single council which treats matters of piety instead of palliums,[30] ranks, incomes, and other profane trifles which no one but a madman could attribute to the Holy Spirit. And nevertheless they are called the church, even though all of them (at least those who live so) are lost and are anything but the church. But even under them he saved his church, but not in such a way that it was said to be the church. How many holy men do you think that these inquisitors of heretical depravity[31] alone have burned and killed for some centuries now, such as Jan Huss[32] and persons like him, in whose times many holy men undoubtedly lived by the same Spirit.

Why are you not astounded instead, Erasmus, that from the beginning of the world there have always been more outstanding talents, greater

29. Arianism, a fourth-century heresy which denied the full divinity of Christ, spread widely for more than a hundred years, especially through the patronage of some emperors. There were indeed times when orthodox bishops were in a minority, but by the end of the fifth century the heresy had mostly died out.

30. The pallium is an ecclesiastical vestment bestowed by the pope on metropolitan and primatial bishops as a papal confirmation of their authority.

31. A technical term for special judges (often Dominicans) in matters of heresy appointed by the pope. The institution was founded by Gregory IX in 1231 and spread throughout Europe, especially in the South; to many its judgments and procedures seemed cruel and unjust, so that Luther could count on it as an instrument of antipapal propaganda.

32. Jan Huss (1369–1415), a theologian and rector of the University of Prague, was a supporter of John Wyclif, some of whose teachings (about the eucharist and the nature of the church) had been declared heretical. Huss himself was finally excommunicated in 1410, condemned by the Council of Constance in 1515, and burnt at the stake.

learning, more eager inquiry among the pagans than among Christians
or the people of God, as Christ himself confesses that the children of this
world are wiser than the children of light (Luke 16:8)? What Christian
could be compared with Cicero alone (to say nothing of the Greeks)
in talent, learning, and diligence? What, then, shall we say kept any of
them from being able to acquire grace? Certainly they exercised free
will with all their might, did they not? Who, then, would dare to say
that not one of them sought the truth with the utmost effort? And yet
it is necessary to assert that none of them achieved it. Here, too, do you
say it is unbelievable that in the whole course of history God abandoned
so many great men and allowed them to struggle in vain? Certainly if
free will had any existence or power, it should have had them in these
men in some single case or other. But it had no such power; indeed it
had the opposite power, so that this one argument alone is enough to
prove that free will has no existence, since not a single trace of it can be
shown from the beginning to the end of the world.

But to get back to the matter at hand, why is it surprising that God
should allow all the principal figures of the church to go their own
way, since in this same manner he permitted all the gentiles to go
their own way, as Paul says in Acts (14:16)? The reality of the church
of God, my dear Erasmus, is not as commonplace as the name "the
church of God," and the saints of God are not to be found everywhere
that the name "the saints of God" occurs. There is a pearl and there
are noble gems which the Spirit does not throw before swine, but, as
Scripture says, he keeps them hidden so that the wicked do not see
the glory of God.[33] Otherwise, if they were openly recognized by
everyone, how could it be that they are so afflicted and persecuted in
the world? As Paul says, "If they had known, they would not have
crucified the Lord of Glory" (1 Cor. 2:8).

I do not say these things because I deny that those you cite are saints
of the church of God but because, if anyone should deny that they
are in fact saints, it cannot be proved that they are and it must be left
uncertain; thus any argument based on their holiness is not sufficiently
reliable to confirm any dogma. I profess and consider them to be holy;
I call them and I believe them to be the church of God by the rule of
charity, not by the rule of faith. That is, charity, which thinks the best
of everyone, is not suspicious, but believes and presumes everything
good about its neighbors, calls every baptized person a saint;[34] nor is

33. Matt. 13:44–46, 7:6, 11:25.
34. 1 Cor. 13:7, Rom. 1:7.

there any danger if it is mistaken, since it is of the nature of charity to be deceived because it is vulnerable to all the uses and abuses of everyone since it is the general servant of the good and the bad, the faithful and the unfaithful, the truthful and the deceptive. But faith calls no one a saint except by the express and open judgment of God, because it is of the nature of faith not to be deceived. Thus, although all of us should consider each other to be saints by the law of charity, still no one ought to be judged to be a saint by the law of faith, as if it were an article of faith that one person or another is a saint, according to the way that the pope, that enemy of God, sets himself up in God's place (2 Thess. 2:4) and canonizes his own adherents, about whom he knows nothing. Rather, I say only that when those saints of yours, or rather of ours, disagree with one another, those should have been followed who have spoken best, that is, against free will and in favor of grace, and that those should be ignored who follow the weakness of the flesh and have borne witness to the flesh rather than to the Spirit. So too, when they are inconsistent, they should have been sifted and accepted when they speak according to the Spirit but rejected when they savor of the flesh. This is the way of a Christian reader as a clean animal which has cloven hooves and ruminates (Lev. 11:3). But nowadays we abandon judgment and gobble up all and sundry or, what is even worse, we judge perversely and spit out what is better and approve what is worse in one and the same author, and then we bestow on those worse judgments the title and authority of the holiness which those authors have earned because of good deeds and only because of the Spirit, not because of free will or the flesh.

Internal and external clarity of Scripture is the best test of who has the Spirit.

What, then, shall we do? The church is concealed, the saints are hidden. What to do? Whom shall we believe? Or, according to your very subtle argumentation, who makes us certain? Where will we discover the Spirit? If you consider learning, both sides have eminent teachers; or if their lives, there are sinners on both sides; or if Scripture, both sides embrace it. And the dispute is not so much about the canon of Scripture, which may not yet be sufficiently clear,[35] as about the meaning of Scripture. But there are proponents on both sides, and

35. What books constitute the canon of Scripture was still being discussed by Erasmus, Luther, and others. The reformers generally ended up rejecting the so-called deuterocanonical or intertestamental books of the Old Testament.

neither their numbers nor learning nor rank contribute anything to their case, much less their scarcity, lack of learning, or low status. And so the matter remains doubtful and a verdict has not yet been rendered,[36] so that it seems that the prudent thing for us to do is to accept the opinion of the Skeptics—unless perhaps you do the best of all by saying that you seek the truth and are in the process of learning; and in the meantime, until the truth becomes quite apparent, you incline to the side which asserts free will. My reply is this: you say something but not everything. For we will not discover who has the Spirit by arguments based on learning, manner of living, talent, large numbers, rank, ignorance, lack of learning, small numbers, or humility. And I do not approve of those who take refuge in boasting that they have the Spirit. For I have waged battles enough this past year, and still do so, with those fanatics who subject Scripture to their spirit;[37] by the same token I have fought up to now against the pope, in whose kingdom there is no proposition more widespread and well received than the proposition that Scripture is obscure and ambiguous and that the spirit to interpret it should be sought from the apostolic see of Rome, whereas in fact nothing could be more pernicious than this, because wicked men have relied on it to elevate themselves above Scripture and to make of it whatever they wish, until it has been completely crushed and we have been both believing and teaching nothing but the dreams of madmen. In brief, that proposition is not just a human invention but rather a poison spread throughout the world by the incredible malice of the very prince of all the demons (Mark 3:22).

This is what I say: spirits are to be investigated and proved in two ways. One is by means of the inner judgment, through which someone enlightened by the Holy Spirit or by the unique gift of God, for the sake of himself alone and his own salvation, distinguishes and judges with complete certainty concerning the dogmas and opinions of everyone. This is spoken of in 1 Cor. 2:15: "the spiritual person judges all things and is judged by no one." This pertains to faith and

---

36. Horace, *Ars poetica* 78.

37. Luther refers to his German book *Against the Heavenly Prophets in the Matter of Images and Sacraments* (1525), directed against the *Schwärmer,* or enthusiasts, who were more extreme in reformation than Luther himself—primarily Karlstadt, his main opponent and former collaborator, whose ideas about the eucharist and images were forcefully rejected by Luther. Karlstadt's view of the human will as capable of performing only evil acts is one of the opinions Erasmus takes up in *A Discussion.*

is necessary for all Christians, even private persons. Earlier we called this the interior clarity of Holy Scripture. Perhaps this is what was meant by those who replied to you that all things are to be decided by the judgment of the Spirit.[38] But this judgment is of no use to anyone else and has nothing to do with the question at issue here. No one, I believe, no one has any doubt about this judgment. But quite another matter is the exterior judgment, by which we judge spirits and dogmas with full certainty, not only for ourselves but also for others and for the salvation of others. This judgment belongs to the external ministry of the word and to public office and pertains above all to the leaders and heralds of the word. We employ it when we strengthen those weak in the faith and confute its adversaries (Tit. 1:9). Above we called this the external clarity of Holy Scripture. This is what we say: by the judgment of Scripture all spirits are to be proved in the presence of the church (1 Thess. 5:21). For among Christians it should above all be fixed and most firmly established that Holy Scripture is a spiritual light far clearer than the sun,[39] especially in matters necessary for salvation. But because we have long been wrongly persuaded of the opposite by that pestilent claim of the sophists that Scripture is obscure and ambiguous, we are first of all forced to prove our very first principle, which is needed to prove everything else—something which the philosophers consider to be absurd and impossible to do.[40]

First of all, Moses says in chapter 17:8–11 of Deuteronomy that if any difficult case arises, they should go to the place the Lord has chosen for his name's sake, and there they should consult the priests, who should give judgment about it "according to the Law of the Lord." He says, "according to the Law of the Lord." But how will they judge unless the Law of the Lord is outwardly quite clear, so that they can give a proper judgment? Otherwise, it would have been enough to say "they will judge by their own spirit." Indeed this is the way it is in all government of the people, so that all the cases of all the litigants can be settled by law. But how could they be settled if there were no very certain laws to be guiding lights of the people? For if the laws were ambiguous and uncertain, not only could no cases be dispatched but there would be no certain moral criteria, since, in fact, laws are made so that morality can be regulated and cases decided according to

---

38. See *A Discussion,* p. 5.

39. Cf. 2 Pet. 1:19.

40. First intellectual principles (like the principle of noncontradiction) were held to be inborn and incapable of demonstration. See Aristotle, *Posterior Analytics* 1.3.

a certain standard. Therefore it is necessary that what is to be the rule and measure of others should be completely certain and clear, such as the Law is. But if the light and certainty of laws is necessary in civil governments, which are concerned with temporal matters and have been granted as a free gift from God to the whole world, would he not grant to his Christians, namely the elect, even clearer light and greater certainty in laws and regulations for their guidance and the settlement of their cases? Especially since he wants his people to consider temporal matters to be quite unimportant. For if God so clothes the grass of he field, which stands today and tomorrow is thrown into the oven, how much more will he care for us? (Matt. 6:30)

But let us proceed to use Scripture to destroy that pestilent proposition of the sophists. Psalm 18:9 says, "The precept of the Lord is like a clear light shining in our eyes." I believe that what shines in our eyes is not obscure or ambiguous. So too Psalm 118:130: "the opening of your words shines and gives understanding to the little ones." Here he speaks of the word of God as if it were a door or an aperture because it is open to all and illuminates even the little ones. In chapter 8:20, Isaiah submits all questions "to the Law and to testimony," and he threatens that if we do not do this we will be denied the light of dawn. In chapter 2, Zachary[41] commands that the people seek the Law from the mouth of the priest, since he is the angel of the Lord of Hosts, and what a splendid angel or ambassador of the Lord he would be if his message were so ambiguous to him and unclear to the people that neither he knew what he was saying nor they what they were hearing. And in the whole Old Testament, what praise is more often given to Scripture, especially in Psalm 118:105, than that it is a most certain and manifest light? For he celebrates its brightness as follows: "Your word is a lantern for my feet and a light on my path." He does not say "A lantern for my feet is your Spirit alone," although he recognizes the task of the Spirit, saying, "Your good Spirit will lead me to level land" (Ps. 142:10). And he speaks of both the way and the path, out of overabundant certainty.

Let us proceed to the New Testament. In Romans 1:2, Paul says that the gospel was promised by the prophets in Holy Scripture, and in chapter 3:21 that the Law and the prophets have testified to justification by faith. And how can it testify if it is obscure? Indeed, throughout his epistles he makes the gospel a word of light, a gospel of clarity, as he does so deliberately and abundantly in chapters 3:7–11

---

41. Mal. 2:7. Either Luther or the printer miswrote *Zacharia* for *Malachia*.

and 4:3–6 of 2 Corinthians, where he presents a glorious discussion of the clarity both of Moses and of Christ. Peter also says in 2 Peter 1:19, "We have the very sure word of prophecy; you do well to attend to it as a lantern shining in a dark place." Here Peter makes the word of God a bright lantern, all else being in darkness. And shall we make the word into obscurity and darkness? Christ often calls himself the light of the world (John 8:12) and John the Baptist a bright and burning lantern (John 5:35), undoubtedly not because of holiness of life but because of the word, just as Paul in Thessalonians[42] speaks of the bright lamps of the world, "because," he says, "you keep the word of life." For life without the word is uncertain and obscure.

What are the apostles doing when they prove their preaching by means of Scripture?[43] Darkening what is dark by means of more darkness? Making something more known by what is less known?[44] What is Christ doing in John 5:39, where he tells the Jews to examine Scripture, which bears witness to him? Making them more doubtful about believing in him? In Acts 17:11 what are the people doing who, having heard Paul, read Scripture day and night to see whether these things were true or not? Do not all these places prove that the apostles, like Christ himself, call upon Scripture to give the clearest testimony to the truth of what they say? And we have the effrontery to make Scripture obscure? I ask you, are the following words of Scripture obscure or ambiguous: "God created heaven and earth" (Gen. 1:1), "the word was made flesh" (John 1:14), and all those teachings which the whole world has accepted as articles of faith? Where did it get them if not from Scripture? And even today, what are they about who preach, interpret Scripture, and clarify it? And if the Scripture they clarify is obscure, who will make us certain that their clarification is certain? Another new clarification? And who will clarify that? And thus there will be a regression to infinity.[45]

---

42. Phil. 2:15–16. By a slip of Luther (or his printer) "Thessalonians" appeared instead of "Philippians."

43. For example, Peter in Acts 2:14–20.

44. *Obscurum per obscurius* (what is obscure by what is more obscure) is a well known saying (Stevenson, 2536.5) but I have not been able to pinpoint an example earlier than Luther.

45. In an infinite regression there can be no starting point for the series and hence it cannot exist. Erasmus turns the argument from infinite regression concerning the necessary accesses of grace against Luther in *The Shield-Bearer* 2, CWE 77 p. 723.

In sum, if Scripture is obscure and ambiguous, what need was there for God to hand it down to us? Were we not already sufficiently obscure and ambiguous without having heaven increase our obscurity and ambiguity and darkness? Then what room is left for what the Apostle says: "All Scripture inspired by God is useful to teach, to reprove, to refute" (2 Tim. 3:16). No, it is completely useless, Paul; what you attribute to Scripture is to be sought from the fathers who have been accepted throughout the ages and from the See of Rome. Hence we should reject the opinion you write to Titus that a bishop should be proficient in encouraging sound doctrine and confuting gainsayers and in stopping the mouths of babblers and those who deceive and lead minds astray (Tit. 1:9–10). How will he be proficient if all you leave him is Scripture that is obscure, that is, weapons of flax and thin stubble-straws[46] for swords? Then Christ will also have to take back the false promise he made us when he said, "I will give you speech and wisdom so that your adversaries will not be able to resist you" (Luke 21:15). How will they not resist if we fight against them with obscure and ambiguous weapons? And you, too, Erasmus, why do you give us an outline[47] of Christianity if Scripture is obscure to you? But I think that I have long since become tiresome even to dullards by wasting so much time and trouble about a matter that is so obvious. But so much was necessary to eradicate that shameless and blasphemous proposition that Scripture is obscure, so that you could see, my dear Erasmus, what you are saying when you deny that Scripture is quite clear. For at the same time you will necessarily also be asserting that all those saints you cite are much less clear. For who is there to make us certain about their light if you make Scripture obscure? And so those who deny that Scripture is completely lucid and manifest leave us nothing but darkness.

But at this point you will say: all of this has nothing to do with me; I do not say that Scripture is obscure everywhere (who could be that insane?) but only on that point and ones like it. I reply: I do not say these things only against you but rather against all who think as you do. And then, against you I am speaking about all of Scripture; I mean that no part of it can be said to be obscure; what we reported from

---

46. Ovid, *Metamorphoses* 1.492.

47. Luther may be referring to the straightforward attitude of a good Christian, given by Erasmus in *A Discussion* (CWE 76 pp. 9–10), or perhaps to the more detailed verse catechism Erasmus wrote for Colet's school at St. Paul's (CWE 85, No. 49 pp. 92–106).

Peter is unbending on this point, that the word of God is a lamp for us shining in a dark place (2 Pet. 1:19). But if part of this lamp does not shine, it will be part of the dark place rather than of the lamp itself. Christ has not enlightened us in such a way that he intended some part of his word to be left obscure to us, at the same time commanding us to pay attention to it;[48] for there is no point in commanding us to pay attention to it if it gives no light. Therefore, if the dogma of free will is obscure or ambiguous, it has nothing to do with Christians or Scripture and should be ignored, and it should be numbered among those fantasies condemned by Paul among quarreling Christians.[49] If, however, it pertains to Christians and Scripture, it should be clear, open, and manifest, just like all other manifest articles. For all the articles of Christianity should be such that they are not only completely certain to Christians themselves but also confirmed by manifest and clear Scripture against others, so that they shut up others and keep them from saying anything against such articles, according to Christ's promise to us: "I will give you speech and wisdom so that all your adversaries will not be able to resist you" (Luke 21:15). If our mouths are weak on that point, so that our enemies are able to resist, then he is not speaking the truth when he says that no adversary can resist what we say. Therefore, either we will have no adversaries concerning the dogma of free will (which will be the case if it has nothing to do with us) or if it does have something to do with us we will indeed have adversaries, but they will not be able to resist us.

But our adversaries' inability to resist (since that is the case here) is not such that they are forced to change their opinion or be persuaded to yield or remain silent. For if someone is unwilling to believe, who will force him either to admit his error or to keep quiet? For, as Augustine says, who babbles more than a blockhead?[50] But because their mouth is stopped so that they have no real reply but still go on making many replies, common sense still judges that they are saying nothing. It is easier to show this by examples. In Matthew 22(:23–32), when Christ silenced the Sadducees by citing Scripture to prove the resurrection of the dead from the words of Moses in the third chapter in Exodus, "I am the God of Abraham," etc. "He is not a God of the dead but of the living,"[51] they could not resist him on this point or

48. Cf. John 5:39.
49. 1 Tim. 4:7, 2 Tim. 2:14.
50. *City of God* 5.26.2 (PL 41 174).
51. Exod. 3:6, Matt. 22:32, Mark 12:26–27, Luke 20:37–38.

say anything against him. But did they in fact yield to his argument? And how often did he refute the Pharisees by very manifest scriptural texts and arguments, so that the people saw that they were overcome and even they themselves perceived their defeat? Nevertheless, they continued to be his adversaries. In chapter 7 of Acts, as Luke bears witness, Stephen spoke in such a way that they could not resist the wisdom and the spirit which spoke in him (Acts 7:54–57). But what did they do? Did they yield? By no means! Ashamed to be defeated and unable to resist, they went mad; closing their eyes and ears, they brought false witnesses against him (Acts 8).[52] And as he was standing before the Council, see how he confuted his adversaries. When he had reckoned up the gifts of God to that people from the very beginning and had proved that God had never commanded that a temple be built for him (for that was the charge against him and the issue at hand), he finally granted that a temple was indeed built under Solomon (Acts 7:2–50). But he took that into account in this way: "But the most high does not dwell in the works of human hands" and as proof he cited the prophet Isaiah (66:1), "What is this house you are building for me?" Tell me, what could they say at this point against such manifest Scripture? Nevertheless, they were not affected and remained fixed in their opinion. Wherefore he inveighed against them, saying, "Uncircumcised in your hearts and ears, you always resist the Holy Spirit, etc." (Acts 7:51). He says they resisted though they were unable to resist.

Let us come to our own opponents. Jan Huss cites Matthew 16:18 against the pope: "the gates of hell do not prevail against my church" (is there any obscurity or ambiguity in this text?), "but the gates of hell will prevail against the pope and his adherents, since they are well known throughout the whole world for their manifest wickedness and crimes" (is that also obscure?); "therefore the pope and his adherents are not the church about which Christ is speaking."[53] What could they say against this? Or how could they resist the speech which Christ himself had given Huss? But nevertheless they did resist and went on doing so until they burnt him—so far were they from yielding to that interpretation. And Christ does not remain silent on this point when he says, "the adversaries will not be able to resist"

---

52. Acts 6:13. Somehow the wrong number, 8, displaced the correct number, 6, where the false witnesses against Stephen are mentioned.

53. John Huss, *De ecclesia (The Church),* tr. and ed. David S. Schaff (New York: Charles Scribner, 1915) chapter 7, pp. 56–66.

(Luke 21:15). "They are adversaries," Huss says; therefore they will resist, for otherwise they would not be adversaries but friends, and yet they will not be able to resist. How is that any different from saying that by resisting they will not be able to resist? And so if we are also able to refute free will so that our adversaries cannot resist even if they persist in their belief and resist contrary to their conscience, we will have done enough.

For I have had enough experience to know that no one wants to be vanquished, and (as Quintilian says)[54] there is no one who would not rather appear to know than to learn, just as in that proverbial saying of ours which everyone quotes, using it rather than truly feeling its force, indeed abusing it: "I choose to learn; I am ready to be taught and to accept advice and follow the better course; I am human, I can err."[55] In fact, under that specious mask of humility they can confidently say, "I am not satisfied; I do not understand; he does violence to Scripture; he stubbornly asserts," certain as they are that no one would suspect such humble souls of stubbornly resisting and even fighting strongly against truth they recognize. Thus they make it appear that their refusal to assent must be attributed not to their malice but rather to the obscurity and ambiguity of the arguments. This is also what the Greek philosophers did: none of them wanted to seem to yield to someone else, even if he was clearly vanquished. So they began to deny first principles, as Aristotle reports.[56] At the same time we flatter ourselves and others in the conviction that there are many good men on the earth who would willingly embrace the truth if there were someone to teach it with clarity, and we claim it should not be presumed that so many learned men throughout the ages erred or did not recognize the truth—as if we did not know that this world is the kingdom of Satan, where, apart from the natural blindness inborn in us from the flesh, we are hardened in that blindness by most wicked spirits reigning over us, holding us captive in the inhuman darkness of demons.

If, then, Scripture is quite clear, you say, why have such powerful minds been blind on this point for so many ages? I reply they were blind in their praise and glorification of free will in order that its vaunted power, by which humanity applies itself to what pertains to eternal salvation, might be revealed as a power which does not see what is

54. Luther paraphrases a remark made by Quintilian (*Institutio oratoria,* preface).

55. *Humanum errare est* was a frequently repeated saying. See Otto, homo 3, and Stevenson, 707–8.

56. I have not found the place in Aristotle to which Luther refers.

seen or hear what is heard, much less does it understand or desire it
(1 Cor 2:14). This is the point supported by what Christ quotes from
Isaiah and what the apostles so often assert: "Hearing you will hear
but not understand; seeing you will not see."[57] What does this amount
to except that free will or the human heart is so overburdened by the
power of Satan that, unless it is marvelously aroused by the Spirit of
God it cannot on its own either see or hear what strikes its eyes or ears
so clearly as to be palpable? Such is the wretchedness and blindness
of the human race. For the evangelists themselves were amazed that
the Jews were not persuaded by the works and the words of Christ,
which were clearly irrefutable and undeniable, and in this place in
Scripture they found themselves an answer, namely that mankind left
to itself seeing does not see and hearing does not hear. What could be
stranger? "The light shines in the darkness," he says, "and the darkness
does not comprehend it" (John 1:5). Who would believe this? Who
ever heard of such a thing? A light shines in the darkness and still the
darkness remains dark and is not illuminated? In fact, in matters divine
it is not surprising that powerful minds were blind for so many ages; in
human matters it would be surprising. In matters divine, however, the
wonder would be that one or two persons should not be blind, but
it is not surprising that everyone should be blind. For apart from the
Spirit, what is the whole human race but the kingdom of the devil,
as I said, a confounded chaos of darkness (Gen. 1:2)? Hence Paul
calls devils "the rulers of this darkness" (Eph. 6:12). And in the first
chapter[58] of 1 Corinthians, he says, "None of the princes of this world
has known the wisdom of God" (1 Cor. 2:8). What do you suppose
he thinks of the others if he asserts that the princes of this world are
the slaves of darkness? For by "princes" he understands the foremost
and loftiest in the world, the ones you call powerful minds.

Why were all the Arians blind? Were there not among them men
of powerful intellect? Why was Christ "foolishness to the gentiles"?
Are there not powerful minds among the gentiles? Why was he "a
stumbling-block to the Jews" (1 Cor. 1:23)? Have there not been
powerful minds among the Jews? Paul says, "God knows the thoughts
of the wise, that they are empty."[59] He chose not to say "of men,"
as the text has it;[60] he meant the first and foremost of men so that

---

57. Matt. 13:14–15, Isa. 6:9–10.

58. An error on Luther's or the printer's part: the second chapter is meant.

59. 1 Cor. 3:20, Ps. 93:11.

60. That is, the text Paul is citing from Psalm 93:11.

by them we might judge the rest. But about this I will perhaps say something later. It is enough to set down in the introduction that Scripture is perfectly clear and by it we can defend our positions so thoroughly that our adversaries cannot resist them. And what cannot be defended by it is alien and unchristian. But if there are any who do not see this clarity and are blind or scandalized in the full light of day, if such persons are wicked, they make it clear how great is the majesty and power of Satan among the children of men, so that they neither hear nor understand the perfectly clear word of God, just as if someone deceived by a magic trick should think that the sun is a cold piece of charcoal or imagine that a stone is a piece of gold. But if they are pious persons, they may be reckoned as among the elect who are sometimes[61] led into error so that the power of God in us may be made clear, without which we cannot see or understand[62] anything at all. For it is not the weakness of our minds (as you argue) that prevents us from understanding the word of God. Indeed, nothing is more suited to understanding the word of God than such weakness, for Christ came because of the weak and to them he sends his word.[63] [What prevents us is the wickedness of Satan enthroned in our weakness, reigning and resisting the word of God. If Satan did not do this, if we heard God speak to us just once, everyone in the world would be converted and nothing more would need to be said.]

What need for me to say much about it? Why not make this introduction also the conclusion of my case and render a judgment against you in your very own words, according to what Christ says, "By your own words you will be justified, by your own words you will be condemned" (Matt. 12:37)? For you say that Scripture is not very clear on this point. Hence, without commitment you give arguments on both sides, what can be said for it and against it; you do nothing more than that in that whole book of yours, which for that reason you call *A Discussion* rather than *A Decision*[64] or some other name, because

---

61. WA and the first edition of 1525 read *aliquanto* ("somewhat") but I have corrected to *aliquando* ("sometimes") as Otto Clemens does in his edition of the Latin (*Luthers Werke in Auswahl,* vol. 3, 5th rev. ed. [Berlin, 1959].

62. I supply "understand" (*capere*) here because the parallelism and the *capiant* of the next sentence show it has been carelessly omitted.

63. Matt. 9:12, 11:25; cf. 1 Cor. 9:22.

64. Luther's *apophasin* (a Latinized Greek word) is an argument that negates everything but the true conclusion. In Erasmus' case it would mean eliminating all views of free will except the one he holds to be true. But Erasmus actually

you were writing to discuss everything but affirm nothing. If, then, Scripture is not quite clear, why are those people you boast about so much not only blind on this point but also ready to define free will so rashly and boldly as if on the basis of certain and very clear Scripture?— I mean that large body of very learned men who have been approved throughout so many centuries right up till our own day, many of whom are recommended not only by a wonderful skill in interpreting Scripture but also by the holiness of their lives, some of whom not only defended the teachings of Christ by their writings but also gave witness for it with their blood. If you mean what you say, you firmly hold that free will is asserted by writers endowed with a marvelous command of Holy Scripture, so much so that they have also borne witness to it with their blood. If that is true, they considered Scripture to be quite clear; otherwise, what would that marvelous command of Holy Scripture be? Then, too, how light headed and reckless would they be to shed their blood for something uncertain and obscure! For this is not Christian but rather diabolical martyrdom.

And then you, too, should take a serious look and consider well whether you think more credence should be given to the precedent of so many learned and orthodox men—so many saints and martyrs, so many ancient and modern theologians, so many universities, councils, bishops, and popes who thought Scripture is very clear and confirmed it both in their writings and with their blood—or rather should be given to your isolated private judgment that Scripture is not very clear, a judgment coming from you, who have perhaps never sighed or shed a single tear for the teachings of Christ. If you think they judged rightly, why do you not imitate them? If you do not think so, why do you put out such mouthfuls of boasts, such copious rhetoric, as if you wanted to overwhelm me with the storm and flood of your oratory, which actually rushes mightily back on your own head, while my ark is lifted up to the safety of the heights (Gen. 7:17)? For you attribute to these numerous great men the very height of both folly and recklessness when you write that they were very learned in Scripture and defended it with their pens, their lives, their deaths, while you, on the other hand, contend that it is obscure

---

compares the various views of free will, and, though he clearly favors one, he does not completely negate all the others. He discusses or discourses (Διατριβή sive Collatio) without firmly deciding. Luther (or his alleged helper) personifies *A Discussion* as a woman (the Latin and Greek designations in the title Διατριβή sive collatio de libero arbitrio are feminine).

and ambiguous, that is, you do nothing more than make them very ignorant in their knowledge and very foolish in their assertions. I would not have honored them as little by scorning them privately as you have by praising them publicly.

I have caught you on the horns of a dilemma, as they say. For one of the two must be false: either what you say about how marvelous they were in their command of Scripture, their lives, and their martyrdom, or what you say about the lack of clarity in Scripture. But when you are carried away by your belief that Scripture is not very clear (and that is your point throughout your whole book), all we can think is that you are merely amusing yourself or flattering them, that you are not at all serious when you say that they were very learned in Scripture and suffered martyrdom for Christ, for you say it simply to pull the wool over the eyes of the people and to make trouble for Luther and to heap scorn and contempt on his case by means of empty words. But I say that neither horn is true but that both are false: [I say first that Scripture is quite clear and then that those writers, insofar as they upheld free will, were quite ignorant of Holy Scripture and finally that they upheld it not with their lives or deaths but only with their pens and that their wits were wandering when they did so.]

And so I conclude this little disputation as follows: [if Scripture up till now is unclear, according to your own testimony, then it has not been and cannot be used to define anything about free will. Moreover in the lives of mankind, from the beginning of the world, nothing has been shown to support free will, as was said above.] Therefore, to teach something that not a single word of Scripture prescribes and that is not demonstrated by any human deed outside of Scripture has nothing to do with Christian dogma but belongs with the *True Histories* of Lucian,[65] except that Lucian's jokes and his deliberate satire of human folly do not deceive or harm anyone, whereas these adversaries of ours put forth their insanities about a serious matter which pertains to eternal salvation, and they do so to the perdition of innumerable souls. And in this way I might have resolved this whole question of free will, even by the testimony of my adversaries, which supports me and refutes them—since there is no stronger proof than the testimony and confession of a guilty man against himself.

65. Lucian of Samosata (c. 120–180), Greek rhetorician, orator, and satirist. His *True Histories* (which he begins by announcing that they are totally false) recounts a fantastic voyage (by ship and in the belly of a whale) to the moon and the Elysian Fields. He was a popular author among the humanists: More and Erasmus translated (c. 1505) some dialogues of Lucian.

But since Paul teaches us to refute[66] let us go on with the case
and treat the matter in the order in which *Discussion* takes it up, first
by confuting the arguments brought forth to support free will, then
by defending our arguments against attempts to confute them, and
finally by fighting against free will on behalf of God's grace.

Refutation of Erasmus' Passages from the Old Testament Supporting Free Will

Three views of grace and free will—or, rather, three statements of one view

Out of one opinion about free will you fashion three. One that you
think hard but sufficiently probable is held by those who deny that
anyone can will the good without peculiar grace[67]; they deny that
anyone can begin, they deny that anyone can continue, complete, etc.
You approve of this opinion because it leaves to mankind effort and
endeavor but it does not leave to them the right to ascribe anything
to their own powers. A harder opinion is held by those who contend
that free will can achieve nothing but sin, that only grace effects
anything good in us, etc. The hardest is held by those who say that
free will is an empty expression, that God works both good and bad
in us, and that everything that is done happens by necessity only. You
claim that you are writing only against the last two opinions. Do you
have any idea what you are saying, my dear Erasmus? You fashion
three opinions as if they stemmed from three sects because you do not
understand that one and the same thing, expressed in different words,
is being propounded by all of us who belong to one and the same sect.

But let me show and demonstrate the lassitude[68] or rather
the stupidity of your judgment. I ask you, how does the definition of
free will which you gave earlier jibe with this first, sufficiently probable
opinion? For you said that free will is a power of the human will by
which a person can apply himself to what is good. But here you give

---

66. Titus 1:11. The Latin text here has a transliteration, *epistomisin* for ἐπιστομίζειν,
"to refute." Luther is showing his familiarity with the Greek New Testament first
published by Erasmus (1515).

67. See *A Discussion,* n. 22.

68. The definitive modern editions have *oscitantem,* a participle which is
syntactically impossible in this context. Luther probably intended *oscitationem,* and
I have so translated.

the opinion, and approve of it, that a person cannot will anything good without grace. The definition affirms what this instance of it denies. In your free will we find "it is" and "it is not"; at one and the same time you approve of and condemn us; you also condemn and approve of yourself in one and the same dogma and article. Don't you think it is a good thing to apply oneself to what concerns eternal salvation, which is what your definition attributes to free will? But then there would be no need of grace if free will alone could apply itself to what is good. And so the free will you define is different from the one you defend. And now Erasmus has two free wills, totally inconsistent with one another and with free will as conceived by others.

But apart from the free will fashioned by the definition, let us see what this opinion itself brings up against it. You admit that without peculiar grace a person cannot will the good (for we are not disputing about what the grace of God can do but about what a person can do without grace). Therefore you grant that free will cannot will the good, and that is as much as to say that it cannot apply itself to those things which pertain to eternal salvation—the happy tune sung by your definition. Indeed a little before that you say that the human will after sin[69] is so depraved that it has lost its freedom and is forced to serve sin and cannot recall itself to a better course. And, if I am not mistaken, you make this the opinion of the Pelagians. Here, I think, there is no escape open to Proteus.[70] By his clear language he is held fast, admitting that the will has lost its liberty and is constrained and held captive in slavery. Oh wonderful free will!—which Erasmus himself says has lost its freedom and become the slave of sin. When Luther said this, nothing could be more absurd and unheard of, nothing more useless could be spread abroad than this paradox, which would need to be countered by many a discussion. But perhaps no one will believe that Erasmus said these things. Just read this passage in *A Discussion* and you will be surprised. But I am not very surprised. After all, a person who does not take the matter seriously and is not at all concerned about it but rather considers it with complete detachment, is bored by it, languid about it, or even sick of it—how can such a person keep from always saying what is absurd, irrelevant, or contradictory, since he always handles the case as if he were drunk or snoozing, and as he snores away he belches up "is" or "is not" according to the varying statements that re-echo in his ears? For that reason rhetoricians require

69. Original sin is meant.
70. See n. 22 above.

true engagement in an advocate; all the more must the commitment of a theologian be watchful, sharp, focused, wise, and energetic.

[And so if free will without the grace of God has lost its freedom, is forced to serve sin, and cannot will the good, I would like to know what that effort is, that endeavor that remains behind according to that first and probable opinion. It cannot be a good effort or a good endeavor because it cannot will the good, as the opinion states and concedes.] What remains, then, is an evil effort, an evil attempt, which, after the loss of freedom, is forced to serve sin. What does this amount to, I ask you? This opinion leaves behind effort and endeavor but it leaves behind nothing to which to ascribe them. Who can conceive of such a thing? If the effort and endeavor are left behind for free will, why are they not ascribed to it? If they are not ascribed, how can they be left behind? Do the effort and the endeavor which are still present before grace belong to future grace and not to free will, so that they both remain and do not remain as belonging to free will? If such ideas are not paradoxes, or rather absurdities, what can be absurd?

But perhaps Discussion is dreaming that there is something between these two—to be able to will the good and not to be able to do so—a middle state, an absolute will with no regard to good or evil, so that by this dialectical subtlety we can avoid the reefs by saying that in the human will there is a certain act of willing, which (it is true) cannot choose the good without grace and yet does not by that fact choose nothing but evil, but rather is a pure and simple will which grace lifts up to the good and sin casts down to the evil. But then how can it be valid to say that freedom is lost and the will is forced to serve sin? Where is that effort that remains, that endeavor? Where is that power to apply itself to what pertains to eternal salvation? [For that power of applying itself to salvation cannot be pure indeterminate will unless salvation itself is said to be nothing. Hence the effort and the endeavor also cannot be said to be pure will, since the endeavor and the striving must be directed at something (that is, toward the good) and not at nothing, and the effort cannot be mere quiescence.] In short, in whatever direction Discussion turns, she cannot escape contradictions and inconsistencies, so that she herself is more of a captive than the free will she defends. Thus, she is so entangled in liberating free will that she is bound together with free will by unbreakable chains.

Then, too, the notion that in man there is a middle state of pure will is merely a figment of dialectic and those who assert it cannot prove it. It springs from an ignorance of things and an attention to words, as if the being of things were immediately determined by words, as numberless realities are among the sophists.[71] Rather the truth is what Christ says: "Whoever is not with me is against me."[72] He does not say, "Whoever is not with me and is not against me is in a middle position," for if God is in us, Satan is absent, and the only thing in us is to will the good. If God is absent, Satan is present and there is nothing in us but to will what is evil. Neither God nor Satan allows there to be in us a pure and simple will, but rather, as you rightly said, when liberty is lost we are forced to serve sin, that is, we will speak sin and evil, do sin and evil. See where invincible and almighty truth has driven unwise Discussion and made her wisdom foolish (1 Cor. 1:20), so that when she wants to speak against us she is compelled to speak for us and against herself, just as she makes free will something good and then turns around and makes it into something evil by the endless evil it does against the good, so that Discussion speaks as badly as free will acts. In fact, Discussion altogether is nothing but a marvelous work of free will, damning by defending, defending by damning, that is, doubly foolish when she wants to seem wise.[73]

Such is the case when elements of the first opinion are compared with one another: it denies that a person can will the good and yet it says that there is left to it an effort, which nevertheless does not belong to it. Now let us compare it with the other two opinions. The second one is harder: it holds that the will has no power to do anything but sin. And this is the opinion of Augustine in many places, but particularly in his book *On the Spirit and the Letter,* Chapters 4 and 5, if I am not mistaken, where he uses these very words.[74] The third opinion, the hardest of all, is that of Wyclif[75] and Luther, who hold that free will is an empty name and that all things are done out of pure necessity. Discussion takes issue with these two. At this point I say that perhaps I do not know Latin or German well enough to be able to explain the actual facts. But I call God to witness, I did not mean or want anyone to understand anything different in the language of

---

71. Luther is thinking of the reality (or lack of it) expressed by such technical words as "essence," "quiddity," or "prime matter."

72. Matt. 12:30, Luke 11:23.

73. Luther may be echoing Erasmus: "Among mortals those men who seek wisdom are . . . fools twice over" (*Praise of Folly*, 54).

74. *De spiritu et littera* 3.5 (PL 44, 203): "For free will is capable of nothing but sinning." Chapters 4 and 5 mentioned here deal mainly with the related fact that the Law makes evil desirable to human will without grace.

75. See *A Discussion,* n. 5.

these two latter opinions than what is contained in the first one. And I do not think Augustine meant anything but what is contained in the first opinion, and that is what I understand from his words, so that the three opinions presented to me by Discussion are no more than my single opinion. For after it has been granted and accepted as correct that free will, having lost its freedom, is forced into the slavery of sin and cannot will anything good, all I can gather from such language is that free will is an empty phrase, since its reality has been lost. According to my grammar, lost freedom is no freedom, and to give it the title of freedom when it has no freedom is to assign to it an empty phrase. If I am wrong, let anyone who can correct me do so. If these arguments are obscure or ambiguous, let anyone who can illuminate and establish them do so. As for me, I cannot call lost health actual health, and if I attribute such health to a sick man, it is apparent that I am attributing nothing but an empty name.

But away with these verbal monstrosities. For who can put up with such misuse of language as to say that a person has free will, while asserting at one and the same time that he has lost freedom and is forced into slavery to sin and cannot will anything good? Such statements fly in the face of common sense and make language totally useless. In fact, Discussion herself should be accused of chattering away in a doze, paying no attention to what others say. She does not consider, I say, what it is and what it means to say: "Mankind have lost their freedom, they are forced to serve sin, and they cannot will anything good." For if she were awake and paid attention, she would clearly see that the three propositions which she considers to be diverse and inconsistent with one another are actually one and the same opinion. For if someone has lost freedom and is forced to serve sin and is not able to will anything good, what could be more correctly inferred about him than that he necessarily sins and wills what is evil? For this is the way even the sophists draw conclusions by means of their syllogisms. Therefore Discussion is most unfortunate in taking issue with the latter two propositions and approving of the first, since the latter two are the same as the first. Once more she acts as she usually does: she condemns herself and proves our point in one and the same article.

Ecclesiasticus 15:14–18: the foolishness of Reason

Now let us take up the passage in Ecclesiasticus[76] and also compare it with that first, probable opinion. The opinion says that free will cannot

76. Ecclus. 15:14–18.

will the good. The place in Ecclesiasticus is cited to prove that free will is something and can do something. The opinion to be confirmed by Ecclesiasticus, however, says one thing, and Ecclesiasticus is cited to prove something else, as if someone who was supposed to prove that Christ is the Messiah were to cite a text proving that Pilate was the prefect of Syria or some other point, totally off the mark. This is also the way free will is proved here, to say nothing of what I insisted on earlier, namely, that nothing is said or proved clearly and certainly about what free will is or what it can do. But it is worthwhile to examine the whole passage in detail. First it says "God established man in the beginning" (Gen. 1:26). It is speaking here about the creation of mankind and says nothing yet about either free will or commandments. After that comes "And left him in the hand of his own counsel." What do we have here? Does this introduce free will? But here, too, there is no mention at all of commandments that would require free will, and we read nothing on that point in the creation of mankind. If something different is meant by "the hand of his counsel," it refers rather to the fact that in chapters 1 and 2 of Genesis man is established as the master of created things and has free dominion over them, as Moses says: "Let us make man, who is to preside over the fishes of the sea" (Gen 1:26). No more than that can be elicited from this passage. For man could treat things according to his own decision, because they are subject to him. Finally, he speaks of the counsel of man as something distinct from that of God. For after that, when he had said that man was established and left in the hand of his counsel, he went on to say: "He added his orders and commandments." What did he add them to? To the counsel and decision of man, over and above the establishment of human dominion over other things. By these commandments he took away from man dominion over one part of creation (namely, the tree of the knowledge of good and evil) and willed rather that man should not be free. Then, after adding the commandments, he came to man's choice with reference to God and the things of God: "if you wish to keep the commandments, they shall preserve you, etc."

Thus from this point ("If you wish"), the question of free will is taken up so that from Ecclesiasticus we should understand that mankind is divided between two realms: in one they are directed only by their choice and counsel, with no commandments or orders from God, namely in the realm of things below them. Here they are rulers and lords, left in the hand of their own counsel. Not that God leaves them to themselves in such a way that that he does not work with them in all things, but rather he allows them their own choice in the use of things and does not constrain them with any laws or commandments. [As if you should say, by way of analogy, "the gospel has left us in the hand of our own counsel," so that we rule over and command things just as we wish. But Moses and the pope have not left us to our own counsel but rather have bound us with laws and subjected us to their choice. But in the other realm man is not left in the hand of his own counsel but is conducted and led by the counsel and choice of God, so that, just as he is conducted by his own choice in his own realm with no commandments from anyone else, so too in the realm of God he is conducted by the commandments of another with no choice of his own. And this is what Ecclesiasticus says, "He added commandments and orders. If you wish, etc."] And so, if these things are sufficiently clear, we have carried our point that this passage does not support free will but undermines it, since it subjects mankind to the commandments and choice of God and deprives him of free will. If they are not sufficiently clear, we have at least made it plain that this passage cannot support free will, since it can be understood in a way different from their interpretation, namely in the one that I have given, which is not absurd but quite sound and agreeable with Scripture as a whole, whereas their interpretation of it contradicts Scripture and is sought out from this passage alone, contrary to all of Scripture. Thus I stand secure in a good interpretation, one that is against free will, until they confirm their difficult and strained interpretation in favor of free will.

[And so when Ecclesiasticus says, "If you should wish to keep my commandments, they will keep you, to keep them with acceptable faithfulness,"[77] I do not see how free will is proved by these words. For the verb is in the subjunctive mood (if you should wish [*si volueris*]),[78] which asserts nothing, as the dialecticians say that a conditional asserts nothing indicatively, such as "If the devil is God, he is rightly adored," "if an ass flies, an ass has wings," "if there is free will, there is no grace."[79] However, if Ecclesiasticus had wished to assert free will,

---

77. The Latin displaces the phrase "to keep them with acceptable faithfulness" to a position after the main clause "they will keep you," thus detaching "faithfulness" from the conditional clause. This may be a careless slip on Luther's part or perhaps an error of the printer.

78. Luther assumes that *volueris* is perfect subjunctive, though it is more probably future perfect indicative. But for the purposes of his argument it does not matter much, since his point is that conditional clauses say nothing about actual facts.

79. The examples Luther gives are indeed conditional clauses, but they are not in the subjunctive mood.

he should have said "Man can keep the commandments of God" or "Man has the power keep the commandments." But here Discussion will argue, "When Ecclesiasticus says, 'If you wish to keep,' he signifies man has the will to keep or not to keep. Otherwise what good would it do to say 'If you wish' to someone who has no will. For it is ridiculous to say to a blind man 'If you wish to see, you will find a treasure' or to say to a deaf person 'If you wish to hear, I will tell you a good story.' This would simply be to ridicule their misery." I reply: these are the arguments of human Reason, which is accustomed to put out such words of wisdom. For we must disagree not with Ecclesiasticus concerning this inference but rather with Reason, which interprets the Scripture of God with inferences and syllogisms and twists it however it wishes. And we will disagree all the more willingly and confidently as knowing that Reason babbles away with nothing but foolish absurdities, especially when she sets out to display her wisdom in sacred matters.

And, first of all, if I should ask how it is proved that free will is signified or inferred whenever we say "if you wish," "if you do," "if you hear," she will say "because it appears so from the nature of words and the ordinary human use of language." Therefore she measures divine matters and language by ordinary human usage. What could be more perverse, since one is heavenly and the other earthly? And so the foolish creature trips herself up, showing that she thinks about God in a purely human way. But what if I should prove that the nature of words and even ordinary human usage does not always intend to ridicule the incapacitated when it says "if you wish," "if you do," "if you hear"? How often do parents play with their children by ordering them to come to them or do something or other, precisely to make it clear that they cannot and to make them ask their parents to lend a hand? How often will a trustworthy physician tell a refractory sick person to do something that he cannot do or that would hurt him, in order to make the patient learn by his own experience when there is no other way to persuade him? And what is more ordinary and common than to insult or challenge either friends or enemies to show them what they can and cannot do? I say this just to show Reason how foolishly she applies her inferences to Scripture and also how blind she is, since she cannot see that they do not always have any place in human affairs and language. But if she sees that such an inference can sometimes be drawn, she applies it generally to all the language of both God and men, making a particular into a universal in her usual wise way.

Now if God should treat us like his children to enlighten our ignorance and make us aware of our inability, or make our disease known to us like a trustworthy physician, or if he should insult his enemies who proudly resists his counsel, and if he should lay down laws (as the most efficient way to do this) saying "do," "hear," "keep," or "if you hear," "if you wish," "if you do," should we infer from this as a solid conclusion, "Therefore we are free to do it, or else God is mocking us"? Why does this not rather follow: "Therefore God is testing us, so that, if we are his friends, he leads us by the Law to an awareness of our inability, or else, if we are proud enemies, he truly and rightly insults and mocks us"? For this is the reason for divine legislation, as Paul teaches (Rom. 3:20). For human nature is so blind that it does not know its own powers, or rather diseases. And then, in its pride, it imagines it can know and do everything. God cannot provide a more effective remedy to this pride and ignorance than by laying down his Law. We will say more about this in the appropriate place. Here it is enough to touch upon it to confute this inference of a carnal and foolish wisdom, "If you wish, you are therefore free and able." Discussion dreams that mankind is whole and sound, as it seems to be in its own affairs; therefore she prattles away, arguing that the words "if you wish," "if you do," "if you hear," ridicule mankind if there is no free will. Scripture, however, defines mankind as corrupt and captive, proud in their contempt and ignorance of their own captivity; therefore in these words it pinches him and wakes him up so as to know by his own certain experience that he can do none of these things.

But let me single out Discussion directly. If you truly believe, my lady Reason, that these inferences ("if you wish, you are free and able to do it") are valid, why do you yourself not hold to them? For you say that, according to that probable opinion, free will cannot choose anything good. What kind of inference is this to be derived from that very passage ("if you wish to keep them"), from which you say it is possible to derive that a man can freely will and not will? Do sweet and bitter waters flow from he same fountain? Or are you here mocking mankind by saying that they can observe things which they cannot will or choose? And so either you do not seriously believe that this is a valid inference ("if you will it, you are free and able to do it") even though you contend for it so strongly, or else you are not serious when you propose that probable opinion which holds that mankind cannot will the good. Thus Reason is so trapped by the inferences and words of its own wisdom that it does not know what it is saying or what it is talking about—unless (as is quite proper) free will should be defended by such contradictory and self-destructive arguments, just as the Midianites perished in mutual self-slaughter when they assaulted Gideon and the people of God (Judges 7:22).

Indeed, I will take even greater exception to this wisdom of Discussion. Ecclesiasticus does not say "if you make an effort and an endeavor, which is not ascribed to your power," as you imagine he does, but rather he says this: "if you wish to keep the commandments, they will keep you." Now if we wish to draw inferences in the manner of your wisdom, we will infer this: "Therefore man is able to keep the commandments." But in this way we will leave mankind not just a bit of effort or endeavor, but rather we will attribute to them a full and abundant power to keep the commandments. Otherwise Ecclesiasticus would be mocking the misery of mankind by ordering them to keep a commandment which he knows they cannot keep. It would not be enough that they have the ability to make an effort or to endeavor; he could not evade the suspicion of mockery unless he meant that they actually have the power to keep it.

But let us imagine that this effort and endeavor on the part of free will is actually something. What will we say, then, to the Pelagians, who used this passage to deny grace altogether and attributed everything to free will?[80] Clearly the Pelagians would be victorious if the inference of Discussion is valid. For the language of Ecclesiasticus expresses keeping commandments, not endeavoring or making an effort to keep them. But if you deny the Pelagians any inference about keeping commandments, they in turn will be even more justified in denying any inference about endeavors. And if you take free will in toto away from them, they will take away from you any remaining bit of it, since what you deny as the whole you cannot assert as a part. And so whatever you say based on this passage against the Pelagian position of attributing everything to free will, I will say even more forcefully against that little bit of effort on the part of your free will. And the Pelagians agree with me to the extent that, if their opinion cannot be proved from this passage, then much less can any other opinion be proved from it, because, if the case is to be decided on the basis of inferences, then Ecclesiasticus would argue most strongly of all for the Pelagians, since he speaks in clear language about the totality of keeping: "If you wish to keep the commandments." Indeed, he also speaks about faith, "if you wish to keep the faith acceptably," so that

80. See *A Discussion*, n. 15.

by the same inference keeping the faith ought to be in our power, even though it is a special and rare gift of God, as Paul says (Eph. 2:8). In short, since so many opinions in support of free will can be reckoned up, and since there is none that does not seize upon this passage in Ecclesiasticus, and since they are diverse and contradictory, it cannot but be that they consider Ecclesiasticus to express contradictories in exactly the same words. Therefore nothing can be proved from this passage—although if any inference is allowable, it makes for the Pelagians alone, against all others. Therefore it also makes against Discussion, who is dispatched by her own sword.[81]

But, as I began to say, this place in Ecclesiasticus offers no support at all to those who assert free will, but rather undermines their whole position. For the inference "if you wish, therefore you can" is not admissible, but we are to understand that this and similar passages let a man know about his own impotence, which, in his ignorance and pride, he does not recognize or perceive without these admonitions from God. But here we are talking not only about the first man but about any man whatever, though it makes little difference whether you understand it to apply to the first man or to any others whomsoever. For if the first man was not powerless when he was assisted by grace, nevertheless in this precept God clearly shows him how powerless he is when grace is absent. But if that man, to whom the Spirit was present, even with his new willpower, could not will the good newly proposed to him, that is, if he did not have obedience because the Spirit had not bestowed it upon him, what will we be able to do lacking the Spirit and having lost the good? Therefore, in that man we are given a fearful example to wear down our pride: we are shown what our free will can do left to itself if it is not continually and increasingly driven and amplified by the Spirit of God. That man could do nothing to amplify the Spirit, though he had the first fruits of the Spirit but fell away from the first fruits of the Spirit. How, then, can we do anything, having fallen into the loss of the first fruits of the Spirit, especially since the full power of Satan reigns in us, whereas Satan did not yet reign in him, but was still able to lay him low simply by tempting him? No stronger argument against free will can be formulated than a consideration of this passage in connection with the fall of Adam. But this is not the place for that; perhaps there will be an occasion for it later. In the meantime it is enough to have shown that in this passage Ecclesiasticus says nothing at all in favor of

---

81. Terence, *Adephoe* 5.8.35.

free will (even though they take it as a chief proof-text) and that this passage and others like it ("if you wish," "if you hear," "if you do") do not show what mankind can do but what they ought to do.

Other Old Testament passages: the imperative and indicative moods

Another passage cited by Discussion is from chapter 4:7 of Genesis, where the Lord says to Cain: "the desire to sin will be subject to you and you will have lordship over it." This passage shows (says Discussion) that the base impulses of the mind can be overcome and do not bring with them any necessity to sin. This point (that the base impulses of the mind can be overcome), even though it is ambiguous, is distorted by the purport of the statement, the consequence, and the circumstances, to mean that free will can conquer base impulses and that the impulses do not impose any necessity upon it. Once more, is there anything here that is not attributed to free will? What need for the Spirit, for Christ, for God, if free will can conquer the base impulses of the mind? Once more, where is the probable opinion which says that free will cannot so much as will the good? But here victory over evil is attributed to something which does will or choose the good. The thoughtlessness of this Discussion of ours is excessive beyond all excess. Here is the sum and substance of it: such sayings, as I said, show mankind what they ought to do, not what they can do. And so Cain is told that he ought to have lordship over sin and make desire for it subject to himself, but he neither did nor could do this because he was overwhelmed by the foreign dominion of Satan. It is also well known that in Hebrew the future indicative is frequently used for the imperative, as in chapter 20 of Exodus: "You will not have foreign Gods," "You will not kill," "You will not fornicate," and numberless such commands (Exod. 20:3–17). Otherwise, if they were taken to be indicative (as they seem to be),[82] they would be promises made by God, whereby, since God cannot tell a falsehood, no man would sin, and then there would be no need for any commandment. Our translator would have done better if he had rendered it thus: "But let your desire for it be subject to you and exercise lordship over it," just as concerning the woman he ought to have said, "Be subject to your husband and let him rule over you" (Gen. 3:16). That it was not spoken indicatively to Cain is proved by the fact that then it would

82. That is, they are literally in the indicative mood but actually in the imperative mood in their meaning.

have been a promise from God. But it was not a promise, because it turned out that Cain did the opposite (Gen. 4:8).

The third passage is from Moses: "I have placed before you the way of life and of death. Choose what is good, etc." (Deut. 30:15, 19). What, says Discussion, could be said more clearly than this? He leaves to mankind the freedom to choose. I reply: what could be clearer than that here you are blind? Where, I ask you, does he leave the freedom to choose? In the fact that he says "choose"? When Moses says "choose," does that mean that they immediately do choose? And so once again the Spirit is unnecessary. And so since you keep on repeating and hammering away at the same things, I am permitted also to repeat the same things over and over. If there is liberty to choose, why did the probable opinion say that free will cannot will the good? Can it choose without willing to do something or willing not to do it?

But let us listen to your comparison. It would be ridiculous to say to someone standing at a fork in the road, "walk whichever way you want," if only one way were open to him. This is the same thing we said above[about the argument of carnal Reason, where it says a man would be mocked by an impossible command, whereas we say such a command admonishes and incites him so that he can see that he is powerless.]And so we are indeed at a fork in the road, but only one way is open to us, or rather no way, since the Law shows us that the one road, the one to the good, is impossible for us unless God grants us the Spirit and the other is wide and easy for us if God allows it. And so it is not ridiculous but weighty and necessary to say to someone standing at the fork "go whichever way you choose" if that person, however weak, wants to seem strong and contends that neither way is closed to him.

[Thus the words of the Law are spoken not to affirm the power of the will but to enlighten blind Reason so that she may see that its light and the power of the will are nothing. Paul says "knowledge of sin through the Law" (Rom. 3:20), not the elimination or avoidance of sin.]The whole scheme and the force of the Law is to be fulfilled only in knowledge, and that of nothing but sin; it is not to reveal or to confer any power. For knowledge is not power and does not confer power but rather it instructs and shows that there is no power there nor anything else but weakness. For what can the knowledge of sin be except a knowledge of our weakness and our sinfulness? For he does not say "through the Law comes a knowledge of virtue and goodness." But according to Paul, all that the Law does is make sin known.

And that is the passage to which I replied that by the words of the Law mankind is admonished and instructed what they ought to do, not what they are able to do—that they recognize sin, not that they believe they possess some power. Therefore, my dear Erasmus, as often as you bring up against me the words of the Law, I will bring up against you the statement of Paul: "through the Law comes the knowledge of sin," not the efficacy of the will. And so gather together into one heap all the imperative verbs even from the larger concordances, as long as they are expressions not of promises but of obligation and Law, and I will immediately say that they signify what mankind ought to do, not what they do or are able to do. And even grammarians and schoolboys[83] know that verbs in the imperative mood signify no more than what ought to be done. But whatever is done or can be done should be expressed in the indicative mood. How is it, then, that you theologians talk such nonsense, as if you were in your second childhood, so that as soon so as you encounter an imperative verb, you infer an indicative meaning, as if, the moment something is commanded, it must necessarily be done or be capable of being done? For there's many a slip 'twixt the cup and the lip, so that something you have commanded, even something which can be done, is nevertheless not done. There is very great difference between verbs in the imperative and those in the indicative, even in common, everyday affairs. And yet in matters whole worlds above us, things in fact impossible, you immediately change for us an imperative into an indicative, so that the moment something is observed, done, chosen, and fulfilled, you consider it to be done by our own power the moment you hear the words of command, "do," "observe," "choose."

In the fourth place you cite from chapter 3 and from chapter 30, verses 15 to 17[84] of Deuteronomy many similar texts about choosing, avoiding, and observing, such as "if you observe," "if you turn away from," "if you choose," etc. All of these, you say, would be spoken inopportunely if the human will were not free to do the good. I reply: you also, my dear Discussion, quite inopportunely deduce the freedom of choice from these words. For you were supposed to

---

83. Otto Clemen translates *Gassenjungen* (street children), which the Latin *in triviis* makes a possibility. But it is more likely Luther is thinking of boys learning Latin as part of the trivium (grammar, logic, and rhetoric), since boys in the streets know nothing at all about imperative and indicative moods.

84. Erasmus has the error "3," which Luther corrects to "30," though he retains the erroneous "3."

prove only the endeavor and the effort of free will, but you adduce no passage which proves such an endeavor. Rather you cite places which, if your inference is correct, would attribute everything to free will. And so let us here once more distinguish the words cited from Scripture and the inference Discussion adds to them. The words cited are imperative; they say nothing but what should be done. For Moses does not say "you have the force or the power to choose," but rather "choose," "observe," "do"; he hands down commands to do something, but he does not describe the human ability to do them. But the inference added by this dabbler Discussion is this: "therefore mankind can do such things; otherwise they would be commanded in vain." To this the response will be: "Lady Discussion, your inference is false and you do not prove the conclusion you draw, but rather in your blindness and laziness you think it follows and is proved."[85] But these commands are not inopportune or vain but are given so that mankind in their pride and blindness may perceive through them their diseased impotence if they try to do what is commanded.

Thus your comparison is also invalid, where you say that it would be like saying to a person tied in such a way that he could not extend his arm except to the left, "Look there, on the right you have the very best wine. On your left you have poison. Reach out your hand to whichever you wish." I think you preen yourself on these comparisons of yours. But at the same time you do not see that if the comparisons are valid, they prove much more than what you set out to prove. Indeed they prove what you deny and consider not to be proved, namely that free will can do everything. [For in your whole treatment you have forgotten that you said free will could do nothing without grace; you prove that free will can do everything without grace. For the effect of your inferences and comparisons is to say that free will, all by itself, can do what is said and commanded or else the commands are vain, ridiculous, inopportune.] But these are the old tunes of the Pelagians, which even the sophists have refuted and which you yourself have condemned. And at the same time, through this forgetfulness and failure of memory, you show how little you understand and how little you care about the issue. For what can be more shameful for a rhetorician than to be always discussing and proving something irrelevant to his case, indeed to be holding forth against his case and against himself?

And so I say once more: the passages you cite from Scripture are imperative and prove nothing, establish nothing about human

---

85. In this sentence Luther mockingly uses the respectful plural *vos*.

capability but rather prescribe what is to be done and avoided. As for your inferences or additions or comparisons—if they prove anything, they prove this: that free will can do everything without grace. But this is not what you set out to prove; indeed, you deny it. Hence, proofs of this sort are nothing more than the strongest disproofs. But allow me to make an argument that perhaps can arouse Discussion from her lassitude: if I note that Moses says "Choose life and keep the commandment," and that he would be ridiculous to command mankind to do this unless they can choose life and keep the commandment, have I proved by this argument that free will can do nothing good or that any endeavor it makes does not spring from its own powers? Quite the contrary—I have proved most conclusively that either mankind can choose life and keep the command, as he is ordered to do, or else Moses is giving a ridiculous precept. But who would dare to say that Moses is doing so? It follows, then, that mankind can do what is commanded. This is the way Discussion continually argues against her own profession and promise not to argue for this point but rather to show that free will merely makes some endeavor—a point she hardly remembers in the whole course of her argument; she is so far from proving it that she proves the opposite, so that she is the one whose speech and arguments are always ridiculous.

[Now, just as, according to the comparison you make, it would be ridiculous if someone whose right arm is tied were commanded to hold out his right hand, since he could only hold out his left, would it also be ridiculous if someone who had both arms tied up but still proudly contended and ignorantly presumed he could reach out in either direction were then commanded to reach out in either direction, not in order to make fun of his captivity but to eliminate his false presumption of freedom and power or to make it crystal clear to him that he is ignorant of his captivity and his misery—would that also be ridiculous?] Discussion is always imagining a person who can do what is commanded or at least is aware that he cannot. But there is no such person anywhere. And if there were, either it would truly be ridiculous to make impossible commands or else the Spirit of Christ would be in vain.[86] But Scripture presents mankind as not only bound, miserable, captive, sick, dead (Eph. 2:1), but also as instigated by their prince, Satan, so as to add to their own miseries the misery

---

86. That is, if he can do them, he does not need the Spirit of Christ; if he knows he cannot, he does not need the impossible commands to show him that he cannot.

of blindness, by thinking they are free, happy, liberated, powerful, healthy, alive. For Satan knows that if man were aware of his misery Satan could never keep him in his kingdom, because if man recognized his misery and cried out, God could not but immediately take pity on him and help him, for God is very often praised throughout Scripture as being near to contrite hearts (Ps. 33:19), as in Isaiah 61:1. Christ bears witness that he was sent to preach the gospel to the poor and to heal the contrite (Luke 4:18). [Thus, if Satan is to keep hold of men, it is necessary that they should not be aware of their misery but presume they can accomplish everything they are told to do. But for Moses and any lawgiver the opposite is necessary, so as to reveal to mankind their own misery by means of the Law and thus to prepare them for grace when they are contrite and confounded by knowledge of themselves, and to send them to Christ, and thus to save them.] And so what the Law does is not ridiculous but extremely serious and necessary.

Now whoever understands these things also easily understands that Discussion in the whole course of her argument accomplishes nothing by collecting imperative verbs from Scripture, not understanding what they mean and why they are spoken; and then by adding her inferences and carnal comparisons, she mixes up a strong brew that asserts and proves more than she intended, and she argues against herself, so that there is no need for me to run through any more of the single points of her argument. For one solution solves them all, since all of them rely on one argument.

But so as to crush the argumentative abundance with which she wanted to crush me, I will proceed to recount some of them. Isaiah 1:19: "If you are willing and listen to me, you will eat the good things of the earth," where Discussion judges that if there is not freedom of the will, it would have been more suitable to say "if I am willing," "if I am unwilling." The answer is clear from what I have already said. Then, too, how would it be suitable there to say "if I am willing, you will eat the good things of the earth"? For does Discussion, in the riches of her wisdom, think that the good things of the earth can be eaten if God is unwilling, or that it is a new and extraordinary idea that we cannot receive good things unless God is willing? So too with that passage from Isaiah 21:12: "If you are seeking, seek; turn and come." What good does it do to encourage them to do something they have no power to do? According to Discussion, it is like saying to a man in shackles "bestir yourself and come here." Quite the contrary, what good does it do, I say, to cite passages which in and of themselves prove nothing and to add inferences that distort them so as to attribute everything to free will, whereas only a certain endeavor is what was supposed to be proved, and even that not to be ascribed to free will? I will say the same about that passage in Isaiah 45:22: "Gather together and come, turn to me and you will be saved." And in 52(:1–2): "Arise, arise, shake off the dust, loose the halter from your neck." Likewise Jeremiah 15:19: "If you change your ways, I will change you, and if you distinguish the precious from the base you will be as my mouth." But even more clearly Zachary points out the endeavor made by free will and the grace prepared for one who tries: he says, "turn back to me, says the Lord of hosts, and I will turn back to you, says the Lord" (Zech. 1:3).

Erasmus fails to distinguish between Law and gospel.

In these passages our dame Discussion makes no distinction whatever between the language of the Law and that of the gospel; she is so blind and ignorant that she does not see what the Law or the gospel is. From all of Isaiah—with the exception of this one place, "If you are willing"—all the passages she cites are not expressions of the Law but of the gospel; by speaking of grace offered to us, they call the contrite and afflicted to be consoled. But Discussion makes these into expressions of the Law. But I ask you, in matters of theology or biblical exegesis, what can a person do if he has not gotten far enough to know what the Law is, what the gospel is, or (if he knows) scorns to observe the difference? Such a person is bound to mix up heaven, hell, life, death and he will make no effort at all to know anything about Christ. But on this point I will instruct my dear Discussion later.

Consider the passages from Jeremiah and Zachary: "If you change your ways, I will change you." and "turn back to me and I will turn back to you." Does it follow from "turn back" that you have the power to turn back? Does it follow from "love the Lord thy God with your whole heart"[87] that you have the power to love him with your whole heart? What, then, follows from such arguments but that free will does not need the grace of God but rather can do everything by its own power? How much better it is to take these words in their context? "If you should change your ways,[88] I will change you," that is, "if you stop sinning I will stop punishing you" and "if you should convert and live well, I will also act well toward you, turning

87. Matt. 22:37, Deut. 6:5.

88. Luther shifts from *converteris* (present or future indicative) to *conversus fueris* (either future perfect indicative or perfect subjunctive).

away your captivity and your afflictions." But it does not follow from this that a person is changed by his own power, nor do the words themselves say that; the words simply say "if you should change your ways,"[89] which instructs a person what he ought to do. But once he has seen and recognized that he cannot do it, he looks for a way to be able to do it, unless the Leviathan (Job 40:20) of Discussion (that is, her addition and inference) intervenes by saying that it would be pointless to say "change" if a person could not change by his own power. But enough said about that sort of thing and what it accomplishes.

Surely it is some mental daze or lethargy that makes you think that those words "change" or "if you change" and other such expressions confirm the power of free will and do not observe that by the same token it would be confirmed by the command "love the Lord God with your whole heart," since in both cases the expression is a command to do something required. But the love of God is no less a requirement than our changing or our observance of all commands,[90] since the love of God is our true change or conversion. Nevertheless, from this command to love no one argues for free will. But they all do argue for it from such expressions as "if you will," "if you hear," "turn back," and such like. Therefore, if from that expression ("Love the Lord God with all your heart") it does not follow that free will exists or can do something, it is certain that it does not follow from those expressions, "if you should wish," "if you should hear," "change," and the like, which demand less or demand less vehemently than the command "love God, love the Lord." And so whatever is said to show that the expression "love God" does not imply anything in favor of free will can also be said to show that all other expressions of command or requirement do not imply anything in favor of free will. Thus the expression about loving takes the form of a Law showing what we ought to do, not the power of our will or what we are able to do—in fact, it shows what we are unable to do. The same is shown by all other expressions of what is required. For it is clear that even the scholastics, with the exception of the Scotists and the Moderns, assert that mankind cannot love God with their whole heart.[91] Thus they cannot fulfill any other precept, since all the others depend on this

89. Luther shifts from *converteris* (present or future indicative) to *convertaris* (present subjunctive).

90. In the Latin, a word such as *observatio* was clearly omitted before *mnium praeceptorum* (of all commands) by Luther or his printer.

91. See *A Discussion*, nn. 17–20.

one, as Christ testifies (Matt. 22:40). Therefore what it comes down to, even according to the scholastic doctors, is that the words of the Law do not argue in favor of free will but rather show what we ought to do but cannot do.

But when this Discussion of ours cites that text from Zachary, "turn back to me," she even more ineptly brings in not only the indicative but also strives to demonstrate the endeavor of free will and the grace provided to one who endeavors. And here, now and then, she finally remembers her own endeavor. And in her new grammar "to turn to" means the same as "to endeavor" so that the meaning is "turn back to me," that is, "endeavor to turn," and "I will turn," that is, "I will endeavor to turn to you"; she sometimes attributes an endeavor even to God, perhaps also ready to provide grace even to his endeavor. For if "turn to" means "endeavor" in one place, why not everywhere? So too she says that text from Jeremiah 15:19, "if you distinguish the precious from the worthless," proves that not only the endeavor but also the very freedom to choose, which she formerly taught, is lost and changed into the necessity of serving sin. Thus you see that Discussion does indeed have free choice in handling Scripture, so that in her hands the same set of words is distorted in one place to prove an endeavor, in another place—to prove freedom, just as she sees fit.

But enough of these inanities! In treating Scripture the phrase "turn back" is used in two senses, the one legal, the other evangelical. In the legal usage it expresses a precept or command which requires not an endeavor but a complete change of life, as Jeremiah often uses it, saying "Every one of you, whoever you may be, turn back from your evil way of life," "turn back to the Lord."[92] This, it is clear, requires fulfillment of all the commands. In the evangelical usage it expresses consolation and the promise of God, which requires nothing from us but rather offers us the grace of God, as in that text from Psalm 13:7, "When God turns away the captivity of Zion," and that from Psalm 22:3,[93] "turn, my soul, to your rest." And so in this brief expression Zachary manages to preach both the Law and grace: the sum and substance of the Law when he says "turn back to me," and grace when he says "and I will turn back to you." For free will is no more proved by the expression "love the Lord" or any other particular legal command than it is by this phrase summing up the

92. Jer. 25:5, 35:15, 4:1.
93. Ps. 114:7 is closer to the wording Luther gives. See *A Discussion*, pp. 00–00.

Law, "turn back." And so a wise reader of Scripture will observe which expressions apply to the Law and which apply to grace, so that he will not mix up everything in the manner of these sordid sophists or this dozing Discussion.

For see how she treats that remarkable passage in Ezekiel 18:23–4,[94] "I live, says the Lord, and I do not want the death of the sinner, but rather that he turn back and live." First of all, she says: "In this chapter the terms 'turn away,' 'do,' 'perform' constantly recur, in both a good and a bad sense. And where are those who claim that man does nothing?" See, I beg you, the extraordinary logic of this conclusion. She set out to prove the endeavor and effort of free will and she proves that everything is done and all is achieved by free will. Where are those, I ask you, who insist on grace and the Holy Spirit? For this is how she spins out her argument: Ezekiel 18:27 says "But if the wicked man turns away and does what is right and just, he will live"; therefore the wicked man does so and is able to do so. Ezekiel signifies what ought to be done; Discussion understands that it is done and has been done, once more setting out to teach us by her new grammar that it is one and the same thing to owe and to have, to be required and to be accomplished, to demand and to comply. And then she interprets that sweetest of evangelical pronouncements, "I do not want the death of the sinner, etc." as follows: "Does the good Lord lament the death of his people which he himself brought about in them? If he does not want our death, we must indeed ascribe it to our own will if we perish; but what can you ascribe to someone who can do nothing, good or bad?" This is the same tune Pelagius sang when he attributed not merely effort and endeavor to free will but the total power to fulfill and accomplish everything. For, as we said, that power is what is proved by those inferences, if they prove anything, so that they are quite as strong or even stronger against Discussion herself (who denies such a power to free will and aims only at endeavor) than they are against us, who deny such power altogether. But leaving her ignorance aside, I will speak of the reality itself.

The evangelical message is also a very sweet consolation to miserable sinners where Ezekiel says, "I do not want the death of a sinner but rather that he turn back and live," and it is so in all manner of ways, such as the saying in Psalm 28:6,[95] "For his anger is a moment and his will is life instead," and Psalm 68:17, "How sweet,

94. The wording is closer to Ezek. 33:11.
95. In the Vulgate numbering, Ps. 29:6.

O Lord, is your mercy," and likewise "because I am merciful,"[96] and what Christ says in Matthew 11:28, "Come to me all you who labor and I will refresh you," and likewise that text in Exodus 20:6, "I will show mercy in thousands of ways to those who love me." And what is almost half of Holy Scripture but promises of grace, by which God offers mankind mercy, life, peace, salvation? But what do the words of promise proclaim but that saying "I do not want the death of a sinner"? Isn't it the same thing to say "I am merciful" as to say "I am not angry," "I do not wish to punish," "I do not want you to die," "I want to forgive," "I want to spare you"? And unless these divine promises stand firm, so that consciences tormented by a consciousness of sin and terrified by a fear of death and judgment can be lifted up, what place could there be for pardon or hope? What sinner would not despair? But just as free will is not proved by other texts about mercy or promise or consolation, so too it is not proved by this one: "I do not want the death of a sinner, etc."

But once again this Discussion of ours makes no distinction between the language of the Law and that of the promise and takes this passage from Ezekiel as an expression of the Law, interpreting it as follows: "I do not want the death of a sinner," that is, I do not want him to sin mortally or to be a sinner deserving of death, but rather I want him to turn away from any sin he may have committed so that he may live." For if she does not explain it in this way, it has nothing to do with the issue. But to do this is to completely overthrow and eliminate that most sweet saying of Ezekiel, "I do not want the death." If we wish to read and understand Scripture in this way, according to our own blindness, is it any wonder that it is obscure and ambiguous? For he does not say "I do not want anyone to sin" but "I do not want the death of a sinner," clearly showing that he is speaking about the punishment of sin, which the sinner feels because of his sin, namely the fear of death. And he lifts up and consoles the sinner who finds himself in such affliction and despair, so as not to snuff out the smoking wick or snap the crushed reed (Isa. 42:3) but rather to give hope of pardon and salvation, so that the sinner may turn away—that is, be saved from the punishment of death—and may live, that is, may be well and may rejoice in a carefree conscience.

We should also note this: just as the word of the Law applies only to those who do not feel or recognize their sinfulness (as Paul says in Romans 3:20, "through the Law comes the knowledge of sin"), so

96. Exod. 22:27, Jer. 3:12.

too the word of grace comes only to those who feel their sinfulness, are tortured by it and tempted to despair. Thus in all the expressions of the Law you see that sin is revealed inasmuch as it shows what we ought to do. On the other hand, in all the expressions of the promise you see that what is revealed is the evil under which sinners labor and from which they need to be lifted up, just as this text, "I do not want the death of a sinner," clearly mentions death and the sinner, both the evil the sinner feels and the person who feels it. But this text, "love God with your whole heart," indicates the good which we ought to do, not the evil which we feel, so that we may recognize how incapable we are of doing that good.

And so no passage could be more ineptly cited to demonstrate free will than this passage from Ezekiel; indeed, none refutes free will more forcefully. For it shows what free will amounts to and what it can do for someone who has recognized his sin or turned away from it; namely it can only fall deeper and add despair and impenitence to sin, if God did not immediately come to his assistance, calling him back and lifting him up by the word of promise. For God's care in promising grace to recall the sinner and lift him up is a very great and reliable argument that free will by itself can only fall further and sink to hell as Scripture says (Prov. 5:5), unless you think that God is so frivolous that he speaks such abundant words of promise not out of the need for our salvation but out of sheer loquacity; thus you can see that not only do all the words of the Law stand against free will but also all the words of promise refute it totally, that is, all of Scripture contradicts it. Thus you see that the text "I do not wish the death of a sinner" does nothing but preach and offer the world God's mercy, which only those who are afflicted and tormented by death receive with joy and gratitude, since in them the Law has already completed its function, that is, has made them know their sin.

But those who have not yet experienced the efficacy of the Law and do not recognize their sinfulness or feel their death scorn the mercy expressed in this passage. But why some are touched by the Law and others are not, so that some accept and some scorn the offer of grace, is another question, one not treated in this passage from Ezekiel, which speaks of the preached and offered mercy of God, not of that secret and fearful will of God, who decides according to his own counsel what persons and what sort of persons he wishes to be capable of sharing and to actually share the mercy he proclaims and offers. This will we must not pry into but must reverently worship as something secret and worthy of the uttermost adoration, reserved only to the divine majesty and forbidden to us, far more to be venerated than any number of Corycian caverns.[97]

Now Discussion quibbles: "Is the good Lord lamenting the death of his people, which he himself actually caused? This seems quite absurd." I reply, as I have already said: we must discuss God in one way when we speak of his will as preached, revealed, offered, worshipped, and in another way when we speak of God as not preached, not revealed, not offered, not worshipped. Therefore, insofar as God hides himself and does not wish to be known by us, there is nothing for us to be concerned about. Here the saying "what is above us does not concern us"[98] is truly valid. And lest anyone should think this is a distinction of my own, I follow Paul, who wrote to the Thessalonians that the Antichrist would be lifted up above all that is called God or that is worshipped, clearly meaning that someone can be lifted up above God insofar as God is preached and worshipped (2 Thess. 2:4), that is, above the word and worship by which God is known to us and has dealings with us, but nothing can be lifted up above God as he is not worshipped or preached, that is, in his own nature and majesty, but rather all things are subject to his almighty hand.

And so God in his own nature and majesty must be left alone, for at that level we have nothing to do with him nor did he want us to have anything to do with him. But insofar as he is clothed and presented in his own word, by which he offered himself to us, we do deal with the beauty and glory with which the psalmist celebrates him as clothed (Ps. 20:6). This is what we say: the good Lord does not lament the death of his people, which he himself actually caused; rather he laments the death which he finds in the people and aims to remove. For this is what God as preached does: he seeks to save us from sin and death. For "he sent his word and healed them" (Ps. 106:20). But God as hidden in his majesty neither laments nor takes away death, but he works life, death, and all things in all things (1 Cor. 12:6). For there he did not limit himself by his word but kept himself free over all things.

---

97. Pomponius Mela (*De chorographia* 1.72.7) tells of a cave which, alluring at first, became more horrific the deeper one penetrated. In *A Discussion* (CWE 76 pp. 8–9), Erasmus compared the attempt to go deeper and deeper into Scripture to the dangers of these caverns.

98. *Adages* 1.6.69.

God preached, God hidden; God's will revealed, God's will secret

But Discussion is deluded by her ignorance, making no distinction between God as preached and God as hidden, that is, between the word of God and God himself. God does many things which he does not reveal to us in his word. He also wills many things which in his word he does not reveal to us that he wills. Thus he does not will the death of a sinner, in his word, that is, but he does will it by that inscrutable will. But now we should pay attention to the word and leave that inscrutable will alone. For we should be guided by the word, not by that inscrutable will. And in fact, who can guide himself by that totally inscrutable and unknowable will? It is enough simply to know that there is a certain inscrutable will in God. But it is absolutely not allowed to inquire, hope for, take pains about, or touch upon what and why and to what extent it wills, but only to fear and adore it. And therefore it is rightly said that if God does not will our death, it is to be imputed to our will if we perish—rightly, I say, if you are talking about God as preached. For he wishes all men to be saved (1 Tim. 2:4), since he comes to everyone with the word of salvation, and the fault is in our will if it does not accept him, as is said in Matthew 23:37: "How often did I wish to gather your children and you did not want it?" But it is not allowable to inquire why that majesty does not take away that fault of our will or change it in everyone, since mankind cannot do so, or to ask why he should impute to mankind something which they cannot avoid, and no matter how much you inquire you still will never find out, as Paul says in chapter 11 of Romans:[99] "Who are you to answer back to God?" Let this suffice for that passage in Ezekiel; let us go on to the rest.

After this, Discussion argues that so many exhortations in Scripture—and also so many promises, threats, expostulations, reproaches, entreaties, blessings and curses—such swarms of commands would necessarily be pointless if it is not in anyone's power to observe what is commanded. Discussion always forgets the main issue of the case and does something other than what she undertook to do; she does not see how all of it works against her and not against us. For from all these places she proves the power and ability to keep all commandments, as does the inference she draws from the language, even though she

99. Rom. 9:20. The inversion of the true number IX probably produced the false number XI.

wants to prove a free will that can will nothing good without grace and to affirm a certain endeavor which is not to be attributed to its own power. I do not see that any such endeavor is proved by any of these passages but only that they require what ought to be done, as I have said so often—but I have to repeat it so often because Discussion so often harps on the same wrong note,[100] putting readers off with a useless, copious gush of words.[101]

Just about the last text she cites from the Old Testament is from Moses, in Deuteronomy 30:11–14: "This commandment that I lay upon you this day is not beyond you nor is it located far away. It is not in heaven, that you might say 'Which one of us is strong enough to go up to heaven and bring it back to us, that we may hear and fulfill it?' But the word is very near to you, on your lips and in your heart, that you may do it." Discussion claims it is clear from this passage not only that we do have it in us to do what is commanded but that we have a proclivity for it, that is, that it is easy for us, or at least not difficult. We are very grateful for such learning! If, then, Moses declares so clearly that we not only have the power to observe all commandments but also can do so easily, why are we working away so hard at it? Why didn't we just bring out this passage right away and assert free will in a free field?[102] What need is there now of Christ? What need of the Spirit? Now we have found a passage which shuts everyone's mouth (Rom. 3:19) and which not only asserts free will but also teaches that commands can be observed easily. How foolish was Christ to shed his blood to purchase a Spirit we do not need, to make it easy for us to observe the commandments when we can do so from our own nature! Indeed, Discussion herself should withdraw what she said about free will not being able to will anything good without grace. Now she should say that free will is so powerful that it not only wills the good but also effortlessly keeps all the commandments, including the greatest. See, I beg you, what is accomplished by a mind distracted from the main issue, how it cannot avoid betraying itself. Is there still any need to confute Discussion? Could anyone confute her better than she herself does?

100. Horace, *Ars poetica* 355–56.

101. Luther's phrase *inutili verborum copia* is a glancing blow at one of Erasmus' most famous works, *De duplici copia verborum et rerum* (CWE 24, *The Double Abundance of Words and Things*).

102. Latin *libero campo,* that is, in an open field with no obstacles, straightaway. Luther mockingly parallels the phrase *libero arbitrio*.

This is indeed that beast that eats itself up.[103] How true it is that a liar needs a good memory![104]

We have spoken about that passage in Deuteronomy. Now we will take it up again briefly and discuss it apart from Paul, who handles it very powerfully in Romans 10:6–8. In this passage you clearly see that not a single syllable is said about ease or difficulty, about the power or the impotence of the free will of mankind to observe or not observe, except that those who lay hold of Scripture with their inferences and excogitations make it obscure and ambiguous on their own hook so as to get something out of it. If you cannot look at it, at least listen to it, or touch it with your fingertips. Moses says, "It is not beyond you nor is it located far away. It is not in heaven, nor across the sea." What is meant by "beyond you"? By "far away"? By "in heaven"? By "across the sea"? Will they make even grammar and ordinary usage so obscure to us that we can say nothing with certainty, just to gain their point that Scripture is obscure? According to our grammar, these words do not signify the quality or quantity of human powers but the distance between places. For "above you" says nothing about any power of the will but about a place above us. So too "far away," "across the sea," "in heaven" say nothing about human abilities but rather about a place at a distance from us, above, to the right, to the left, behind us, in front of us. Someone may laugh at me for explaining the obvious and offering great men such an elementary tidbit of syntax, as if I were teaching boys learning their alphabet. What am I to do when I see them seeking out darkness in full daylight and making a deliberate effort to be blind, reckoning up so many centuries, so many talents, so many saints, so many martyrs, so many doctors, and boasting with so much authority about this place in Moses, and still not deigning to look at the syllables and not curbing their thoughts so as to actually consider the place they are boasting about? Let Discussion go on now and tell us how it can be that one private person sees what so many public and leading authorities throughout so many centuries did not see. Certainly this passage, as even a little boy could judge, convicts them of having been all too often blind.

---

103. Augustine, *Contra Julianum* 3.21.47 PL 44, 726. Augustine's opponent Julianus had said Augustine was like a quack who promised to produce a serpent that eats itself up, because Augustine wrote a sentence in which the second half contradicted (consumed) the first half. Luther says the accusation applies nicely to Erasmus.

104. Quintilian, *Institutio oratoria* 4.2.91.

And so what does Moses mean by these very open and clear words but that he has very remarkably fulfilled his duty as a faithful lawgiver? He means that on his part there is no reason why they should not know everything, having had the laws laid before them, and that there is no room for excuses, such as not having or not knowing the commandments or having to seek them elsewhere, so that if they do not observe them, the fault lies not with the Law or the lawgiver but with themselves, since the Law is there and the lawgiver has taught it; hence there is no room for ignorance as an excuse but rather they should be charged with negligence and disobedience. There is no need, he says, to bring laws from heaven or from shores across the sea, or from far away, and you cannot use as a pretext that you did not hear them or have them. You have them near at hand, for you have heard me issue God's commandments, you have perceived them in your hearts (Heb. 8:10), and you have received them by the constant instruction of the Levites among you, as my words and my book testify. All that remains is that you put them into practice. What, I ask you, is here attributed to free will? Nothing but the requirement that it put into practice the laws it has, without any excuse from ignorance or the absence of laws.

This is just about all the evidence that Discussion cites from the Old Testament in favor of free will; now that it has been explained, there is nothing left to do—no matter whether she cites more texts or intends to do so—since she can cite nothing but imperative or subjunctive or optative expressions, which signify not what we can do or actually do (as we have so often said to Discussion, just as she so often brings them up) but what we ought to do or are required to do, so that our powerlessness becomes quite clear to us and we attain to the knowledge of sinfulness. Or if anything is proved by the added inferences and the comparisons sought out by human Reason, it is only this, that we should attribute to free will not some slight endeavor or pursuit but rather the fully free power to do everything without the grace of God, without the Holy Spirit. And so all that copious, repetitious, insistent disputation proves nothing less than what was supposed to be proved, namely that probable opinion which defines free will as so impotent that it cannot will anything good without grace and is forced into servitude to sin and makes endeavors which should not be attributed to its own powers; in other words, it demonstrates a monstrous thing that can do nothing by its own powers and yet makes attempts by its own powers, and so it constitutes a blatant contradiction.

A Display of Forces on Luther's Side

We have come to the last part of this book, where, as we promised, we should bring forth our troops against free will. But we will not bring forth all of them, for who could do this in a little booklet, whereas all of Scripture, down to the tiniest jot and tittle, stands on our side. Nor is there any need to do so, since free will has already been vanquished and laid low by a two-pronged argument: on the one hand, we prove that everything she thinks makes for her actually stands against her, and on the other we show that what she intended to confute still stands unvanquished. Then, too, even if she were not yet vanquished, it should be enough if she is struck down by one or two spears. For if an enemy has been killed by one spear, what need is there to transfix the dead man with many others? I will now proceed more briefly, insofar as the material allows it. And from such a multitude of armed forces, I will bring forward two leaders with some of their legions, namely Paul and John the Evangelist.

St. Paul: universal sinfulness nullifies free will

Paul, writing to the Romans, takes issue with free will in defense of grace as follows: "the wrath of God is revealed from heaven," he says, "upon all the wickedness and injustice of mankind, who hold back the truth of God in injustice" (Rom. 1:18). Don't you hear in this judgment the general sentence against all mankind because they are under the wrath of God? What does this amount to but that they are deserving of wrath and punishment? And Paul gives the reason for the wrath—that what they do is worthy of nothing but wrath and punishment, namely because they are all wicked and unjust and hold back the truth in injustice. Where now is this power of free will to endeavor to do some good? Paul makes free will worthy of the wrath of God and he decrees that it is wicked and unjust; and whatever deserves wrath and is wicked strives and works against grace, not for it.

But here some ridicule the dullness of Luther for not examining Paul carefully, saying that Paul in that sentence is not speaking about all mankind and not about all their endeavors but only about those who are wicked and unjust, and, as the words themselves say, about those who hold back the truth in injustice.[105] Hence it does not follow that

---

105. That is, they say, in grammatical terms, that the relative clause "who hold back . . ." is restrictive, not general or nonrestrictive (as a comma before "who" makes it). See *Shield-Bearer* 2, n. 65.

this applies to everyone. Here I say that for Paul to say "upon all the wickedness of mankind," is the same as to say "upon the wickedness of all mankind." For he frequently follows Hebrew idiom, so that the meaning is: "All men are wicked and unjust and hold back the truth in injustice and for that reason are all deserving of wrath." And then in the Greek there is no relative pronoun "those who," but rather the definite article, giving the meaning "the wrath of God is revealed upon the wickedness and impiety of the suppressors of truth in injustice." Thus the fact that they hold back truth in injustice is an adjectival modifier of "all mankind," just as "Our father who art in heaven" is as much as to say "Our heavenly father or father in heaven." The expression differentiates them from the faithful and the pious.

But these words would be irrelevant and empty if they were not reinforced and confirmed by Paul's argument. For Paul has just said: "the gospel is the power of God for the salvation of all who believe, first the Jews and then the Greeks" (Rom. 1:16). The words are not obscure or ambiguous: "the Jews and the Greeks," that is, "the gospel of truth is necessary for all mankind so that believers may be saved from the wrath that is revealed." How, I ask you, can he proclaim the Jews (who rely on the Law of God and the power of free will) to be indiscriminately without justice and lacking the power of God to be saved from the wrath that is revealed, and still say that this power is necessary for them, if he thinks that they are not under that wrath? What men, therefore, can you offer who are not deserving of God's wrath, since you are forced to believe that the greatest men in the world, that is, the Jews and the Greeks, do deserve it? And then, among those Jews and Greeks, what exceptions can you find, since Paul subjects all of them to the same judgment, including them indiscriminately under the same judgment? Should we think that these two superlative nations did not provide some persons who strove to be responsible, none at all who exerted themselves by the power of free will? But Paul does not hesitate in the least: he places them all under wrath, he proclaims all of them to be wicked and unjust. By the same token, should we not believe that the other apostles also used similar language to consign all other gentiles, of whatever sort, to this same wrath?

And so this passage from Paul stands strong and confirms that free will—however remarkable it may be in itself or in extremely remarkable men, however they may be furnished with the Law, justice, wisdom, and all the virtues—is nevertheless wicked, unjust, and deserving of the wrath of God. Otherwise Paul's argument has no validity. If it does, the division it makes allows for no middle ground but assigns salvation to those who believe in the gospel, and wrath to all others; it makes believers just and unbelievers wicked, unjust, and subject to wrath. It means only one thing: the justice of God is revealed in the gospel, which springs from faith. Therefore all mankind are wicked and unjust. For it would be foolish for God to reveal justice to mankind if they already knew it or had the seeds of it. But since God is not foolish, and yet he reveals the justice of salvation to them, it is obvious that free will, even in the greatest men, not only does not have and cannot do anything but does not even know what is just in the eyes of God—unless perhaps the justice of God is revealed not to those lofty persons but only to the lowly; and yet that is contrary to Paul, who glories in owing a debt to the Jews and the Greeks, to the wise and the unwise, to the barbarians and the Greeks.[106] In this passage, therefore, Paul lumps absolutely all mankind into one mass and concludes that they are all wicked, unjust, and ignorant of justice and faith—so far are they from being able to will or do anything good. And this conclusion is confirmed by the fact that God reveals the justice of salvation to them as ignorant people sitting in darkness; therefore in themselves they are ignorant. But being ignorant of the justice of salvation, they are certainly subject to wrath and damnation; and they cannot extricate themselves because of their ignorance, or even try to do so. For how can you try to do something if you do not know what, or how, or why, or to what degree you must try?

Reality and experience agree with this conclusion. For in the whole race of mankind show me one person—let it be the most just and the holiest of all—who ever had the slightest notion of this way to justice and salvation, namely belief in him who is at once God and man, who died because of mankind's sins and rose up again and is placed at the right hand of the Father, or whoever so much as dreamed of this wrath of God which Paul here says is revealed from heaven? Look at the greatest philosophers who knew about God, see what writings they left behind about the wrath to come. Look at the Jews, schooled by so many miracles and prophets, see what they knew about this way; they not only did not accept it, they even hated it so much that no nation under the heavens persecuted Christ more bitterly, and they do so even till the present day. But who would dare to say that among such great people there was not even one

---

106. Rom. 1:14. That is, Paul says he must bring the gospel to all, whether of high or low status.

person who cherished free will and endeavored to do something by its power? How is it, then, that they all endeavored to do the opposite, and this remarkable power in the most remarkable men not only did not cherish this method of salvation, not only did not know it, but even when it was proclaimed and revealed they hated it, rejected it, and wanted to destroy it?—so much so that Paul says in chapter 1 of the first epistle to the Corinthians that this way was a stumbling block to the Jews and foolishness to the Greeks (1 Cor. 1:23).

But since he mentions the Jews and the Greeks indiscriminately and since it is certain that the Jews and the Greeks were the most prominent peoples under the heavens, it is likewise certain that free will is nothing more than the greatest enemy of justice and human salvation, since it could not but be that some among the Jews and gentiles would act and endeavor by that supreme power of free will, and yet all they did was wage war against grace. Go on now and tell me what good free will endeavors to do, since it considers goodness itself and justice to be a stumbling block and foolishness. And you cannot say that this applies to some but not to all. Paul speaks indiscriminately about all when he says: "foolishness to the gentiles and a stumbling block to the Jews," and he makes an exception for no one but believers. "To us," he says, that is, to those who are called and sanctified, "it is the power and wisdom of God" (1 Cor. 1:18). He does not say "to some gentiles, to some Jews" but he says simply "to the gentiles and to the Jews" who do belong to us, clearly separating believers from unbelievers, leaving no middle position. And we are speaking about the gentiles acting without grace; to them, Paul says, the justice of God is foolishness which they abhor. So much for that praiseworthy endeavor of free will to do the good!

Look, then, doesn't Paul himself bring up the loftiest of the Greeks when he says that those who were wisest among them were made into fools, and their hearts were darkened so that they became vain in their reasonings, that is, their subtle arguments (Rom. 1:21)? I ask you, is he here not touching upon what is highest and most remarkable among the Greeks, when he touches upon their reasonings? For these were their highest and best thoughts and opinions, which they considered to be solid wisdom. But just as elsewhere he called this wisdom foolishness, here he says that in them it is vain, and that the further they progressed in it by their frequent endeavors, the worse it became, so that their hearts were darkened and they worshipped idols and gave themselves over to the monstrosities which he goes on to mention.

And so, if the best endeavors and works of the best of the gentiles are wicked and impious, what do you think about the vulgar herd, representing the worst of the gentiles? For here, too, he makes no distinction among the best but condemns the efforts of their wisdom with no respect of persons. But if their efforts and works are condemned, so too are those who make the efforts, even if they do so with the full power of free will. Even their very best endeavors, I say, are asserted to be vicious—how much more then, those who are engaged in them? Likewise, he goes right on to reject, without any distinction, the Jews who are Jews in the letter, not in the Spirit. "By the letter and circumcision," he says, "you dishonor God." Likewise, "a Jew is not one who is a Jew outwardly but who is a Jew inwardly" (Rom. 2:23–29). What could be clearer than this distinction? An outward Jew is a transgressor of the Law. But how many Jews do you think there were who were without faith but were extremely wise, religious, ethical and strove mightily to achieve justice and truth? How often he testifies that they have zeal for God, that they follow the justice of the Law, that they endeavor day and night to achieve salvation, that they live without quarreling.[107] And yet they are transgressors of the Law because they are not Jews in Spirit, indeed they stubbornly resist justice by faith. What remains, then, but that free will at its very best is the very worst and that the more it endeavors the worse it becomes and behaves? The words are clear, the division is certain, nothing can be said against it.

But let us listen to Paul as his own interpreter. In the third chapter, making (as it were) his concluding summary, he says: "What then? Do we surpass them? By no means. For we have charged both Jews and Greeks, that they are all subject to sin" (Rom. 3:9). Where is free will now? All Jews and Greeks, he says, are subject to sin. Are there any figures or knotty problems here? What value would any interpretation whatsoever have against this utterly clear statement? Someone who says "all" makes no exceptions. Someone who delineates them as subject to sin, that is, as the slaves of sin, leaves no room for anything good. But where did he hand down this sentence that all the Jews and gentiles are subject to sin? Precisely in the place we have pointed out, namely where he says, "The wrath of God is revealed from heaven upon all the impiety and wickedness of mankind" (Rom. 1:18). And he goes on to prove from actual experience that they are unpleasing to God and subject to very many vices, convicted (as it were) by the fruits

107. Rom. 10:2, Phil. 3:6.

of their impiety, as neither wanting nor doing anything but evil. Then he passes judgment on the Jews separately, saying that a Jew by the letter is a transgressor (Rom. 2:27). And in a similar way he proves this by their fruits and actual experience, saying, "You preach against stealing and you steal. You abhor idols, yet you commit sacrilege" (Rom. 2:21–22). He makes no exceptions whatever except for Jews in the Spirit. And here there is no room for you to escape by saying, "they are subject to sin and yet what is best in them, that is, reason and will, makes some attempt to do good." If some good endeavor remains in them, then it is false for him to say that they are subject to sin. When he names the Jews and the gentiles, he encompasses whatever is included in the Jews and gentiles (Rom. 3:9), unless you want to turn Paul upside down by making him say: "the flesh of all the Jews and gentiles, that is, their baser desires, are subject to sin." But the wrath that is revealed from heaven upon them will condemn them totally, unless they are justified by the Spirit, and that would not be the case if they were not totally subject to sin.

But let us see how Paul proves his judgment from Holy Scripture, whether the words as found in Paul are more condemnatory than in their original context. "As it is written," he says, "that 'there is not any one who is just, who has understanding, who seeks for God. All have fallen away; all together have become useless; there is no one who does what is good, no, not even one,'" (Rom. 3:10–12) and so on. Here let anyone who can, give a suitable interpretation; let whoever dares argue that these words are ambiguous and obscure, let him defend free will against these condemnations. Then I, too, will willingly yield and recant; I myself will profess and assert free will. It is certain that these things are spoken about all mankind, for the prophet presents God looking over all mankind and handing down this judgment against them. For this is what Psalm 13 says: "the Lord looked out from heaven over the children of men to see if there was anyone who had understanding or sought after God. But all have fallen away, etc." (Ps. 13:2–3). And lest the Jews should think that this does not apply to them, Paul anticipates the objection by stating that it applies especially to them. "We know," he says, "that whatever the Law says it says to those who are under the Law" (Rom. 3:19). This is the same thing he meant when he said "to the Jew first, and then to the Greeks" (Rom. 2:10). And so you are told that all the children of men, all who are under the Law, that is, both the gentiles and the Jews, are judged in the eyes of God to be unjust, to have no understanding, not to seek after God, not even one. But all fall away and are useless.

And I think that among the children of men, among those who are
under the Law, there are to be numbered also those who are the best
and the most virtuous, who strive by the power of free will after what
is virtuous and good, and who Discussion boasts have awareness and
inborn seeds of virtue—unless, perhaps, she contends that they are the
children of angels![108]

If everyone is universally ignorant of God, does not care about
him or seek him, how can there be anyone who strives after what
is good? If everyone falls away from the good and is utterly useless,
how can anyone have any useful power to do good? Do we not know
what it means not to know God, not to understand, not to seek after
God, not to fear him, to fall away and be useless? Aren't these words
perfectly clear and do they not teach that all men are both ignorant
of God and contemptuous of him, so that they fall away to what is
evil and are useless for what is good? For here we are not dealing
with ignorance about getting food or with contempt for money but
with ignorance and contempt for religion and piety. And undoubtedly
that ignorance and that contempt are not in the flesh or in the lower,
base desires but rather in the highest and most excellent powers of
mankind, where justice, piety, knowledge of God, and reverence for
him ought to reign, namely in our reason and will and even in that
very power of free will, in that very seed of virtue and in the most
excellent quality in mankind.

And where are you now, my dear Discussion? You promised before
that you would gladly agree that what is most excellent in mankind
is fleshly, that is, wicked, if it was proved by Scripture. Agree now,
therefore, since you are told that the most excellent part of all mankind
is not only wicked but also ignorant of God, contemptuous of him,
inclined to evil, and useless for good. For what does it mean to be unjust
except that the will (that feature which is one of the most excellent
of all) is unjust? What does it mean not to understand God or what is
good except that reason (the second of the two highest functions) is
ignorant of God and what is good, that is, blind in recognizing piety?
What does it mean to fall away and be useless except that mankind,
in all of their features, especially in the most excellent, have no power
to do anything good but only what is evil? What does it mean not to
fear God, except that mankind in all their abilities, especially in the
most powerful, are contemptuous of God? But to be contemptuous

108. That is, since Paul has condemned "all the children of men," those who
Erasmus claims are not totally unjust must be the children of angels, not of men.

of God is also to be contemptuous of all the things of God, namely his words, deeds, Law, commandments, and his will. How can reason point out what is right if it is blind and ignorant? What good can the will choose if it is evil and useless? Indeed, what can the will follow if reason directs it only to the darkness of its blindness and ignorance? And so, since reason errs and the will turns away, what good can a man do or try to do?

But perhaps someone might be so bold as to make a sophistic[109] distinction: although in act the will may fall away and reason may be ignorant, nevertheless the will can attempt something and reason can know something by their own powers, since we are able to do many things which in fact we do not do. For we are disputing about the force of potency, not about act. I reply: the words of the prophet include both act and potency. It is the same thing to say, "A man does not seek God," as to say, "A man cannot seek God." You can gather this from the fact that if there were a potency or a power in a man to will the good—since by the motive force of divine omnipotence, he is not allowed to be quiescent or inactive, as I showed earlier—it could not be that his power would not be moved in some persons or at least in some one person so as to show itself by being put to some use.

But this does not happen, since God looks out from heaven and sees not even one who seeks or tries; from this it follows that there is nowhere any power which tries or wills to seek but rather all fall away (Ps. 13:2–3). And then if Paul were also understood not to be talking about the entire lack of potency, his argument would have no effect, because in this place Paul is focused completely on showing the necessity of grace for all mankind. But if mankind were able to begin anything on their own, there would be no need for grace. But as it is, because they cannot, they need grace. Thus you see in this passage that free will is completely eliminated and that there is nothing good or virtuous left in man, since he is delineated as unjust, ignorant of God, contemptuous of God, turned away, and useless in the eyes of God. And the prophet makes this point quite emphatically, both in the original context and as quoted by Paul. And it is no small matter to say that man is ignorant of God and contemptuous of him: for these vices are the sources of all crimes, the cesspool of sin, the inferno of evil deeds. For what evil can be lacking wherever there is ignorance and contempt of God? In short, there could be no briefer or fuller description of the reign of Satan in mankind than to say that they are

109. Luther means: in the manner of the Scholastic theologians.

ignorant of God and contemptuous of him. Where such vices reign, there is incredulity, disobedience, sacrilege, blasphemy against God, ruthlessness toward neighbors, and self-love in all the affairs of God and men. There you have the glory and power of free will!

But Paul goes on to bear witness that he is speaking both about all mankind, and especially about the best and most outstanding among them, when he says, "that the mouths of all may be stopped, and the whole world may be liable to God, because from the works of the Law no flesh is justified in his eyes" (Rom. 3:19–20). I ask you, how are the mouths of all stopped if there is still a power by which we can do something? For it will be allowable to say to God, "It is not absolutely nothing that is here. There is something which you cannot condemn, such that you yourself will grant that it can do something. This, at least, will not be silent and will not be accountable to you." For if that power of free will is sound and can function, it is not true that the whole world is accountable to God and guilty, since that power is no small thing and not limited to one part of the world but is a most excellent feature and widespread throughout the whole world and its mouth ought not to be stopped, or if it should be, then it ought to be liable to God and guilty together with the whole world.

But how can anything rightly be called guilty if it is not unjust and wicked, that is, deserving of punishment and vengeance? Please let me see what interpretation can free that human power from the guilt in which God binds the whole world or what skill can make it an exception to being included with the whole world. Great thunderclaps, piercing lightning bolts, and truly "the hammer," as Jeremiah says, "which crushes stone" (Jer. 23:29) are those words of Paul: "all have fallen away," "the whole world is guilty," "not anyone is just." They crush whatever there is, not only in one man or in some men or other or in some portion of humanity but also in the whole world, in all mankind, with no exceptions, so that at these words the whole world should tremble, fear, and flee. What could be more sweeping or forceful than to say, "the whole world is guilty," "all the children of men are turned away and useless," "no one fears God," "there is no one who is not unjust," "no one understands," "no one seeks God." Nevertheless so great was and is the hardness and the insensate stubbornness of our hearts that we still neither hear nor feel this thunder and lightning but instead, in spite of all this, with one voice we extol and establish free will and its powers, so that we truly fulfill that text in the first chapter of Malachi, "they build, I will destroy" (Mal. 1:4).

Free will may do the works of the Law but not fulfill the Law.

There is the same sweeping eloquence in the text, "From the works of the Law no flesh is justified in his eyes" (Rom. 3:20). "From the works of the Law" is a sweeping statement, as is "the whole world" or "all the children of men." For we should notice that Paul refrains from referring to persons but rather mentions endeavors so that he includes all persons and whatever is most excellent in them. For if he had said that ordinary Jews or the Pharisees or some wicked persons are not justified, it might seem that some others had done something by the power of free will and the help of the Law to keep them from being completely useless. But since he condemns the works of the Law itself and makes them wicked in the eyes of God, it is quite clear that he condemns all who were proficient in the pursuit of the Law and works. And it is only the very best and most excellent who were diligent in pursuing the Law and doing works, and they did so only by means of their highest powers—reason and the will.

And so if some practiced the Law and works with the greatest eagerness and endeavor of both reason and will, that is, with all the power of their free will, and were aided by the divine assistance (as it were) of the Law itself, which instructed and aroused them, if (I say) they are condemned as wicked because they are not justified but are delineated as flesh in the eyes of God, what, then, is left in the whole human race that is not fleshly and wicked? For those who do the works of the Law are condemned one and all. It makes no difference whether they practiced the Law with great application or moderate devotion or none at all. For they could perform only the works of the Law, but the works of the Law do not justify. If they do not justify, they convict those who perform them and leave them in their wickedness. But the wicked are guilty and deserve the wrath of God. These points are so clear that it is not possible even to mutter against them.

But at this point they usually avoid and evade Paul by saying he means ceremonial works, which are deadly after the death of Christ. I reply: this is the ignorant error of Jerome; though Augustine strongly resisted it,[110] yet in the absence of God and with the power of Satan

---

110. In *Epistola* 82.2.17–18 to Jerome (PL 33, 282–83), Augustine points out that Jerome had misunderstood him and says he agrees with Jerome's assertion that it was sinful for any of Christ's apostles to take part in any Jewish ceremonies, even if only as a dissimulation for new converts, and that Paul did not do so. But Augustine also points out that Christ himself was circumcised and that he told a

it spread throughout the world and persisted even to this day, making it impossible to understand Paul and necessitating that the knowledge of Christ be obscured. And if there had been no other error in the church, this single one was pestilent and powerful enough to destroy the gospel; because of this, if it were not for the intercession of a special grace, Jerome would have deserved hell rather than heaven, so far would I put him (I dare to say) from being canonized as a saint. In fact, it is not true that Paul was speaking only of ceremonial works; otherwise, how could he prove his conclusion that all are wicked and in need of grace? For someone might say, "Granted that we are not justified by ceremonial works, but it might be possible for some to be justified by the moral commands of the Decalogue. Hence your syllogism does not prove that grace is necessary for them." And then, how useful is that grace that frees us only from ceremonial works, which are the easiest of all to perform and can be wrested from us merely by fear or self-love? And it is also erroneous to say that the ceremonial works are deadly and forbidden after the death of Christ. For Paul never said this. He says that they do not justify and are of no avail to mankind to free them from wickedness in the eyes of God. From this it is clear that someone can perform them without doing anything forbidden, just as eating and drinking are works which do not justify and do not commend us to God (1 Cor. 8:8), and yet someone who eats and drinks does not do anything forbidden.

And they also err on this point, because the ceremonial works were just as much commanded and required in the Law as the Decalogue, and therefore they have neither more nor less validity than it does. And Paul speaks first to the Jews, as he says in Romans 1:16. Therefore let no one doubt that by the works of the Law he understands all he works of the whole Law. For they should not be called the works of the Law at all if the Law is abrogated and deadly; for an abrogated Law is not a Law at all. Paul was fully aware of this; hence he does not speak of an abrogated Law when he mentions the works of the Law but of a valid and still obligatory Law. Otherwise it would have been very easy for him to say, "the Law is now abrogated." That would have been very open and clear. But we claim that Paul himself is his best interpreter. In Galatians 3:10 he says, "All who belong to

---

leper he had cured to offer sacrifice according to the Law of Moses (Mark 1:44). This is a small distinction, not a major discussion about the inadequacy of the Law to justify; and from Augustine's response it is not at all clear that Jerome thought Paul was speaking only about the ceremonial Law in chapter 1 of Romans.

the works of the Law are under a curse. For it is written: 'Cursed is everyone who does not abide in all things that are written in the book of the Law, so as to do them'" (Deut. 27:26). Here you see that when Paul is making the same case as in Romans, and does so in the same words, he speaks of all the laws written in the book of the Law whenever he mentions the works of the Law.

And what is even more remarkable, he even quotes Moses, who curses those who do not abide in the Law, whereas Paul preaches that those who are of the Law are cursed, citing a contrary place with a contrary meaning, the one expressed negatively, the other positively. But he does this because what holds in the eyes of God is that those who apply themselves most diligently to the works of the Law fulfill it the least because they lack the Spirit, the one who consummates the Law. Indeed they try with all their power but they accomplish nothing. Thus both statements are true: according to Moses they are accursed because they do not abide; according to Paul they are accursed because they belong to the works of the Law. For both demand the Spirit, without whom the works of the Law, however much they are performed, do not justify, according to Paul, and because they do not abide in all things that are written, according to Moses.

In brief, by his division Paul quite confirms what we say. For he divides those who comply with the Law into two groups: those who act in the Spirit and those who act in the flesh, leaving no middle ground. For this is what he says: "No flesh shall be justified from the works of the Law" (Rom. 3:20). What does this mean but that they comply with the Law without the Spirit, since they are flesh, that is, wicked and ignorant of God, so that their works are of no avail to them? Thus in Galatians 3:2 he makes the same division, saying: "Did you receive the Spirit from the works of the Law or from hearing about the faith?" And again in Romans 3:21: "Now the justice of God has been manifested without the Law." And once more: "We think that a man is justified by faith without the works of the Law" (Rom. 3:28). From all of this it is clear and obvious that according to Paul the Spirit is opposed to the works of the Law in the same way as it is to all things that are not spiritual and to all the powers and pretentions of the flesh, so that it is certain that Paul's opinion agrees with what Christ says in John 3:6, that everything that is not of the Spirit is flesh, however attractive, holy, and excellent it may be, and this applies even to the most beautiful works of the divine Law itself, with whatever powers they may finally be performed. For the Spirit of Christ is necessary and without it all things are nothing but damnable.

Take it as settled, then, that Paul understands by the works of the Law not the ceremonial laws but all the works of the whole Law. Take it as also settled that whatever in the works of the Law is without the Spirit is condemned. But that power of free will about which we are disputing is without the Spirit, though it is the noblest power of mankind. For to be engaged in the works of the Law is the most excellent thing that can be said about a man. For he does not say "those who are engaged in sin or wickedness against the Law" but "those who comply with the Law," that is, the best and most conscientious followers of the Law, who, apart from free will, were assisted by the Law, that is, they were instructed and urged on by the Law. And so if free will, even when it is aided by the Law and exercised in the Law by the greatest men, is unavailing and does not justify but remains in wickedness and in the flesh, what must we think it could do all by itself, without the Law?

"Through the Law," he says, "comes knowledge of sin" (Rom. 3:20). Here he shows how much the Law can do and how far it can go. Namely, he shows that free will all by itself is so blind that it does not even recognize sin but needs the Law to teach it. But what can anyone do in an attempt to remove sin if he does not even know what it is? For this reason: that he will judge what is sin to be not sin, and what is not sin to be sin. Experience makes it quite clear how the world hates and persecutes the justice preached by the gospel and does so by means of those whom it judges to be the best and the most diligent in pursuing justice and piety, how they call it heresy, error and brand it with the worst names, whereas they vindicate and boast about their own works and counsels, which are in fact sin and error, as if they were wisdom and justice. With this sentence Paul shuts the mouth of free will by teaching it that the Law reveals its sin to it, since it is ignorant of its own sin—so little does he grant it any power to attempt what is good.

And here is the answer to that question so often repeated by Discussion throughout her tract: If we cannot do anything, what is the use of so many laws and commandments, so many threats and promises? Here Paul responds: "Through the Law comes knowledge of sin." This is a quite different response to that question than mankind or free will imagines. Paul says free will is not proved by the Law; it does not cooperate in pursuing justice, for by the Law comes not justice but rather the knowledge of sin. For the fruit, the effect, the function of Law is to be a light to the blind and the ignorant, such a light as shows the disease, the sin, the evil, the death, the inferno, the wrath of God, but it does not help, does not liberate from these afflictions; it is content merely to show them. And when a person has recognized the disease of sin, he is grieved, afflicted, desperate. The Law does not help, much less can he help himself. But there is need of another light to show the remedy. This is the word of the gospel, showing that Christ is the liberator from all these afflictions. He is not shown by reason or free will. And how could it show him, since it is in itself darkling, needing the light of the Law to show it its disease, which it does not see by its own light but imagines instead that it is healthy?

Also, in Galatians 3:19 he treats the same question, saying: "Why, then, was the Law?" But Paul does not reply in the manner of Discussion, who argues that it entails free will, but says this: "It was established because of transgressions until the seed should come to whom he made the promise." "Because of transgressions," he says, not to put a stop to them, as Jerome dreams,[111] (since Paul argues that it is promised to the future seed to take away and put a stop to sins by the gift of justice) but to make sins abound, as he says in Romans 5:20: "the Law entered in that sin might abound," not because sins would not have existed or abounded without the Law but because they would not have been recognized as transgressions or serious sins but rather most of them, even very serious sins, would have been thought to promote justice. And if sin is not known, there is no room or hope for a remedy, because sinners do not tolerate the treatment of the physician, thinking they are healthy and do not need a physician. And therefore the Law is necessary to make sin known, so that, once its wickedness and magnitude are known, the person who is proud and seemingly healthy may be humbled so as to sigh and long for the grace established in Christ. See, then, how simple the language is: "Through the Law comes knowledge of sin," and yet this all by itself is quite sufficient to undermine and confound free will. For if it is true that by itself it does not know what sin and evil are—as Paul says here and in Romans 7:7, "For I would not have known that lust is a sin if the Law had not said, 'Thou shall not lust'"—how will it ever know what is just and good? Not knowing justice, how can it strive for it? We are ignorant of the sin in which we are born, in which we live, move, and have our being (Acts 17:28)—indeed which lives, moves,

---

111. *Commentariorum in Epistolam ad Galatas libri tres* 3.2, verses 19–20 (PL 26 366A–B). Jerome points out that Moses gave the Law to the Israelites after such defections as the worship of the golden calf—that it was intended to keep them from going astray.

and reigns within us. And how could we know justice, which reigns in heaven, outside of us? Certainly these sayings make nothing at all, absolutely nothing at all, for that miserable free will.

This being so, Paul speaks with full confidence and authority when he says: "But now the justice of God, testified to by the Law and the prophets, is manifested without the Law, the justice (I say) of God through faith in Jesus Christ unto all and over all who believe in him. For there is no distinction: all have sinned and lack the glory of God, being justified freely by his grace through the redemption which is in Christ Jesus, whom God has established as a propitiation through faith in his blood, etc." (Rom. 3:21–25). Here Paul speaks sheer thunderbolts against free will. First he says, "The justice of God is manifested without the Law." He separates the justice of God from the justice of the Law, because the justice of faith comes from grace without the Law. What he says here, "without the Law," can mean only that Christian justice stands without the works of the Law so that the works of the Law have no value and do nothing to obtain it, just as he says a little later, "We think that mankind is justified by faith, without the works of the Law" (Rom. 3:28), and as he said above, "From the works of the Law no flesh is justified in his eyes" (Rom. 3:20). From all of this it is abundantly clear that the endeavor or effort of free will counts for absolutely nothing. For if the justice of Gods stands without the Law and without the works of the Law, how could it not stand even more firmly without free will? For it is the highest aim of free will to be proficient in moral justice or the works of the Law, by which its blindness and helplessness are assisted. This word "without" removes morally good works, it removes moral justice, it removes any preparations for grace. Finally, imagine whatever you can about the ability of free will, Paul will stand firm and say: "Without such ability the justice of God stands."

And even if I should grant that free will makes some progress though its endeavors—namely, in good work or in the justice of civil and moral law—it makes no progress in the justice of God nor does God deign to account its effort toward the justice of God in any way, since he says that his justice is valid without the Law. But if it makes no progress toward the justice of God, what does it gain if by its own works and efforts it should progress (if that could be) to the sanctitude of the angels. Here I do not think there is ambiguous and obscure language or room for tropes, because Paul clearly distinguishes between two justices, attributing one to the Law and the other to grace, and asserting that the one from grace is granted without the

Law and its works, and that the other, without grace, does not justify
or have any value. I would like to see, then, how free will can stand
and be defended against such evidence.

There is another thunderbolt which says that the justice of God is
manifested and has force unto all and over all who believe in Christ,
and that without any distinction (Rom. 3:21–22). Once more, in the
clearest language, he divides the whole human race into two groups:
he assigns the justice of God to those who believe and he takes it
away from those who do not. Now no sane person has any doubt
that the force or endeavor of free will is something different from
faith in Christ. But Paul says that whatever is outside this faith is not
just, in the eyes of God. If it is not just, in the eyes of God, it is
necessarily sin. For with God there is no middle ground left between
justice and sin, no neutral space, as it were, as being neither justice
nor sin. Otherwise Paul's whole argument would be invalid, since it
proceeds from the division that whatever men perform or do belongs
either to justice or to sin, in God's eyes: justice if faith is present,
sin if it is not. Among men it is certainly true that some things are
medial or neutral, when men neither owe anything to each other
nor provide anything. But a wicked man sins against God whenever
he eats or drinks or whatever he does, because he abuses a creature
of God with wickedness and perpetual ingratitude and does not for a
single moment seriously glorify God.

And it is a thunderbolt not to be taken lightly, when he says, "All
have sinned and lack the glory of God, nor is there any distinction."[112]
I ask you, what could be said any more clearly? Give me an operative
of free will and answer me, does he also sin by that endeavor of his?
If he does not sin, why does Paul not make an exception of him but
rather includes him without any distinction? Certainly someone who
says "all" makes no exception for anyone, at any place or time, for any
work or endeavor. If you make an exception for anyone's endeavor or
work you make Paul into a liar, because that operative and endeavorer
by free will is also numbered among all and with all, and Paul should
have had more respect for him than to number him so freely and
generally among sinners. So too when he says they are empty of the
glory of God. Here you can take the glory of God in two ways—as
active or passive. And Paul does this according to his Hebraisms, as he
often does. The active glory of God is the glory he himself takes in
us; the passive glory, that which we take in him. But now it seems

---

112. The last five words are from Romans 3:22; the first part is from Romans 3:23.

to me that it should be taken passively, just as the Latin *fides Christi*
means "the faith which Christ has," but the Hebrew for *fides Christi* is
understood as "the faith which is placed in Christ." Thus, according
to the Latin idiom, the justice of God is said to be that which God
has, whereas according to the Hebrew idiom it should be taken as
the justice we have from God and in his eyes. Thus, according to the
Hebrew, not the Latin idiom, we take the glory of God to apply to
the glory which is had from God and in his eyes, which can be said to
be our glory in God. And so whoever knows with certainty that God
favors him and deigns to look upon him with benevolence, so that
what he does is pleasing in his eyes or, if it is not pleasing, is at least
condoned and tolerated—such a person glories in God.

And so if the effort or endeavor of free will is not a sin but good
in the eyes of God, it can glory and, with confidence in that glory,
say, "This is pleasing to God, this he favors, this he deigns to accept,
or at least tolerates and forgives it." For this is the glory of the faithful
in God; whoever does not have this, however, is confounded in the
eyes of God. But Paul denies they have it, saying they are completely
empty of this glory. And he proves this also by experience: ask all of
those who endeavor by free will, and if you can show me a single
one who can say seriously and from the bottom of his heart about
any endeavor or effort of his, "I know this pleases God," I will yield
and grant you the palm of victory. But I know that no one will be
found. And so if this glory is lacking, so that conscience does not
dare to know with certainty or to trust that this is pleasing to God,
then it certainly is not so. The fact accords with the belief, for he
does not believe with certainty that he is pleasing, but it is necessary
that he do so because it is in itself a sin of unbelief to have any doubt
about the favor of God, who wishes us to believe with rock-firm
faith that he favors us. Thus we convict them by the witness of their
own conscience that for all its powers, endeavors, and attempts, free
will, when it lacks the glory of God, is continually guilty of the crime
of unbelief.

Congruous merit and condign merit

But what will the defenders of free will say to what follows: "They
are justified gratis, through his grace" (Rom. 3:24)? What about this
"gratis"? What about "through his grace"? How can endeavor and
merit be compatible with justice freely given and bestowed? Here
they will perhaps say that they attribute as little as possible to free will,

by no means any condign merit.[113] But these are empty words. For what is asked about free will is whether there is any room for merit. In her argument Discussion always demanded, "If there is no freedom of choice, where is any room for merit? If there is no room for merit, where is the room for reward? To whom should justice be imputed if someone is justified without merit?" Here Paul replies that there is no merit whatever but that whoever is justified is justified gratis and that this is not imputed to anyone but rather to the grace of God. For with the bestowal of justice comes the bestowal of the kingdom and life eternal. Now where is the endeavor? Where the effort? Where the works, where the merits of free will? Of what use are they? You cannot argue from obscurity or ambiguity; the fact and the words are absolutely clear and simple. Granted that my opponents attribute as little as possible to free will, nevertheless they teach that we can achieve justice and grace through that little bit. For there is no other way for them to answer the question, "Why does God justify one and abandon another?" except by positing free will, namely, that this one tried and the other did not, and that God is mindful of the one who tried and scorns the other, so as not to be unjust by acting otherwise.

And though they pretend in their speech and writing that they do not acquire grace by condign merit and they do not even call it condign merit, nevertheless they play with words, and yet they hold it as a fact. For what kind of excuse is it not to call it condign merit and yet to attribute to it everything that applies to condign merit, namely that the person who tries gets grace from God, and the person who does not try does not get it? Isn't this clearly a function of condign merit? Do they not make God a respecter of works, merits, and persons,[114] since, after all, the one lacks grace through his own fault, because he did not try, and the other person gets it because be did try, and would not have gotten it if he had not tried? If this is not condign merit, I would like to be instructed about what in fact can be said to be condign merit? In this way you can play with all the words and say: "Certainly it is not condign merit, but still it does what condign merit does." A thorn tree is not a bad tree but it produces nothing but what a bad tree does; a fig tree is not a good tree but it produces what a good tree usually does (Matt. 7:16). Certainly Discussion is not wicked but she speaks and acts only as a wicked person does.

113. See *A Discussion,* n. 20.
114. Cf. Rom. 1:11, Gal. 2:6.

These defenders of free will fall under the saying, "By trying to avoid Charybdis he runs into Scylla."[115] For in their attempt to dissent from the Pelagians,[116] they begin by denying condign merit, and then by their very denial they affirm it. In their speech and writing they deny it, but in fact and in their hearts they affirm it, and in two respects they are worse than the Pelagians. First, because the Pelagians profess and assert condign merit[117] simply, candidly, and honestly, calling a spade a spade and a fig a fig, teaching what they think. But our fellows, though they teach and think the same as the Pelagians, nevertheless delude us with deceptive words and false appearances, as if they disagreed with the Pelagians, whereas that is the last thing they do, so that if you view our hypocrisy we seem to be the bitterest enemy of the Pelagians, but if you view the fact and our hearts we are doubly Pelagians. And secondly, because by this hypocrisy we reckon and purchase God's grace far more cheaply than the Pelagians. For they claim that it is not some tiny thing in us whereby we acquire grace, but rather that our works and endeavors are total, complete, perfect, great, and manifold. But our fellows say that it is a tiny thing, almost nothing, whereby we merit grace.

And so if we must err, it would be more honest and less proud to err with those who say that the grace of God costs a great deal, considering it to be precious and dear, than to agree with those who say that it costs only a little, tiny bit, considering it to be cheap and contemptible. But Paul smashes both camps with one blow when he says that all are justified gratis and likewise that they are justified without the Law, without the works of the Law. For someone who says that justification is gratuitous in all those who need to be justified, leaves no one to work, merit, or prepare; and he leaves no work which can be said to be congruous or condign; and he strikes with one bolt of lightning both the Pelagians with their total merit and the sophists with their tiny bit of merit. Gratuitous justification does not tolerate that you should set up those who "work," because to be given something gratis manifestly contradicts the idea of working to achieve something. Then, too, to be justified by grace does not tolerate that

---

115. Homer, *Odyssey* 12.235–47.

116. Semi-Pelagianism, the teaching that no grace is necessary in order to will the acceptance of initial (or impelling) grace, was condemned by the second Council of Orange in 531, but the decrees of this council were not widely known when Erasmus and Luther were disputing about free will.

117. See *A Discussion*, n. 18.

you bring forward the worthiness of any person, as Paul says later in chapter 11:6: "If from grace, then not from works; otherwise grace would not be grace" (Rom. 11:6). As he also says in chapter 4, verse 4, "For to him who works, a reward is attributed not as a grace but as a debt." Therefore my Paul stands as the unconquered destroyer of free will, and with one phrase he lays two armies low. For if we are justified "without works," all works are condemned, whether they are tiny or great; he makes no exceptions but fulminates equally against all.

And see here how dull we all are and how much it matters if someone has relied on the ancient fathers, revered throughout so many centuries. Were they not blind, one and all; did they not neglect the absolutely clear and manifest words of Paul? I ask you, what could be said clearly and manifestly on behalf of grace and against free will if the language of Paul is not clear and manifest? He proceeds by refuting and he boasts of grace against works and he uses utterly clear and simple language to say that we are justified gratis and that grace is not grace if it is acquired by works, most manifestly excluding all works in the process of justification so as to establish grace alone and gratuitous justification. And yet in this light we still seek out darkness, and where we cannot attribute great things and all things to ourselves, we try to attribute small and tiny things to ourselves, just so as to reach the idea that justification through the grace of God is not gratuitous and without works—just as if God, who negates all the greater things we do, would not even much more deny that tiny, little things should help us in our justification, since he has decreed that we are justified by his grace alone, without all works, and even without the Law itself, in which all works are included, whether great or small, congruous or condign. Go on now and boast about the authority of the ancients and rely on the words of absolutely all those who you see have neglected Paul, that most clear and manifest teacher, who have deliberately fled from that morning star, indeed that very sun, simply because they were taken up with their carnal notion that it would seem absurd to leave no room for merit.

The righteousness of works and of faith, and a summary of St. Paul's testimony against free will

Let us cite the example that Paul goes on to cite concerning Abraham. "If Abraham," he says, "is justified by works he has glory, but not before God. What, then, does Scripture say? Abraham believed in God and it was imputed to him unto justice" (Rom. 4:3). Notice,

I beg you, that here also Paul makes two categories when he speaks of the justice of Abraham. One concerns works, that is, moral and civil justice, but by this he says no one is justified in the eyes of God, even if he is justified by it in the eyes of men. Then he has glory among men but he himself lacks the glory of God, even with that justice. Nor is there any reason for anyone to say that here the works of the Law or of ceremonies are condemned, since Abraham lived so many years before the Law. Paul is simply talking about the works of Abraham, and about only the very best of them. For it would be ridiculous to dispute about whether anyone is justified by evil works. Therefore if Abraham is not justified by any works but rather both he and all his works would have remained in the realm of wickedness if he had not been clothed in another justice, namely that of faith, it is obvious that no man can make any progress toward justice by his works, and then that no works, no endeavors, no efforts by free will have any value in the eyes of God, but rather all are judged to be wicked, unjust, and evil. For if he himself is not just, his works and endeavors are also not just. If they are not just, they are damnable and deserving of wrath. There is another justice, by faith, which consists not in any works but springs from the favor and imputation of God through grace.

Notice how Paul stresses the word "impute" by emphasizing it, repeating it, and hammering on it. "To him who works," he says, "a reward is not imputed according to grace but as a debt owed him. But to him who does not work but believes in him who justifies the wicked, his faith is imputed toward justice according to the plan of God's grace." Then he also cites David concerning the imputation of grace, saying, "Blessed is the man to whom the Lord has not imputed his sin, etc."[118] In this chapter he repeats the word "impute" about ten times. In brief, Paul brings together those who work and those who do not, and he leaves no middle ground between the two; he denies that justice is imputed to the one who works, but he asserts that justice is imputed to the one who does not work, as long as he believes. Here there is no way for free will to evade or escape with its endeavor or effort. For it will be reckoned either with the one who works or with the one who does not. If with the one who works, you hear in this passage that no justice is imputed to him. If with the one who does not work but nevertheless believes in God, justice is imputed to him. But then there will not be any power of free will but rather a creature

118. Rom. 4:8, citing Ps. 31:2.

renewed by faith.[119] If, however, justice is not imputed to the one who works, then it is clear that his works are nothing but sinful, evil, and wicked in the eyes of God. At this point no sophist can have the effrontery to argue that even if a man is evil his deed may still not be evil. For Paul does not seize upon simply a man but a man who works, and thus he very clearly states that the works and endeavors of a man are condemned, whatever they may be and to whatever name or category they may be assigned. And he is talking about good works, because he is talking about justification and meriting. And since he is talking about one who works, he is speaking universally about all who work and about all their works, but especially about good and honorable works. Otherwise his distinction between one who works and one who does not would not make sense.

At this point I pass over the very strong arguments drawn from the plan of grace, from the promise, from the power of the Law, from original sin, from the election of God—any one of which taken alone could totally eliminate free will. For if grace comes from the plan or predestination of God (Eph. 1:11), then it comes by necessity, not from any effort or endeavor of ours, as I explained above. Likewise, if God promised grace before the Law existed, as Paul argues here and in Galatians, then it does not come from works or the Law; otherwise it would not be a promise. So too, if works had any value, faith would be of no value (and yet Abraham was justified by it before the Law). Likewise, since the Law is the power of sin, showing it only but not taking it away, it makes the conscience guilty in the eyes of God, and it threatens wrath; this is what is meant by the saying, "The Law works wrath" (Rom. 4:15). How, then, could it be that justice is provided through the Law? But if we are not helped by the Law, how can we be aided by the sole power of free will? Likewise, since we are all under sin and damnation by the single offense of a single man, Adam (Rom. 5:12), how can we attempt anything that is not sinful and damnable? For when he says "all" he makes no exceptions, not for the power of free will, nor for any doer of works; whether he works or not, whether he endeavors or not, he is necessarily included among "all" the others. And we would not sin or be damned by the single offense of Adam if it were not also our offense. For who would be damned by the offense of someone else, especially in the eyes of God?

---

119. 2 Cor. 5:17, Gal. 6:15. In both places the Vulgate has *nova creatura* but here Luther has *renovata creatura*. The syntax suggests that he may have intended *renovatatur*.

But it becomes ours not by imitation or any action of ours, for it could not be the single offense of Adam if it were committed not merely by him but also by us; rather it becomes ours by birth.

But this argument must be taken up elsewhere. And so original sin in itself will not allow free will to do anything at all except sin and be damned. These arguments, I say, I will pass over, both because they are quite clear and strong and because I said something about them before. But if I wished to recount all the arguments against free will in Paul alone, I could do nothing better than to compose a continuous commentary on him and show that in almost every single word this vaunted power of free will is confuted, as I have already done in the third and fourth chapters, which I discussed mainly to show how thick headed we all are when we read Paul and find even in the clearest passages anything but these very strong arguments against free will, and also in order to show the folly of that trust based on the authority and writings of the ancient fathers, and at the same time to make us think about how very clear these arguments will become if they are handled with care and judgment.

As for me, I must say that I am astounded that when Paul uses so many universal words—"all," "none," "not," "never," "without"— such as "all have fallen away," "no one is just," "there is no one who does what is good, not a single one," "because of the offense of one man we are all sinful and damned," "by faith without the Law," "we are justified without works,"[120] so that even if a person wanted to, he could hardly have spoken more clearly and manifestly—I am astounded, I say, that in the face of these universal words and statements, contrary, even contradictory, opinions have prevailed, such as "Some are not delinquent, not unjust, not evil, not sinful, not damned," "there is something in man which is good and strives toward the good," as if anyone who strives toward the good, whoever he may be, were not included in such words as "all," "none," "not." I would have nothing to oppose or respond to Paul, even if I wanted to, but I would be forced to include the power of my free will, together with its endeavors, among the "all" and the "none" of which Paul speaks, unless a new grammar or a new verbal usage is introduced. And perhaps it might be permissible to suspect there is a figure of speech or that words are being taken out of context and twisted if he had used such designations once or in only one passage. But as it is, he uses them constantly and he combines both positive and negative

120. Rom. 3:12, 3:10, 5:12, 5:15, 3:28.

forms, and he handles his opinion by arguments from contrast and by divisions into two universal groups on both sides in such a way that not only the nature of the words and the language itself but also what precedes or follows, the circumstances and the intention and the whole body of the disputation focus on the common meaning intended by Paul, that outside of faith in Christ there is nothing but sin and damnation. And in this way I have promised I would confute free will so that all opponents could not put up any resistance. And I think I have done just that, even though the vanquished will not grant that my opinion is right or will remain silent. For this is not something I can do; this is a gift of the Holy Spirit.

But before we listen to John the Evangelist, let us add a final flourish from Paul,[121] being prepared, if this is not enough, to construct a continuous commentary on Paul against free will. In Romans 8:5, where he divides the human race into two groups, the flesh and the spirit (as Christ also does in John 3:6), he says, "those who are according to the flesh, are wise in the things of the flesh, but those who are according to the Spirit, are wise in the things of the Spirit." That Paul here designates as fleshly all those who are not spiritual is manifest both from the division itself and the opposition between the Spirit and the flesh and also from the following words of Paul himself: "You are not in the flesh but in the Spirit if, in fact, the Spirit of God dwells in you. But if someone does not have the Spirit of Christ, he is not one of his" (Rom. 8:9). For in this passage what is the meaning of "You are not in the flesh if the Spirit of God is in you" except that those who do not have the Spirit are necessarily in the flesh"? And if someone does not belong to Christ, to whom does he belong except Satan? And so it is established that those who lack the Spirit are in the flesh and subject to Satan. Now let us see what he thinks about the endeavor and the power of free will in the fleshly. "Those who are in the flesh cannot please God," and again "The understanding of the flesh is death," and again "The understanding of the flesh is enmity against God." Likewise, "He is not subject to the Law, nor can he be so" (Rom. 8:6–8). At this point, let the defender of free will answer me this: how can there be any attempt toward the good by something which is death, displeasing to God, enmity against God, disobedient to God, and incapable of obedience? For Paul did not mean that the understanding of the flesh is dead or hostile to God, but rather that it is death itself, enmity itself, which cannot possibly be subject to the

---

121. He moves from chapter 3 of Romans to chapter 8.

Law of God or please God, just as he had said a bit earlier: "For what is impossible for the Law in that it was weakened by the flesh, God did, etc." (Rom. 8:3).

I am also aware of Origen's fairy tale about the three mental dispositions, one of which he calls the flesh, another the soul, and another the spirit; but the middle disposition is the soul, which can turn in either direction, toward the flesh or the spirit.[122] But these are merely his dreams; he says them but does not prove them. Here Paul designates as flesh whatever is without the Spirit, as we have shown. Therefore those lofty virtues of the best men are in the flesh; that is, they are dead, inimical to God, neither subject to the Law of God nor capable of being so, and not pleasing to God. For Paul says not only that they are not subject but also that they cannot be so. So too Christ, in Matthew 7:18: "A bad tree cannot produce good fruit"; and in 12:34 "How can you speak what is good when you are bad?" Here you see that we not only speak what is bad but that we are not able to speak what is good. And when in another place he says that though we are bad, we nevertheless give good things to our children (Matt. 7:11), he still denies that we do what is good, even in the very act of giving what is good; that is to say, though the creature of God which we give is good, nevertheless we are not good and we do not do good when we give those good things. For he is talking to everyone, even to his own disciples, so that this twofold opinion of Paul stands firm: "The just man lives from faith" (Rom. 1:17) and "Everything that is not from faith is sin" (Rom. 14:23). The second statement follows from the first, for if there is nothing by which we are justified except faith, it is evident that those without faith are not yet justified. But those not justified are sinners, and sinners are bad trees and can do nothing but sin and bear bad fruit. Therefore free will is nothing but a slave of sin, death, and Satan, doing nothing and able to do or attempt nothing but what is bad.

Add that text cited from Isaiah (65:1) in Rom. 10:20: "I was found by those not seeking me; I openly appeared to these who did not ask for me." He says this about the gentiles, because it was granted them to hear and acknowledge Christ, even though before that, they could not even conceive of him much less seek him or prepare themselves

---

122. Origen often explains that man consists of three parts: the spirit, the flesh, and between them the soul, which can join itself with the spirit above it or with the flesh beneath it. See his *Commentary on the Epistle to the Romans* 1.5, 1.18, 6.1, 9.24 (PG 14 850, 866, 1057, 1226).

for him by the power of free will. From this text it is sufficiently clear that grace comes so gratuitously that no conception of it precedes it, to say nothing of endeavor or effort. So too Paul, when he was Saul, what did he do by that lofty power of free will? Certainly in his mind he went about doing the very best and most moral deeds, if we consider reason alone. But look, see the endeavor by which he found grace. He not only did not seek it but he received it when he was raging against it. On the other hand, he says about the Jews: "The gentiles who did not pursue justice obtained the justice which is from faith; but Israel, by pursuing the Law of justice did not arrive at the Law of justice" (Rom. 9:30). What can any defender of free will mutter against this? The gentiles, when they were overflowing with wickedness and all manner of vices, received justice gratuitously by the mercy of God. The Jews, while they struggled for justice with the greatest endeavor and effort, struggled in vain. Is this not as much as to say that the attempt by free will is in vain even when it attempts to do the very best deeds, and that instead "it rushes into what is worse and slipping away falls back"?[123] And no one can say they did not pursue the highest endeavors by the power of free will. [In Romans 10:2 Paul himself bears witness that they had zeal for God, but not according to knowledge. And so the Jews lacked nothing which is attributed to free will, but with no result, indeed with the opposite result. The gentiles possessed nothing which is attributed to free will and yet the result was the justice of God.] What is this but a confirmation, based on the quite manifest example of the two peoples and likewise on the utterly clear testimony of Paul, that grace is given gratuitously to those who have not earned it and do not deserve it at all and is not obtained by any effort, endeavors, works (whether tiny or great), even those of the best and most moral men who seek and pursue justice with burning zeal?

St. John: free will is of the world and the flesh; grace is of Christ by faith. The two are opposites.

Let us also come to John, who is also a fully furnished and powerful destroyer of free will. Right at the beginning he makes free will so blind that it does not even see the light of truth, much less can it make an effort to conform to it. For this is what he says: "the light shines in the darkness but the darkness does not comprehend it." And right after that: "He was in the world and the world did not recognize him. He came to his own and his own did not accept him" (John 1:5, 10–11).

---

123. Virgil, *Georgics* 1.200.

What do you think he understands by "world"? Do you think you can separate any human being from this designation unless he is recreated by the Holy Spirit? Also the use of this word "world" is special in this apostle; by it he understands absolutely the entire human race. Therefore whatever he says about the world is understood to apply to free will as the most excellent feature of mankind. And so according to this apostle the world does not know the light of truth. The world hates Christ and his own. The world does not know or see the Holy Spirit. "The whole world is situated in wickedness." "All that is in the world is the concupiscence of the flesh and of the eyes and the pride of life." "Do not love the world." "You are of the world," he says. "The world cannot hate you; it hates me because I bear witness that its works are evil."[124] All these statements and many like them are proclamations about free will, namely about the most outstanding part reigning in the world under the imperial rule of Satan.[125] For John himself uses antithetical contrast when he speaks about the world, so that the world is whatever has not been taken up out of the world into the Spirit, as when Christ says to the apostles, "I have taken you out of the world, and I have placed you, etc." (John 15:16–19) Now if there were anyone in the world who tried to do good by the power of free will, as there would have to be if free will could do anything, John would rightly have softened his language out of respect for them, lest by general language he should have involved them in the many evils of which he accuses the world. Since he does not do his, it is evident that he makes free will guilty in all the same respects as the world, since whatever the world does, it does by the power of free will, that is, through reason and will—its most excellent features.

The passage goes on as follows: "to those who accepted him he gave the power to become children of God, to those who believe in his name, who are born not of blood nor of the will of the flesh nor of the will of man but of God" (John 1:12–13). Here, by an all-encompassing division, he rejects the blood, the will of the flesh, and the will of man from the kingdom of Christ. I think "the blood" means the Jews, that is, those who wished to be the children of the kingdom because they were the children of Abraham and the fathers, and so gloried in their blood.[126] "The will of the flesh" I understand to be the endeavors of the people, which they expended in the Law

124. John 1:10, 15:19; 1 John 3:1, 5:19, 2:16, 2:15; John 8:23, 7:7.

125. Luther means the most outstanding part of the man, his highest powers.

126. For example, John 8:33–39.

and works. For "flesh" here signifies those who are fleshly without the Spirit, who, though they may indeed have the will and the effort, possess them in a fleshly way because they do not have the Spirit. "The will of man" I understand to be the efforts of all people, whether with the Law or without it (that is, of the gentiles) and of all people whosoever—so that the meaning is that they become the children of God neither by the birth of the flesh nor the pursuit of the Law or any other human pursuit, but only by a divine birth. And so, if they are neither born by the flesh nor brought up by the Law nor prepared by any human discipline but are born from God, it is obvious that in this respect free will is unavailing. For I think that "man" in this passage is taken in the Hebraic sense of "whoever" or "any person whatsoever," just as "flesh" should be taken antithetically to mean persons without the Spirit, and "will" to refer to the highest power in mankind, namely to free will as their principal feature.

But even granted that we should not understand the words individually, still the gist of the matter is very clear: in his division John rejects whatever is not generated by God and at the same time says that they do not become children of God except by being born of God, which happens (as he understands it) by believing in God's name. And the will of man, or free will, is necessarily included in this rejection because it is not faith or a birth from God. And if free will had any value, John should not have rejected the will of man or drawn mankind away from it and sent them to faith alone and rebirth, lest what Isaiah says should be applied to him: "Woe to you who call good evil" (Isa. 15:20). But now, since he equally rejects blood, the will of the flesh, the will of man, it is certain that the will of man is of no more use in making anyone a child of God than blood or fleshly birth. But no one doubts that the birth of the flesh does not make anyone a child of God, as Paul says in chapter 9 of Romans, "those who are the children of the flesh are not the children of God" (Rom. 9:8), which he proves by the examples of Ishmael and Esau.

John also brings in the Baptist speaking thus about Christ: "And of his fullness we have all received grace for grace" (John 1:16). He says that grace was received by us out of the fullness of Christ. From what merit or effort, then? "For grace," he says, that is, the grace of Christ, as Paul says in Romans 5:15: "the grace of god and the gift by the grace of one man, Jesus Christ, has abounded unto many." Where now is the endeavor of free will by which grace is obtained? Here John says that grace is received not only not by any effort of ours but also by the grace and merit of another, namely of the one man

Jesus Christ. And so it is either false that our grace is received through the grace of another or it is evident that free will counts for nothing (for the two are not consistent with one another), and that the grace of God is so cheap that it can be obtained anywhere and everywhere by any man's puny effort, and at the same time is so dear that it is given to us in and through the grace of such a great man. Moreover, in this passage, I want the defenders of free will to be advised that they deny Christ when they assert free will. For if I obtain the grace of God by my own effort, why is the grace of Christ necessary for me to receive grace? Or what do I lack, since I have the grace of God?

Now Discussion has said, and all the sophists say, that through our own effort we procure the grace of God and are prepared to receive it, though not by condign but by congruous merit. But this is clearly to deny Christ, through whose grace the Baptist testifies that we receive grace. For I have earlier confuted that fabrication about "condign" and "congruous," showing that they are empty words and they really mean condign merit; and they do so more wickedly than the Pelagians, as I have said. And so it comes about that the wicked sophists, together with Discussion, deny the Lord Christ, our redeemer, more grievously than did the Pelagians or any other heretics—so thoroughly does grace exclude any particle or power of free will. And that the defenders of free will deny Christ is proved not only by this Scripture but also by their lives. This is the reason they do not treat Christ as a kind mediator but make him into a fearful judge whom they seek to placate through the intercession of his mother and the saints by discovering so many works, rites, religious orders, vows, by all of which they believe that Christ will be placated and grant them grace, and they do not believe that he intercedes with God and procures grace for them through his blood and his grace (as is said here) for grace.[127] And the fact conforms to their belief. For Christ is truly and rightly their inexorable judge, while they desert him as their mediator and most merciful savior and value his blood and grace as cheaply as the efforts and endeavors of free will.

Let us also hear an example of free will. Surely Nicodemus (John 3:1–14) is a man in whom you could ask for nothing more that is in the power of free will. For what does he lack in the way of effort or endeavor? He professes that Christ was genuine and came from the Father, he speaks openly of the signs, he comes by night to hear and discuss the rest. Doesn't he seem to have sought by the power of

---

127. John 1:16; cf. Rom. 8:344.

free will the things that pertain to piety and salvation? But see how he resisted when he heard Christ teach the true way of salvation by rebirth. Did he recognize that way or confess that he had sometimes sought it? No, he was so horrified and confounded that he not only said he did not understand it but even shied away from it as impossible. "How can these things be?" he said. And no wonder. For who ever heard that a man must be regenerated unto salvation by water and the Spirit? Who ever thought that the Son of God must be lifted up so that everyone who believes in him will not perish but will have eternal life? Did the best and most brilliant philosophers ever mention such a thing? Did the princes of this world ever conceive or know of such a thing? Did anyone's free will strive toward such a thing? Did not Paul profess that there is a "wisdom hidden in mystery," preached indeed by the prophets but revealed by the gospel, so that it was silent and unknown from all eternity (1 Cor. 2:7–8)?

What can I say? We will ask what experience can tell us. The whole world itself, human reason itself, even free will itself is forced to confess that it did not know or hear of Christ before the gospel came into the world. And if it did not know him, so much the less did it seek him, so much the less could it seek him or strive for him. But Christ is the way, truth, life, and salvation (John 14:6). Therefore it must confess, willy nilly, that by its own powers it could neither seek nor know those things which pertain to life, truth, and salvation. Nevertheless we rave on against this very confession and our own experience, and in empty words we argue that there is left in us a certain power which can know and apply itself to the things that pertain to salvation—that is to say, to Christ the Son of God lifted up for us—whereas no one ever knew this nor was anyone able to think of it; but nevertheless, in this case ignorance was not ignorance but a conception of Christ, that is, of those things which pertain to salvation! And do you not yet see and put your very finger on the fact that those who assert free will are clearly out of their minds when they give the name "knowledge" to what they themselves confess to be ignorance? Is this not calling darkness light, as in Isaiah 5:20? This is how powerfully God stops the mouth of free will by its own confession and experience; but even so, it cannot be silent and give glory to God.

[Furthermore, since Christ is called the way, the truth, and the life (John 14:6)—and that by way of contrast, so that whatever is not Christ is not the way but deviation, not truth but a lie, not life but death—it must needs be that since free will is neither Christ nor in Christ, it must comprise deviation, lies, and death.] And so where and

whence do we get that middle, neutral ground, namely that power of
free will which is not Christ (that is, the way, the truth, and the life)
and yet does not have to be deviation, lies, or death? For if everything
said about Christ and grace is not spoken by contrast with what is
contrary—namely, that apart from Christ there is nothing but Satan,
apart from grace nothing but wrath, apart from light nothing but
darkness, apart from the way nothing but deviation, apart from the
truth nothing but lies, apart from life nothing but death—what, I
ask you, would be the use of everything said by the apostles and of
Scripture altogether? In fact, all this would be in vain if it did not
require that Christ be necessary—and they do their best to remove
that requirement by finding some middle ground which in itself is
neither bad nor good, neither of Christ nor of Satan, neither true
nor false, neither living nor dead, perhaps also neither anything nor
nothing, and they call it the most excellent and lofty quality of the
whole human race. And so choose whichever you want. [If you grant
that Scripture speaks by contrast, then you can say nothing about free
will except what is contrary to Christ, namely, that deviation, death,
Satan, and all evils reign in it. If you grant that Scripture does not
speak by contrast, you debilitate it so that it is of no use and does not
prove that Christ is necessary, and thus, while you establish free will,
you debilitate Christ and undermine all of Scripture.]

And then, while you pretend in your words that you profess Christ,
nevertheless in your hearts you deny him. For if the power of free
will is not totally deviational and damnable but rather sees and wills
what is moral and good and what pertains to salvation, it is sound and
does not need the physician Christ (Matt. 9:12), and Christ does not
redeem that part of man. For what need is there of life and light where
there *is* life and light? But if that part is not redeemed by Christ, what
is best in man is not redeemed but is in itself good and saved. Then
God is also unjust if he damns that man because what he damns in
man is best and sound, that is, innocent. For there is no man who does
not have free will. And though a bad man may misuse it, they teach
that the power itself is not extinguished so as not to strive or to be
unable to strive for the good. And if it does so, it is undoubtedly good,
holy, and just. Hence it should not be damned but should be separated
from the man who is to be damned. But this cannot be done. And if it
could be done then the man without free will would then not even be
a man, nor would he merit or not merit, nor would he be damned or
be saved, but he would clearly be a brute animal, no longer immortal.
We are left with the conclusion that God would be unjust if he damns

a good man and, together with him, that good, holy, and just power which does not lack Christ.

But let us go on with John. "Whoever believes in him," he says, "is not judged. Whoever does not believe has already been judged because he does not believe in the only begotten Son of God" (John 3:18). Answer me, does free will belong to the number of believers or not? If it does, it has no need of grace, since it believes in Christ on its own—though on its own it neither knows nor conceives of him. If it does not, it has already been judged. And what does this mean but to be damned in the eyes of God? But God does not damn anything but what is wicked. Therefore it is wicked. But what piety can a wicked thing strive for? And here I do not think that the power of free will can be an exception, since John is speaking about the whole man, who he says is damned. And so unbelief is not a gross emotion but sits and rules aloft in the citadel of will and reason, just as its opposite does, namely belief. But not to believe is to deny God and to make him into a liar, as in 1 John 1:10 "If we do not believe, we make God into a liar."[128] How, then, can that power which is contrary to God and makes him into a liar strive toward the good? If that power were not unbelieving and wicked, he should not have spoken about the whole man, "he has already been judged," but rather he should have said, "Man according to his gross emotions has already been judged, but according to what is best and most excellent in him he is not judged, because he strives toward the faith or rather he is already a believer."

Thus wherever Scripture says, "Every man is a liar,"[129] we will say, on the authority of free will, "On the contrary, it is Scripture that lies, because man is not a liar in his best part, that is, reason and will, but only in his flesh, blood, and marrow, so that the whole portion from which he takes the name "man," namely reason and will, is sound and holy." So too that pronouncement of the Baptist, "Whoever believes in the Son has life eternal; whoever does not believe in the Son will not see life but the wrath of God remains over him" (John 3:36) should be understood to mean "over him, that is, over the gross emotions of man the wrath of God remains, but over that power of free will, that is, of will and reason, grace remains and eternal life." By this method, in order to maintain free will, whatever Scripture says against wicked men you can twist by synecdoche to that brutal part of man,

---

128. Luther refers to a similar text in the first chapter of 1 John, but 1 John 5:10 is closer to the actual wording he quotes.

129. Ps. 115:11.

so that the rational and truly human part is saved. Then I, for my part, will thank those who assert free will; I will sin with confidence, safe because reason and will or free choice cannot be damned, insofar as it is never extinguished but remains continually sound, just, and holy. But by means of will and blessed reason I will rejoice that the filthy and brute flesh is separated and damned—so far am I from hoping that it be redeemed by Christ. Do you see where that dogma of free will takes us—even to the point of denying everything divine and human, temporal and eternal, and making a mockery of itself by so many monstrosities?

Likewise the Baptist says, "A man can receive nothing unless it be given to him from heaven" (John 3:27). At this point Discussion should stop displaying the abundance of all the things we have from heaven, numbering them up. We are disputing not about nature but about grace; we are not inquiring about how we are on earth but how we are in heaven in the eyes of God. We know that man has been established as the lord of things beneath him, over which he has free will and the right to have them obey him and do what he thinks and wishes. Rather we are inquiring about whether he has free will with regard to God, whether God should be obedient and do what man wishes or whether God instead has free will over man, who should do what God wishes and can do nothing but what God wishes and does. Here the Baptist says that he can receive nothing unless it be given to him from heaven. Hence free will must be nothing. Likewise he says, "He who is from the earth is of the earth and speaks of the earth; he who comes from heaven is above everyone" (John 3:31). Here again, he makes everyone earthly and says that those who are not of Christ savor and speak of earthly things, and he does not leave anyone in a middle position. But certainly free will is not "he who comes from heaven." Hence it is necessarily of the earth and it savors and speaks of the earth. Now if there were any power in man, at any time, in any place, or in any deed, which does not savor of earthly things, the Baptist should have made an exception for it and should not have spoken generally about all who are apart from Christ, saying, "They are of the earth, they speak of the earth." So too farther on, in chapter 8, Christ says, "You are of the world, I am not of the world. You are from below, I am from above" (John 8:23). But those he was speaking to had free will, namely, reason and will, and nevertheless he says they are of the world. But what would be new about saying that according to their flesh and their grosser emotions they are of the world? Did not the whole world already know that? What need was there to say that mankind in its brutal component is of the world, since brute beasts are of the world in that manner?

Now, that text in the sixth chapter of John where Christ says, "No one comes to me unless my Father has drawn him" (John 6:44), what does it leave for free will? For he says that it is necessary for everyone to hear and learn from the Father himself and that everyone should be taught by God. Here, indeed, he teaches not only that the works and endeavors of free will are in vain but also that it is useless to hear even the word of the gospel (about which he is speaking in that passage) unless the Father himself addresses, teaches, and draws the interior man. No one, he says, can come, including that power by which a man can strive toward Christ, that is, he asserts that it is nothing in obtaining what pertains to salvation. Nor is there any help for free will in that passage cited by Discussion from St. Augustine[130] in order to besmirch this very clear and forceful text, namely that God draws in the same the way that we draw a sheep by showing a branch. This comparison is intended to prove that there is within us a power of following the drawing force of God. But this comparison has no application to this text, because God shows not only one good but all his goods, even his Son, Christ, and yet no one follows him unless the Father shows something else within him and draws him in another way; instead the whole world persecutes the Son, whom he shows. The comparison fits the pious very well since they are already sheep and recognize God as their shepherd; living and moved by the Spirit, they follow whereseoever God wishes and whatever he shows. But a wicked person does not come, even if he has heard the word, unless God draws him and teaches him inwardly, which he does by bestowing the Spirit. This is a different sort of attraction than that which comes from the outside; it shows Christ by the illumination of the Spirit, by which a person is swept to Christ with the very sweetest seizure and submits himself to God, who speaks to him and draws him, instead of doing his own seeking and running.

Let us cite one more text from John, where he says in 16:8–9, "The Spirit will convict the world of sin, because they have not believed in me." Here you see that it is a sin not to believe in Christ. But certainly this sin is seated not in the skin or hair but in reason and the will. But since he makes the whole world guilty of this sin, and since it is well known from experience that this sin was no more

---

130. *A Discussion,* CWE 76 pp. 66–67, referring to *In Ioannis evangelium tractatus CXXIV* 26.5 (PL 35, 1609; CCSL 36 262).

known in this world than Christ (since it is revealed when the Spirit convicts the world as guilty of it), it is obvious that free choice, together with its will and reason, is reckoned as captured by this sin and damned in the eyes of God. Hence, as long as it does not know Christ or believe in him, it cannot will or attempt anything good but necessarily serves that sin which it does not recognize. In brief, since Scripture everywhere preaches Christ by contrast and antithesis (as I said), so that it subjects whatever is without the Spirit of Christ to Satan, wickedness, deviation, darkness, sin, death, and the wrath of God, scriptural evidence contravenes free will whenever it speaks of Christ—that is innumerable times, indeed everywhere throughout. Therefore if we plead our cases by Scripture, I will be completely victorious and not one jot or tittle will be left which does not condemn the dogma of free will. Scripture preaches this by contrast and antithesis, and if great theologians and defenders of free will do not know it (or pretend not to know it), nevertheless all Christians know it and commonly profess it.

The two kingdoms of Christ and of Satan.
The assurance of faith

They know, I say, that there are two kingdoms in the world totally at odds with each other, that one is ruled by Satan, whom Christ calls the prince of the world and Paul calls the god of this age,[131] who holds captive to his will all those who have not been snatched from him by the Spirit of Christ (as Paul also says) and does not allow them to be snatched from him by any forces except the Spirit of God (2 Thess. 2:6–8), as Christ testifies in the parable about the strong man keeping his court in peace (Luke 11:20–23). In the other kingdom Christ reigns, continually resisting and fighting against the kingdom of Satan; we are carried over into that kingdom not by our power but by the grace of God, which frees us from the wicked present age and snatches us from the power of darkness. The awareness and profession of these kingdoms continually fighting each other with might and main would be sufficient in itself to confute the dogma of free will, because we are forced to serve in the kingdom of Satan unless we are snatched from it by the power of God. These things, I say, the people know and profess well enough by their sayings, their prayers, their efforts, and their whole life.

I omit that truly Achillean argument of mine which Discussion, by chance, passed over untouched, namely that in Romans 7:14–25 and

131. John 12:31, 2 Cor. 4:4.

Galatians 5:16–17 Paul teaches that in holy and pious persons there is a struggle between the flesh and the spirit which is so substantial that they cannot do what they wish to do. From that fact I argued as follows: if human nature is so bad that even in those who are reborn in the Spirit it not only does not strive for the good but even fights and struggles against it, how can it strive for the good in those who are not reborn and still serve Satan in the old man? For in that passage Paul is speaking not only about the gross emotions, which Discussion usually employs as the ordinary escape from all scriptural evidence, but he also numbers heresy, idolatry, and dissentions among the works of the flesh, which certainly reign in those lofty powers, namely reason and will. If, then, in such emotions the flesh fights against the Spirit in holy persons, it fights against God much more in the wicked and in free will. For that reason, in Romans 8:7 he also calls it an enemy of God. This is the problem, I say, that I wish he would solve for me, and I wish he would defend free will against it.

As for me, I firmly confess that if it were possible I would not wish to be given free will or to have anything left in my power by which I could endeavor to be saved, not only because, in the midst of so many adversities and dangers and also so many assaults by devils, I would not be able to stand firm and keep hold of it (since one devil is stronger than all men put together and no person would be saved), but also because even if there were no dangers, no adversities, no devils, I would still be forced to struggle continually toward an uncertainty and beat the air with my fists;[132] for no matter how long I should live and do works, my conscience would never be certain and sure how much it had to do to satisfy God. For no matter how many works I did, there would always remain a scruple about whether it pleased God or whether he required something more, as is proved by the experience of all self-justifiers and as I learned over so many years, much to my own grief. But as it is, since God has removed my salvation from my own choice and taken it into his own and has promised to save me not by my own work or pursuit but by his grace and mercy,[133] I am certain and safe, because he is trustworthy (1 Cor. 1:18) and will not lie to me, and also because he is so powerful and great that no devils, no adversities could break him or snatch me from him. "No one," he says, "will snatch them from my hand, because the Father who gave them to me is greater than all" (John 10:28–29). And so it comes

132. 1 Cor. 9:26. Paul has only "beating the air"; the fists are Luther's addition.
133. Rom. 9:16.

about that, if not all, still some and even many will be saved, whereas absolutely no one would be saved by the power of free will but all of us would perish without exception. Then, too, we are safe and certain that we please God, not by the merit of our works but by the favor of his mercy which he has promised us, and if we do less than we should or act badly, he will not impute it to us but rather will forgive and correct us like a father. This is how all the saints are glorified in their God.

The mercy and justice of God in the light of nature, grace, and glory

But if there is some difficulty about defending the mercy and fairness of God because he damns those who do not deserve it, that is, those who are wicked in such a way that they were born wicked and can find no way not to be wicked, and if they remain so and are damned and forced by the necessity of their nature to sin and perish—as Paul says: "We were children of wrath, like the rest" (Eph. 2:3)—since they were created so by God himself from seed vitiated by the sin of Adam alone, then at this juncture we should honor and revere God in the fullness of his mercy because he saves and justifies those who are most unworthy of it, and we should at least concede something to the wisdom of God by believing him to be just even though he seems unjust to us. For if his wisdom were such that it could be judged to be just by human capacity, it would clearly not be divine and would not differ from human justice. But since he is the one and only true God[134] and hence totally incomprehensible and inaccessible to human reason, it is proper, indeed it is necessary, that his justice also should be incomprehensible, as Paul cries out, saying, "Oh the depth of the riches of the wisdom and of the knowledge of God, how incomprehensible are his judgments and how unsearchable his ways!" (Rom. 11:33). But they would not be incomprehensible if we could thoroughly understand why they are just. What is man compared to God? How much can our power do compared with his power? What is our strength compared with his might? What is our knowledge compared with his wisdom? What is our substance compared with his substance? In sum, what is everything of ours compared with everything of his?

And so if we grant, even by the teaching of nature, that human power, strength, wisdom, knowledge, substance, and all that we have are absolutely nothing if compared with the power, strength, wisdom,

---

134. Jer. 10:10, Gal. 3:20.

knowledge, and substance of God, how perverse it is of us to object to God's justice alone and to his judgment and to claim so much for our own judgment, that we want to comprehend, judge, and evaluate the judgment of God? Why do we not likewise say on this point, "Our judgment is nothing compared with God's judgment"? See if reason itself is not vanquished and forced to admit that it is foolish and reckless in not allowing the judgment of God to be incomprehensible, since it admits that the other divine qualities are incomprehensible. Thus in all other matters we yield to the majesty of God; we are prepared to deny him only concerning his judgment, and we cannot believe, even for a little while, that he is just, even though he has promised us that when he reveals his glory, all of us will then see and feel down to our fingertips that he was and is just.

I will give an example to confirm this faith and to offer consolation for that wretched viewpoint which suspects that God is unfair. Consider, God controls this corporal world in external matters in such a way that if you view and follow the judgment of reason, you would be forced to say either that there is no God or that he is unfair, according to the poet, "I am often tempted to think there are no gods."[135] For see how evil men are very prosperous, while the good, on the other hand, are very wretched, according to proverbs and the experience underlying them: "The more wicked they are, the better off they are";[136] "The tabernacles of the wicked," says Job, "abound" (Job 12:6); and Psalm 72:12 complains that "sinners in the world abound in riches." I beg you, does not everyone think it most unfair that the wicked are fortunate and the good afflicted? But such is the way of the world. On this point even the loftiest minds have sunk so low as to deny that there is a God or to imagine that fortune turns everything randomly, as the Epicureans[137] and Pliny do. And then Aristotle, to free that supreme being of his from misery, imagines that the deity sees nothing but himself only, because he thinks it would be most distressing to see so

---

135. Ovid, *Amores* 3.9.36.

136. A well-known saying (Stevenson 2491.9), though I have not been able to pinpoint an example before Luther.

137. Epicurus of Samos (342–271 BCE) held that everything consisted of the random motion of atoms of different sorts and that the gods did not interfere in the working of the world. But he held that the happy man through reason has become superior to the fluctuations of fortune. Lucretius' didactic epic *De rerum natura* is the fullest and best known expression of Epicureanism.

many evils, so many injuries.[138] But the prophets, who believed that
God does exist, are even more tempted concerning the unfairness
of God, like Jeremiah, Job, David, Asaph, and others. What do you
imagine Demosthenes and Cicero thought when they did everything
they could and still suffered a miserable death as their reward?[139] And
yet this extraordinarily probable unfairness, which is handed down
with arguments that reason and the light of nature cannot resist, is
easily removed by the light of the gospel and the knowledge of grace,
which teaches us that the wicked may indeed flourish in the body but
that their souls perish. And this insoluble question is entirely answered
by the single statement that there is a life after this life, in which
whatever is not punished and rewarded here will be punished and
rewarded there, since this life is nothing more than a trial run, or
rather a beginning, of the future life.

And so if the light of the gospel, which is validated only by the
word and faith, is effective enough to resolve and easily dispose of
this question, which was handled but never answered throughout all
ages, what do you think will happen when the light of the word
and of faith ceases and the reality of the divine majesty is revealed
in itself? Don't you think that then the light of glory will very easily
resolve the question which was insoluble in the light of the word or of
grace, since the light of grace so easily answer the question which was
insoluble in the light of nature? Posit three lights—the light of nature,
the light of grace, and the light of glory, according to the usual (and
valid) distinction. In the light of nature it is insoluble how it is just
that the good should be afflicted and the bad should be well off. But
this is resolved by the light of grace. In the light of grace it is insoluble
how God damns someone who with all his exertions can do nothing
but sin and be guilty. Here both the light of nature and that of grace
dictate that the fault is not that of a wretched human being but of an
unjust God, nor can they judge otherwise of a God who gratuitously
and undeservedly crowns a wicked man and not only does not crown
but even damns another man who is perhaps less wicked, or at least
not more wicked. But the light of glory dictates something else: it
will then show that the judgment of God which was once insolubly
unjust is now most just and most manifestly just, so much so that in

138. *Metaphysics* 12.9.

139. Demosthenes (384–322 BCE) and Cicero (106–43 BCE), leading orators
and statesmen in Greece and Rome, were hounded to death by their enemies:
Demosthenes took his own life, and Cicero was brutally murdered.

the meantime we believe it because we are instructed and confirmed by the example of the light of grace, which completes a similar miracle in the light of nature.

Conclusion: the case against free will is unanswerable; Erasmus must yield.

Here I bring this little book to an end, prepared, if necessary, to plead this case further, though I think that what I have done is quite enough for a pious person and one who wishes to believe the truth with no stubborn resistance. For if we believe it is true that God foreknows and foreordains everything and that he can be neither deceived nor hindered in his foreknowledge and foreordination, and then if we believe that nothing happens unless he wills it—which even reason is forced to concede—then reason itself likewise testifies that there is no free will, whether in man, angel, or any creature. Likewise if we believe that Satan is the prince of the world, continually scheming and fighting against the kingdom of Christ, so that he does not release captive humanity unless driven to do so by the divine power of the Spirit, then it is also clear that there can be no free will. Thus if we believe that original sin has so undone us that even in those driven by the Spirit it wreaks havoc by struggling against the good, it is clear that in a person empty of the Spirit there is nothing left that can turn to the good, but what is left can only turn to what is evil. Likewise, if the Jews, who pursued justice with all their might, fell instead into injustice, and the gentiles, who pursued wickedness, arrived at justice gratuitously and beyond all hope, it is manifest by this very action and experience that mankind without grace can will nothing but what is evil. But in sum, if we believe that Christ redeemed mankind by his own blood, we are forced to confess that all of humanity was lost; otherwise we will make Christ either superfluous or the redeemer of the most worthless part of human nature—which is blasphemous and sacrilegious.

Now, my dear Erasmus, I beg you in the name of Christ to carry out at last what you have promised; and you promised that you are willing to yield to anyone providing better teachings. Put aside respect of persons. I grant you are great and endowed by God with many most noble gifts—with talent, learning, eloquence which is almost miraculous, not to mention others. But I have and am nothing, except that I venture to glory in being a Christian. This also I proclaim and extol in you, that you alone, beyond everyone, have gone to the heart

of the matter, that is, to the basic issue of the case, and do not wear
me out with such side issues as the papacy, purgatory, indulgences
and similar trifles (rather than issues), in which up to this point almost
everyone has hunted me down, without success. You are the one and
only assailant who has seen the central issue and gone for the jugular,
and for this I am deeply grateful to you, for I am willing to be engaged
in that matter insofar as time and leisure allow. If those who have
attacked me up till now had done this, if those who boast of their new
spirits, their new revelations, were still doing as you do, we would
have less sedition and factionalism and more peace and concord. But
God has taken vengeance on our ingratitude by means of Satan.

Still, if you cannot handle this case other than you have done in
this Discussion, I very much wish that you would rest content with
your gift and that you would favor, adorn, and advance letters and
languages, as you have till now done with much fruit and praise. In
these pursuits you have benefited me not a little, so that I confess that
I owe a great deal to you, and certainly in that matter I venerate and
look up to you with all sincerity. God has not yet willed or granted
that you be up to this case of ours. I beg you not to think this is said
out of arrogance. But I pray that very soon God will make you as
superior to me as you are in other matters. For there was nothing
strange about God instructing Moses through Jethro or Paul through
Ananias.[140] As for your saying that you are far from the mark if you
do not know Christ, I think you yourself know how this is. For all
will not go astray simply because you or I do. God is such that he is
proclaimed to be amazing in his saints (Ps. 67:36); indeed it is amazing
that we think those to be saints who are furtherest from sanctity. For
it is not difficult for you, human as you are, to understand incorrectly
or not to examine with enough care those writings or saying of the
fathers which lead you to think you have hit the mark. You give a
good indication of this when you write that you assert nothing but
rather discuss. This is not the way a person writes if he has seen deeply
and understood rightly. But as for me, in this book I have NOT
DISCUSSED BUT ASSERTED AND I DO ASSERT, and I wish to
be under no one's judgment, but I urge everyone to obey. And may
the Lord, whose case this is, enlighten you and make you a vessel of
his honor and glory (Rom. 9:21), AMEN.

THE END

---

140. Exod. 18:13, Acts 9:10.

ERASMUS

The Shield-Bearer Defending A Discussion Part 1 (1526)

Erasmus' Response to Luther's Review of Erasmus' Introduction

The centrality of Scripture in the debate must also include its interpreters.

Afterwards, in the very vestibule of the disputation, using language as copious as it is vehement, you handle what I desired you to teach me, arguments which would make us believe with certainty that you and your few adherents teach the truth, while so many Doctors of the church, so many universities, councils, and popes, etc. were blind, even though both sides have Scripture in common. This is the knot I wish you could really untie. For I have often enough tried to get your adherents to do it, but I have not yet found anyone who could. I frankly admit it, this worry really torments my mind, and if (as you say) you want to "win over your most beloved brother,"[1] the first thing you should do is to remove this obstacle. I will put up with the blows and fisticuffs of your insults provided you furnish what I want. It would take too long to repeat here what I said on this point; whoever wants to can reread the passage in *A Discussion*.[2] As for now, note how you do not perform the task you undertook with such dust and heat. You immediately charge that I said in my preface that in this discussion I would not make use of the assistance of orthodox teachers or councils but only of the authority of Holy Scripture so as to avoid laboring to no avail among those who accept nothing except Holy Scripture. I frankly confess this is true. Nor do I make use of these authorities except occasionally in explaining a passage in Scripture, for you would immediately have rejected my interpretation even before you had heard all of it.

1. *De servo arbitrio* WA 18 602:21–22, LW 33, 18.

2. *A Discussion*, pp. 1–2.

Moreover, I do not deny that I do not judge those writers to be entirely useless in deciding an issue. For even though I attribute primary authority to Holy Scripture, I am not scornful if such great men can contribute something to the understanding of the holy books, even if I am not unaware that as men they sometimes fall into error. I do not see why you would think you should say this, unless perhaps you also consider it impious and blasphemous to attribute something to the fathers, to whom the catholic church has granted so much authority over the centuries, whose testimony even you do not hesitate to cite whenever it suits your purpose. But you are wrong to appropriate that entire comparison to yourself, since I make an exception of you by name lest I should seem to be directing at you everything I say against "certain persons better known to me."[3] It goes without saying that in number, dignity, authority, and even in duration of time you people are inferior to them. I attributed learning, insight, spirit, holiness to them in such a way as not to detract from you, and I avoided making any odious comparisons about morals or way of life in order not to offend anyone. Hence it is irrelevant for you here to mention your way of life, since I never said so much as a word touching your way of life. For I am not so shameless as to attack the life of a person I do not know, nor so discourteous that, when the argument is about doctrine, I should bring forth any baseness of life or pull skeletons out of any closets, even if I knew anything reprehensible.

So too in another place you disavow any suspicion of greed or vainglory, defending yourself when no one is accusing you. For in such matters I will allow you to plead your case with God, before whom you stand or fall. But if the splendid reputation, the holiness, dignity, authority of those whom I set over against you has sometimes affected your outlook so that you felt as I now do and you completely despaired of being able to overthrow such a thoroughly reinforced authority, you should be so much the more equitable towards me, who know less and therefore dare less. And I beg you to show me by what methods you banished this uneasiness from your own mind and gained so much self-confidence. Indeed, you call God as your witness, swearing that your conscience is clean. But what I was after was for you to tell how we could be sure that what your adherents claim for themselves is true, especially when we see those who struggle equally to claim the Spirit for themselves disagree so violently among themselves about so many things. An easy believer is light headed, and you would

3. *A Discussion*, p. 5.

rightly find us lacking in manly constancy if we rashly defected from the universal catholic church unless the matter was proved to us with ironclad arguments. Otherwise you would have to fear that you have disciples who are not very firm, since they so readily departed from the ancient fathers and went over to your opinion.

For I am not disturbed by such insults as these: "You are nothing but a voice"[4] and "but if I were to ask you what a manifestation of the Spirit is, what miracles are, what holiness is, to these three questions, so far as I know you from your writings and books, you would seem too inexperienced and ignorant to be able to make them clear by so much as a single syllable."[5] If you, O most learned of all, would only teach us what we want to know! But you remind me, Luther, of some schoolmasters who are fond of flogging:[6] though they have undertaken to instruct their tender-aged students, they spend a good part of their time beating, scolding, and insulting their charges. You are so omniscient (it seems) that you are not permitted to use the most ordinary words, to call a spade a spade and tell it like it is. And I think you would define Spirit, holiness, and miracles so cleverly that you would make it clear there is no Spirit, is no holiness, are no miracles in the church. How the apostles manifested their spirit, I know only from the Acts of the Apostles and the gospel, except that their writings seem to me to breathe a certain fragrance of the Holy Spirit which I do not find in the writings of very many persons. From the same writings I know of the miracles performed by the apostles and I read how their speech was confirmed by God through subsequent signs. By similar tracks I detect the Spirit, holiness, and miracles in other reputable men. There breathes a certain something in their books— though far less than with the apostles—which manifests the Spirit and their holiness. And then I have learned of their lives and miracles in histories, the authority of which is confirmed for me by the consensus of the church, which reveres their memory so devoutly.

Against such arguments not much weight can be given to that proverb which is bruited about in the universities: "Many pass for saints on earth whose souls are in hell."[7] Though you picked up this saying from the street corner, nevertheless you upbraided me a little before because "I employ many expressions commonly used and

---

4. *The Enslaved Will*, n. 4.

5. *The Enslaved Will*, p. 33.

6. Cf. Horace, *Epistles* 2.1.70.

7. *The Enslaved Will*, n. 5.

accepted in ordinary speech which are remarkably inappropriate if they are called to the judgment bar of conscience."[8] But my point there was that, since we have not been given the gift of discerning spirits (1 Cor, 12:10) and therefore cannot be sure about your conscience, we should be shown some reason why we can safely believe in your teaching, rejecting the doctrine handed down by so many learned and famous men and accepted by the whole Christian world with such an overwhelming consensus. You try many ways to avoid this knot. First you claim that none of the ancients ever performed any miracles in the name of free will but rather in the name of Jesus Christ. But a little earlier you taught us that this name, Jesus Christ, also embraces these doctrines which you now teach. From this it follows that whoever performed a miracle in the name of Jesus while believing that free will works together with his grace performed a miracle in the name of free will.

And I do not teach that "free will is not of the Spirit but is something human"; rather I think that among the perfect, the apostles taught that free will works in us together with the grace of God, especially since this is the opinion which very learned men affirm from their writings. You open another crack to get away. You say that however spiritual they were, as human beings they sometimes perceived things according to the flesh. I do not deny it, but what you object against them you have in common with them, and so we come back to the comparison: Should the Spirit be attributed to you or to them? I do not demand miracles from you, but I argue that, other things being equal, we should place more faith in those who are famous for their miracles than in those who come recommended by no miracles. Likewise, it is not right for you in turn to demand miracles of us. For we are not the authors of this new teaching, but rather we follow the authority of those who are famous for their holiness and miracles. Likewise it is as immodest of you to demand that we confirm free will with miracles as it would be for someone to demand that theologians should prove the truth of the gospel with miracles. For it is enough that it has been proved once and for all by miracles and the consent of the whole world.

But whereas you say in jest that proof is required from those who affirm, not from those who deny, and bring up again that proverb from the schools of the sophists and lawyers, "The negative side proves nothing," I reply first of all that that sophistical rule has no

8. *The Enslaved Will*, p. 33.

place in the decisions of the church, unless perhaps someone who denies that Christ was born of the Virgin Mary or that his mother was a perpetual virgin is not required to offer any proof. Moreover, you not only deny an accepted teaching but also assert your own. It is just as if someone should come to another person's farm and drive away by force the person whose family has owned it for many generations, denying that it belongs to him and asserting that it belongs to himself. Would he not be required to offer some proof? Indeed, the law will favor an owner by the right of possession even if there is a defect in his proof of ownership. If fifty years of possession invalidates any claim and establishes the right of ownership, we have held this teaching more than a thousand years. And so you are to be rejected even if all you do is deny our teaching; as it is, you assert your new teaching in such a way as to drive us out of such an ancient possession. And since I see you are so conversant with matters rhetorical, I imagine you know that in counterpleas, since the accusation of an alleged crime has been turned back by the defendant against the plaintiff,[9] both sides are equally required to provide proof, as in that controversy between a blind man and his stepmother: "You killed my father"—"Not I but you." Here each one becomes both defendant and plaintiff, and the judge expects proofs from each of them. Likewise you say, "My teaching is pious; yours is heretical." In the same words, we direct the charge back to you. You see how foolish you were to be so taken by that proverb "The negative side proves nothing."

Finally, you talk as if none of the ancients had ever proved free will, even though that matter is treated in a great many books even today, and not merely by one person. Granted, they differ, but they agree on the point that free will is something which, when grace works with it, contributes something to salvation. But you will not accept human proofs without miracles and the authority of Holy Scripture. I have already spoken about miracles; and these writers also confirm their opinion by the testimony of Holy Scripture, but you reject their interpretation. But by the same token we can reject yours in the absence of miracles. Accordingly, falling back on insults and jests which are not suited to the role you are undertaking or to such a serious discussion, you challenge our Baal (3 Kings 18:17–30) to let us create, by means of free will, just one frog or kill just one louse: you have the impudence, first of all, to identify Baal with the God of our

---

9. On counterpleas (*anticategoria*) see Quintilian, *Institutio oratoria* 2.10.5, 7.2.9, and 12.1.2. By a counterplea, the defendant turns the charge back on the plaintiff.

church, who is adored by so many thousands of saints that supported and support free will, and then to claim the true God for your flock. But at the same time you contribute nothing to solving the difficulty.

No more to the point is what you throw together in the next section. For you demand that we show you what good deed the saints have done by the power of free will. And here you imagine that we will all be "more silent than frogs or fish."[10] Anyone could readily ask, in turn, what good deed grace has done in us. If you name one, he will say it was done by free will. But if you prefer a more appropriate response, no one is so ignorant or tongue tied that he would not immediately respond, "We are not dealing with asserting or denying free will by means of miracles, for instead of a miracle we have the authority of Scripture together with the definition of the church." What then are we dealing with? We are dealing with this: would a stable mind depart from the opinion handed down by so many men famous for holiness and miracles, depart from the decision of the church, and commit our souls to the faith of someone like you, who has sprung up just now with a few followers, although the leading men of your flock do not agree either with you or among themselves—indeed, though you do not even agree with yourself, since in this same *Assertion* you say one thing in the beginning and something else later on, recanting[11] what you said before?

For where you argue in passing that free will is not of the Spirit but is a human invention, arguing from my initial concession that this question was bruited about by the philosophers before Christ, I think you see how feeble your reasoning is. Plato and the poets teach that the world was created,[12] and for that reason is it wrong for Christians to assert that the world was created, refuting those who teach that the world had no beginning? Plato teaches that souls survive the death of the body,[13] and is that a reason we should not assert the same? The philosophers taught that God is mind, all

10. *The Enslaved Will*, n. 15.

11. In the beginning of chapter 36 of *Assertio* (CWE 76 p. 301), Luther quotes the article to be defended ("After sin free will exists in name only"), but later in the chapter he says: "For I misspoke when I said that free will before grace exists in name only; rather I should have simply said 'free will is a fiction among real things, a name with no reality'" (CWE 76 p. 306).

12. Plato, *Timaeus* 29a; Ovid, *Metamorphoses* 1.5–88.

13. For example, *Apology* 40c.

powerful and all good, present everywhere, though no place can hold him.[14] Do not Christians piously assert these same things? In his treatise *Household Affairs,* Aristotle teaches that between husband and wife there should be a mutual love and a lasting friendship closer than any other human relationship,[15] and is that a reason to think Paul was wrong to command, "Husbands, love your wives, etc."? (Eph. 5:25). And there are innumerable other points we have in common with pagan philosophers, but that fact does not diminish the authority of our teachings but, rather, confirms that by the light of nature they saw some of the things handed on to us by Holy Scripture. But we do not believe the philosophers unless they agree with Scripture. True enough. And we assert free will from Scripture—wrongly understood, you will say. Therefore the argument is about interpretation. A little earlier you proved the necessity of all occurrences from Virgil,[16] and you think free will should not be asserted simply because it has been treated by the philosophers?

As for the rest, the more copiously you pursue it, the more words you waste, since it has nothing to do with what I proposed. You demand that we describe to you the form and power of free will, what it is, what it can do, what it does. But you already confessed earlier that all this has been set forth by the sophists: what it is, what it avails, what it does, how it is related, etc.[17] Your rhetoric, namely, demanded that in order to cast aspersions on me, you should praise the sophists; though you are always calling them impious and blasphemous, you there deny that they blaspheme the way I do. If they are blasphemous, impious, enemies of Christianity, blind when they teach what they have in common with me, how can you exonerate them from the blasphemy you charge against me? In agreement with the church, we described to you the nature, power, and action of free will, but the description which suits the catholic church does not suit you and your adherents. We prove it from Holy Scripture, but our interpretation does not suit you. You prove necessity from Virgil and Holy Scripture, but your interpretation does not suit the

14. For example, Cicero, *De natura deorum* 1.2.4.

15. Pseudo-Aristotle, *Oeconomia* 1343b.

16. At *De servo arbitrio* WA 18 617.23–618.18 Luther cited *Aeneid* 10.467, 6.146, 6.882, and 2.291, also attributing Manilius, *Astronomica* 4.14, to Virgil.

17. These questions are discussed by Peter Lombard in *Sententiarum libri quatuor,* II, dist. 24–26. Elaborations and refinements on them were produced by the many commentators on the *Sententiae.*

church. How, then, will you prove your teaching to us? You stipulate that we should not ask for or accept anything but Holy Scripture, but you do it in such a way as to require that we permit you to be its sole interpreter, renouncing all others. Thus the victory will be yours if we allow you to be not the steward but the lord of Holy Scripture. And then, as for your insulting here the holy and orthodox men praised by me, that is hardly something unusual for you to do. It is tiresome to respond to such loquacity when everything is beside the point. When will you begin to get down to brass tacks? Put an end to my discussion and indicate whom we ought to believe: you or such an august assembly. You cannot tolerate my speech because I am nothing but a voice,[18] and we are supposed to tolerate such an endless clickety-clatter, grating on our ears with so much that is superfluous, abusive, and insulting?

At this point my writings are once more brought up against me: I advised that we should ignore the mere inventions of men and go to the springs of Holy Scripture, and now I contradict myself and do not practice what I preached. How so? Because "I write discussions, I celebrate the decisions of popes, I boast of the authority of men." In *A Discussion* I do not employ the authority of either popes or councils or orthodox teachers to support free will, and even if I had done so, that would have been somewhat more tolerable than your citing of Melanchthon's pamphlet[19] as if it had the same authority as canonical Scripture. But I introduce this comparison for one purpose only, to get you to show us why we should believe you rather than them. So too you yourself see how shameless and baseless is the accusation you add, that I leave nothing untried in my attempt to divert you from the simplicity of Christian piety. In *A Discussion* I do not defend my teaching but that of the church, but I do so without the assistance of the church, and I defend it from Holy Scripture, not as a fabrication of men but as the determination of Holy Scripture. And you are so little ashamed of this patent nonsense that you always add impudence to impudence. For this is the way you go from false premises to a totally false conclusion: "From that," you say, "we can

---

18. See *The Enslaved Will*, n. 4.

19. Philip Melanchthon (1497–1560) was a professor of Greek at Wittenberg and a close collaborator of Luther. Melanchthon's *Loci communes rerum theologicarum* (Wittenberg, 1521) was a compendium of theological fundamentals. Luther compared Erasmus' book unfavorably with Melanchthon's at *De servo arbitrio* (WA 18, 601:4–11).

easily understand that you were not sincere in giving us that advice or serious in any thing you wrote, but you were confident that with the empty bubbles[20] of your words you could lead the world wherever you wanted. And nevertheless you do not lead it anywhere, since you utter absolutely nothing but sheer contradictions, always and everywhere."[21]

This is truly what you said, Luther. Before, you decided to excuse my outlook but now you make this pronouncement about it: I was not sincere in what I wrote, even when I wrote correctly, according to your judgment. What could be more shameless than for me to want to lead the world with my writings, since I always wanted to stand alone and I never allowed the tiniest faction to be attached to me— something which you do in the most ambitious way? Nor do I regret this attitude; I prefer, certainly I prefer, to be a sheep in the flock than a leader of a herd of pigs or goats. Now, though "I utter nothing but sheer contradictions world without end and everywhere," nevertheless you have not yet been able to bring forward one place where I am not consistent. You should not have laid this charge against Erasmus before you yourself had responded to those writers who have published books accusing you of many contradictions excerpted from your writings You add: "as was quite rightly said by the person who called you a perfect Proteus or Vertumnus."[22] Did I not know that you would borrow something from scurrilous books to hurl against me? And nevertheless the person, as I conjecture, who you said had spoken quite rightly, seems to your Philip to have been out of his mind when he wrote those things, as he also testified in a letter of his.[23] And if that person spoke quite rightly, you spoke quite wrongly when you made me into a supreme theologian.[24] But it is no wonder that instead of a supreme theologian I have become a Vertumnus, since I was once called in your writings an extraordinary ram caught

20. Latin *bullis*, which could mean either "bubbles" or "papal bulls."

21. *The Enslaved Will*, p. 39.

22. Otto Brunfels published a scurrilous attack on Erasmus in 1524, calling him more changeable than Vertumnus. On Proteus and Vertumnus, see *The Enslaved Will*, n. 22.

23. In a letter of August 23, 1523, Melanchthon says that someone who wrote against Erasmus (perhaps Brunfels—see the preceding note) was out of his mind.

24. Luther had praised Erasmus in glowing terms in *In Epistolam Pauli ad Galatas Commentarius* (1519), WA 2 pp. 449, 452, 460, 476, 482, 502, 508, and 618.

in a thorn bush (Gen. 22:13)[25] and now I have become a pig from the herd of Epicurus.[26]

After that, you absurdly repeat for us that we are on the affirmative side, you on the negative; I have spoken about that before. And you call us utterly insane because we require you to grant the doctrine of free will for no other reason than that it has been asserted by many great and ancient men. Could anything more shameless be imagined, since I profess during the course of the struggle in *A Discussion* that I will yield if I do not cite testimony from Scripture to prove what I assert?[27] And here once more you have the impudence to scoff at orthodox Greek writers whom you deprive of all authority by a marvelous assumption, that the saints have sometimes erred because they are human, and you point out the danger of believing that because Peter was a saint, he was right when he admonished the Lord not to suffer.[28] Such a method of arguing we have from one who says nothing that is not clever, nothing that is not apt. It is brilliant, to be sure, to compare Peter when he was still a Jew with Peter inspired by the Holy Spirit. And how could anyone think Peter was right to say, "Let this not happen to you, Lord," since he was immediately rebuked by the Lord: "Get behind me, etc." (Matt. 16:22–23).

And as if it were not enough to set forth these clever sayings once, you add in the next section that those who cite the opinion of ancient saints "are like those who, for the sake of a joke, babble that not everything in the gospel is true, alleging that question from John, 'Are we not right to say that you are a Samaritan and have a demon? (John 8:48)' or again, 'He deserves to die.'"[29] What are you about, Luther, or what do you mean by these truly blasphemous comparisons of yours? A person who cites something from the books of those whose memory has been sacrosanct to the church for so many centuries, whose writings are read publicly in church, does no better than buffoons who cite the sayings of wicked Jews from the gospel. But how often do you also cite the testimony of Augustine or Gregory? How does your comparison apply any less to you than to us? Did they speak in the Spirit when they say what makes for you but according

25. Luther applied this simile to Erasmus in his reply to the theologians of Louvain and Cologne (WA 6 184).

26. Horace, *Epistles* 1.4.16.

27. *A Discussion* p. 1.

28. *The Enslaved Will*, p. 40.

29. Matt. 26:66; Mark 14:64.

to the flesh when they say what counts against you? Therefore do not insist that on the issue of free will you have the advantage of having Augustine so often on your side—as you boast, though I will soon show that this is quite false—lest we turn your comparison back against you. Or if you deprive them of all authority, stop making use of their testimony. If they said many things devoutly, many things excellently, although they sometimes made mistakes, allow us to make use of what they said well, as you claim the right to do also.

But you command us to choose what is better in their books, passing over what they said according to the flesh.[30] We chose what is better; you likewise chose what is better. But we say that what is better is what agrees with the teachings of the church; you say it is what makes for your teachings. Who can settle the dispute here about which side chooses better? But this is the question posed by my comparison, to which as yet you have given no response, nor is it likely that you ever will. It seems that up to now you have not ranted and raved enough against the most approved Doctors of the church unless you accuse St. Jerome of impiety, sacrilege, and blasphemy because he wrote, "Virginity fills heaven; marriage, the earth."[31] Clearly impious, sacrilegious, and blasphemous, as you have perverted it! "As if," you say, "patriarchs, apostles, and Christian spouses were entitled to earth, not heaven, or as if pagan vestal virgins without Christ were entitled to heaven." How shamelessly you distort it! Was Jerome talking there about virginity which is celibate without Christ? Was he so crazy that he would promise heaven to such persons? Again, does he exclude the patriarchs from heaven because they had wives? What, then, is he saying? He sets holy virginity above holy marriage because marriage was instituted so that the human race might grow and be propagated, according to the command "increase and multiply and fill the earth" (Gen. 1:28). Virginity, however, although it does not increase the number of people on earth, nevertheless, by teaching and by the greatest purity of life draws people to heaven and begets them, as it were, for heaven. Hence the Lord calls blessed those who make themselves eunuchs because of the kingdom of God (Matt. 19:11–12). Of this number were the apostles: just as we read that some of them had wives,[32] we

---

30. *The Enslaved Will,* p. 45.

31. *The Enslaved Will,* n. 24.

32. The gospels record that Christ cured Peter's mother-in-law; see Matt. 8:14–15, Mark 1:30–1, and Luke 4:38–9).

also do not read that after undertaking the business of the gospel they
made use of their wives.[33]

In your disputation how irreverently you take Jerome to task for this
reason: he wrote that some testimonies from Scripture offer support as
Paul cites them, but not in their own context.[34] Here it is not enough
to call him a dim-sighted, silly trifler without finally execrating his
mouth as sacrilegious. Even if Jerome should have made a mistake,
we can courteously find an excuse for him, or if there is no room for
an excuse, the decent thing to do is to correct the error modestly.
That, I suppose, is the service you would want to be furnished to
you if something similar should happen. For you knew that Jerome
had the highest opinion of Paul, nor did he make that charge against
him because he misused scriptural testimony but because there was
nothing so recondite in Scripture that he could not accommodate it to
proving the gospel. You rant and rave thus against Jerome, but you do
not allow anyone to disagree with you, however courteously.

Now whereas I said it is not credible that God for so many centuries
should have overlooked such a harmful error in his church without
revealing to some of his saints the point which you contend is the
keystone of the teachings in the gospel,[35] you play the sophist and
refute this by saying that no error whatever was overlooked in any of
the saints or in the church, since "no one is a saint unless he is moved
by the Spirit of God"—and the Spirit cannot be in error—and since
"Christ remains with his church till the end of time." But the whole
drift of your reasoning is to make us understand that it is unknown
who the saints are and what the church is. You even go so far as to
try to persuade us that God guides the affairs of mortals in such a way
that the church of the saints seems to be where it is not, and, on the
other hand, is where it does not seem to be, and likewise that those
who are wicked are always considered to be saints, and that those
who are saints are considered to be wicked. But when you declaim
all this so copiously, you do nothing but confound and entirely
subvert all judgments made by the church, and you claim authority
for all heretical conventicles. You deny that "if God allowed the most
learned men to err over a long series of centuries, it immediately

33. Erasmus' phrasing is careful: "we do not read that they made" is quite different
from "we read that they did not make."
34. Acts 17:23, discussed by Jerome in his commentary on Titus 1:12. Erasmus'
Folly cited the same passage in *Praise of Folly* (CWE 27 p. 145).
35. *A Discussion*, p. 35.

follows that the church erred,"—I mean that church you say is hidden and cannot be shown. How, then, are you sure that Wyclif[36] was a holy man and the Arians were heretics? Is Wyclif holy precisely because he was condemned by the church which you call papistical? By the same token you will say that Arius[37] was holy because he was condemned by the same church.

At this point if you appeal to Scripture, did the Arians have any lack of Scripture? No, they did not, you will say, but they interpreted it wrongly. But how can we be sure of that except that the church rejected their interpretation and approved that of the other side? The same could be said of Pelagius,[38] whom you also hold to be a wicked heretic, not so much, I imagine, because he was condemned by the Roman church as because he disagrees with your teaching. But even if we grant it is possible that a general council is so corrupt that either there is no one moved by the Spirit of God, or if there is, he is not listened to, and that a conciliar decree is issued from the opinion of evil men, nevertheless it is more probable that the Spirit of God is there than in private conventicles, where the spirit of Satan is quite likely to be detected. If the church of God cannot be shown, but there is a need for some certain judgments, then I think it is safer to follow public authority rather than the opinion of someone or other who scorns everyone and boasts of his own conscience and spirit. If it is enough to say "I have the Spirit," then we will have to believe many people urging various opinions upon us, and if the opinions disagree with one another they cannot be true. But in fact I did not discuss whether we must believe whatever the saints have taught or whether whatever the church has defined is undoubtedly true, but rather I wanted to show that, other things being equal, the greater probability lies on the side of what is approved by such men and confirmed by the public authority of the church rather than with what someone or other brought up on his own.

But even you do not dare to say that "from the beginning of the world the condition of the church on earth has been such that those

---

36. *A Discussion*, n. 5.

37. *The Enslaved Will*, n. 29.

38. A lay ascetic (360?–420?) who argued that the will is free to do either good or evil and that grace is conferred in proportion to merits as a mere facilitator of what the will itself could perform. He was attacked by Augustine, Orosius, Jerome, and others, and he was condemned at the Council of Carthage (418). See *A Discussion*, n. 15.

who were not the people of God were said to be so and, on the other hand, some others who were both saints and the people of God were not said to be so," but rather you set forth the proposition in this way: "Who knows?" If you confess that you don't know, what are you about in your *Assertion,* which rejects the authority of all councils and orthodox teachers and rescinds just about all the decrees of the church?[39] If we were sure that the Spirit of God is in your church, we would rightly reject this church, since it conflicts with yours. As it is, since you confess that you are not certain where the saints are, where the true, inerrant church is, either we will waver in uncertainty or we will follow what is nearer to the truth. But whereas you challenge me to bring forward from the reign of the pope even one bishop who fulfills his duty or one council in which anything was decreed which contributed to the Christian religion rather than to profane trifles about palliums,[40] dignities, and revenues—as for the first point, just as I confess that there are few bishops who truly play the role of bishops, so too it is possible to bring forward some in whom you will not find anything lacking in the duties of a pious prelate, among whom I number John, the bishop of Rochester.[41] But you will immediately reject him because he wrote against you (and so your rejection has no weight). Nor is there any reason for you to cry out here that I write to gain his favor: I neither receive nor desire any income from him—and on many points he disagrees with my opinions—nor does he have such a high regard for my studies.

Finally, nothing could be less comparable than the comparison you propose: God permitted Cicero to err in the case of free will; therefore it is not unlikely if someone should say that God permitted the most learned and holy men of the church to err like Cicero.[42] At the moment we are not investigating what God revealed to pagan

39. In his *Assertio omnium articulorum* (WA 7 91–151) Luther explicitly rejects the authority of the visible, recognizable church on many points.

40. *The Enslaved Will,* n. 30.

41. St. John Fisher (1469–1535), patron of Erasmus, had a high reputation for learning and holiness. He wrote a Latin treatise against Luther, *A Confutation of Luther's Assertion* (Antwerp, 1523).

42. Cicero wrote on free will, fate, and divine foresight in his *De natura deorum* (especially in book 3), in the fragmentary *De fato,* and in *De divinatione.* Both Luther and Erasmus were certainly familiar with Augustine's extended polemic against Cicero on this subject in *De civitate Dei.* Luther's argument here, however, is not so much that Cicero erred about free will as that free will did not get Cicero or pagan philosophers grace and salvation.

philosophers or orators but rather what eluded men who have tasted the Spirit of God and devoted themselves most diligently to Holy Scripture for many years. Did they not achieve anything precisely because their opinions vary or because they dispute without rendering any opinion? So too you people disagree in your teachings. And here you say, "Who knows?" But do Christians fail to believe most firmly in the resurrection of the body simply because the greatest philosophers vacillate and argue about it? You add that God conceals his saints like a splendid pearl which is not to be cast before swine "lest a wicked man should see the glory of God." And nevertheless the gospel says, "By their fruits you shall know them."[43] If a good tree as well as a bad one is known by its fruit, we can make some judgments about the pious and the wicked even in this world, though the most certain judgments are those of God. And this would be the place for a discussion comparing fruits, if I had not decided not to stir up such a hornets' nest.

At this point, Luther, I seem to be dealing with the rhetorician,[44] whose modesty I wish you had imitated in all of your writings; you would have alienated far fewer from yourself or, if we give you any credence, from the gospel. Your insults know no bounds, and you do not approve of anything at all in a person who opposes your opinion. This rhetorician, though he engages in sufficient buffoonery by dallying with my Discussion—"What are you about, my little Discussion?" and "Lady Discussion,"[45]—still he is more moderate than you are, unless he strove to preserve the decorum of the role he is playing. But in fact his arguments about saints and the church do not have much validity against me, because I am not using their authority but rather Holy Scripture to refute your opinion. But if we posit an equal balance in the things by which you wish to be judged and if the opinion of men is wavering in the balance, I ask you whether the authority of the ancient fathers and the church should have any weight. This was the drift of my discussion, to which you should have directed your arguments. You confess that the church I allege does exist, you confess that the saints I bring up do exist, but you distinguish the rule of charity, which can be deceived, from the

---

43. Matt. 7:16–20 and Luke 6:43–4; *Adages* 1.9.39.

44. Erasmus refers to some less aggressive rhetorician (perhaps Melanchthon) whose help he thinks Luther has engaged in his reply to Erasmus.

45. Luther (or his alleged helper) personifies *A Discussion* as a woman (the Latin and Greek designations in the title Διατριβή *sive collatio de libero arbitrio* are feminine).

rule of faith, which cannot—a distinction aimed at preventing us from believing anyone is a saint unless God declares him to be so. Charity believes that all who are baptized are saints, but faith does not.[46]

Although this is the case, nevertheless, because "charity, which hopes for all things" (1 Cor. 13:7). and which is also confirmed by many arguments, believes that the orthodox fathers were saints, it should have enough weight, when the scale is evenly balanced, to incline us towards those who have been commended for so many centuries by the public favor of the whole world than towards those who are commended for no other reason than that they are baptized. And so, if you insist that their authority has no value in confirming an opinion, then neither does yours or anyone else's. I have already answered about choosing the better parts as well as about the testimony of Scripture, since each side chooses and interprets. Likewise I am unaffected by that old song of yours about some who fail to exercise judgment and devour everything indiscriminately, or by a perversion of judgment spit out what is better. Though there may be some such, still charity is not so wrongly suspicious as to conceive such an opinion about the leaders of the church unless what they prescribe is manifestly wicked.

But finally you approach the heart of the matter. "If the church is concealed" you say, "if the saints are hidden, what and whom shall we believe? And as you argue very pointedly, who will give us certainty? Where will we discover the Spirit? If you consider learning, there are erudite teachers on both sides. If you look for morals, there are sinners on both sides. If you look to Scripture, both sides embrace it." But if we make Scripture the judge, the interpretation of it is uncertain in many places, and both sides pull Scripture towards their meaning. Hence it follows that here we play the Skeptics, "unless you take the best line of all when you express your doubt in such a way as to aver that you are seeking to learn the truth, inclining in the meantime towards the side that supports free will, until the truth shines forth."[47] Imagine, if you like, that I have no feeling for talent or phrasing: do you really think, Luther, that it is unclear to me who wrote this? One voice is as different from the other as a parrot from a quail.[48] Could you ever bear to say "as you very pointedly argue," since for you I always speak ignorantly and stupidly? Could you say such a thing as

46. *The Enslaved Will*, pp. 44–45.
47. *The Enslaved Will*, p. 46.
48. Cf. Martial 10.3.7.

"unless you take the best line of all," since up to now you have so shamelessly ranted and raved against Erasmus as a Skeptic and worse than a Skeptic, namely, a thoroughgoing Lucian and Epicurus?[49] Again, could you say "there is something in what you say but not the whole truth," since you always bawl out that I have nothing to say and utter nothing but verbal bubbles and bombast? But however this may be, it doesn't much matter.[50]

Not all of Scripture is fully clear

Finally, when you are ready to untie the knot, you do what you regularly and wrongly blame the sophists[51] for doing: you introduce a twofold clarity of Holy Scripture and likewise a twofold judgment to test spirits. The first is the one by which everyone "enlightened by a special gift of God judges and discriminates all teachings with full certainty." Paul is speaking about such a person in 1 Corinthians, 2:15: "The spiritual man judges all things and is judged by no one." And you call this "the interior clarity of Holy Scripture." "This," you say, "is perhaps what was meant by those who replied to you that all things were to be decided by the judgment of the Spirit."[52] Indeed, I know someone[53] who I did not believe had this Spirit, which he claimed for himself, since I had learned by most certain evidence that he was a consummate liar—brimful of vainglory, and an insatiable backbiter—but then he did not understand this matter as you interpret it. For when I agreed with him so far as to allow that some person or other might be certain because of his own spirit, I went on to ask how that would give me any certainty, since I do not have the gift of distinguishing the spirits[54] of others and I said that in

49. Lucian of Samosata (c. 120–180) was a rhetorician and philosopher who wrote satiric dialogues, some of which were translated jointly by Erasmus and Thomas More. Epicurus (342–271 BCE) was a philosopher and moralist who upheld atomism, denied the immortality of the soul and divine providence, but did not deny the existence of the gods.

50. That is, it doesn't much matter whether someone (perhaps Melanchthon) helped Luther in the writing of *The Enslaved Will*.

51. Erasmus refers to the distinctions often drawn by scholastic theologians, whom Luther regularly mocks as "sophists."

52. *The Enslaved Will*, p. 47. In *A Discussion* (p. 5) Erasmus had spoken of the *indicio* (sign) of the Spirit, but Luther misread the word as *iudicio* (judgment).

53. Erasmus' reference is unclear. Was it Ulrich von Hutten or someone else?

54. Cf. 1 Cor. 12:10.

this way, as you also confess, his certitude did not remove my doubt. He brought the argument back to Scripture, but when I objected that the interpretations are various, he had no answer but "Spirit, Spirit." Hence if you can solve the difficulty you have taken in hand, you will be performing no mean task. And so you confess that this judgment does no good for others but only for the person provided with this spirit. Otherwise we would have to have faith in all the fanatics who boast more contentiously about having the Spirit than those who truly have this special gift.

And so you display also the other clarity of Scripture, namely that which is external, and also the external revelation of the spirit by which we promote the salvation of others also by judging quite certainly about spiritual things and the teachings of everyone. Come on, then, I am waiting for this certainty with bated breath. You add that "This judgment is mainly the concern of leaders and heralds of the word," which I take to mean either bishops or theologians; if they should agree among themselves in explaining Holy Scripture, we would have something certain to follow. As it is, our heralds teach something different than you do, and your adherents disagree among themselves and even go so far as to cry out boldly against you. Where, then, even in the church, is this certain judgment by which we prove or disprove teachings drawn from Holy Scripture, a rule which is completely certain, "a spiritual light brighter than the sun?" But you yourself perceive and confess that you will get nowhere unless you prove what you assume, even though it is debatable, and you promise you will do it. Come on, we will follow you if you perform what you promise; certainly we want to. In Deuteronomy 17:8–13 Moses speaks of referring judgment to the priests if there is any difficulty about which the judges disagree and which they cannot resolve, etc. "How," you say, "how can they give a judgment about a controverted matter according to the Law unless the Law is externally quite clear?" I reply in two ways. First, if the Law had been externally quite clear to anyone who has common sense, why did the judges themselves not unravel the knot, since it is probable that they were not ignorant of the Law? They are said to have differed in their opinions not because they did not know the Law but because the case was difficult, and therefore the case was referred to the priests as more skilled in the Law. Secondly, I reply that in that place Moses did not mean difficulties which arise concerning the question of free will or the like but rather concerning more material affairs, of which he gives some examples there, such as a case of blood against blood, lawsuit against lawsuit, leprosy or not leprosy.

[Then too, when you try to confirm your argument by adducing secular laws, by which suits cannot be settled unless they are quite clear, you work against yourself. For just as I do not deny that many disputes are settled by the laws, it is also obvious that there are many obscurities in the laws of princes. Otherwise what point would there be in devoting so much effort over many years to learning secular law if it were so obvious that it would be completely clear to anyone at all who knows the language and is not lacking in common sense? Therefore those who wrote so many volumes in an attempt to iron out the difficulties of the law were wasting their energy. Judges and senates are foolish to wear themselves out for years sometimes to understand just one case. The poet was wrong when he said, "Who unties the knots of justice and solves the riddles of the law."[55] Nor is this conclusion of yours valid: if there is so much lucidity in secular laws, how much more should there be in writings which pertain to eternal salvation? [First of all, the matters treated in Holy Scripture are more obscure. Next, it was not impious either for other orthodox fathers or for Augustine, to whom (not without cause) you attribute so much, to say that God deliberately left some obscurity in Holy Scripture to stir up in us a greater desire to scrutinize it.[56]

From Psalm 18:9 you bring up the verse: "the command of the Lord is clear, enlightening the eyes." But he says the command is clear, not all of Scripture; and even if all of Scripture were clear to David and others inspired by a prophetic spirit, it is not immediately clear to all who know grammar and have common sense, as you so often affirm. Again, from Psalm 118:130 you bring in the verse: "The disclosure of your speech illuminates and gives understanding to children." I will accept this testimony if you mean such children as David was and those upon whom the Spirit of God rests; but if you apply it to whoever knows the language, that is quite another matter. Then too, in what you cite from Isaiah, chapter 8, verse 2. "Go rather to the Law and the testimony, etc.," the prophet is not saying there is no obscurity in the sacred books, but rather he is threatening that darkness will come upon those who consult soothsayers and ventriloquists. For he adds in the same place,[57] "Shall the common people not ask God" for vision, etc.? Christ lay hidden in the Law, but the words of the Law were not clear to everyone who knew Hebrew; rather, they

---

55. Juvenal, 8.50.

56. *De doctrina christiana* 2.6.7–8 / CCSL 32 35–36.

57. Isa. 8:19.

asked the Scribes, who were well versed in the Law, for advice from
the Law, as when Herod consulted them about where the boy Jesus
would be born (Matt. 2:2–4). Again, the second chapter of Malachi
verse 7 commands the people to ask for the Law from the mouth of a
priest. "A very fine messenger indeed," you say, "who will announce
what is both ambiguous to him and unclear to the people." Why then
do you people not follow the advice of Malachi and ask for the Law
from the mouths of priests and bishops?

Moreover, what need was there to learn the Law from the mouth
of a priest, since anyone of the people who knew the language and
had common sense could easily understand a Law that was perfectly
clear. Therefore, someone who orders that the Law be sought
from the mouth of a priest indicates that the Law is not clear to
just anyone, but rather he points out the fitting interpreter of the
Law. Again, Psalm 118:105, "Your word is a lamp to my feet and a
light on my paths," does not deal with intricate questions, but rather
with the rules of a good life which shine forth and show what we
ought to seek and what we ought to avoid. And even if you twist it
violently so as to extend it to the whole Law, what applies to David
does not apply to just anyone skilled in grammar. So much for Old
Testament passages, but of texts such as these you could have brought
up hundreds.

You go on to the New Testament. In the second chapter of
Romans,[58] Paul says that the gospel was promised in Holy Scripture.
"What sort of witness is it," you say, "if it is obscure?" If nothing is
obscure in the predictions of the prophets and in the figures of the
Law, why are they called shadows? (Heb. 10:1). And why do we
speak of the light of the gospel, if not because what is wrapped and
covered up by figures in the Law is brought out into the open by the
gospel? Is nothing there predicted about Christ which is not perfectly
clear to all, provided they know Hebrew? Indeed, even the disciples
of the Lord, after hearing so many sermons, after seeing so many
miracles, after so many signs and tokens which the prophets foretold
concerning Christ, did not understand Scripture until Christ opened
up the meaning so that they understood Scripture. Now in Paul's
letter to the Corinthians, when he discusses the brightness of Moses
and Christ, he makes the brightness of the gospel so preeminent that
he says, "The brightness of that part"—he is speaking of the Law—
"was not even glorified" (2 Cor. 3:7–11).

---

58. The correct reference is Romans 1:2.

What if God deliberately wanted prophecies about Christ not to be clear to just anyone at all, just as on earth he also did not want anyone to preach before his death that he was the Messiah (Matt. 16:20), because that was expedient in carrying out the program of saving mankind? But when the apostles announced that the predictions of the prophets had been fulfilled, both the Law was clearer through a comparison with the events, and it also turned out that the Law contributed to belief in the gospel and the gospel threw light on the enigmas of the Law. Surely this is what Peter meant when he compared the speech of the prophets to a torch "shining in a dark place" (2 Pet. 1:19), nor did he take everything else to be dark, since Paul attributes even to the pagan philosophers enough light for them to know God and his sempiternal divinity (Rom. 1:19–20). All truth is light. And many truths promulgated by them agree with the teachings of Christians. John was a burning lamp (John 5:35), because he preached the word of God. For the same reason Paul called the Thessalonians lights of the world[59] because they knew the word of life. But that was not reason enough for any of them who knew grammar to understand whatever is difficult in Holy Scripture. Christ was "the light of the world,"[60] but nevertheless the divine nature was hidden in him, nor do we immediately grasp whatever is in Christ. You could have thrown together hundreds of such testimonies, even from indexes, where light is mentioned.[61]

What follows is even more banal: "What are the apostles doing when they support their preaching by Scripture? Do they do it to add darkness to darkness so as to make what is obscure to us even more obscure or to prove what is better known by what is less known?" At this point when will you stop throwing prophets, baptists, and apostles at us? No one doubts their Spirit, and their authority is sacrosanct. Because they had the Spirit teaching them from within, they explained what is obscure in the writings of the prophets. We were talking about your spirit and that of your followers, who profess that there is nothing in Holy Scripture which is obscure to you as long as you know →

---

59. Phil. 2:1. "Thessalonices" in the two Basel editions of 1526 and in the Leiden edition of 1703–1706 is a slip of the pen (or the printer) for "Philippenses."

60. John 8:12, 9:5.

61. Luther cited the scriptural passages on light which Erasmus has just discussed. The first concordance of the Bible was completed in 1230. Fuller concordances were printed in 1470, 1475, 1485, and 1496; see *The Catholic Encyclopedia* 15 vols. (New York, 1907–1912) iv 195.

grammar, and we demanded that you establish the credibility of this certainty, which you still fail to do, try as you may.] In John, you say, Christ commands the Jews to search the places in Scripture which speak of him (John 5:39); if they are obscure, he is throwing them into doubt. Indeed, if there is no obscurity in them, what is the meaning of that word "search"? For we do not search for the sun, which is open to all eyes, but we search to find something that is hidden. And nevertheless, when the Lord added "for those places speak of me," he added a good deal of light, pointing out the aim of the prophecy.

Just so in Acts; when Paul had taught and admonished them, they compared the scriptural passages with what had been carried out and what had been propounded to them (Acts 17:11), and there was much they would not have understood if the Apostle had not supplied this additional light. Therefore, I am not making the passages obscure, but rather God himself wanted there to be some obscurity in them, but in such a way that there would be enough light for the eternal salvation of everyone if he used his eyes and grace was there to help. [No one denies that there is truth as clear as crystal in Holy Scripture, but sometimes it is wrapped and covered up by figures and enigmas so that it needs scrutiny and an interpreter, either because God wanted in this way to arouse us from dullness and also to set us to work, as Augustine says,[62] or because truth is more pleasant and affects us more deeply when it has been dug out and shines forth to us through the cover of darkness than if it had been exposed for just anyone to see, or because he did not want that treasure of wisdom to be prostituted to anyone no matter who.] And so you accomplish nothing at all by bringing up one place or another where there is no obscurity.

"God created heaven and earth" (Gen. 1:1). You propose this place as not at all obscure, for in the words there is no figure of speech or ambiguity. But yet you see how here too the interpreters have sweated over what is meant here by "heaven," what by "earth," or whether he created individual things in series or all things together with one nod. And when all this is explained, there remains the cloud of allegory, as Jerome calls it.[63] You will say: "a knowledge of such difficulties is not

---

62. See n. 56, above.

63. Jerome, Ep. 74.6 (CSEL 55 28). That allegory clouds or veils the truth was a hermeneutical commonplace deriving from the Alexandrian school of literary criticism. Its principal exponent among patristic exegetes was the pioneering theologian Origen of Alexandria (c. 185–254). Jerome accepted his tripartite division of scriptural senses into the historical, tropological, and spiritual (Ep. 12 [PL 22, 1005]) and often employed allegory to elucidate Scripture.

necessary to salvation." The same thing was meant by the Corycian caverns, which upset you so much:[64] when we search in Holy Scripture more deeply than is necessary or than we are capable of understanding, then the vision of our minds encounters the darkness in which the majesty of the eternal wisdom is concealed, to be worshipped rather than investigated. When you yourself teach the same thing in different words, distinguishing the light of glory from the light of grace, what was impious when I taught it becomes pious when you teach it. "The word was made flesh" (John 1:14). What could be clearer? But it is so to us, to whom the mystery has been explained. If the same words were read by Demosthenes,[65] come to life once more, he would not understand them, and certainly we all know and profess that the Son of God took on a human nature. And yet many points are handled concerning these words: how only the Son took on a human nature; and how the divine nature, by means of a human soul, combined with itself a mortal body into the same hypostatic union; and how that holy little body was fashioned by the Holy Spirit from a little drop of the purest blood, as big (they say) as a tiny spider; and whether the soul of Christ, immediately after it was created and infused into the body, was granted the beatific vision; and whether God could have imparted to him more grace than he did.[66] These questions and countless others like them exist about those words, "The word was made flesh."

You say the same thing about the articles of the faith: since there is no one who does not understand them, we have drunk them in from Holy Scripture that is most clear; otherwise how could we believe or teach them with certainty? You add: "What are those who preach about Holy Scripture doing still today, interpreting and expounding it? If it were obscure, "who could make us certain that their exposition is certain? Another new exposition? And who will expound that? And so there will be a regression to infinity." This is what you say, Luther, in a very declamatory strain.[67] But if, as you teach, nothing

---

64. *The Enslaved Will,* n. 97.

65. Athenian orator and statesman (384–322 BCE).

66. For example, Thomas Aquinas, *Summa theologiae* III q 3 aa 4–8, q 2 a 3, q 31 a 5, q 34 a 4, q 7 a 12. The hypostatic union in Christ means that he has two natures, divine and human, neither of which has a separate being of its own but both of which are united into one being or substance (hypostasis).

67. In classical times and during the Renaissance, declamations were oratorical exercises defending either side of fictitious and improbable cases, with little or no regard for real issues. See Quintilian *Institutio oratoria* 3.8.55–9, 7.9.4–8.

is needed for Holy Scripture except grammar, what need is there to hear a preacher expound and interpret it? It would be enough to read out a prophet or the gospel to the common people, who do not have the sacred books, without explaining anything at all, unless there might perhaps be some underlying difficulty about the words. But if you press the point about what the heralds of the gospel are doing, I will say this: often from the same words, which you would like us to think are most clear, they elicit various opinions, as if from the same flint one person would strike fire, another water. Nor is there any reason for you to shout back that this happens among the papists and the carnal sophists; it happens among the heralds of your communion, who claim the Spirit for themselves no less immovably than you do. If Holy Scripture is perfectly clear in all respects, where does this darkness among you come from, whence arise such fights to the death about the meaning of Holy Scripture?

You prove from the mysteries of Scripture that the body of the Lord is in the eucharist physically;[68] from the same Scripture Zwingli, Oecolampadius, and Capito[69] teach that it is only signified. This is the main point of this disputation, that you make us certain that you alone teach what is most true and most certain on issues about which up till now the orthodox fathers have been deluded, the leaders of the church have been deluded. If you will not allow us to consider their judgment certain in any respect, certainly you will allow us simple and unlearned folk to give as much weight to the judgment of such men as to yours or Wyclif's.[70] But if you claim the right to rescind the decisions of the church insofar as you find it convenient to do so, you will permit the church also to give tit for tat by rescinding and condemning yours. And if you think it is right for the whole assembly

---

68. Although Luther had rejected transubstantiation in *De captivitate Babylonica ecclesiae praeludium* of 1520 (WA 6 502:1–526:33), he defended the real presence of Christ in the eucharist in many polemics.

69. Zwingli (1484–1531) was a Swiss reformer who, unlike Luther, denied the physical presence of Christ in the eucharist. He circulated an open letter (published in March 1525) in which he argued for his view of the eucharist. He reaffirmed his view at length in *De vera et falsa religione* (Zurich 1525). Johann Oecolampadius (1482–1531), a leading reformer at Basel, agreed with Zwingli's teaching about the eucharist and criticized Luther's view in *De genuina verborum Dei: 'Hoc est corpus meum,' etc. expositione* (Basel 1525). Wolfgang Faber Capito (d. 1541) was a Strassburg reformer who took Zwingli's side against Luther concerning the eucharist.

70. *A Discussion*, n. 5.

of the church, together with so many orthodox fathers, to yield to you, a newly arisen prophet, you also ought to yield to the others who arise after you.[71]

Consider all this as said for the sake of argument. But I will follow the course of your speech. "if Scripture," you say, "is obscure or ambiguous, what need was there for God to deliver it to us? Do we not have enough obscurity and ambiguity without having our obscurity and ambiguity and darkness increased from heaven?" You say this as if I said that all Scripture is obscure and ambiguous, whereas I confess that it contains a treasure of eternal and most certain truth, but in some places the treasure is concealed and not open to just anybody, no matter who. The sun is not dark if it does not appear when it is covered by clouds or if a dim-sighted person gropes about in full daylight. But actually all this I am saying to you is beside the point; I was dealing with intricate questions which arise from Holy Scripture as it is interpreted first in one way and then in another. Here was the place you should have brought forth that most certain light of yours by which you convict the whole church of blindness. For, as to that quibble of yours that this light is always concealed in that church which is hidden and not thought to be the church, even if I granted you this (which you cannot prove), it is more probable that the holiest and also most learned men belonged to that hidden church than that you and your few adherents do.

You still do not perform what you promised, but rather you go on: "All divinely inspired Scripture," you say, "is useful for teaching, rebuking, and censuring" (2 Tim. 3:16). And here you indulge in marvelous rhetorical flourishes, or rather someone else under your name,[72] for you are not able to set forth ten words without insults. "No, Paul, it is completely useless; rather, such things as you attribute to Scripture we must seek from the fathers accepted over the course of the centuries and from the see of Rome. Hence you must revoke your opinion when you wrote to Titus that a bishop should be powerful in exhorting and reproving objectors by sound doctrine, etc. How

---

71. Luther had cited 1 Corinthians 14:29 ("Let two or three prophets speak, and let the others judge") to refute Erasmus' submission to the church, since that would deprive everyone of the liberty Paul attributes to the "others." Erasmus replies that Paul's text would also require that Luther yield to those who arose after him and disagree with him, such as Karlstadt and Zwingli.

72. Here Erasmus refers to some unidentified rhetorician-helper who he claims has learned all his eloquence from Erasmus; he also says this unnamed helper has not read good authors.

will he be powerful," you say, "when you leave to him an obscure Scripture, that is, arms made of tow and thin blades of grass instead of a sword?"[73] I have no doubt that you imagine this is quite cleverly said, though it does not untie the knot I proposed and is false besides. Leave out the Titus's and Timothy's here, one of whom was conversant with Holy Scripture from his childhood, and both of whom had Paul for a teacher, and, besides that, they had a spirit not subject to any doubt. Is it so that no bishop today can use divinely inspired Scripture to teach or rebuke if he is at a loss in certain places? Does a physician have no advice to give a patient if he has doubts about some passage in the medical books? Is no one powerful in sound doctrine unless he can truly claim that there is no place in the mysteries of Scripture where he is at a loss? I hardly know whether the apostles would have dared to profess so much as this.

How did it happen that for thirteen hundred years the Doctors of the church have been shutting the mouths of heretics (as so many of them arose, one after the other) against the truth of Scripture? Did they fight with arms made of tow, and instead of the sword of the word, which you brandish, did they have flimsy blades of grass? And yet those men, who had such strength with the help of Scripture, confess that in Holy Scripture some things are obscure, some things are beyond human understanding. And how did it happen that the church suspended judgment for so long concerning the procession of the Spirit from both[74] if the light of Scripture is so bright that a knowledge of grammar is enough to understand it? Why should it be so monstrous if, when some ambiguity or other arises in Scripture, we ignorant souls should prefer to consult the See of Rome rather than that of Wittenberg, which is full of disagreements at that?[75] And who would believe the church of Rome if it should make pronouncements without Scripture? Nor does it interpret Scripture without the help of a council made up of learned men. You interpret at your own whim, with the help of your spirit, which is unknown to us (not to say that we do know it).

73. Cf. Titus 1:9. See *The Enslaved Will*, p. 000.

74. A reference to the debate over the *filioque* clause in the Nicene Creed— whether the Holy Spirit proceeds from the Father only (the Greek position) or from both the Father and the Son (the Latin, *filioque*, position). The dispute was settled (briefly) in favor of the Latin side at the Council of Florence in 1439.

75. The word is, of course, ironic as applied to Wittenberg, which was never a bishopric.

There is no reason why Christ should be forced to recant his saying, "I will give you speech and wisdom, which all your adversaries will not be able to resist" (Luke 21:15). Why do you throw up the apostles to me when we are dealing with your spirit? Christ provided his apostles with what he promised them. He did not promise it to you or to just anybody, and if he also provided it for you, prove to us with irrefutable arguments that he gave to you alone what he denied to that numberless multitude. This is what we are dealing with, this is the knot which must be untied, and in the meantime you waste our time with prolix declamations and do not provide what you promise. [As for me, I do not compare you with Christ or the apostles, but rather I compare a person whose spirit is unknown with so many orthodox teachers, with the leading men of the church; though we admit we are not certain about their spirit, nevertheless, according to your own rule, charity has had a good opinion about them for so many centuries past, even though faith approves of nothing except what has been commended to us by God. And yet you demand that we reject their authority, that we hold to your teachings as if they were articles of the faith. At least grant us, for their teachings as well as yours, the same right to suspend judgment about either] I do not say these things as my sincere opinions, but rather in order to confute you.

Finally your speech diverges from the apostles and Christ. Why, you say, "do you prescribe a formulation of Christianity[76] if Scripture is obscure to you?" On my behalf I reply: I do not prescribe a formulation of Christianity in *A Discussion;* I only show how far the inquiry of ordinary people should go. Nor do I wish to attribute anything more to my formulation than other orthodox writers wished to attribute to their writings, to whom we owe a good deal that contributes to piety. If you also profess this, since they confess that they find not a few places in Scripture obscure, either recant what you have often confessed, that they discoursed about many things correctly, or grant us the right to teach some things as best we can, even though we do not deny that we find some obscurity in the sacred books. [But if you abrogate all faith in these writers, why do you demand that we have faith in your writings, since you confess that you are at a loss in some places and since you sometimes bring forth varying interpretations—which you would hardly do if there were no obscurity or ambiguity?] The same thing also happens to

76. *The Enslaved Will,* n. 47.

your followers: Bugenhagen[77] and Oecolampadius[78] speak about some places with doubts and hesitation, as in the end even Philippus[79] does, for whom there is no end to your praises. Everything which you thundered with such vehemence and lavishness against those who think there is anything obscure in Scripture recoils on the heads of your followers and even on your own.

Finally, you yourself confess that obscurity occurs in the mysteries of Scripture because of ignorance about words, and you will add, I think, because of corruptions in the manuscripts, figures of speech, and places which conflict with one another. Once you admit this, all the disadvantages return which you attributed to obscurity. For it does not matter where the obscurity comes from as long as some is there. Such obscurity you certainly cannot deny. But if you eliminate all faith in those who are at a loss anywhere, you yourself are at a loss and so are your adherents, in whom you wish us to have wholehearted faith. They are not only at a loss, but they also disagree so much among themselves that they boldly reject and condemn your teaching as well, with no other aid except Scripture. Now bring out all the copiousness and power of the eloquence you pretend not to have, and say against yourself and your adherents what you have said against us.

As for the argument you add—that if you deny that Scripture is clear, you profess that the saints I bring up are even less clear—you might have said it against me with some appearance of probability if I had used them to assail your teaching; as it is, I use Holy Scripture to engage you. And I do not bring up how numerous and gifted they were except to force you to bring forth a manifest argument by which we may know that we can safely believe in you and piously diverge from them. Although you have accepted this position, still, after so many blows and fisticuffs, after so much spitting, you teach nothing to the point. You grant that I do not mean all of Scripture but only those places from which such question arise. If you grant this, what is the point of speaking so many words as if I had said all of it is obscure?

---

77. Johann Bugenhagen (1485–1558), known in Latin as Pomeranus, was city pastor at Wittenberg and, next to Melanchthon, the most influential member of Luther's circle there.

78. Johannes Oecolampadius (1482–1531) was a learned Greek scholar who assisted Erasmus in his edition of the *New Testament*. But he later became one of the leading reformers in Basel. Though he attacked Erasmus' position on free will and denied the real presence in the eucharist, the two never fully broke with each other and continued to respect each other's learning.

79. That is, Melanchthon. See n. 19 above, and n. 101 below.

But what applies to me, as you say, is that I confess that some things are obscure; you want no part of Scripture to be obscure. I hear "I want," a word of command, but I preferred the voice of a teacher. What you affirm, I wish; what you say you know, I desire to learn; nor is it enough for me that you firmly assert this—I demand the certitude which you profess to have. Teach us the external clarity of Scripture, seeing that you take it away from the church herself and the luminaries of the church and claim it for yourself, throwing the world into the most tumultuous uproar.

Nor is your assumption true that the church drew upon obscure places in Scripture in her pronouncement about free will, although I confess that the abyss of this question is unsearchable and therefore should not be penetrated more deeply than is sufficient; but I am persuaded that the ancient fathers and the church asserted what they asserted on the basis of passages in Scripture that are quite clear in themselves. Even so, the authority of the church did not put forward a judgment on this matter immediately but rather turned her eyes for a while on the light of Scripture and finally, having perceived the manifest truth, made a pronouncement. For it often happens that when someone comes out of the dark, he does not see anything even in full sunlight unless he has focused his eyes for a while, and some things we do not see immediately through the darkness, but as we focus our eyes what was doubtful before gradually begins to be clear to us, and the same thing happens when things are far away from us. But out of courtesy I pretended that the interpretations on both sides were ambiguous so that on a level playing field you might show something that would incline towards your side those of us who were vacillating in the middle. With similar restraint I called it a discussion, not an assertion, and I conclude that I follow the probable opinion, not because I have any doubts about the received opinion but because it is dangerous to put yours forth before crowds, either because in this way the people learn to disbelieve the decrees of the church (and it could turn out that they will finally begin to doubt even the most certain articles of faith), or else because it is not safe to debate for and against received articles before uneducated people, or else because this question has such profound depths that the unlearned should be kept away from them, since it is enough for them to hold to the teachings handed down by the church.

I also do not agree with you when you make all the articles of faith equal. For some are so evident that it would be wrong to argue about them, such as these: that Christ was born of a virgin, that he suffered under Pontius Pilate.[80] Some are such that only after long investigation were they finally approved by public authority. Concerning some there is not sufficient agreement even now. Some had doubts about the perpetual virginity of Mary[81] until their mouths were shut by arguments from Scripture rightly interpreted. Some ancient fathers had doubts about whether the bishop of Rome is the universal pastor of the church, and it was permissible to do so until the church made a decision.[82] And there is still controversy in the schools about whether the authority of the bishop of Rome is greater than that of a general council.[83] Accordingly, if you want your teaching to be believed with faith equal to that we have in the Apostle's Creed, bring forth testimony from Scripture which is equally clear, show that your teaching came down to us directly from the time of the apostles together with the gospel.

Therefore, just as I believe those things most firmly, so too I had no doubts about the dogma of free will after the catholic church had pronounced on it. Why then, you say, are you arguing as if you would follow something more correct if anyone could show it? Why did you prefer the title *A Discussion* rather than *A Confutation?* Why do you not exhort everyone to reject my teaching and hold firmly to what the church has handed down? I had no lack of words I could have applied to my discussion and to your teaching (and they are not new to you), but I was disposed to try to see whether I could either heal you by this courtesy or invite you to respond more gently. Then, since I saw that human affairs were more than sufficiently inflamed, I did not want to have the fierceness of my pen pour oil, as it were, on the fire. Finally, I would not have argued at all if you had not promulgated this fable of yours so that now in weavers' shops and cobblers' stalls it is argued everywhere that there is no free will but

80. Articles of the Apostles Creed, affirmed by both the Catholic and the Lutheran interlocutors in Erasmus' colloquy "An Examination concerning the Faith" (CWE 39 p. 419–47).

81. The teaching that Mary was a virgin not only when she conceived but also when she gave birth and thereafter (as affirmed, for example, by Thomas Aquinas in *Summa theologiae* III q 28 aa 1–3), although never directly defined, was accepted by the Council of Chalcedon (451) and the Lateran synod of 649.

82. Erasmus had detailed the ancient controversy about Matthew 16:18 in his *Annotations on the New Testament* (LB VI 88C–F). Later he asserted that the papal primacy was divinely instituted (LB IX 388A).

83. The conciliarist doctrine that a general council constitutes the supreme authority in the church. The question was hotly debated in Erasmus' times.

rather that everything is done by sheer necessity. And as if you hadn't done enough already, they say that this disputation of yours is being translated into German by Jonas[84] so that you can stir up weavers and farmers against me, and once they have been stirred up I cannot placate them because I do not know the language.[85]

When you have been driven hither and thither by all the arguments, you finally escape by making common sense the arbiter[86] of those who fight about the clarity of Scripture. For, as you say, even those who have been vanquished by the most clear testimony of Scripture offer resistance, but common sense shows that they have nothing they can rightly say in reply.[87] Thus when the Sadducees were confuted, they were indeed silent, but they did not relinquish their error (Matt. 22:31–33). It would be foolish to suggest what replies the Sadducees might have made: they could have said, first, that the souls of the dead cannot rightly be called human beings; secondly, that, while it is not absurd to speak of the God of Abraham, Isaac, and Jacob, who worshipped him while they were alive, just as in the ordinary way of speaking fathers are still called fathers even when they have survived their children,[88] yet at that point they were dealing with the resurrection of the body, which cannot be proved from these words. You will say, "Why, then, were they silent?" Because there was divine power in the words of Christ which attracted the minds of believers and overthrew the consciences of the wicked. But this is beside the point. And so if you also wish to shut our mouths

84. Justus Jonas (1493–1555) was provost at the Castle Church of All Saints and professor of canon law at Wittenberg. He translated Luther's *De servo arbitrio* into German (Wittenberg: Hans Lufft 1526).

85. In fact *De libero arbitrio* was translated into German by Nicolaus Herman of Altdorf (1526), and so was *The Shield-Bearer* 1 translated by Jerome Emser (Leipzig: Melcher Lotter 1526). Emser (sig Aa1) makes Erasmus' meaning more explicit ("because the high-German tongue is unknown to me"); Erasmus knew only Dutch or low-German (*Plattdeutsch*).

86. Latin *arbitrum*, with wordplay on *liberum arbitrium* (free choice), which is normally translated as "free will" in English.

87. *The Enslaved Will*, pp. 51–52.

88. To Jesus' first reply about marriage in heaven (that it is spirits which survive in the afterlife) the Sadducees could have replied that a spirit is not properly a human being. To Jesus' second argument, that the God of Abraham must be a god of the living, they could have replied that "God of Abraham" is a common figure of speech, meaning the God whom Abraham once worshipped, just as men who survive their children are still called "father."

so that we do not dare to open them, bring forth similar testimony from Scripture; show us the Spirit speaking in you, so that if we attempt to resist you the common sense of everyone will condemn us and approve of you. But even today plenty of people who seem to have common sense cry out against you. And who would deny that those orthodox fathers and the whole Christian people had common sense? It is more likely that you and your adherents lack common sense: you, because you rant and rave with such uncontrollable abuse against those who contradict your teachings even for the sake of discussion; your adherents, because with unrestrained factionalism in support of you they approve of whatever you have taught: *ipse dixit*.[89] If you appeal to the Spirit, once more I demand a manifest sign. The rest of what you bring up, I pass over, since it has no force against me.

Nor is it my place to judge Jan Huss.[90] He had his judges among men—would that he has found God to be a more merciful judge. I will only say this: I thought less badly of the man before I sampled the book he wrote against the Roman pontiff.[91] What does such laborious abuse have in common with the Spirit of Christ? And in our discussion it does not matter what sort of pope condemned Huss; he is unknown to me, and popes have their own judge before whom they stand or fall. They are my judges; I am not theirs. Now where you say some people feign simplicity so that they can have a better excuse to resist the truth they know, saying "I am a man, I can err, I want to learn" and then adding "it does not satisfy me, he is doing violence to Scripture, etc.," whether you are saying this about me or about others, I for one certainly exclude myself from the number of those who knowingly and willingly reject known truth, especially concerning the articles of the faith. As for you, see to it that you find a way to excuse what you are doing. But I do not yet hear anything that cuts the knot so as to give us clear proof of your spirit.

But you seem to me to fight like that dog sent by the king of Albania as a gift to Alexander: when the dog fought with an elephant, he skillfully ran around in circles barking on one side and then the other, until he wore the beast out, making it dizzy from turning

89. That is, "he himself has spoken" (*Adages* 2.5.87); though it is given here in Latin, Erasmus gives the saying in Greek.

90. *The Enslaved Will*, n. 32.

91. Asserting that Christ is the only head of the church, Huss challenged the primacy of the bishop of Rome as originating merely in Constantine's sanction.

around so often, and in this way brought it down.[92] You do not deny
that very many men distinguished for ability, learning, and rank—and
some also for their miracles and martyrdom—reject your teachings;
you confess that they were saints, or rather you grant it and we accept
it. In other respects my case is as good as yours. At this juncture it
remains for you to bring forward a most manifest argument to show
why we ought to take sides with people such as you rather than
with men such as they—not to go over the whole comparison once
again. You excuse them by saying that perhaps they came to their
senses before they died, but that otherwise they must be damned. It is
hardly likely that those who firmly held the same opinion in so many
volumes should change their opinion on their deathbed. But when he
was about to die, Bernard said "I have wasted my time because I have
lived wastefully."[93] But is this a recantation? What saint didn't say such
things? This is the voice of modesty, not of recantation.

You have not yet been able to make a convincing case for the
clarity of Scripture, and I will soon touch on this point somewhat.
And if you had made a case, it is more probable that you are blind
than that they were. If you bring up their spirit, a charitable judgment
inclines towards them, though I grant we cannot be certain. If you
call for choosing what is preferable, it is reasonable to think that they,
together with the church, chose what is preferable. If you rely on
common sense, the opinion of common sense comes down on their
side. If you respond that it is not surprising that such spiritual men
sometimes perceived according to the flesh, the identical words of
your response can be turned back against you. If you respond that the
world is the kingdom of Satan, and therefore it is not surprising that
so many great men throughout the long course of centuries were so
blinded that they did not see the light of Scripture, all of this, with
much more probability, will be turned back against you. For you too
are carrying the flesh around with you, and you dwell in the world
you share with them, in which Satan reigns.

And in getting out of this tight spot you are not helped by your
lengthy additions about those blinded for the glory of free will, those

---

92. Pliny, *Naturalis historia* 8.61.149–50.

93. St. Bernard of Clairvaux, *Sermones super Cantica canticorum* (*Opera omnia,*
ed. J. Leclerc et al., vol. 1, [Rome 1957], 114–17). St. Bernard of Clairvaux
(1090–1153), Doctor of the church, was an abbot and an illustrious exponent
of monastic theology. His views about free will can be found in *Treatises III:
On Grace and Free Choice*, trans. Daniel O'Donovan, in *The Works of Bernard of
Clairvaux* 7, Cistercian Fathers Series 19 (Kalamazoo, MI, 1977).

who hearing do not hear and understanding do not understand
(Matt 13:13), for this applies more to you than to the luminaries of
the church. Nor is it appropriate to this topic for you to compare
yourself to Christ, your disciples to the apostles, the Doctors and
leading men of the church to the Jews, and for you to call your
doctrine light and the decision of the fathers and the church darkness.
If you wish to press us with comparisons, you will have to look for
others; those we do not accept. It is much more stupid for you to
bring up the Arians and the philosophers.[94] The church has judged
the Arians, and you approve of her judgment. But the same church
condemned your teachings. And yet here I do not burden you with
the authority of the church. We have nothing in common with the
Jews, since we recognize Christ as our savior. Even the most learned
philosophers erred, as if I had written that learned men endowed with
great intelligence could not be blind. You hang your argument from
one tiny thread. Gather together a heap of likely conjectures and from
that show us that we should believe you rather than them.

But how sophistical you are when you deny that what I said is true,
namely that Scripture is sometimes not understood because of the
weakness of the human intellect. "Nothing," you say, "is more suited
to grasp the words of God than the weakness of the intellect; because
of the weak and to the weak Christ both came and sent the word of
God."[95] If you mean by "weak" what I mean, that is, ignorant and
feeble—like the Galatians (Gal. 4:9) and like many whom we see—
and unsuited for the study of the humanities, why do we not seek for
a knowledge of Scripture from such persons rather than from learned
theologians or from you, who claim to have such great knowledge?
But if you call weak those who are unassuming and obedient to the
Holy Spirit, I agree with you. But it is amazing how little of this
weakness is in your writings! Just as if you had won the victory in
every battle, you hasten to the final goal of the disputation, but before
I allow that, I will say a few words about the obscurity of Scripture,
though I think enough has been said before about that matter.

For unless you show us that Scripture is clearer than the sun as long
as skill in grammar is available, you confess that you cannot untie the
knot of proving what your spirit is. Here if I sing you the old song
about how much all the ancient fathers constantly complain about the
difficulties of Scripture, how they sweat in order to explain Genesis,

---

94. On the Arians, see *The Enslaved Will*, n. 29.

95. Cf. Mark 2:17, Luke 5:32. See also *The Enslaved Will*, p. 55.

how much darkness Jerome saw in the beginning and conclusion of Ezekiel,[96] and how often Augustine was at a loss, you will respond that it is no wonder that dim-sighted men even in sunlight collided with something. And if I propose to you from the psalm "Deep calls to deep," which Augustine and Jerome interpret as meaning the darkness of the mysteries of Scripture, or likewise "Day utters a word to day and night shows knowledge to night,"[97] which they explain similarly, or the passage from Ezekiel about the torrent whose waters swell up and cannot be crossed,[98] just as in Psalm 17:10, "and darkness beneath his feet" is cited as referring to the profundity of Scripture, and again the verse "He placed the darkness as his hiding place" is interpreted by Jerome as meaning that Christ's birth, which you want to be perfectly clear, is obscure to us, and the verse "dark water in the clouds of the air"[99] is interpreted as referring to the obscurity of Scripture, and if I should propose other testimony like this, you will reject the exposition of the ancient fathers and present me with a new interpretation, twisting Scripture to the advantage of your cause.

But I wish you would disentangle this puzzle: if linguistic skill and common sense are enough for a clear understanding of Scripture, why was there any need in Paul's time for prophets among those who spoke in tongues? Paul distinguishes the gift of tongues from that of prophecy, and he places the gift of prophecy on a much higher level than the gift of tongues (1 Cor. 14:1–6). This clearly argues that there are hidden things in Scripture which are not clear to just anybody who knows languages. If what you say is true, that whoever has the Spirit of God perceives no obscurity in the sacred volumes, why is the person who prophesied earlier commanded to be silent when another prophet arises to whom something has been revealed? (1 Cor. 14:30) Many persons had the gift of prophecy, and yet what was clear to one was obscure to others, for this reason: the Spirit does not bestow everything on everyone but distributes gifts to individuals according to his own

---

96. In his *Commentarium in Hezechielem* (CCSL 75 3–4), Jerome says that the beginning and end of Ezekiel (together with the beginning of Genesis and the Song of Songs) were traditionally considered so difficult by the Jews that no one under the age of thirty was allowed to read them.

97. Ps. 41:8; Ps. 18:3.

98. Ezekiel 47:5; Jerome interpreted the passage as referring to insurmountable thoughts but did not associate it specifically with scriptural obscurity; see *Commentarii in Hezechielem* (CCSL 75 711).

99. Ps. 17:12.

will. And so you are marvelously fortunate, since you profess that there is nothing in Holy Scripture which is not perfectly clear to you.

And after the prophecies have been heard, Paul wants a judgment about what has been said: "Of the prophets," he says, "let two or three speak, let the rest be silent" (1 Cor. 14:29). Then, too, among the gifts of the Spirit he reckons the distinguishing of spirits (1 Cor. 12:10). These facts argue that Scripture is not as manifest and obvious to just anybody as you want to make it seem. Again, Paul says, "We see now in a puzzling mirror, but then face to face" (1 Cor. 13:12). You hear "puzzling," and you proclaim to me clarity of the very clearest. We see by faith and the light of faith is in Holy Scripture. And he says there: "We know partially and we prophesy partially," and a little further on "now I know partially, but then I shall know as I am known" (1 Cor. 13:9, 12). By "prophecy," Paul means the interpretation of the mysteries of Scripture; why would he profess that it is imperfect if there is nothing which is not perfectly clear? And if Paul here acknowledges imperfection, where are those who now boast of omniscience? I wish that they would at least clarify for us "as I am known." Is there anyone who knows or will know God in the same way as he is known by God? I think it is peculiar to God himself to know himself perfectly. The eunuch read Isaiah, and he was undoubtedly fluent in the language, and yet he did not understand the hidden meaning. (Acts 8:27–31).

Now I imagine that you number the epistles of Paul among the writings of Scripture. But here is Peter's pronouncement upon them: "Our most beloved brother Paul wrote to you according to the wisdom given to him, as he does in all his epistles, speaking in them about some points which are difficult to understand etc." (2 Pet 3:15–16). You will reply, "They were difficult for the ignorant." But you don't demand anything more than skill in grammar. If you say they lacked the Spirit, the inquiry comes full circle, since this is what you promised us, that you would prove to us you have the Spirit. But it is easy to wiggle out of this if you will only prove what you assume; you will say that out of stubborn malice we oppose the known truth, as the Pharisees did. Who can catch someone who has gotten ready so many bolt-holes for his escape?

Who has the Spirit that understands Scripture?

Well now, I come to those to whom you attribute the Spirit, which, as you write, they have drunk in from your books. Where do the quite substantial disagreements in their writings come from? If they are all moved by the same Spirit and are dealing with the same Scripture, there cannot be such perspicuous clarity that linguistic skill and common sense are sufficient. But you will say that Zwingli and Oecolampadius[100] lost the Spirit after they started writing against you. Does not Philippus Melanchthon sometimes speak hesitantly and suspend judgment in his brief commentaries?[101] But you say it is wrong to do this in dealing with Holy Scripture, where the clear truth is to be boldly asserted. When Oecolampadius had not yet disagreed with you, he did not deny that there was any obscurity in Isaiah, but he thought it sufficient if he could keep the pious and persistent reader from falling into despair, and in his preface he was so far from professing that there is nothing he has not explained that he confesses that his attempt would have been futile if he had not been aided by the Hebrew commentaries, at the same time speaking of Jerome with somewhat more reverence than you do[102] when you make out such a man to be a sacrilegious blasphemer in this book of yours, so perfect as it is in all respects. Is not Bugenhagen, whom you praise so much, a Skeptic in some places in his commentary on the Psalms, walking on eggshells, as you say, with hesitant steps?[103]

But perhaps you will find a way to evade what others have said; I will press you with what you yourself have said, since you consider it an affront and blasphemy against Holy Scripture if someone attributes any obscurity to it. Note how this paradox agrees with your preface to

---

100. See n. 69, above.

101. In his *Commentarius in Genesin* of 1523, Melanchthon says he has not yet made up his mind what it means that man is God's image; he also says that there are many things in Scripture that are uncertain, so that it is better to linger over things that contribute to faith and charity rather than questions which are over-curious rather than useful.

102. In the preface of his *In Iesaiam Prophetam . . . Commentariorum . . . Libri Sex* (Basel: Andreas Cratander 1525), Oecolampadius says what Erasmus attributes to him here (sigs b4v–b5), and he repeats it in a second preface to the city council of Basel.

103. See n. 77, above. Bugenhagen's *In Librum Psalmorinn Interpretatio* (Basel: Adam Petri 1524) was published with a foreword by Luther (WA 15 8). In this commentary Bugenhagen says, for example, that the Hebrew title of Psalm 4 has been interpreted in so many ways that its meaning is uncertain; hence he has recourse to the Greek (sig B6v-7). He notes that Psalm 7:11 is ambiguous (sig d3v). He also finds Psalm 17:8–17 so obscure that he presents various opinions before giving his own (sig H6v).

the Psalms. There you say as follows: "I am teaching the Psalter, etc., but I teach it in such a way that I would not want anyone to presume to get from me what none of the most learned and holiest men has yet been able to furnish, that is, an understanding and explanation of the proper meaning of the Psalter in all respects. It is enough to understand some of its meaning and that only partially. The Spirit keeps many things to himself, so that he may always have students; many things he displays only so as to lure us on, he hands down many things to move our feelings. And, as St. Augustine has excellently said, 'no one ever spoke so as to be understood by everyone on every point.'[104] Even more so, the Holy Spirit himself is the only one who understands all his own words. Hence, I must frankly confess that I do not know whether or not I have a proper understanding of the Psalms, etc."[105] Again, somewhat further on: "What, then, remains but that we help each other, forgiving those who make mistakes because we ourselves have erred or will err?" Again, in that place: "I know that it would bespeak a most shameless recklessness if anyone should dare to profess that he understands any one book of Scripture in all respects. Indeed who would dare to presume that he understands one psalm entirely?" There is an enormous difference between your language here, Luther, and the paradox about the wonderful clarity of Scripture which you teach in this book with such earnest perseverance, asserting that unless this point is granted everything will be transformed into darkness and there will be no certainty in human affairs. Who would believe that it is the same man who wrote these things when he was about to comment on the Psalms and who now challenges all corners to bring forth even one place which is obscure to you?

But what good does it do now to pick out places from your commentary where you profess that you have been abandoned by the interpreters, who disagree with each other, and are following what your own mind has dreamed up, or again, where you confess you do not understand at all how a verse hangs together with the preceding verse and you call your opinion mere folly. Thus on Psalm 17 you say, "The doctrine of the church is beyond the grasp of human understanding," and now skill in grammar is enough! On

---

104. *De Trinitate* 1.3.5 (CCSL 50. 32:14–15)

105. Here and in the following paragraph, Erasmus quotes Luther's *Operationes in Psalmos* of 1519–1521 (WA 5 22–23, 508, 531, 580, 583). He congratulated Luther on his psalm commentaries in Allen, *Ep.* 980:52–54, CWE 6 p. 393 (May 30, 1519).

Psalm 19 you speak as follows: "I have expounded this psalm as an example of the faith of some king or other, nor is it certain that I have reached the right meaning," and then you put off onto your reader what judgment to make about your interpretation. Once more, on Psalm 20 you confess you are uncertain "whether to understand it as concerning Christ or rather some king," and you accuse me of a theology of Skepticism because I would not dare to make pronouncements on the intricate difficulties of scholastic questions! Where was that Stoic asserter then? Where was that know-it-all? [You say to me, no one but a Lucian or an Epicurus speaks so hesitantly,[106] and you forgive yourself for speaking the same way in a profoundly religious work.] At the end of this book you say, "I do not want anyone to have the right to judge, but I urge everyone to assent," and on the psalm you pass the judgment on to your reader. You make me into a Proteus,[107] but in doing such things how are you consistent with yourself? Did you not have the Spirit at that time? I imagine you will say "I did not."

But if you had only persevered in such modesty! There you call the ancient, orthodox writers consummately orthodox, holy, and learned; here you laugh at me for attributing holiness to them while you charge them with blindness, ignorance, even blasphemy and sacrilege. And you can find no other excuse that would enable them to be saved except that they meant something different from what they wrote or repented of their error before they died. And since you require internal clarity from all Christians in such a way that without it you give them no hope of salvation, what can we think but that they all perished because concerning such a necessary article of the faith they were, I will not say ignorant, but recalcitrant, overthrowing necessity and professing free will? You call me blasphemous so often because I have doubts about your teaching and argue about it, and do you imagine it is not clear what such a judgment would lead you to pronounce about them?

And here again is a new paradox: if someone has the Spirit, nothing is obscure to him; if he does not, he understands not even a single iota. There is nothing in between. Therefore if someone professes that he is in doubt about some places in Scripture, either he has the Spirit and is lying about a nonexistent obscurity or he does not have it and does not understand a single iota. Tertullian, an outstanding Doctor

---

106. On Lucian and Epicurus, see n. 49, above.
107. *The Enslaved Will*, n. 22.

of the church, later slipped over into the teachings of Montanus[108] and left the communion of the church.[109] When he lost the Spirit, did he not understand a single iota? But you take "he did not understand" to mean "he did not feel, he was not affected." But we were dealing with the certainty of doctrine, not with a person's unknown feelings, about which you confess that no one can pronounce with certainty except God alone. For since, according to Paul, some only pretend to have the Spirit, and an angel of Satan "transforms himself into an angel of light" (2 Cor. 11:14), even someone who believes he is moved by a good spirit can be deceived.

But if you attribute a total understanding of the Holy Scripture to the Holy Spirit, why do you make an exception only for ignorance of grammar? In a matter of such importance, will the Spirit allow grammar to stand in the way of man's salvation? Since he did not hesitate to impart such riches of eternal wisdom, will he hesitate to impart grammar and common sense? Whoever attributes even the tiniest bit to free will blasphemes against God; and are you pious when you grant such importance to grammar that it alone darkens the supremely bright light of Scripture? Those who complain that there is darkness in Scripture hardly deny that it is perfectly clear to the Spirit who is the author of Scripture, but rather they impute this darkness to the weakness of human nature. Though you profess this most openly in the preface which I just cited, here you most boldly deny it, affirming that nothing is more capable of understanding Holy Scripture than human weakness. But, to press you to deal with the matter at hand, show us by what arguments we can be sure that you have the Spirit as your master and are not deceived in explaining Scripture, even though all the Doctors of the church were deluded about it. You confess that some obscurity arises from ignorance of languages. On this point, then, since many disagree with each other and each one of them claims to have skill in languages, how will I be certain who is blind about language and who is not? For on this, as you say, depends the certitude of interpretation.

---

108. The founder of an elite and ecstatic movement originating in Phrygia in 156, he believed himself to be the charismatic vessel of a new effusion of the Holy Spirit, whose oracles supplemented Scripture.

109. Tertullian (c. 160–c. 230) was a Roman jurist who converted to Christianity and was for a time an orthodox church father. Later, as an instructor of catechumens, he broke with the church, joining forces with the heretical Montanists.

You do not entirely deny that some obscurity arises from figures of speech, and even though you teach that they should not be rashly allowed in exegesis, nevertheless, whether you like it or not, they occur frequently in the prophets, in parables, in enigmas. I too do not like far-fetched figures of speech, especially when they undermine the historical sense; but if you exclude figurative speech from Holy Scripture, we lose a good deal both of the pleasure and the utility in the secrets of Scripture. Moreover, if you confess that obscurity comes from ignorance of grammar, you will at the same time also confess that darkness arises from translations and from corrupt copies. Oecolampadius also complains about this in Isaiah.[110] Therefore, when one person says there is a figure of speech and another denies it, or if they both agree there is a figure of speech but disagree in interpreting the figure, how can I be certain which one of them has hit the mark? By comparing passages? Both sides have passages to compare; I am still stuck in my doubts. Similarly, when I hear several interpreters disagreeing with one another while each contends that his copy is free of corrupt readings, what can clear away all ambiguity for me? Now who will dare to affirm that obscurity does not frequently arise from places that conflict with one another? Or if someone does affirm it, who will believe him? What is simpler than the story of the gospel? And yet how many talented men have sweated to harmonize inconsistencies in it? Augustine tried with all his might and did not accomplish what he wished.[111] Do us this service at least, so that we may not lack faith in you.

Many fail to grasp what is taught in Sacred Scripture because they are dull-witted, many because they are lazy, many because their minds are devoted to human desires; for the contentious twist Scripture to fit their own teachings, while the opposite is what should be done. Finally, the Spirit does not reveal everything to everyone. So many are the ways, then, in which we will have doubts about the interpreter. And all the abuse you heaped up against those who think there is some obscurity in Scripture, all the insults you hurled at them—this will be thrown back at you, since you cannot avoid confessing that in some fashion there is obscurity in Holy Scripture. But for you there is no obscurity. Let us stipulate that what you say is true, but how will you make this clear to us? For this is what you undertook to prove, confessing that you have no reply to my question unless you did prove

---

110. See n. 102, above.

111. *De consensu evangelistarum* (*The Agreement of the Gospels*), PL 34 1223–24.

it quite clearly. But after you tried everything and were not able to do it, like Proteus bound tightly in chains, you return to your native form[112] and heap hatred upon me because I make Scripture obscure, just as if I denied there is any light at all in it. I said there is darkness in many places, but the Spirit wills that they should be clarified sufficiently to provide for our salvation, for he keeps some things hidden away for future ages. If you infer from this that nothing can be certainly proved from Scripture, tell me this: how did the orthodox fathers instruct the people of Christ for so many centuries, how did they drive heretics out of the church? By means of Scripture that is ambiguous and not understood? Finally, you cast the blame on Satan: it is his work that Scripture is clear to so few; if he would take a rest, a single word of God heard only once would convert the whole world.

At this point, although you have run completely aground, you nevertheless act as if you had done very well, threatening to trap me with my own snares, and you wield against me a syllogism with a horn on each side, so twisted that there is no escape. "From your own words," you say, "you will be justified, and from your own words you will be condemned [Matt 12:37]. You say Scripture is not clear on this point. But if that is not true, why do you suspend your judgment in *A Discussion*? If it is true, what are those orthodox people doing, the ones whose intelligence, learning, sanctity, miracles, martyrdom, dignity, antiquity, and numbers you boast about, who used doubtful Scripture to assert free will?" Where shall I turn, hemmed in as I am by horns blocking me on both sides? In fact, I will cut off one horn of your syllogism; then I will deal with the other. My Discussion does not say that Scripture is obscure on this matter. Her words are as follows: "But the debate here is not about Scripture; the quarrel is over its meaning. In interpreting it etc."[113] Do you hear? I say "quarrel," not "obscurity." Were the scriptural passages that were used to vanquish Arius[114] obscure because he opposed them? And if I had granted that on this question Scripture was obscure—which I do not—I would have granted it for the sake of argument, as many things are conceded to opponents in the universities.

If you choose to seize upon this concession, you will still have to admit that the interpretation on both sides is doubtful. You will say:

---

112. *The Enslaved Will,* n. 22. Only when he was tightly bound could Proteus be forced to assume his true shape (Homer, *Odyssey* 4.354–569).

113. *A Discussion,* p. 3.

114. *The Enslaved Will,* n. 29.

"If Scripture is clear in the parts used by the ancient fathers to assert free will, why did you like the title 'Discussion'; why do you profess to be an inquirer, not an asserter; why did you say in the conclusion, 'I have discussed the issue; let others pass judgment?'"[115] I reply: When they are disputing in the universities, one disputant proving what is in Scripture and the other refuting him with other scriptural passages and arguments from reason, why do they refer the decision to the senior professors or to the one who is presiding, as they say? For it could be that the ancient fathers correctly asserted free will from perfectly clear passages in Holy Scripture but that I have defended it with insufficient skill against the battle-line of your arguments. And once before I already gave you the reason for my procedure: to find out whether you could dispute without insults and, since the whole matter has been rubbed raw, not to throw oil on the fire, as they say. And this courtesy of mine you throw back in my face time and again, whereas instead you ought to have approved of it and imitated it. And if you take such pleasure in assertion, why do you need to find it in me, since the church long ago handed down her judgment on the matter and recently confirmed it?[116]

And so, you say, "They considered Scripture to be clear." I grant it, insofar as it was enough to dispel any doubt about free will. And what then? Why then, you say, do you make Scripture obscure on this point? My *Discussion* does not do so; rather you pretend that she does, as I said just now. If you contend that there is no obscurity whatever in Holy Scripture, do not take up the matter with me but with all the orthodox fathers, of whom there is none who does not preach the same thing as I do. But whenever my *Discussion* mentions obscurity in this matter, she is either speaking in your person or conceding for the sake of argument something she could refuse to grant. For example, she says this: "If you then say Scripture is not clear on this point, on which so many eminent men have been blind, etc."[117] Do you think I am speaking for myself when I say "on which so many eminent men have been blind"? Such words are attributed to you, and I seize on them to use against you because you want your interpretation to be taken as if it came from an oracle. Here is a similar example: "If it is so

---

115. *A Discussion*, n. 78.

116. Erasmus probably refers to the condemnation of Wyclif's teachings at the Council of Constance (May 4, 1415) and to the condemnation of Luther's teachings in the bull *Exsurge Domine* (June 15, 1520).

117. *A Discussion*, p. 5.

clear, why have such distinguished men throughout so many centuries been blind, precisely on a matter of such importance." These words do not convict the ancient fathers of blindness; rather they urge you either to confess that they speak the truth or to stop demanding that we consider your interpretation to be an oracle from on high. Again, when I say "if [this gift of the spirit has come] to no one (seeing that many obscurities torment scholars even today), then no interpretation is certain,"[118] what is the thrust of this argument but to get you to let others reject your interpretation by the same right you claim to reject the interpretations of everyone else?

And then behold how fiercely but irrelevantly you say this: "What a frivolous and foolhardy outlook it takes to shed your blood for something uncertain and obscure! This is done not by Christian martyrs but by demons."[119] Don't you see that this horn has been cut off? But where was your mind when you wrote, "This is done not by Christian martyrs but by demons?" Do demons have blood to shed? Then who ever said that these holiest of men shed their blood for free will? You will say: they shed it for Holy Scripture, which you claim is obscure. Once more you talk as if I had said that all of it is obscure or as if, though it might be obscure to me and you, it would also be obscure to those who defined the doctrine of free will. Cyprian[120] shed his blood. Let us grant that he shed it for Scripture. Does it follow that nothing in all of Scripture was ever obscure to Cyprian? Imagine that Augustine had been slain when the Donatists tried to ambush him.[121] He would have been reckoned among the martyrs. Would you think this canonization absurd if he had found something unclear? On this frivolous foundation rests what you say at the end of the section: "That is nothing but making them perfect dullards in what they knew and total fools in what they asserted."[122]

---

118. *A Discussion*, p. 3.

119. *The Enslaved Will*, p. 56.

120. St. Cyprian (c. 200–258), bishop of Carthage, was martyred during the Valerian persecution. Erasmus edited his *Opera* (Basel: Froben 1520).

121. Augustine, as bishop of Hippo, was the chief polemicist against the Donatists, a rigorous heretical sect in North Africa, which claimed that the holiness of the church resided in it alone and held that the sanctity of the ministers was necessary for the validity of the sacraments. The Donatists made several attempts on Augustine's life; for one he foiled, see *Enchiridion ad laurentium de fide et spe et caritate* 5.17 (CCSL 46 57:32–8).

122. *The Enslaved Will*, p. 57.

Scripture correctly or
and on the basis of this
owing why we should
. In the schools, you
r the sake of argument
nent. If someone in an
[132] and you are Apollo,
cessions were serious?[133]
t in the entire course of
argue that Scripture is
me in refuting manifest

n even more shameless
I attribute knowledge of
present a false face to the
ble for Luther and to use
h hatred and contempt."
would not have tempered
circumspect in avoiding
cussion, I would not have
ithout being vexatious. If
with princes, the best way
rave against you with the
written so unvexatiously
to some people; and yet
ely you had thought and
t I am resolved in matters
feelings. Do you take it as
with so many luminaries of
he universities? What then
u the object of far different
you are silent about them
in Latin, "I put on a false
ee to it that this disputation

sometimes spoke as if they were

e that Luther had a low opinion

I have broken up that horned syllogism, but alas, here comes another. "If you think they judged correctly," you say, "why do you not imitate them? If you do not think so, why do you boast with such abundant bombast, etc.?"[123] I think that those who asserted free will, as the church does, judged correctly. Why, then, you say, do you not assert instead of arguing? Is someone in doubt because he argues? I do not argue because I am in doubt but, rather, in order to refute you for attacking our assertion. Equally irrelevant is what you then stuff in: "Now you should also place before your eyes and ponder in your mind whether you judge that we should place more weight on the judgment of so many learned men, so many orthodox teachers, so many saintly fathers, so many martyrs, so many ancient and modern theologians, so many universities and councils, so many bishops and popes who thought that Scripture is clear and confirmed that view in their writings and with their blood, or rather on the private judgment of you alone, who deny that Scripture is clear but who perhaps never shed a tear or breathed a sigh for the teachings of Christ."

I will pass over the judgments you make in your usual manner about what tears I shed or what sighs I breathe out. What is your point here, Luther? That the scriptural passages on which the ancient fathers based their assertion of free will were clear to them? How, then, do you have the nerve to say they blasphemed when they defined doctrine on the basis of clear Scripture?

And time and time again you sing me the old lying tune that I make out that Scripture is obscure on this point. I say the interpretations vary, and I called into question which interpretation we should follow, that of the ancient fathers, which has been approved for so many centuries, or yours, which has sprung up so recently. In that place I certainly do my best to show that the Doctors of the church did not err in asserting free will but rather that you are blind about it. This is what I say: "If you then say that Scripture is not clear on this point, about which so many eminent men have been blind, we have come full circle."[124] You see that I am not speaking for myself when I say "about which so many eminent men have been blind." These are your words, not mine. And if what you say is true, either Scripture was obscure to them or they wickedly resisted the Holy Spirit.

Nor is there any danger in saying that on this subject Scripture was sometimes obscure to them but that their assertion was nonetheless

123. *The Enslaved Will*, p . 56.
124. *A Discussion*, p. 5.

correct and certain, seeing that in councils what is c
revealed to others by the Spirit, so that through disc
individuals obscurity disappears as each brings f
revelation. But if you push us to include all of Scriptu
that some things in it are obscure to me and the likes
immediately object that more weight should be given
of such a large crowd of eminent men than to the pri
me alone. What are you saying? Is it the private judgm
when in fact none of the most praiseworthy men, wl
the sake of irony, has not professed the same? For wl
explaining the mysteries in these volumes, does not
the obscurity of Scripture—not because they blame S
falsely charge, but because they deplore the dullness
mind; not because they despair but because they impl
him who alone closes and opens to whomever he wi
wishes, and as much as he wishes? Since you confess t
in your commentaries,[125] why do you call it the privat
me alone and make me out to be an enemy of those w
side? You make out that Scripture was obscure to them
boldly reject their interpretations. If you had not done so
be no quarrel.

It is amusing that you turn against me the very compa
between you and the ancient fathers. I do not require any
the opinion of all of them on a matter of such great im
to believe me alone—which is what you do, and not on
alone, entreating and even demanding assent as rightfully
threatening to trample in the mire of the streets whoever r
you preach the word of God. Therefore fairness requires tl
us firm arguments showing us why your judgment alone s
more weight with us than that of so many great men (not t
their qualities so often). If your belief is certain, you say,
meaning of the words "discussion" and "discourse"? Wh
suspend judgment and argue on both sides, sometimes for,
against?" If that is proof of a divided mind, let all the sch
summoned to court. Thomas asks whether the eucharist is a
of the church, and he gives arguments on both sides.[126]
mean he has doubts on the matter he is arguing about? Jeron

125. See n. 105, above.
126. Thomas Aquinas, *Summa theologiae* III q 73 a 1.

men, so numerous and so great, interpreted
whether you with your few adherents do so,
supposition I require from you firm proofs sl
abandon them and get on your bandwago
have often seen, if I am not mistaken, that f
something not true is conceded to an oppo
argument should imagine that he is Tarquin
would you bear down on the man as if the co
You add a shameless hyperbole, namely, tha
the pamphlet *A Discussion* I do nothing bu
not clear. What good can it do to waste t
nonsense?

Not satisfied with all this, you add a
fabrication: you deny that I am serious when
Scripture to very holy men; "I do it only to
ignorant mob, intending really to make trou
empty words to overwhelm his position wi
If I had in mind to do what you imagine, I
my style so much, I would not have been s
any appearance of tooth and claw in *A Dis*
taken such care to handle a vexing subject v
I had published *A Discussion* to curry favor
to please them would have been to rant and
full force of my eloquence. As it is, I have
that my restraint has rendered me suspect
it was not unclear to me how affectionat
written about me for some time now.[134] B
of faith not to give any weight to private
contemptuous of you that I compare you
the church, with general councils, with all
will you say about those who have made y
comparisons in their published books? An
and complain about my courtesy. Writin
face before the ignorant multitude." You

132. An Etruscan tyrant (Livy 1.49–60).
133. In declamations or mock debates, students
historical characters.
134. As early as August 1523 Erasmus was awa
of him.

of yours is translated into German[135] so that you can expose Erasmus to ridicule among farmers, sailors, and cobblers, to whom he cannot speak,[136] and do you think learned men do not see what you are doing? Insurrection is what you have in mind; you see that that is what has so often resulted up to now from your German pamphlets.[137] That is what the apostles did, indeed! I debated with you subject to the judgment of the community of learned men; you transfer your case to the ignorant mob, and you make false charges against me among workmen, tanners, and farmers, who favor you and do not know me. They understand you when you make false charges; they do not understand me when I reply. What a pretty victory you are out to get!

What you add next, I do not fully understand. For this is what you write: "As for me, I say that neither is true but both are false. First, that Scripture is perfectly clear; then that they, insofar as they assert free will, were most ignorant of Holy Scripture; then that they asserted it with neither their lives nor their deaths but only with their pens—and that while their wits were wandering."[138] Up to now you have contended that Scripture is perfectly clear, and now you say that is false. And then, you have always asserted that the ancient fathers proved free will from scriptural passages wrongly understood, and now you say that this is also false. To these two statements you add a third, apparently also false, which up to now you have insisted was very true. But let us not indulge in verbal chicanery: what you wrote is clear for all to see, but what you mean I can guess well enough— though if I had blurted out such a mistake, there would have been no end to your misrepresenting and berating me. But here is a fine way for you to excuse the ancient orthodox fathers: they thought and lived and died quite differently than they wrote concerning free will. You say that only their pens sputtered out this blasphemy, but "their wits were wandering." This is how we excuse those who commit a sin out of madness.[139]

And you can find no other excuse for the church, which approved of their opinion, or for the universities but that, when they assert free

135. See nn. 84 and 85, above.

136. In fact, *The Enslaved Will* was translated into German (Leipzig 1526) by Jerome Emser, a humanist opponent of Luther.

137. Erasmus refers to the Peasants' War (1525–1526).

138. *The Enslaved Will*, p. 57.

139. St. Thomas Aquinas teaches that *stultitia* is not sinful if it results from a congenital indisposition (*Summa theologiae* II–II q 46 a 2).

will, their mind is not at home but is wandering in the wilderness. How likely is it that writers who assert free will in books clearly devoted to that subject, who often inserted into their commentaries what they taught about it, and who fought against those who disagreed with them about it, should make a mistake about it merely through a slip of the pen when they were out of their minds? If St. Augustine thoughtlessly asserted free will, why did he not at least come to his senses in the books of his *Retractions?* And there he asserts what he asserted before,[140] and the authority of his judgment is all the weightier because he rebukes himself for some places in which he attributed more than he should have to free will. Someone who criticizes his own work and cuts away what is superfluous gives strong confirmation to what he leaves untouched. Are their deaths and their lives inconsistent with their pens because they had no confidence in their own merits but ascribed their salvation completely to the mercy of God? Those of us who assert free will do the same. What a convenient crack you have found here, one through which you can slip away whenever you are confronted with the authority of the ancient fathers: they didn't mean this, but rather they brought such things forth with a wandering pen and a meandering mind. And all the time you do not see that this device of yours can be turned back against you, not only by us but also by your followers.

And so, Luther, since you cannot escape from the snare of my question and have poured forth clouds of smoke before our eyes, playing the part not so much of Proteus as of Cacus,[141] I once again place before your eyes the gist and the upshot of the whole business. In my *Discussion* I say that I do not wish to fight with you using the authority of the ancient orthodox fathers or the previous judgment of the church, which condemned your teaching long ago, not because I think their opinion has no weight but because these weapons would get me nowhere with you. But rather, if it should happen that we seemed equal in testimonies out of Scripture and judgment hung in the balance, wavering in either direction, I asked whether it seemed right in this state of affairs that the authority of the ancients, together with the decision of the church, should certainly have a tiny bit of influence to make us more inclined towards their judgment rather

140. Namely, that free will does exist (*Retractationum libri duo* 1.9.1–7 [CCSL 57 23–9]).
141. On Proteus, see *The Enslaved Will,* n. 22 and n. 112. Cacus was a monster who breathed fire and smoke when he was slain by Hercules (Virgil, *Aeneid* 8.252–61).

than yours. And I do not speak this way because my opinion truly wavers, but I made this supposition so that you would approve of my fairness and could not complain that the victory was wrung from you by unfair rules. Place, then, free choice in the middle, held in good faith by the catholic church for more than thirteen hundred years. Place yourself on one side assailing it with the assistance of Scripture and me on the other side defending it with the same assistance. Add spectators who, like me, think all our evidence is equal, although you demand to be at one and the same time both contestant and umpire and superintendant of the games. Who will award the prize[142] either to you or to me, and by whose choice shall free choice be preserved or else destroyed?

Whenever opposite judgments in trials are balanced on either side, circumstances are usually taken into account, and at that point opinions are not counted but evaluated. The defendant is given the benefit of the doubt; some allowance is made for the age, dignity, and authority of the other side. Likewise I suggested that when opinions waver, the circumstances on either side ought to have some weight. On the right-hand side we have placed you together with Manichaeus, Jan Huss, and Wyclif, all of whom have been struck by the thunderbolt of the church;[143] as for the judgments of God, they are unknown to us. Add, if you like, Lorenzo Valla, though he does not positively defend your opinion but gives up, overcome by the difficulty of the question. And I don't know whether you set much store by Lorenzo, first because he is a rhetorician and then because he treats the question of foreknowledge not out of Holy Scripture but by human reasoning and secular examples.[144] Now, when you say Augustine is completely on your side, I cannot get over my amazement: in the books of his *Retractions* he excuses himself for some things he wrote in those three books he began in Rome and finished in Carthage after his ordination,[145] because in them he seemed to attribute more than enough to free will and to take too little account of grace, but

---

142. The rare Latin (and Greek) word used here (*brabeum*) shows that Erasmus is alluding to 1 Cor. 9:24.

143. That is, excommunication.

144. On Valla, see *A Discussion*, n. 6. In fact, Valla based his position about free will on Paul's Epistle to the Romans.

145. Of the three books of Augustine's *De libero arbitrio*, the first was written in Rome (388) and the last two in Hippo (391); see Chronological Table B on page 74 of Peter Brown, *Augustine of Hippo* (London, 1967).

he still persevered in the opinion that free will is something.[146] What more need I say? If Augustine thought like you, why did he write a book in his old age against those who rushed to opposite errors, some denying free will entirely because they heard so much attributed to grace, others attributing too little to grace because they heard free will asserted? We find this in the first chapter. The second chapter begins as follows: "So he has revealed to us through Holy Scripture that man's will has free choice."[147] You hear free will being asserted not from the dreams of the philosophers but by the authority of Holy Scripture. And in another place he recants something he wrote following Origen, if I am not mistaken, to the effect that we can will good deeds but cannot accomplish them without the assistance of grace; but he does not renounce free will.[148] Now, as for what he says somewhere about God performing both good and bad deeds in us,[149] in the proper place I will show how that is so. Now we are dealing with another matter.

And so we will allow Lorenzo, Jan Huss, and Wyclif to stand on your side; but the first was in grave danger because of his opinion,[150] the other two were condemned by the judgment of the church, and

146. *Retractionum libri duo* 1.9.1–7 (CCSL 57 23–9).

147. *De gratia et libero arbitrio* 1.1 and 2.2 (PL 44 881–2).

148. In *De diversis questionibus ad Simplicianum* 1.1.11 (CCSL 44 5:188–92) Augustine had quoted Paul (Rom. 7:18), "For to wish for the good lies in my power but not to perform it," arguing that it did not deny free will but rather affirmed it. In his later anti-Pelagian works, however, he emphasized another text of Paul (Phil. 2:13), "For it is God who works in you the will and the performance," arguing that grace is necessary from the very beginning of our good deeds. See *De gratia Christi et de originali peccato* 4.6 (CSEL42 129:16–26) and *Contra duas epistulas Pelagianorum* 2.9.21 (CSEL 60 483:10–18).

149. Augustine comes close to this in *De gratia et libero arbitrio* 43 (PL 44 909): "This testimony makes it clear that God works in the hearts of men to incline their will wherever he wishes, whether to good deeds out of his mercy or to evil ones because of what they deserve." In *De praedestinatione sanctorum* 16.33 (PL 44 984) Augustine says: "Malicious persons have it within their power to sin: but whether in that malice of theirs they commit this or that sin is not within their power but rather within that of God, who divides the shadows and orders them." Erasmus fears the effects of widespread stress on this teaching but does not deny its truth.

150. For Lorenzo Valla's brush with the Neapolitan Inquisition, see Giovanni di Napoli, *Lorenzo Valla: Filosofia e religiose nell'umanesimo italiano* (Rome, 1971), 279–312.

one of them was also burned at the Council of Constance.[151] Here do not immediately shout back at me that this was done by the judgment of Satan, not of the church; now I am only reporting what happened. Let your friends also stand with you, though their vote has less weight, either because they have sworn to uphold your teachings or because they do not constantly adhere to the same wisdom either among themselves or with you. And you know that a witness from one's own household is rejected,[152] and you are not unaware that nothing impairs the credibility of witnesses more severely than inconsistent testimony. This is your chorus.[153] On the opposite side stand those famous luminaries of the house of God, among whom are so many men outstanding for their intelligence and well versed in the philosophy of God: first the Greeks, who always had the highest authority in treating Holy Scripture, then the Latins,[154] who emulated the Greeks—and among them many recommended by very holy lives, some also illustrious because they gave witness with their blood, men whose memory to this very day has always been sacrosanct to the whole people of Christ—so many bishops, so many popes whose opinion has been accepted and approved down through many centuries and confirmed finally by the public decision of the church. In agreement with these add the judgment of all the universities, add the repeated assessment by theologians and by the church, add finally a precept strengthened by the long time it has endured.

Don't we need, then, most manifest evidence for you to convince us that such a venerable chorus of fathers together with the leaders of the church were utterly blind to Holy Scripture, that they were driven by the spirit of Satan, or (to put it quite mildly) were out of their minds to have given their verdict for a dogma which is heretical, impious, blasphemous, against the clearest evidence of Scripture, and most dangerous to the human race? Do we not need such evidence for us to abandon our fathers, by whose teaching, laws, and authority we have been nourished and guided up to now, to spurn our mother

151. For Huss' heresy and trial see Gordon Leff, *Heresy in the Later Middle Ages* (Manchester, UK, 1967), 606–707.

152. This was in fact a feature of Justinian civil law.

153. Erasmus may well be thinking of the choir of a church, where the two sets of choir stalls face one another.

154. That the Greeks were superior to the Latins in exegesis is a characteristic judgment of Erasmus, expressed most famously in his assertion that he benefited more from one page of Origen than from ten pages of Augustine (Ep. 844:272–4).

whose milk has nourished us, to desert such a large confraternity of Christian people with whom we have associated for so many years, and, with the highest risk to our property, lives, and souls, to assent to your covenant, in which (apart from a few persons and even those in disagreement with each other) we see nothing but fierce assertions? You seem willing to yield to them in dignity, authority, antiquity, intelligence, and learning. You call their miracles into question, but they have been approved for a long time now by the public and unshaken opinion of the Christian people, whereas there is not even a suspicion or a rumor of such a thing about you.

As for your quibble that none of them worked miracles by means of free will, I have already answered that. Then again, you call into question the holiness of their lives; but opinion is on their side. Nor do I wish to press that side of it. We are moved by their authority, we are moved by the steadfastness with which you and yours make your assertions—for I had pretended it was so—but we do not dare to withdraw from our church and to commit our salvation to your faith. What sign do you show us that we should believe you rather than them? Now, even if we should grant that you have the spirit you so boldly claim, that you alone find all of Scripture perfectly clear, though this may be true, it is true for you; for us, as you yourself confess, it does no good. And so you promised that the external clarity of Holy Scripture would persuade everyone that your interpretation is the truest of all and that the opinion of all others, however numerous and great, however holy and learned, is false, blind, and deadly, and that whoever follows it is hurrying straight to hell. No one in his right mind believed the Donatists[155] when with their mighty assertions they tried to show that everyone in the other churches had lost the grace of baptism and that it remained uncorrupted only in their own church. And you want us to go right ahead and believe that for so many centuries the gospel has been shrouded by Satan, that it is now unveiled by you, and that there is no pure interpretation of Scripture anywhere but in Wittenberg. In a matter so hard to believe and so dangerous that it cannot be enough to deal in assertions and commonplace arguments, you must bring forth manifest, firm, indeed Achillean arguments.[156]

And now that the testimony of Scripture has been brought forward on both sides, will you call upon common sense to settle

155. See n. 121, above.
156. As invincible as Achilles, the hero of Homer's *Iliad*.

the controversy? Both the Spirit and common sense and the clarity of Holy Scripture are claimed by both sides. As the case now stands, your prolix discourse about the obscurity or the light of Scripture has little or nothing to do with the matter. Grant that Scripture is perfectly clear: what will we unlearned people do when we see both sides contending with equal assertiveness that they have the Spirit who reveals mysteries and that they find Scripture absolutely clear? Grant that it is obscure in some places: what will we do when each side accuses the other of blindness? However these things may be, we are certainly left wavering in doubt, and in the meantime you neither acquit your faith by fulfilling your promise nor set us free by removing our doubt.

Perhaps you will go back to those suppositions you began to lay out for us earlier: I know that my conscience is clear, I know that I am moved by the Spirit of God, I neither have nor desire money, I am not looking for glory—and what pleasure could I hope for in the midst of such great labors and dangers? Such statements, Luther, we accept from you in such a way as to hope they are true, but they do not persuade us and they do not provide that full conviction[157] about external clarity, but instead you try to force people rather than draw them on. It may be that you are such a man as you proclaim yourself to be, but we would be more ready to believe it if there were less arrogance in your writings, less bitterness, less trickery and craftiness. If I saw as much of these in the writings of the apostles, I doubt if I would have faith in them. For I imagine the Manichaeans and Donatists said such things as "I do not desire money or glory or the other advantages of this world." For some spirits are impostors, according to Paul, and the spirit of Satan "transforms himself into an angel of light," (2 Cor. 11:14) and it is not safe to believe just any spirit.[158] As far as fame is concerned, you could not hope for more, and you have gained it in a brief period of time: you reign far and wide in the minds of men; you are armed with very many partisans; you have a theater ringing with wonderful applause; to the nobles you are more to be feared than loved; you have your bodyguard; you have your spies and couriers, you have people to collaborate in your writings, you have translators to turn them into German. What is left but a crown? Even an incorrupt mind could be corrupted by so fortunate a

---

157. Erasmus borrows a transliterated Greek word (*plerophorian*) from Paul (Col. 2:2; 1 Thess. 1:5; Heb. 6:11 and 10:22).

158. Cf. 1 John 4:1.

turn of events. I do not care how much money you have, but in other matters also I think you are a little better off than you would have been if you had not stirred up this hornets' nest. Certainly I know many people for whom this gospel of yours has brought forth both revenue and a wife and many other benefits, although they were out of luck before.

Now if you want to hear the reward of my flattery (for such you consider it to be), I have lost half of the little fortune I had so as not to go into the arena against you, I have gained much suspicion and ill will, but I am not a penny the richer; and the fact that I have more than once refused a fortune joined with dignity argues that I have an attitude which scorns such things.[159] But I do not allow myself to judge your attitude; it has its own judge who alone knows the secrets of the heart (3 Kings 8:39). This is what we demand: that you make us certain concerning your teaching—which you had taken upon yourself to do. If you can't do it, allow us little sheep and simple souls to follow the voice of the church.[160] You will say that those who drank in the Spirit from your writings are satisfied. I only wish that you could impart a good spirit by laying on your hands,[161] for I have grave doubts about the spirit which is drunk in from your writings. Here I am not reporting my own experience, but am only saying what is public knowledge: very many persons imitate the violence and superciliousness of your pen. Formerly Jonas seemed to me to have a gentle and sound temperament.[162] I began to read attentively the book he wrote against Johannes Faber,[163] desiring to see what arguments he

159. Erasmus is denying charges that he attacked Luther for reasons of material gain. In January 1522 Pope Adrian VI encouraged Erasmus to write against Luther and invited him to come to Rome, where he would find well-stocked libraries and the company of pious and learned men. He also promised Erasmus he would be well recompensed for this journey and "most pious labor" (Epp. 1324:117–33, 1338:59–64). In 1520 Erasmus was promised a bishopric if he would write against Luther, an incentive he evidently ignored (Ep. 1141:36–37 and n. 12). See also Epp. 1408:11–13, 1477:26–29, 1477b:64–67, 1510:23–25.

160. Cf. John 10:3–5.

161. As in the ordination of a priest by a bishop.

162. See n. 84, above.

163. Johannes Faber (1478–1541) became a doctor of civil and canon law at the University of Freiburg in 1510 or 1511. In 1517 he became vicar-general of Constance and in 1521 he was appointed suffragan bishop of Constance. His first book against Luther (1522) was fairly conciliatory. Luther scorned it and asked Jonas to reply to it. Jonas' response, *Against Johannes Fabri in Defense of the Marriage*

would use to win his case, but there he was so raucously insulting that I was driven by disgust to put the book down—there were no bounds or end to it. The same thing happened to me with your *Abolition of the Mass*[164] and some other little works of yours.

At this point, naturally, you distinguish faith from charity; you say that faith is fierce, charity puts up with everything. But we see the fierceness; we do not perceive that charity which puts up with everything. At the same time you do not consider how much harm you do your cause by directing the licentiousness of your pen first at one person, then at another, egged on by frivolous persons. And unless my guess is completely wrong, you were driven to this last burst of ranting by some of your adherents who were offended by nothing more than this: when asked for my opinion, I disagreed with Karlstadt about the eucharist.[165] They wanted you to take vengeance for this vexation of theirs, even though on this point I agree with you.[166] If you had overwhelmed *A Discussion* with untrammeled reasoning and strong arguments, you would not have offended me in the least. Perhaps you would have drawn me over to your opinion—which I would not find so abhorrent if we were dealing merely with a doctrine of the schools, and not also with a doctrine of the church—and you would have gained less hostility and more credibility in the minds of others.

As for me, I challenged you to a struggle of arguments, not of insults, and you see how large a part of your volume you devote to insults. But enough of such things. With the following conclusion you end the

---

of Priests (Wittenberg, 1523) was vitriolic and insulting. See also *The Enslaved Will*, n. 25.

164. Luther's *De abroganda missa privata Lutheri sententia* of 1521 (WA 8 411–76; LW 36 133–230) was mentioned disparagingly by Erasmus in Ep. 1342:829–31.

165. Andreas Bodenstein von Karlstadt (c. 1430–1530) was a Thomist by education, dean of the theology faculty at Wittenberg, and originally a colleague of Luther's in reformation. But in communion services Karlstadt initiated in Wittenberg and in a series of German tracts published in Basel in October and November 1524, he denied the physical presence of Christ in the eucharist, thus launching the Sacramentarian controversy, which was later taken up by Zwingli and Oecolampadius. Luther sharply rebuked Karlstadt in a series of sermons in 1522 and in a major polemic of 1525.

166. Erasmus agreed with Luther against Karlstadt's denial of the real presence, but he does not say he agrees with Luther's doctrine of the eucharist. Luther accepted the orthodox doctrine of the physical presence of Christ in the eucharist, but he disagreed with the church by asserting that the bread remained after consecration, a view which goes under the name "consubstantiation."

prolix disputation assailing the preface of my *Discussion:* "Therefore I conclude this little disputation as follows: up to now nothing has been certainly laid down by Scripture, since it is taken to be obscure, nor can it lay down anything about free will, as you yourself testify; but in the lives of all men since the beginning of the world nothing has been shown in favor of free will, as was said above. Therefore to teach something which is not prescribed by a single word in Scripture nor demonstrated by any deed—this does not pertain to the teachings of Christians but rather to the *True History* of Lucian,[167] except that Lucian in his intentional jokes and playful treatment of playful matters neither deceives nor harms anyone, whereas these friends of ours on a serious matter, one which pertains to eternal salvation, are raving mad and cause the perdition of innumerable souls. In this way I also might have concluded this whole question of free will, since the testimony of my adversaries themselves makes for me and opposes them—and there is no stronger proof than a defendant's own confession and testimony against himself."[168]

Here we have a pretty conclusion of a well-managed disputation! I have already said enough about obscurity. I supposed that there is obscurity in those places where interpretations vary. If you approve of this supposition, you will thereby confess that the scriptural passages you use to destroy free will are also ambiguous and obscure. But if you reject it, we will make use of our right to take back the concession we made. Neither do I prove free will by the lives of orthodox teachers. But when the testimony is equally balanced in number and weight, I want the commendable lives of the witnesses to be taken into account. Thus, in a trial, if the arguments on each side are equally balanced and the witnesses disagree, we more readily believe a man who has fought bravely for his country, who has been an incorruptible magistrate, than we do someone whose honesty has no public testimony to recommend it and whose dishonesty is notorious. You will say: what do his brave deeds or his magistracy have to do with the case in which he is giving testimony? This is what they have to do with it: no one can easily suspect that in this case he will either lie or be deceived, since in many other circumstances he has been a manifest model of an upright and prudent man.

---

167. A fantastic, satirical narrative. Lucian (born c. 120), a rhetorician and philosopher of Samosata, wrote satiric dialogues, some of which Erasmus translated from Greek into Latin. See *The Enslaved Will,* n. 65.

168. *The Enslaved Will,* p. 57.

Now if there is a ruling about the doctrine of free will in Scripture, why do you reject the testimony of the fathers taken from Holy Scripture? If there is not, why do you assert it without Scripture? If each side rejects the interpretation of the other, claiming there is no obscurity in Scripture, certainly there is doubtfulness for us unlearned souls, except that the decision of the church does not allow us to vacillate. And in my argument I presuppose vacillation precisely because I said at the outset that I would make no use of ecclesiastical judgments. If you will accept nothing apart from Scripture unless it has been directly revealed by God, why do you accept the perpetual virginity of Mary?[169] It is not expressed in Scripture and it has not been revealed by God through any miracle. If you consider the perpetual consensus of the church to be a miracle, we will confront you with that same consensus in favor of free will. And wasn't it enough for you to say that nothing is to be accepted unless it is expressed in Holy Scripture or revealed by a sign from God, without adding your hyperbole about the *True History* of Lucian? Are you saying that whatever the ancient writers set forth about the lives and martyrdom of the saints, whatever church history has to say, and also the exhortations and the practices of the ancient fathers and the regulations of prelates, have no more weight than the *True History* of Lucian? Liturgical readings in which famous Doctors of the church have exercised their eloquence recount the martyrdom of St. Andrew, St. Lawrence,[170] and others.[171] And all this is nothing more than the ridiculous fables of Lucian? You might have cracked this joke more opportunely elsewhere, Luther. And so, where is that defendant with

---

169. Luther defended the virgin birth forcefully—for example, in his sermon against the *Schwärmgeister* (enthusiasts); see WA 19 490:1–491:13. The "virginity of Mary" is the belief that Mary was an intact virgin before her conception of Jesus and remained so during and after his birth.

170. According to legend, St. Andrew the apostle was crucified at Patra in Greece about the year 70. St. Lawrence, a Roman deacon, was put to death by the sword in the year 258, although by legend he is reputed to have been roasted on a gridiron. For their miracles and martyrdom see *The Golden Legend of Jacobus de Voragine*, trans. Granger Ryan and Helmut Rupperger, 2 vols. (London, 1941), 1:7–16 and 2:437–45.

171. Erasmus is thinking here not of readings in the mass but rather of readings in matins of the divine office. Leo the Great tells of the martyrdom of Lawrence in the lessons of matins on Lawrence's feast day (August 10). Gregory the Great praises Andrew in the lessons of matins on Andrew's feast day (November 30).

his confession now?[172] Indeed he denies it loud and clear and shows that everything you assume is quite false. Hence, it follows that your conclusion is also no more true than those things you assume as if they were confessed.

What was the point of throwing this insult into your mixture: "These people, on a serious matter, one which pertains to eternal salvation, are raving mad and cause the perdition of innumerable souls." Don't you understand that this charge of blasphemy falls not only on me or on the theologians and popes of our times, but on all the most approved Doctors of the church almost from the time of the apostles to this very day, on all Christian people, who probably held that opinion, which they had gotten from their teachers? And you add: "and cause the perdition of innumerable souls." But a little before, when my *Discussion* charged that you alienated many by your bitterness and paradoxes, you replied that there is no danger: only the wicked who are perishing are offended, the elect are safe. Are you saying those who follow your teaching are safe and those who agree with so many orthodox teachers and the definition of the church are perishing? And where is that scrupulousness now that made you complain about me because I put you in a bad position where you were forced either to yield or to speak against such great men? You put your own self in that position before I ever put you anywhere. For how often did you assail them as ignorant of Scripture, blind, sacrilegious, blasphemous! Here you add "raving mad," just as a little before you said they were out of their minds. And you complain about me, as if you were not accustomed to say on your own hook whatever you like against them. If you were proclaiming the truth, even then what pious person could bear the wicked licentiousness of your pen? As it is, since you are proclaiming falsehoods, it is even less endurable. This is your triumph before the victory, Luther. Now you are girding yourself for battle, and the victory is in your hands—that is, if we were willing to accept, before the encounter, the laws which the victors usually lay down for the vanquished.

First of all, you usually reject, with marvelous indignation, whatever might be brought up from the scholastic theologians. Now you reduce everything to scholastic reasoning, and for no other reason than to make things dark and difficult for me, since I have little experience in it—this is, as they say, to pull a fish out of water. But

---

172. The "defendant's own confession and testimony against himself" mentioned on p. 184, above.

you usually accept nothing except what is in Scripture, and using that alone I contended with you. But you changed your mind and you drag us off into the midst of these thorns of sophistry, which, if they were as deficient as they are hateful to you, you would frequently be confused and at a loss. And whenever it is convenient, you reject any assistance from them, but you do so by confronting us with another sophistical argument no less sophistical than the previous one, and you devise new cracks for you to slip through. For here there is such a mass of distinctions that you cannot be taken hold of anywhere. You distinguish the Law from the gospel, but in such a way that each is in the other; the internal clarity of Scripture from the external; God from Scripture; God preached from God not preached; the Spirit of the gospel from the spirit of error; a negative opinion which has nothing to prove from an affirmative one which has a duty to prove. You show us a twofold showing of the Spirit; a twofold rule, one of charity and one of faith; a twofold necessity, one of a deed and one of time, and also one of compulsion and one of immutability; a twofold omnipotence of God, one of nature and one of operation; a twofold respect, to what is above and to what is below. Indicative verbs are distinguished from imperatives and subjunctives; writing is set over against life and death,[173] a disputation is distinguished from a prayer; and finally what seems to be the church but is not is distinguished from what seems not to be the church but is, and those who seem to be saints but are not are distinguished from saints who are thought to be wicked although they are truly saints.

I do not list these because I disapprove of all your distinctions, but rather because you claim for yourself in explicating Holy Scripture a privilege you withhold from others and because you ordinarily hiss at the distinctions of others but want your own to be considered oracular. For us you shut up every way out; and for yourself you want all your bolt-holes to be open. Now look at the laws which you prescribe, though you are not yet the victor: lay down whatever arms are supplied by the ancient orthodox teachers, the schools of the theologians, the authority of councils and popes, the consensus of the whole Christian people over so many centuries; we accept nothing but Scripture, but in such a way that we alone have authoritative certainty in interpreting it; our interpretation is what was meant by the Holy Spirit; that brought forward by others, however great,

---

173. Erasmus refers to Luther's distinction between what the fathers wrote about free will while they lived and what they believed on their deathbeds.

however many, arises from the spirit of Satan and from madness; what the orthodox taught, what the authority of the church handed down, what the people of Christ embraced, what the schools defend is the deadly venom of Satan; what I teach is the spirit of life; believe that in Scripture there is no obscurity at all, not even so much as to need a judge; or, though all are blind, I am not blind; for I am conscious that I have the Spirit of Christ, which enables me to judge everyone but no one to judge me; I refuse to be judged, I require compliance;[174] let no one be the least bit moved by the multitude, the magnitude, the breadth and depth, the miracles, the holiness of the church's saints; they all were lost if they meant what they wrote, unless perhaps they came to their senses before the last day of their lives; whoever does not believe my proofs either lacks common sense or commits blasphemy against the Holy Spirit and subverts Christianity.

If we accept such laws as these, the victory is indeed yours. Then again, you demand that we not believe the ancient orthodox fathers because they sometimes disagreed among themselves, whereas the few of you fight very much with each other about the prophets, images, church rules, baptism, and the eucharist; and you want us nevertheless to believe your teachings, especially because every day we expect new ones. And we are called blasphemous because we still cling to the old church and do not dare to join your camp; and you croak at us that text from the gospel: "Whoever is not with me is against me, and whoever does not gather with me scatters" (Matt. 12:30). I am not making any of this up; I am saying what is certain and well known.

Erasmus' definition of free will

Now, it will be worthwhile to see how insincerely you treat *A Discussion*, leaving nothing undistorted, nothing not falsely blamed, nothing not condemned. You would have been more believable if you had approved of some things, for you would have seemed to condemn the other things out of judgment, not because of a diseased mind. For who is such a bad writer than he never puts in something that should be approved? And so you rail especially at my definition which I propose as the subject of our debate: "Free choice is a power of the human will by which a person may be able to apply himself to what leads to eternal salvation or turn away from it."[175] Though I proposed this brief definition only in order to show the scope of the

---

174. Cf. Luther's concluding words in *The Enslaved Will*, p. 126.

175. *A Discussion*, p. 6.

argument and keep it from digressing more than was necessary, you heap up here everything babbled by the boys in the schools of the sophists. You object that I do not unfold the parts of the definition— afraid as I am to be shipwrecked more than once—even though that is usually done by others. It is usually done, but by those who propose to debate about something controversial or less well known; but I undertook a brief little debate on a subject already treated by very many writers, and I did not take it upon myself to teach a class of pupils *ex cathedra* or to write a commentary on a work by a difficult author, so as to need either to defend or to explain individual parts of a definition.

I knew that free choice had been defined by various people in various ways; you make short work of it in your definition, "a name without reality."[176] It would have caused too long a delay to reject or assert or explain the definitions of others. I decided not to delay very long in this arena, and anyway, it was superfluous to describe a well-known and frequently defined phrase. Why define it then? I do not so much define the basic meaning of the phrase as set limits to what I had undertaken to do in this book. Call me a liar if my words do not show this: "And so by free choice in this place I mean, etc." What does "this place" mean? Nothing more than that here we will dispute about free will understood to this extent, lest anyone should expect whatever can be or usually is debated concerning free choice. What good would it have done to explain the individual parts of the definition—as teachers do when they lecture to schoolboys on Aristotle[177]—since that would be done in the course of the debate. Writers usually give a summary of what they intend to talk about, pointing out the target, as it were; that is what I do in *A Discussion*.

And you thrust upon me another sophistical slander: what is defined is broader than the definition itself, for there is the free will of God, which is the only one that can truly be called free, there is a certain free will in the angels, and you limit it to the will of mankind. I have already responded that I said this at the outset precisely to exclude from this little debate any disputing about the choice of God, the demons, or the angels, especially since your *Assertion* attacks nothing but human choice. But a graver crime is that the phrase which I define conflicts with the definition, that is, the "what of the name" with

---

176. *Assertio*, article 36 (WA 7 146:6; CWE 76 p. 306).

177. Cf. Aristotle's *Topics* 6.1–14. Erasmus alludes to the scholastic method of defining in detail, point by point.

that which is the "what of the thing." I recognize the language of
schoolboys. For whoever hears the phrase "free will," you say, takes
it as properly meaning "that which can and does do, in relation to
God, whatever it wishes, constricted by no law, no commanding
authority." For if a slave who lives under the command of his lord
cannot be said to be free, so much the less can the will of man, which
is subject to the commanding authority of God. And so you would
rather it were called "vertible" instead of "free."[178]

First of all, as for your contending that the honor of this phrase
applies properly to God alone, I have already discussed how this is
so, and I do not make man's will free in an unqualified way, as is
sufficiently clear from the debate. Why then use the phrase? I am not
the inventor of the phrase. Hence it would be more appropriate for
you to expostulate with all the ancients and the moderns and even
with Augustine himself, for, though he attributes very little to free
will, nevertheless in the titles of his books and throughout the debate
he uses the accepted phrase.[179]

But as for your saying that by the judgment of everyone's ears this
phrase means nothing but the free power to do, in relation to God,
whatever one wishes etc., the truth is far otherwise among Christians.
Augustine rightly advises us to make it a fixed rule to speak in sober
and appropriate words,[180] but he himself, who gives this advice, very
often hammers away at the phrase "free choice" (*liberum arbitrium*)
in his books. You yourself do not refrain from using the accepted
phrase—how sober you are in changing either the teaching or the
words of the church is known to those who read your writings. And
now you croak Augustine's admonitions at me because I used a phrase
accepted by everyone.

Then too, you demand dialectic and pagan philosophy, which you
usually call the plague of Christianity. But you grant both points: the
use of the phrase and the restriction of the definition to the human will.
But what are you granting me if you concede what is a public right?
Or what are you bestowing upon me if I show the reader within what
limits I intend to speak of free will in this book? For that description
of mine does nothing more than give the reader notice at the outset:

178. WA 18 662:2–14.

179. For example, *De libero arbitrio* (written 388–391) and *De gratia et libero arbitrio*
(426–427).

180. *De civitate Dei* 10.23 (CCSL 47 297); cf. *De doctrina christiana* 4.8.22 (CCSL
32 131–2).

in this book you will not hear about the free choice of God, angels, or demons, or brute beasts if they have any, but about what is attributed to the human will, nor will I discuss what it can do in unimportant matters which do not contribute to eternal happiness but only what it does in those matters which pertain to eternal salvation. If it is a crime to discuss anything unless you go through all its parts and everything connected with them, many writers are guilty of it. If someone does well to show the reader what he should expect and what he should not, what is there, pray tell, for you to forgive me?

But once again there is another false charge against the definition. Peter Lombard and the sophists make the power of free choice twofold: the power to discern, which is a property of the intellect, and the power to select or reject, which is a property of the will;[181] but my definition touches only on the power to select or reject, and so I propose only half of an act of the will. I respond briefly: in this question of freedom the most important point is the will, by which, as Augustine says, a person sins or lives rightly.[182] Though reason is not separate from this will—for we do not properly give the name "will" to what follows sense perception and emotion rather than the judgment of reason—nevertheless I preferred to propose as the subject of this inquiry the principal and the only thing capable of liberty, especially because, once that is proposed, the thing which naturally precedes it is also understood at the same time, just as a person speaking about the pursuit of virtue includes at the same time the points which distinguish virtue from vice. And in the course of the debate I touch sufficiently on the judgment of reason.

And now, just as if we were sitting in the school of Chrysippus,[183] my little definition is laid bare to the very bone. It is accused of obscurity and the individual sections are picked apart and rigorously examined. There is more than one reason for giving a definition: sometimes so that the nature of the thing being discussed can be known; sometimes

181. Peter Lombard was a theologian and bishop of Paris (c 1097–1160) renowned for his compendium of Christian doctrine culled from biblical, patristic, and contemporary texts, his *Sententiae in quatuor libris distinctae* (*Opinions Divided into Four Books*) on which the major scholastic theologians wrote lengthy commentaries. Here Erasmus refers to book II dist 24.5 and 25.1 (PL 192 702 and 706). Cf. Magister Bandinus' commentary (PL 192 1052D): *Est autem liberum arbitrium in voluntate et ratione* (Free will, however, is in the will and in the reason).

182. *Retractationum libri duo* 1.9.95 (CCSL 57 26).

183. A Stoic philosopher (c. 280–207 BCE) who was said to have written seven hundred books and was known for his hair-splitting (Diogenes Laertius, 7.7).

a thing very well known is merely touched on by its label, as, for example, a person of our times discussing anatomy does not need to define anatomy in the company of learned physicians—the label is enough. Sometimes a definition, or rather a description, is added to let the reader know what he should expect, what he should not, as, for example, someone who proposed to discuss animals, intending to keep his readers from expecting to hear what is usually said about their nature, generation, parts, diseases, and remedies, might warn them as follows: "This discussion will treat animals of land and sea, but only those which are harmful because of poison." And that was the only reason I gave that little description of a subject which is presently bandied about and very familiar to all educated persons.

But come on, then, however that may be, I will not beg to escape a severe examination, and I am not as afraid of your judgment, however unfair, as you think I am. I have already replied about the use of the phrase,[184] and I will not tolerate any more objections on that score. According to you these parts are clear: "power of the human will," and also "by which a person can," and also "to eternal salvation." On the other hand these parts are obscure: "apply himself" and "turn away," and also "to eternal salvation," and also "leads." You interpret "power of the human will" as "a power or faculty or ability or aptitude to wish, not wish, select, scorn, approve, resist, and whatever other actions of the will there may be." You do not see how "apply himself" and "turn away" can mean anything but "wish" or "not wish," "approve" or "disapprove," which are actions elicited by the power of the will, and you imagine that power to be some intermediary between the will and the completed action of the will.[185]

And here, for heaven's sake, you cite a rule of law to let us know that you consulted a lawyer[186] when you were writing these things. I know that all the gods brought what they considered to be their principal gifts to this Pandora.[187] But what does this rule of law actually

184. Erasmus means he has already replied to Luther's objection that the phrase "free will" is broader than Erasmus' definition, since it applies to God and angels as well as men.

185. *The Enslaved Will,* p. 60.

186. Erasmus probably alludes to Justus Jonas, who was trained as a lawyer (see n. 84, above).

187. Pandora (the "all-gifted") was endowed by the gods with all the gifts of feminine beauty and charm, but also with flattery and deceit. Hesiod's "Pandora" refers to a work executed by many hands. Erasmus refers to Luther's friends who allegedly contributed to *The Enslaved Will.*

prescribe? That obscure language is to be interpreted against the person who speaks it.[188] But what is prescribed by the rule of charity which you claim for yourself? That everything is to be interpreted in the most favorable sense and that whoever is more steadfast and learned should minister to the weakness of others. See now how far you are from the rule of charity, going beyond even the rule of the law, which was intended to prevent obscurity of language from being an advantage to someone who might have deliberately and intentionally spoken so as to deceive. But you make clear language obscure so as to provide an occasion for slander, as I will soon demonstrate.

But to the matter at hand. Up to this point your interpretation is tolerable: "what leads to salvation" you interpret to mean "the words and works which God offers to the human will so that it may apply itself to them or turn away from them." "The words of God" you divide into "the Law and the gospel; the Law requires works and the gospel faith." For you say you do not see "anything else that leads to the grace of God or to eternal salvation except the word and work of God, because grace or the Spirit is the very life to which we are led by the word and work of God. But this life or eternal salvation," you say, "is something incomprehensible to the human intellect." Therefore I am wrong when I attribute to the human will the power to apply itself, since no one's heart can know what these things are unless the Spirit has revealed them. And to Paul's testimony (1 Cor. 2:9–10) you add an argument from experience: the philosophers, Portius Festus, and Pliny ridiculed the resurrection promised by the gospel.[189] And you add that today there is no lack of those who laugh at this article of the faith as a fable, although in their speech and writings they claim that they believe it.

What you say up to this point is not without piety, but it does no damage to my definition. But when you hope that I am not sprinkled with the same leaven,[190] I willingly accept your prayer, and I in turn pray for the same for you, except that that wish of yours is an insult to my faith. Whether my faith is sufficient for salvation, let the Lord look to it, but certainly it is not feigned; I do not write one thing and think another in my heart, and in my daily prayers I beg that Christ

---

188. In Justinian civil law, obscure language counted against the litigant using it.

189. For Festus, see Acts 24:21 and 26:24–5. Pliny the Younger (c. 61–c. 112), a Roman lawyer and official, wrote about Christian customs in his letters (Ep. 10.96).

190. Cf. 1 Cor. 4:6–7.

in his mercy will increase my faith. But I am surprised that you have anything to do with this wish, since you profess that you are certain you have the Spirit, who bestows all things—how I wish this were entirely true and my suspicion quite groundless! But here you seem to be using a wrestler's trick: you lower yourself in order to throw me down, and you do so with your usual candor.

We have heard a clever interpretation of my definition, indeed one that throws it back at me by a rule of the Law. Now let us hear the terrible additions assembled with the same skill: Erasmus teaches "that free choice is a power of the will, which by itself can will or not will the word and work of God, by which it is led to things which exceed its understanding and its grasp. But if it can will and not will, it can both love and hate, and it can to some degree do the works of the Law and believe the gospel, because, if it can will or not will, it is impossible for it not to be able to perform some of the work by that will, even if someone else prevents it from completing the work. Thus, since death, the cross, and all the evils of the world are numbered among the works of God which lead to salvation, the human will would be able to will both its death and its own perdition. Indeed it can will all things if it can will the word and the work of God." For what is left except God himself? What in the world is left? Here I attribute nothing to grace but I clearly attribute a certain divinity to free will. Come hither, all diviners and soothsayers! Listen to a strange portent: out of nothing Erasmus has made a God.[191]

Throw Helicon open, O goddesses![192] Here is an open field for Luther to display his tragic eloquence: Erasmus goes far beyond the impious sophists, for whatever they think, they certainly speak more sparingly about free will; he is a Pelagian;[193] indeed, he goes far beyond Pelagius, who did indeed attribute divinity to free will, but to the whole of free will, whereas Erasmus attributes the same to half of it![194] O heavens, O earth, O seas of Neptune![195] Is there more? There is: he goes beyond even the heathen philosophers. How so? For this reason: though it is not yet agreed among the philosophers

191. Erasmus plays on the meaning of "create": to make out of nothing. God created the world out of nothing, but by Luther's hyperbole Erasmus has created God.

192. Virgil, *Aeneid* 7.641; Helicon was a mountain in Boeotia sacred to the Muses.

193. *A Discussion*, n. 15.

194. That is, to the part of free will that resides in the will itself, without considering the part that resides in the intellect.

195. Terence, *Adelphoe* 790.

whether anything can move itself, for me free will not only moves itself and does so by its own power, but it also applies itself to things which are eternal, that is, incomprehensible to itself. What horrors you relate! But is there more yet? There is: up till now Erasmus has surpassed everyone in impiety, and now at last he surpasses himself. How so? For this reason: though he confessed before that free will was ineffective without grace, here he lays it down that the human will has a power whereby it may be able to apply itself to what pertains to eternal salvation. For the moment I overlook that you changed "can" to "is effective" and for "ineffective" you put down "entirely ineffective," so as to make the words serve your slander the better, and I take no account of your jeer about my naming grace in jest but leaving it out here when I speak seriously. We come to the highest pitch. What is left but a triumphal chant?

He adds this final flourish: don't you see, my dear Erasmus, that you betray yourself—unwittingly, I believe—by this definition as someone who understands nothing whatever about these matters or else writes about them with total thoughtlessness and contempt for them, unaware of what you are saying or affirming.

Now pay attention to my answer, Luther, and I will show how much you betray yourself as a worker of magic tricks, and reveal how much smoke and how many horrible but empty and baseless pictures of things you pour forth before our eyes. I have already spoken often about the use of the phrase and you have sung that old song in vain time and time again. I have just now refuted your false charge about cutting free will in half. For how can the charge be other than false, since you find wanting in my definition what you immediately condemn in the definition of the theologians? This is what you say: "The sophists are also deficient in that they attribute to free will the power to distinguish good from evil." And so my sin is less than theirs. But from this you conclude that my sin is graver—such is your skill in dialectic. You profess that you wish to speak in plain language but you deliberately introduce darkness even into what is clear. Here, then, is something even more uncultivated: using words taken from the language of ordinary speakers, I call eternal salvation what we enjoy undyingly in the presence of God. Is there any darkness here? For here we live in hope for the time being, we hold the pledge, we look for the promise. And as for what leads to that happiness, I mean everything that arouses our mind to any desire, of any sort, for that happiness, whether it be effective or ineffective. As for "turn away," you know that means: it happens when someone neglects grace that is offered, preferring darkness to the light. And then the opposite of this I called "applying one's self," that is, "making oneself available" to grace.

But you say, "You exclude the grace of God." In fact the very words "applying" and "turning away" signify that it is not excluded: no one applies himself unless he has been admonished by a sense of something to be sought after; no one turns away if nothing has been offered. When you examined the syllables of my definition, you should have examined the implied force of these words, and at the same time you should have noticed that I did not say "is able" but "may be able," because I wanted to include something beyond our natural powers. You will say: "Why did you not expressly include the word 'grace' in your definition, since you earlier professed that free will is ineffective without grace?" Rather why didn't you, as a man full of Christian charity, which never does anything wrong, why didn't you interpret the definition as implying what I so often inculcated in *A Discussion?* Why was it not enough for you that grace was signified by those two words?[196] But if you press me to say why I did not explicitly name grace here, I will tell you: I had not yet distinguished the word "grace" into natural grace, preparatory or imperfect grace, and effective grace which abolishes sin. Even now there is insufficient agreement among theologians about whether or not a person without a special grace can solicit the effective grace of God by means of morally good deeds.[197]

My definition is open to both opinions, since I reject neither one, though I am inclined to the one which attributes more to grace. But according to you I "exclude the Holy Spirit together with all his power as superfluous and not necessary." How do you draw that conclusion, my good man? Evidently from one syllable: "himself."[198] O mighty syllable! In fact that syllable is meant to do no more than let you understand that our natural powers are not completely inactive when we are admonished by grace. And if we accept the opinion of those who teach that without special grace, by our natural powers—which are themselves nevertheless gratuitous gifts of God—anyone can strive to such an extent that the mercy of God will not be lacking to those

---

196. That is, *applicandi* (applying) and *avertendi* (turning away).

197. This issue was especially a matter of contention between the Augustinians and certain of the late medieval theologians of the *via moderna*; see Oberman, *Harvest* 160–65.

198. In Latin the word is one syllable, *se*. The Latin phrases for "apply himself" and "turn away" are both reflexive (*se . . . applicare . . . aut . . . avertere*).

who do the best they can,[199] then it would be true here that the will without grace applies itself to what leads to eternal salvation. For just as no one suddenly becomes most corrupt, so too we are led gradually and step by step to the perfect gift of God, just as when someone is dwelling in the most impenetrable shadows, first the darkness thins out and then a doubtful light appears far away until finally vision becomes clear. For Augustine was fond of this comparison.[200] Just so I include in what leads to eternal salvation those things that admonish us from far off and prod the mind, as it were, to a desire of eternal salvation.

"But no one desires something unless he knows it, and if he knows it he already has it." In fact, if he desires, he neither has nor entirely lacks what he hopes for. But God admonishes us in various ways: sometimes by the light of nature, by which we understand that virtue is to be sought for its own sake and vice is to be avoided because of what it is; sometimes by adversity; sometimes by reading or the admonitions of friends; sometimes also by the soft whistling of the Spirit. Before he drank in the Spirit of Christ, Augustine read the epistles of Paul attentively and made some progress and was brought nearer to the light of grace, but he was even more inflamed by the discourse of Potitianus.[201] Though we admit the grace of God was not lacking here, certainly it was imperfect, not yet freeing him from sin but preparing him for a richer gift; but if he had turned away from that grace, he would have been the cause of his own destruction. As it was, he made himself available to the call of grace and he gained salvation.

And so in what leads to salvation I include not only the words and works of God and his grace but also the natural desire for virtue,[202] which, though it has been overwhelmed, has still not been extinguished in us; I include the love of reading and listening to what stimulates us to a contempt of the world; I include prayers, alms, fasting. But you will say that these things are so far from calling for grace that they are damnable works which stir up the anger of God. But what you assume as axioms is a matter of dispute between us. About Cornelius

199. The doctrine of *facere quod in se est* or *meritum de congruo*: that God will not withhold his grace from those who do their very best. See *A Discussion*, n. 29; and Oberman, *Harvest* 132–33, 468, and 471–72.

200. See *De dialectica* 8.14.3–14 edited by Jan Pinbog and translated by B. Darrell Jackson (Dordrecht and Boston, 1975), pages 104–5.

201. Augustine, *Confessions* 7.21, 86–87. Potitianus, a Roman civil servant in Africa, encouraged Augustine to become a Christian.

202. See Oberman, *Harvest* 467–68 (*Ex naturae rei debita* and *Ex puris naturalibus*).

(Acts 10:1–33) I will say something in the proper place. For it is not surprising that you make such judgments about works performed without grace, since you claim that no one's deed is good even if it is accomplished by God in us after we have been justified by grace. For you, the mass of corruption[203] has such force that even God cannot perform a work in it that is good, much less perfect. Thus you see that the whole melodrama which you stir up out of my definition, once it is examined closely, is nothing but a huge and gross cloud of empty verbal fumes, the empty mockery of a juggler's tricks.

You go on to make false charges against my distinctions: in recounting the opinions of others about free will, I make Pelagius almost evangelical. I attribute a sort of faith and charity to some philosophers.[204] Concerning Pelagius I report nothing except what Augustine professes about him,[205] nor do I make him evangelical, but rather I number him among those whom the church has condemned for heresy. I do not make up a fourfold distinction of grace—and if I did so for pedagogic reasons there would be no danger in it—but rather I drew this distinction from the books of orthodox writers, who confess that whatever we are and can do is attributable to grace and then posit a prevenient grace which invites, as it were, but is imperfect; there is cooperating grace (for so Augustine calls it)[206] which makes our will effective once it has been stimulated by the first grace; there is a grace which perfects the whole process of salvation, for Bernard makes this distinction.[207] And yet I confess that these three are the same grace, although they have different names because of their different effects. You do not like this distinction, though there is no lack of piety in it, because it does nothing to confirm your teaching. Concerning the philosophers, I bear witness only to what Paul writes to the Romans;[208] I wouldn't dare to attribute so much to them if I did not have such a great authority for it. You also, at the end of your work, attribute something to the light of nature, for you know that my citation from the psalm, "The light of your countenance is

203. The phrase is Pauline (Gal. 5:9).

204. Erasmus means that Luther accuses him of doing these things.

205. Although several of Pelagius' writings are extant, he was principally known through polemical writings against him, especially those by Augustine.

206. *A Discussion*, n. 22.

207. St. Bernard of Clairvaux makes this triple distinction in his *De gratia et libero arbitrio* 14–49 (O'Donovan, *Treatises III* 105, 108–9). See note 93, above.

208. Rom. 1:19–20, 2:14–16.

stamped upon us" (Ps. 4:7), is not something I made up. And just as I frankly confess that it is aptly interpreted as the light of faith, so too I deny what you assert, that it cannot be taken as the light of nature: "the light is stamped" because God created man in his own image and likeness,[209] which was obscured but not extinguished by sin.[210]

Therefore I do not misapply the psalm to a blinded reason but rather I accommodate it to a darkened reason. If the light of nature is completely extinguished in us, how did the philosophers know God without the grace of God? How did they bring forward so much about virtue, about living rightly, about the immortality of the soul, the beginning and the end of the world, the differing rewards of the pious and the impious, about not repaying an injury, about the pursuit of virtue for its own sake, avoiding vice because of what it is, about educating children, loving one's wife, fulfilling the duties of office conscientiously, loving one's country? And in their biographies we read of many deeds in keeping with their precepts. And so why was it a crime for me to say that they put forth some ideas that agree with the precepts of the gospel? So too, did not the laws of the pagans punish theft, murder, adultery, perjury just as the Law of Moses also did? Hence I conclude that the light of reason was not entirely extinguished in them, and I add that it seems not improbable that they had a will which was in some way inclined to virtue but not able to achieve eternal salvation without the access of grace through faith. Concerning the faith and charity which you say I attribute to the philosophers in my *Discussion*, I make no firm assertions, although there is some debate about what faith would be sufficient for unlearned Jews and about whether there is some sort of faith whereby a pagan could be saved.[211]

You call my threefold distinction of the laws of nature, works, and faith mere storybook fiction. First of all, the law of nature is not in

---

209. The underlying image is that of a seal: the light of God's countenance is imprinted on man as the design of a seal is impressed on wax or a coin.

210. For Luther's view of the extinction of the divine image in man after the Fall, see Charles Trinkaus "Luther's Hexameral Anthropology" in *The Scope of Renaissance Humanism* (Ann Arbor, 1983), 404–21 (especially 406–7).

211. The most famous examples of saved pagans are Trajan and Ripheus in Dante's *Paradiso* 20.88–129. According to a legend well known in the Middle Ages, Trajan was brought back from hell to life, at the prayers of St. Gregory; see John the Deacon, *Vita Sancti Gregorii* 2.44 (PL 75 105) and John of Salisbury, *Policraticus* 5.8, translated by Cary J. Nederman (Cambridge, 1990), 80–1. According to Dante and to Thomas Aquinas (*Summa theologiae* III suppl q 71 a 5), Trajan was baptized, did penance, and was finally saved.

doubt. My discussion of the law of works and the law of faith I took from Augustine: in the book which he entitled *The Spirit and the Letter*, he followed the opinion of Paul in distinguishing the law of works or deeds from the law of faith. He claims the law of deeds is the Law of Moses, written on the tablets, prescribing without grace. He claims the law of faith is the New Testament, which prescribes the same things as the law of works but by the addition of grace softens the precepts of faith.[212] And among many other things, he says as follows: "What the law of works commands with threats, the law of faith accomplishes by means of belief." And a little later: "By the law of works God says, 'Do what I command.' By the law of faith we say to God, 'Give what you command.' Then again, somewhat later: 'When the works of charity are written on the tablets, it is the law of works and the letter which kills the transgressor. But when charity is poured forth into the hearts of those who believe, it is the law of faith and the Spirit who gives life to those who love.'[213] This is what he says. To be sure, I do not condemn the opinion of those who claim that the Law consists of precepts, the gospel of promises and consolation, so that each is included in the other—that is, the gospel is also in the Mosaic Law and the Law is in the gospel.

But Augustine, though he does not seem very far from this opinion, still does not seem to agree with it completely. For in the same work he distinguishes the Old Testament from the New by the kinds of promises in each: the Old promises what is temporal; the gospel, what is eternal. These are the words of Augustine: "Therefore, just as the law of deeds written on stone tablets and the reward it gets—that promised land which the carnal house of Israel received when it was freed from Egypt—pertain to the Old Testament, so too the law of faith written on the hearts of the faithful and the reward it gets—that species of contemplation which the spiritual house of Israel achieves when it is freed from this world—pertain to the New Testament."[214] He says something in accord with this when he comments on these words from John's gospel: but "the only begotten Son who is in the bosom of the Father has made him known."[215] Though I imitated Augustine, still I come closer than he does to the opinion you approve

212. *De spiritu et littera* 13.22 (CSEL 60 175).

213. *De spiritu et littera* 17.29 (CSEL 60 183).

214. *De spiritu et littera* 24.41 (CSEL 60 194).

215. See Augustine on John 1.18 in *In Ioannis evangelium tractatus CXXIV* 3.19 (CCSL 36 28–9).

of, since among other things I say as follows:[216] "Moses says, 'Do not commit adultery; if you do so, you will be stoned.'[217] But what does the law of faith say, the law which commands us to love our enemies (Matt. 5:44), to take up our cross every day [218] to contemn this life?[219] 'Do not be afraid, my little flock, for yours is the kingdom of heaven' (Luke 12:32). And also: 'Trust me, because I have conquered the world (John 16:33).' And also: 'I am with you until the end of the world, etc.'" (Matt. 28:20). You see that when I want to show what the law of faith is, I bring forward words of trust and consolation. And my intention here was not to discuss in what ways the old law is distinct from the gospel, but the distinction was brought forward in passing so that I could more easily show the reader how the dimmed light of nature could be brightened by the gift of faith, and the corrupted will set right by charity. I think I have made it clear to the reader that thus far I have done nothing reprehensible in *A Discussion* but rather that you distort everything by reporting it wrongly; so much the more do we distrust you when you interpret Holy Scripture because from these distortions we discover your bad faith.

Now behold how much melodrama you stir up out of nothing! These are your words: "If some Christian should put all this together, he will be forced to suspect that you are ridiculing and making fun of the teachings and the religion of Christians. For I find it very difficult to attribute so much ignorance to someone who has read through all our writings and so diligently committed them to memory." This is what you say. Why am I accused of such a horrendous crime? Because I said Pelagius was almost evangelical, that is, a heretic. For what else does it mean to be almost evangelical? Pagans are not called almost evangelical, for they are far removed from the gospel; but Arius was almost evangelical, for he confirmed his teachings from the gospel.[220]

216. *A Discussion,* CWE 76 p. 25–6.

217. Exod. 20:14; John 8:4–5.

218. Luke 9:23; cf. Matt. 16:24.

219. Matt. 10:39, Mark 8:35, Luke 9:24.

220. The Arians compiled a formidable array of scriptural texts to support their teachings. Pages 197–207 of Jaroslav Pelikan's *The Christian Tradition: A History of the Development of Doctrine I: The Emergence of the Catholic Tradition (100–600)* (Chicago, 1971) shows Arius using John 1:18, Gal. 3:19, and Heb. 1:1–4 to support his doctrines (197–202). Arius was an Alexandrian priest (c. 250–336) notorious for his unorthodox denial that the divinity of Christ was of the same substance as the Father. He was condemned at the Council of Antioch (324). At the First

And then I confess that among the philosophers reason was darkened but not extinguished—for they judge well about many things by the light of nature—and likewise that the will was not completely corrupted, since they manifested certain natural strivings towards virtue, for which you substitute faith and charity. I distinguished three kinds of law: the law of nature, of works, and of faith. No one denies there is a law of nature. The distinction between the other two I drew from Augustine. I said that in the opinions and precepts of the philosophers there are some things which agree with the teachings and precepts of the gospel. The verse in Psalm 4, "The light is stamped, etc." I apply to the light of nature in such a way as not to deny that it may rightly be interpreted as meaning the faith by which the light of nature is assisted.

After these points come those monstrous charges which I just now recited: "If some Christian, etc." But where can you show us this Christianity of yours? In your church, opinions vary; in ours, there are no Christians, if we believe you; and then you teach that neither saints nor Christians nor the church can be pointed out. Moreover, since Christian charity does not know how to suspect something is evil, who is this Christian without charity who is so wickedly suspicious that "he is forced" by what is well said "to suspect that I am ridiculing and making fun of the teachings and religion of Christians" I think Christians would suspect this much more readily if I deserted the fellowship of the church and fought to promote your teachings. Here you surely betray how wickedly eager you are to make false charges: up till now I knew nothing, but in everything I say I am thoughtless, addle-pated, and ignorant. Now, in order to get an opportunity for a new slander, you cannot attribute such complete ignorance to me, but rather you give back the knowledge you took away, so that you can brand me with the more serious crime of ridiculing the religion and teaching of Christians. But what are those writings of your camp which I have read through so diligently and retain in my memory? Your own teachings? I have hardly been able to read any of your books all the way through because they are filled with such verbosity and such an insatiable passion for insults. And anyone who is to understand your writings would have to be very learned indeed, since they cannot be understood without your spirit. And I hardly know whether you think there are any Christian teachings besides yours.

Council of Nicaea in the following year, the creed that was formulated adopted the term *homoousios* (having the same substance) in rejection of Arius' error that the Son is not of the same substance as the Father.

As for me, I thought you were talking about the pronouncements of the catholic faith; those I certainly do not ridicule, nor have I ever had any mind to do so, thank God, although I cannot and will not justify how I have lived. So it is that you make up now one thing, now another, no matter what, just as long as I look to you like a suitable target for false accusations. How you ranted and raved in the opening of your book about my skeptical attitude! How often you charged me with not asserting anything in *A Discussion!* And then a little later I am the finest of fellows for the same reason, that I assert nothing and merely debate out of a desire to learn and eagerness to pursue the truth. You are so consistent in your slanders that you can make the same circumstance into a double crime.

And then, as if it were not very slanderous to have charged me with the crime of a wicked and blasphemous mindset, you restrain yourself: "But for the moment," you say, "I will leave that problem alone and will be content to have pointed it out until a more suitable occasion offers itself." And immediately after that I hear "my dear Erasmus" and I am lovingly admonished not to be numbered among those who say "Who is looking at us?"[221] This is a tune you should be singing rather than I: though you play games with such manifold trickery, you think you deceive us and that your spirit is not detected. You say, "Do not try me so." If I try you when I debate with you without any insults, why are you not stirred up against those who harass you and tear you to pieces in large volumes, not debating as I do but calling you and your teachings by their proper names? But if you ignore them because they are outside your church—since Paul did not deign to pass judgment on outsiders (1 Cor. 5:12)—I have always been no less a stranger to your church than they are. Why do you not rage against those who have published books in which they openly rant and rave against your teachings, although up till now they embraced your church?[222] Paul handed over to Satan only those who broke away from the gospel (1 Cor. 5:5). You cannot bring that charge against me: I always wrote and said and thought the same things.

You frequently charge the Roman church with tyranny. If the charge is true, this state of affairs crept in over a long period of time,

---

221. Cf. Ps. 63:6: "They have strengthened their evil speech; they have told tales in order to lay their snares; they have said, 'Who will see them?'" Luther refers to those who sin because they think they are unobserved and will not get caught.

222. Erasmus means books against Luther by Karlstadt, Zwingli, Capito, and Oecolampadius, particularly about the eucharist.

gradually nourished by wealth and worldly power. But if the outlook that breathes from your writings were to acquire the wealth, authority, and power of the Roman pontiffs, it is clear enough what we should expect. Unless I am mistaken, you would send your minions and armed forces here, and you would treat those who disagree with you somewhat less mercifully with the sword than you now do with the pen. And meanwhile, where is that marvelous evangelist who professes that he will defend the gospel against the gates of hell, using only the sword of the Spirit, which is the word of God?[223] You do nothing but stoop to slander, to insults, to threats, and yet you want to appear guileless and undefiled, not led by human emotions but by the Spirit of God. You are right when you teach that God must be believed to be just, even if both the light of nature and the light of grace cannot grasp how he is just, but you are not right to make the same claim for yourself.

Furthermore, I commit an even graver sin in distinguishing opinions, since I make one into three, and if a person sees one thing as three he is certainly afflicted either with insanity or drunkenness. Indeed, I recount several opinions, of which the first is that of Pelagius, which I abandon as condemned. Secondly, I give the opinion of those who attribute the least possible to free will but nevertheless do so in such a way as not to take it away entirely; for they say that of itself it can do nothing effectively without the access of grace, whether stimulating grace or operating or cooperating or consummating. And yet in all of these they profess that there is an application or a turning of the human will or a cooperation, since they posit that the human will has some power which acts somewhat while grace acts. This is the opinion of either Augustine[224] or Thomas,[225] who follows the opinion of Augustine in attributing as little as possible to free will. And I call this opinion probable precisely because it leaves to mankind longing and striving. And here you pour out a tremendous flood of words about how what should be imputed is not imputed and how something that can do nothing of itself is said to be able to do something, although in the debate I make the solution of that difficulty as clear as your hand in front of your face, as they say.

---

223. Eph. 6:17; Erasmus seems to paraphrase *De servo arbitrio* (WA 18 625: 26–626:10; LW 33 51–2).

224. Erasmus synthesizes Augustine's position from many texts, notably *De gratia et libero arbitrio* and *De spiritu et littera* (PL 44 880–912, 199–246).

225. *Summa theologiae* I–II q 111 a 2.

The third opinion that I recount I assign to Karlstadt, who does not altogether take away free will—for the moment allow me to use that phrase, although if someone wants to call it beta or delta,[226] it makes no difference to me—but he says that in the performance of a good work it is not at all active but merely passive, so that grace does not work through our will but in our will, which is merely passive. The fourth opinion I assign to you: in the course of your *Assertion* you deny that free will has any place in the nature of things and you say that our will acts at all when we do good or bad deeds, but that everything is done by sheer necessity.[227] I call this the harshest of all the opinions, and I profess that I must take issue most of all with your opinion and that of Karlstadt. I do not pass over the opinion of Scotus, who thinks that, by morally good works, through the general influence of nature, a person can merit the effective grace of God *de congruo*,[228] because God in his kindness will not allow someone to perish if only he does the best he can[229]—not that he achieves salvation by his own power, but he somehow becomes capable of divine grace. Since the church, so far as I know, has not yet rejected this opinion,[230] I neither defend it nor refute it.

Setting aside, then, the opinions of Pelagius and Scotus, you teach that the three remaining opinions differ only verbally. The first, namely Augustine's, grants that choice or will can do evil by its own power and it does not make God the sole agent, with the will merely being acted upon, as you do;[231] and to this extent Karlstadt agrees with Augustine and dissents from you. For when Augustine calls grace cooperating, he means at least our will does operate to some extent,[232] and then when

---

226. Erasmus probably chose these Greek letters because the first meant "beet" in Latin and the second also referred to the delta of the Nile.

227. *Assertio*, article 36 (CWE 76 p. 306).

228. *A Discussion*, nn. 17 and 20.

229. *A Discussion*, n. 29.

230. This opinion (called semi-Pelagianism) had in fact been rejected in canon 18 of the so-called Second Council of Orange (529), which approved anti-Pelagian canons culled from Augustine's polemics. The decisions of this council were apparently lost by the tenth century. Thus the issue of man's role in the initiation of justification became, in medieval theology, once again a disputed question. The decisions of the council were recovered and published in 1538, two years after Erasmus' death.

231. Augustine, *De gratia et libero arbitrio* 17.33 (PL 44 901).

232. *A Discussion*, n. 22.

they posit a stimulating but imperfect grace, they do not exclude turning towards it or turning away, whereas you completely exclude both by introducing the absolute necessity of all things. For I have no quarrel with the principle which you assert but rather with the recantation by which you correct what you originally said—namely that free will has no power except to sin—and approve the teachings of Wyclif. And those who hold the first opinion make our will vitiated, wounded, and crippled, not extinguished; and so there remains some judgment, though imperfect, some power, though ineffective. You see, then, that this is not the same opinion stated in other terms, as you pretend. But you compare the first opinion, which I say is probable, with my definition, excluding for the moment the opinion of those who think that God's goodness is called upon to confer grace by morally good work without any special grace.[233] But in fact I formulated the definition so that it leaves room even for that opinion, since it has not yet been condemned. But imagine that the opinion of Scotus is rejected. Let the first opinion be that of Augustine, which posits stimulating grace: it does not exclude application and aversion. When Pharaoh was chastised, he began to come to his senses; and if he had not turned away from stimulating grace, he would not have fallen into the abyss of evil.[234] Let us also grant this, according to Bernard: the entire initiation is owing to grace.[235] Certainly, when our will operates with operating grace, it applies itself to grace, accommodating its natural powers to operating grace, just as when the sun rises we open our eyes, or else it turns away, just as if we should close our eyes when the sun is up.[236] Show us then, Luther, the drowsiness or the dullness of my judgment. This is what you do: you say that the first opinion, which confesses that free will vitiated by sin cannot will the good without grace, is probable. And the definition attributes to it the power to apply itself to the good or to turn away from the good without grace. "The definition," you say, "affirms what the example of it denies etc.," as you run on with sufficient impudence and loquacity.

233. Erasmus attributed this position to Scotus, though it could be argued that it is that of William of Ockham or of Erasmus' near contemporary Gabriel Biel (see Oberman, *Harvest* 131–41.

234. Exod. 9:27, 10:17, 12:31–2, 14:5–28. The problem of Pharaoh's fall was very vexed.

235. St. Bernard of Clairvaux, *De gratia et libero arbitrio* 14.46 (O'Donovan, *Treatises III* 105–6). See note 93, above.

236. Cf. Augustine, *De peccatorum meritis et remissione* 2.5.5 (PL 44 153).

Hear now, on the other side, how subtle your slander is: I define free will in general, whether as it was first created, or as it is in those who have been freed by grace, or as it is crippled in those who have not yet been freed from the slavery of sin. What has all this got to do with the first opinion, which is only part of what is included in the definition? The definition also does not exclude special grace, unless we accept the opinion which is closest to Pelagianism,[237] of which you do not approve, but which I may nevertheless use to assist me in making my argument, nor do I see any danger even in defending it. And then you do not notice that I posit two kinds of willing or two kinds of striving for virtue, effective and ineffective. The ineffective is also in those who are subject to sin, according to some by means of the general influence:[238] according to others not without grace but imperfect grace, which indeed does not yet abolish sin but nevertheless prepares for effective grace. Nor am I disturbed because you allow no middle position but make either God or Satan the rider;[239] for what you should have demonstrated, you shamelessly bring forward to refute me. You remember what I said about the light. And that blind man in the gospel first sees nothing, then he sees men who look like walking trees, and then he sees everything clearly (Mark 8:22–25). But I will take this up elsewhere; for here I assert nothing.

You see now that what I have said solves the problems you repeat in the next section, where you hammer away at them, not without wanton insults. You take one part of what is defined, that is, free will vitiated by sin, and with that you compare one opinion: to apply oneself to the good is good; therefore, free will can do good by itself. I grant it, if you are talking about the morally good. Again, I grant it, if you are talking about pious deeds, as long as you join to it preparatory or stimulating grace, as, for example, when from reading the Bible or listening to a preacher, we feel our mind moved to love piety and hate wickedness. This opinion I do not exclude, either in the definition or in recounting the opinions; I exclude only the opinions of Pelagius, Karlstadt, and you. Where, then, are the two free wills in conflict with one another? Does a genus conflict with itself because it includes different species? Will you deny that an ass is an animal because it

---

237. That is, the opinion of Scotus, which allows for merit *de congruo*.

238. *A Discussion*, nn. 25–26.

239. Cf. Ps 72:21. On Luther's image of God and Satan as riders of the human soul, see McSorley 335–40; see also Marjorie O'Rourke Boyle, "Luther's Rider-gods; From the Steppe to the Tower," *Journal of Religious History* 13 (1985): 260–82.

is distinguished from a man by reason of its specific difference and properties?[240] Would you make two purses out of one because it contains gold and silver? Here, then, no Proteus has been caught; rather you yourself are playing Proteus, turning yourself into whatever you wish in your eagerness to slander me, and also making me first one thing and then right away something else, whatever you think suitable for the darts of your slander.

I confess that according to one opinion the human will, corrupted by sin, cannot, insofar as it is corrupted, turn to the good without special grace, whether it be effective or stimulating grace. I confess that in those who have been freed by baptism and faith, the human will in and of itself is more prone to evil than to good. And I confess that according to one opinion the human will by its natural powers can turn to efforts, attempts, and works. If anyone claims these are evil and call forth wrath, I will deny it. If anyone claims that they are not good because they are performed without grace, I will grant it, if he will only confess that they are morally good and do call upon the effective grace of God. Therefore I do not contradict myself when I say different things in the context of different opinions. For here I do not yet declare what I think, but I gather together the subject matter of the ensuing debate for the unlearned reader.

So the triumph which you stage here should have been reserved for the concluding part of the debate where I declare which of all the opinions I favor most; at this point I am only girding myself for the battle. But when did I ever shout at you for professing that free will subject to sin cannot turn to what is better without the help of grace? No, I condemned you instead for teaching that there is no human will either for good or for evil, that it plays no part at all in a good or evil deed, either with or without grace—which you will never read in Augustine. Finally, when you have poured out such a useless spate of verbiage, clearly doing no more than beating the air, as they say (1 Cor. 9:26), then, according to your custom, you set up a triumph, as if you had fought valiantly. You are also afraid that no one will believe you when you recount so many absurdities, so many contradictions: "Read this passage in *A Discussion,*" you say, "and you will be amazed!" Read this passage in *A Discussion,* I say, and whoever reads it will immediately be amazed to find in the herald of the gospel

---

240. Properties are qualities not essential to a species but always connected with it and with it alone—for example, braying as a feature of asses or laughter as a property of mankind.

such a malicious eagerness to slander. It is wearisome to recount the other vainglorious boasts you thunder out in that passage.

Equally intemperate is what you heap up in the next section: how can it be consistent for free will to do something and still for the sum total to be imputed to grace? Since I explain this at length at the end of the debate, what need was there to waste time here with empty verbiage? It should not be imputed, because whatever man can do by his natural power is a gratuitous gift of God.[241] Nor is there any need here for the logician's conception of an absolute act of willing by the human will, with no regard to good or evil, a notion you condemn, though you would approve of it if it helped your case. Why is it absurd if, for pedagogical reasons, someone should posit an absolute when there is in reality no such absolute? How, then, do the philosophers dispute about prime matter and pure elements[242] or the mathematicians about forms abstracted from matter? Nor is it as unlikely as you would like to make out if someone attributes to our will a pure act of willing so that it does not consider its object under the aspect of good or evil but only as a being or as something by its own nature intermediate, even if there are some who deny that there is anything intermediate. Your loquacity is everywhere so troublesome that I think that no Bolanus[243] could have a temperament so felicitous as to put up with your veritable steeplefull of bronze bells, since everything you say is beside the point and yet you never stop talking.

You dispatched the first opinion, that of Thomas or Augustine, and now you attribute the second to Augustine, though it belongs to Karlstadt, who denies that the human will acts at all in a good work,

---

241. This sentence is hardly clear. Erasmus seems to mean that the action of the will need not be imputed to supernatural grace, because the will does make its own contribution; but in another sense all is due to grace, because the ability of the will to do anything is a free gift of God. Or the antecedent of "it" may be the "something" the will does, which should not be imputed to free will because the will's ability to act comes from God.

242. In Aristotelian metaphysics, prime matter is the purely potential principle of being which, when joined with the active principle, form, constitutes an existing material thing (such as those we see around us). The four elements are constitutive principles of all matter: earth (cold and dry), fire (hot and dry), air (hot and moist), and water (cold and moist).

243. Horace, *Satires* 1.9.11–12. Erasmus seems to take the speaker in the satire to mean he wishes he had the patience of Bolanus, who was apparently able put up with fools gladly. But today Horace is thought to mean that he wishes he had the spirit to shake off the bore, as Bolanus might have done.

though he admits it does in a bad one. And from this we can guess how dexterously you handle a topic, since you muddle together even the distinct opinions. Among those which I do not reject I set the opinion of Augustine over against that of Pelagius, from which it is most widely different, and I compare Scotus' opinion with Pelagius as coming the nearest to it. Reread *A Discussion* and you will find that is so. To the opinion of Augustine, I subjoin that of Karlstadt, which I call more harsh; intoxicated with your own endless babbling,[244] you now attribute this one to Augustine. In the third place I put the opinion of you and Wyclif, which I call the harshest of all. I say that my quarrel will be primarily with the last two, that is, with Karlstadt's and yours. I have put you back on track. Now what remains is for you to demonstrate to us that the last two opinions are the same as the first. When Augustine posits co-operating grace, he confesses that free will also does something in a good work; Karlstadt affirms that it does nothing but remains passive; you teach that it does nothing in a good work or a bad one, either before grace or after grace, but that it is a meaningless word, pure and simple. This opinion is in conflict with the first and it goes beyond the second. And here, having fallen off your ass, as they say, or rather having gone off ass-backwards, you do not understand what you are saying and resort to oaths.

"As God is my witness," you say, "I intended to say nothing else, and I intended nothing else to be understood, by the words of the last two opinions but what is said in the first opinion. I think that neither Augustine meant anything else nor do I understand anything else from his words than what the first opinion states, so that the three opinions recited by *Discussion* are for me no more than that one opinion of mine." If I had said anything so mindless as you do here, how you would overwhelm me with insults! There would be no end to your scoffing! And still you never cease to indulge in evasions, returning to your old plea about the name, though I have excluded it often enough and replied to it in more than one way. You yourself seem to be aware of your mistake, but still you did not want to erase what you had written. And so you do not end this section as you usually do, with a triumph, but rather you withdraw crestfallen. "If I am mistaken here," you say, "may I be corrected by anyone who can do so; if these points are obscure and ambiguous, let them be illuminated and firmly established by anyone who can do so." Here you admit a corrector and an enlightener, though in your conclusion you refuse all judgment.

244. Cf. Prov. 10:19 and Matt. 6:7.

But in the next section you pluck up your spirits. "But away with these verbal monstrosities! For who can bear such an abuse of language?" In so many words Echo[245] plays back your utterance: "But away with these verbal monstrosities! For who can bear such an abuse of language?" Concerning the use of an accepted phrase, go quarrel with Hilary[246] and Ambrose,[247] with Augustine[248] and Jerome.[249] Here you had proposed to say that the three opinions are not at all distinct from each other, and skipping over this, you quibble about the term "free will," and you still don't stop asserting what is manifestly false. Is it one and the same thing to say that free will cooperates with grace, that it is only passive in a good work but acts in a bad one, and that it does nothing in either a good or a bad work, but God alone works whatever is done, whether good or evil? You sum up your argument as follows: after sin the human will without grace is free only to do evil; therefore, once freedom is gone, slavery takes its place; that cannot be denied; where there is slavery there is sheer necessity; and where there is necessity free will does nothing; if it does nothing it is purely passive; your grammar cannot call lost health, health. But in order to defend my definition and to pick apart your tangled arguments at one and the same time, I will sum up the matter in stark propositions:

The will of mankind, like that of the angels, after its creation was free to do good or evil in such a way that it could cling to the grace offered to it without the special help of any new grace, and it could turn away from grace.

After the fall of our first parents, this natural liberty was vitiated, not extinguished. For there remained in them some spark of reason

245. A nymph who loved Narcissus in vain and grieved until only her voice remained (Ovid, *Metamorphoses* 3.356–402); Erasmus composed a colloquy entitled "Echo," first printed in *Colloquia* (Basel: Froben, 1526) and based on the acoustical conceit (CWE 40 p. 796–801).

246. St. Hilary (c. 315–c. 367), bishop of Poitiers and Latin church father, wrote the first extensive treatise on the trinity in Latin, *De trinitate*; Erasmus edited Hilary's *Opera* (Basel: Johann Froben, 1523); Erasmus' Ep. 1334 is the preface to this edition. The term *libera voluntas* (or variations on it) occurs, for example, six times in *De trinitate* 9.59 (PL 10 520–21).

247. St. Ambrose (c. 340–397), bishop of Milan, Latin father and doctor of the church, wrote copious exegetical, moral, and dogmatic works, as well as orations, epistles, and hymns. The term *liberum arbitrium* occurs in several of his works.

248. He used the term (with varying inflections) at least 569 times and wrote whole treatises about it.

249. Jerome used the term (with varying inflections) at least fifty times.

which distinguished virtue from vice and likewise some striving of the will which fled from vice and yearned for virtue in some fashion.

But this striving and this reason are ineffective without a special grace, according to some; according to others it has only enough strength to be able to merit grace *de congruo,* whether preparatory or even justifying grace, by means of morally good works. This opinion, I think, has not been condemned by the church, though it has also not rejected the one that precedes it, so that on this point it allows everyone to indulge his own judgment (Rom. 14:5).

Those freed by grace are in the same condition as mankind was when it was first created, in that they can apply themselves to grace when it is offered and can turn away from it, except that, because of Adam's sin and their own, there remains in them a certain darkness of the reason and a certain inclination to sin, which nevertheless does not take away their freedom but rather exercises their piety.

This application and aversion holds good for both kinds of grace, what we have called stimulating grace and justifying grace. For the will applies itself when it makes itself available to grace and at the same time strives with its natural power towards those things to which it is called by grace; it turns itself away when it neglects the whistling of the Spirit and turns to the desires of the flesh. Likewise, it applies itself to justifying grace when, with the little natural power it has, it works with the grace working powerfully upon it; and it turns away when it neglects the gift of God and turns back to the flesh.

My definition, which I made general precisely so as to include all the probabilities, squares with all these opinions, none of which (if I am not mistaken) has been condemned by the church, and it also conforms to every condition of mankind. You accomplish nothing, therefore, when you bear down on this or that opinion and twist the definition in some other direction. Suppose mankind to be in the condition in which it was created: the definition squares with that. Here you bear down on us with the idea that free will was vitiated after the Fall. Suppose mankind to be in the condition of a young person who as a child received the habit of faith[250] through baptism and was cleansed of the sin of the first created man, and has not committed any sin by which grace is lost, although he is nevertheless old enough

---

250. In Aristotelian terms a habit (*habitus*) is a quality by which a power is well or ill disposed to do something (Thomas Aquinas *Summa theologiae* I–II q 49 a 1). According to Aquinas, faith is a habit (*Summa theologiae* II–II q 4 a 5). A child receives "the habit of faith" when it is baptized.

to know the difference between good and evil: my definition squares with that. For he could apply himself to grace or turn away from grace. He will apply himself if he struggles by his natural powers to go where grace leads him; he will turn away if he scorns God's grace and goes off to the flesh.

Finally, imagine a person in the condition Adam was in after he had violated the command of God; here, perhaps, it will seem that my definition does not square with that condition, because once he has been given over to sin he can do nothing but be a slave to sin. Where, then, is the power of applying oneself or turning away? According to the opinion of some, there remains, I say, some freedom by which he can, without any special grace, solicit justifying grace through his natural powers by means of morally good works.[251] This position you oppose with your paradoxes; but you should prove them first before you use them to refute us. According to the opinion of others, which agrees with the opinion of Augustine, he can apply himself to the grace which stimulates and calls him back, and on the other hand he can spurn it; here you see there is some liberty.[252] Then again, he can make himself available to justifying grace; he can turn away from it. And perhaps it would not be absurd to posit a certain middle condition between justification and the lack of it, as, for example, when a person struggles to merit grace by his natural powers or else is aroused by the stimulating grace which we call imperfect so that he applies his natural power to that grace and struggles after innocence. He does not seem entirely unjustified, since he is disgusted with his own wickedness and strives after justification; nor does he seem entirely justified, since he has not yet achieved innocence. And in such a middle condition St. Augustine seems to place Cornelius,[253] in whom both conditions were present but imperfectly (Acts 10), as if, for example, someone

251. A clear statement of the position attributed by Erasmus to Scotus.

252. In his early writings on free will, especially *De libero arbitrio* (388–395), Augustine propounded the view (later endorsed by Pelagius) that man can respond to initial grace by his natural powers, as Erasmus says here that he did; but after 396–397 Augustine recanted that view. For example, in *De spiritu et litera* (412) he says: "Free will is such a neutral power as can either incline towards faith or turn towards unbelief. Consequently a man cannot be said to have even that will with which he believes in God without having received it, since this rises at the call of God out of the free will which he received naturally when he was created (chapter 58; see also chapter 52. See McSorley, 72–76.

253. *Sermones* 269.2 (PL 38 1235–6); *Liber de praedestinatione sanctorum* 7 (PL 44 969–70); *Epistulae ad Romanos inchoata espositio* 8 (CSEL 84 171 10–18).

who is hastening to a place of refuge is neither completely safe nor caught in the very midst of danger, but the further he gets away from danger, the closer he is to safety. Here you croak away about the sudden rapture of the Spirit, which I do not deny. For the moment I am speaking not about what God sometimes does or what he can do, but rather what he generally does with us.[254] But I will discuss this in the appropriate place.

Compare with these opinions those three which you conflate into one. You will find only the first one is true. For when Augustine posits operating and cooperating grace,[255] he clearly confesses that a person is free to apply himself to stimulating grace, if he accommodates his natural power to it. That imperfect effort is aided and fulfilled by cooperating grace, which would not be rightly called cooperating if our will did not operate at all, as Karlstadt claims it does not. What you assert is even less true: that the human will cannot do anything either for good or for ill, but that all things happen by pure and sheer necessity; for I call this opinion yours because you approve of the opinion of Wyclif, which was condemned.[256] What then is left but a quarrel about the name? Free will properly applies only to God. True, but in the same way we use many other names: wise, good, powerful, immortal. But since freedom has been lost through sin, it is now only an empty name, just as in a sick man lost health is not health. I grant that here there is some misuse of the word, but you ought not to blame it on me. And still it is not absurd to say that the reality behind the name remains in a sinner, just as freeborn men captured in a war retain the designation "free" because of their native condition and the hope of regaining their original freedom. Moreover, there are vestiges of original freedom which remain in a person even after he has committed a sin; and these vestiges are not nothing simply because they are in themselves insufficient to regain freedom: it is enough that they do something by their own power and accomplish it also with the assistance of grace. You make lost health into death. Some natural strength remains in a sick man, fighting with the disease as best he can and sometimes winning the battle without the help of a physician. So too you represent reason as totally blind after sin; I say it is dim sighted or blear eyed. For someone whose vision is blurred by rheum is not

---

254. This distinction derives from the late medieval usage of the older distinction between God's absolute and ordained powers.

255. *A Discussion,* n. 22.

256. *A Discussion,* n. 5.

completely blind, and someone who is struggling against a disease is not completely dead.

Now, if you please, summon that sophist, that agreeable drinking companion, and propose to him that comparison to the stone which falls down by its natural force but does not go up except by some violent thrust, and ask him whether he attributes free will to the stone;[257] perhaps he will not be able to keep from laughing and will reply that whoever asks such questions is a stone.[258] For a stone, like every heavy body which lacks reason, has only one natural impetus, but free will, as it was created, was able to turn in either direction. You will say: we are talking about a corrupt will. We will grant that if you will only keep in mind during the debate that it was created free and hence the substance behind the name remains, although the reality is partly lost. But after original sin and even more after actual sin, just as freedom is not totally lost, so too it is not reduced to absolute slavery. Sin introduced impaired vision, not blindness; lameness, not destruction; it inflicted a wound, not death; it brought on weakness, not annihilation. For some spark of reason remains, some inclination of the will towards the morally good remains, although it is ineffective. And it is not nothing simply because in itself it is not enough to recover its original liberty.

But wounded and weak as it is, it is not strong enough to be able to do it, but nevertheless whatever vestiges of power it has it accommodates to the grace which is raising it up—unless perhaps you say that a boy alone has no power because he cannot move a wagon, though he can do it if he combines his effort with someone stronger. But keep your comparison of the stone for men of stone, and do not throw at us your ridiculous conclusions: "no one is everyone and nothing is everything."[259] But what if that sophist of yours should be a Scotist? Will he not immediately shut your mouth for you? Unless, perhaps, you call him agreeable because he responds agreeably to your questions. Finally, so far as the phrase is concerned, Thomas would perhaps concede that after sin it is not properly called free will, but he will deny that it is simply nothing or that it does not act at all together with the action of grace.[260]

---

257. Erasmus himself used Aristotelian dynamics to moralize about sin in his colloquy "A Problem" of 1533 (CWE 40 pp. 1056–69).

258. That is, a blockhead (*Adages* 1.4.89).

259. *De servo arbitrio* (WA 18 666:4; LW 33 109).

260. Aquinas, *Summa theologiae* I q 83 a 2.

This is what I put before the readers at the outset of the debate so that they might be more prepared to understand the rest. For I professed that I am writing for uneducated readers, and you attack this section without having even read, I think, the rest of *A Discussion*, as if I had already made some pronouncement. With the same injustice you pick apart the scriptural evidence which I treat, as if I had made a definitive pronouncement in each case. Indeed I bear witness that I have set out the texts from Holy Scripture, taken from here and there, which seem to contradict one another. And those conclusions which you rail at so mightily are offered by someone who is not defining but rather arguing, not teaching but debating, so that truth may shine forth by the collision of testimonies and interpretations. And for the moment I use the right of debaters, who seek out what is wrong so as to disclose what is right. For a debater frequently does this, not so as to declare what he himself thinks but to snare and trip up his adversary. Furthermore, he not infrequently uses assumptions which are false but have been granted by his adversary, and from them he concludes what goes beyond the truth, so that his adversary may better understand that he is defeated and so stop fighting back and become willing to be taught. And then someone who teaches uses far different methods than someone who is disputing. But for a while now, lack of time has been pressing me to break off this debate. What remains will be handled more carefully and at leisure.

ERASMUS

The Shield-Bearer Defending
A Discussion
Part 2 (1527)

Erasmus' Response to Luther's Critique of Erasmus'
Arguments Supporting Free Will

Imperative and indicative moods

Once more he brings up that superb teaching about the difference between commandments and promises, and from the grammarians he seeks out the difference between the imperative and indicative moods: words of command do not show that a person can do something, but an indicative statement does so. Since this is quite well known to schoolchildren, he is surprised that we theologians talk such nonsense in our second childhood. Whom is he insulting here? Me? I never taught such a thing. But what theologian is so out of his mind that he does not know what this person teaches so superciliously, namely that the imperative mood commands and does not make pronouncements? "You claim," he says, "that something is observed, done, chosen, and fulfilled—and that by our own power—as soon as you hear the voice of someone commanding 'Do,' 'Observe,' 'Choose.'" Can anyone believe this person is sober? Who ever said that what is commanded is immediately accomplished? But if he hadn't spoken in this way, his language would have lacked Lutherly hyperbole. Ordinary, uneducated people know that a person who wants something does not immediately have what he wants and that a condition expresses something undetermined. And yet if someone said to a miser, "If you had taken care of your wife as well as you have taken care of your money, you would have a faithful wife," or "Would that you had taken as good care of your wife as you did of your money," an uneducated layperson would say "I will sue for defamation of character." The defendant will cry out that subjunctive or optative expressions do not state facts, but the judge will fine him out of common sense.

But what do the boys on the street corner[1] know: "Words in the
imperative mood prescribe what should be done, not what the person
addressed can do." But those same boys also know that whoever
commands what cannot be done is either stupid or ridiculous or
tyrannical. Let Luther learn this by experience if he does not believe
me. Let him go into a classroom and command one elementary
student to recite Homer's *Iliad* from memory, command another to
translate Terence into Hebrew, another to fly up to the roof, and
similar feats, one after the other. What would they say? What except,
"This man is either mad or drunk or he is mocking us." "Schoolboys
know the difference between the imperative and indicative moods."
But who ever taught them this conclusion from it that Luther so
mightily ridicules in the theologians? To be sure, nature and common
sense, from which Luther diverges so amazingly as he snatches in all
directions to find support for his too, too beloved dogma. And even
so, if someone spoke that way to the boys, he would be acting less
ridiculously than Luther, who applies his principle to all of God's
commandments. For he commands the boys to do something that
could be done over a period of time. God, if we believe Luther,
issues commands that cannot be obeyed, no matter how much effort
is expended or time spent, not even if the Spirit works in us—laws
such as no tyrant we have ever read about ever issued, laws that are
not worthy of the name. And an opinion so absurd and contradictory
to common sense as this one, which Luther makes the standard of
interpretation for Scripture, he proves by a few words plucked out of
Paul, "Through the Law comes the knowledge of sin" (Rom. 3:20),
as if a law that commands what can be done would not show the
wicked their sins, so that evil men might refrain from wrongdoing
out of fear of punishment (so as to be less guilty or at least less harmful
or, if they don't refrain, so as to have no excuse), and as if it would
not also show sin to good men so that they may avoid it and seek out
what is honorable.

Now that he has found a ready and easy way to invalidate any
evidence from Scripture, he uses the same axe to cut down the
passage quoted by *Discussion* from Deuteronomy 30: "Words in
the imperative mood and the texts cited prove something different
from what he proposes." I proposed that free will could do nothing
without grace, and these texts show that it can do all things, and itself

---

1. The Latin *in triviis* can also refer to the trivium (grammar, logic, and rhetoric),
which was the first part of a university education.

being alone (to talk in a "Lutherly" way).[2] We have to put up with such babble throughout the whole dispute. Hence I want you to remember once and for all, dear reader, that my Discussion sets out various opinions which are not rejected by the church. And in the course of the debate I have not merely one in mind, and my aim is not to support the opinion which I declare at the end to be the one I favor most but to knock Luther's weapon out of his hands by means of scriptural passages that attribute something to free will, whether more according to some or less according to others—for even the orthodox have various opinions in the matter. Regardless of how each of them lays hold of Scripture, I am certainly accomplishing what I wished, namely to make it clear that Luther is wrong when he asserts that Holy Scripture teaches nothing except that there is no free will.[3]

Now, since he twists his scriptural passages most outrageously, if I in turn had twisted mine to win the victory, simply as a debating point, to show that some places in Scripture seem to contradict one another but can be reconciled by comparing one with another, why would it have been absurd for me to do so, especially since that is what *A Discussion* professed to do and actually did? Is Luther so ignorant of the arena of disputation that he does not know the difference between refuting and propounding, between argumentation and pronouncing judgment? St. Thomas very often reasons in this way: "In John 6 the Lord says, 'Unless you eat the flesh of the Son of Man and drink his blood'; therefore this sacrament is necessary for salvation."[4] From a scriptural quotation he draws a false conclusion, sometimes even a blasphemous one, and we recognize that it is legitimate to do so in the arena of debate. Luther endlessly reproaches me for my inferences—or rather not even my inferences but rather, once he has distorted them, his own. But if, in the heat of the debate, I had used absurd allegations and done so to knock the weapon out of the hands of my adversary

2. Erasmus mocks Luther's awkward ablative-absolute construction *se solo* (itself being alone), where *ex se* or *per se* would have been better Latin.

3. The aim Erasmus expresses here explains why his judgments about free will vary considerably.

4. *Summa theologiae* III q 73 a 3. The argument from John 6:54 is the first of three objections to the true position; later in the article Thomas refutes all three objections as false. Erasmus is following the usual form of questions in a scholastic summa: the question, objections to the accepted position, an argument for it, an explanation of it, and refutations of the objections.

and thus defeat him, I would have been doing nothing that is not customary among theologians.

As it is, nowhere in what I say do I draw the conclusion he so often and so scurrilously pounces upon, that free will can do all things without grace and itself being alone.[5] Where did Luther learn such dialectic as this: "He can; therefore he can do all things by himself" and "He cannot do it without assistance; therefore he cannot do anything at all by himself"? If someone says that the emperor can capture a city, is he affirming that he can do it without the help of soldiers? "But in the course of the argument," he says, "you did not mention grace." I did not know that I was dealing with a person so forgetful that I needed to repeat the very same thing for every verse. For I also mention grace frequently. Nor did that have anything to do with the argument. For in that place I cite only passages which, however they are taken, destroy Luther's position, namely, that all the commandments of God are impossible. If such evidence seems to show that free will can do all things by itself—though I did not say that anywhere—it is all the more stupid of Luther to take it so, since he claims it is impossible to show from Scripture that there even is such a thing as free will.

And so, although this insult is partly unjustified, partly false, nevertheless he keeps croaking it at us as if it were a notorious sophism, jumping for joy, mocking me, frisking about, all but triumphing. And all the while, this one and only sharp-sighted debater does not see that he is making a fool of himself in the eyes of men of good judgment as he goes on mocking *A Discussion*. In these two sections, which are not very long, how many tasteless witticisms he utters; he calls her his Discussion; he rouses Discussion from her somnolence; he finds Discussion deficient in memory; he concludes that she either doesn't understand anything or that she doesn't care about her cause; he accuses her of a most shameful offence in an advocate, namely, stupidity, because she brings up points that undermine the case she is making; he ridicules Discussion for flattering herself so very blithely; she always argues against her own position; she is ridiculous in everything she says or does.

But one of his very best sayings is this one: "Lady Discussion," he says, "you make wrong inferences and do not prove your conclusion, but you imagine something follows or is proved because you are blind and somnolent." And yet Augustine uses similar inferences time and

5. See n. 2, above.

time again to assert free will. O companions of Luther, where are you? Why do you not applaud your glorious leader? Why do you not cry out, "Bravo! Very fine! Elegant! Witty! Top notch!" Nomentanus and Balatro in Horace are better buffoons.[6] What could be sillier than such jokes? What more insane than such insults? With such gems as these he made sport of the king of England,[7] and there was no lack of those who applauded him—so true it is that birds of a feather flock together. What does my *Discussion* infer, you idle babbler? No more than that free will is established by Scripture. "Therefore," he says, "free will without grace can do everything."

That is your conclusion, not *Discussion's*. For I promised that I would bring up scriptural texts, some of which seem to eliminate free will completely, some to establish it.[8] After they were cited, what was there left to do? Obviously, to explain those texts that seem to eliminate it completely and then to temper the interpretation of those that establish it so as to ascribe the sum and substance to grace, but to do so in such a way that the human will also plays its part. Didn't *Discussion* perform what she promised? But she did so in the proper place. Therefore *Discussion* did not forget herself, but you did so outrageously by demanding in one place what she promised to do somewhere else. Indeed, one can detect in this debater a special peculiarity: in the individual parts of the argument, he fights as if the victory were located there; in each part he makes preliminary statements, delivers a peroration, and triumphs. And yet he is not so annoying because of his stupid insults as because of his endless repetitions. Therefore, if I were to answer this point every time he brings it up, this volume would become huge; hence I want the reader to understand that whenever I say Luther is cockadoodledooing, I am deliberately passing over such nonsense as this.

The position of man in the presence of grace

In the next section, he repeats the same lie—that my Discussion everywhere imagines that mankind can either do what is commanded

6. Horace, *Satires* 2.8.25–33, 61–74, 83.

7. In 1522 Luther scurrilously attacked Henry VIII in *Contra Henricum regem Angliae* (*Against Henry King of England*) (WA 10/2, 180–222). Thomas More repaid Luther in kind in his *Responsio ad Lutherum* (1523).

8. In *De libero arbitrio* Erasmus cited some scriptural texts supporting free will; but he also discussed scriptural texts which seem to deny free will, including some cited by Luther in *Assertio*, article 36.

or at least understands that it cannot. Discussion holds that, according to the opinion of some, a person by his natural powers can make such progress that God will not deny him grace. She holds that according to the opinion of others free will can and does do all things with the help of grace. What does Luther hold? That the whole of mankind is bound, miserable, captive, sick, dead. Not satisfied with that, he makes all persons so blind that they think they are free and sound. Since no one lacks the law of nature, which tells mankind that many things should be sought or avoided, how can it be that all mankind, even before grace, was such as Luther imagines? What law instructed the philosophers so that they handed down many splendid principles about the habit[9] of virtue and the duties which flow from it? But with Luther, hyperbole always follows hyperbole, just as one handhold leads to another. "Such a person needed the Law to command so many impossible things." For what purpose? "A weighty and serious one: so that he will know his sin and beg for a physician." I have already shown that this could be done more advantageously if the Law had commanded what is possible. "But a person knows his misery better," he says, "if he sees that the Law cannot be observed." But the Pharisees believed they observed the Law. Therefore the Law does not always bring forth knowledge of sin, or if it does, what it brings forth is useless. But let us grant that it does. How does the Law teach that a person can by no means observe what is commanded? And then how will a person be persuaded he ought to observe what is not within his power? Or how will he be persuaded that God is as merciful as Luther here makes him out to be, if he imposes such harsh laws on persons who do not deserve them except insofar as they are descended from Adam?

But let us grant this also, that a person recognizes that his life is a complete disaster. What then? He will beg for God's mercy; God will immediately hear the voice of the person who begs. For at this point, although Luther elsewhere makes God more cruel than any tyrant, since by a sheer whim of his will he commits to eternal fire someone who doesn't deserve it, now he suddenly makes God so merciful that at the first cry he immediately changes flesh to spirit, that is, he turns an instrument of Satan into a temple of God. Why didn't he hear the voice of Balaam in Numbers 23:10 when he said, "May my soul die the death of the justified"? But where does this begging come from? From grace. What, then, does a person beg for:

---

9. On the Aristotelian meaning of "habit" see *Shield-Bearer* 1, n. 250.

what he has or what he does not have? If he begs without grace, he sins by doing so, according to Luther; indeed, he does so even in a state of grace. How, then, will he arouse God's mercy by calling upon him? If the person who begs has what he is seeking, how does God immediately hear him, since he already gave it before it was asked for? But if Luther posits some middle ground between someone who already has sanctifying grace and someone who has not yet attained to it but is being prepared for it, what happens to that hyperbole which makes every person sick, captive, untamed, and self-indulgent? He means that this is the case when a person is beyond the pale of grace, I think: if not, the hyperbole is even more outrageous. Therefore a person appeals for mercy by sinning if he is beyond the pale of grace or on some middle ground between flesh and spirit. Why, then, is Luther always crying out against those who think that a person solicits and obtains grace by almsdeeds, fasting, prayer, spiritual reading, and other pursuits which are, as they say, morally good, when he himself says that grace is immediately achieved at the very first cry? Which is easier, to cry out for it or by good deeds to solicit it long and hard?

Now since Luther so often deals with me as follows: "Free will can do this or that, therefore it can do this or that by its own powers without the assistance of grace," if I have the right to deal with him in the same way, I would reason thus: "The Law brings forth knowledge of sin, knowledge of sin makes us recognize our disastrous condition, recognition brings forth a plea for divine help, the plea brings God's mercy; therefore the Law in and of itself causes a person to recognize sin, and knowledge of sin without grace makes him recognize—that is, confess—his sinfulness, recognition by itself makes him beg for God's mercy, the plea has such force that God cannot deny his mercy to someone who begs for it." Where in this series does Luther place the beginning of grace? After God has listened to the plea? Then whatever came before was done apart from grace under the plenary power of Satan. And yet what was done in that way has such force that it compels God to impart his grace immediately. And how often does the man who teaches such things in his *Assertion* mock and sneer and even charge with impiety those who think that mankind by their natural powers can progress so far by means of morally good works that God in his goodness will not withhold the help of grace from someone who is doing the best he can.[10] How often he proclaims that they are worse than Pelagius himself!

---

10. Erasmus here makes Luther's argument equivalent to the doctrine of *facere quod in se est* (see *The Shield-Bearer* 1, n. 199), which Luther vehemently denies.

But how much more outrageous is what Luther here attributes to knowledge and pleading. For if someone who is dissatisfied with himself because he recognizes his sinfulness goes on to give alms, fasts, becomes familiar with Holy Scripture, goes to mass, listens to sermons, prays, and for all that remains sinful and desires to sin, still he does more than someone who merely understands that the commandments cannot be kept and begs for mercy so that God will confer eternal life on him. For according to Luther grace does not have enough power to enable a person to observe even the least little commandment. What, then, does it do? It turns what would have been mortal sins into venial sins. And so neither knowledge of sin nor pleading brings a person to the point where he can observe the commandments; they bring him only to the point of recognizing his lamentable plight. Then God, who was so harsh when he gave the commandments, suddenly becomes so kind that he will bestow eternal life on someone who does not keep the commandments or who even perseveres in wrongdoing, as long as he cries out and believes with a Lutheran-style faith.

He cites Isaiah 61:1: "He sent me to preach the gospel to the poor, to heal those whose hearts are contrite." (Where some read "to the poor," Jerome translates and the Hebrew means "gentle," "not at all fierce.")[11] But Luther makes everyone blind and self-satisfied. He will say "before the Law." After the Law, then, everyone was dissatisfied with himself? "No, but the Law cast some down, hardened others." The Law does not confer grace. How, then, does it soften some people? "Because it finds material that is softer and more capable of grace." Some of the gentiles and some of the Jews heard the gospel; some immediately submitted to it; others resisted it with all their might. Where does the difference come from? "Because some seed fell on good ground, other seed on different soil" (Luke 8:5–8). Why is soil different? "Because of depraved desires and vicious morals." But where do these corrupting influences come from if not from free will? A simple mind or someone erring out of ignorance is an untilled field, to be sure, but one which is easily capable of growing good seed.

He is also hyperbolical when he says: "Either God commands the impossible or the Spirit is in vain." God does not command what is impossible in an unqualified way, nor is the Spirit in vain, without

---

11. Luther, *Commentarii in Esaiam* 17.61.1/3.1–10 CCSL 73A 706. Erasmus quotes Luke 4:18, which follows the Septuagint version, *evangelizare pauperibus* (to preach the gospel to the poor); Jerome, following the Hebrew, has *ad annuntiandum mansuetis* (to announce to the gentle). See Erasmus' *Annotations on Luke* 4:17 (LB VI 247F).

whose help there is no way to arrive at eternal salvation. Now who are the contrite of heart whom Christ heals? Those who recognize their weakness and beg for God's mercy. If they are healed simply by doing this, what does the healer do? If they are not, then either they must be blind or there must be some middle ground between them and the healed—which Luther denies. The Lord says: "I have not come to call the just but rather the sinful,"[12] meaning by "just" those who think they are just, and by "the sinful" those who recognize the wrong they have done. But the Pharisees clung tightly to the Law, and yet the Law did not bring forth recognition of sin in all of them. This, then, as I said, is not the only effect of the Law, nor does it have this effect in everyone, and this ability or inability arises from free will.

Does Erasmus attribute good works to free will alone and fail to include grace?

In the next section Luther cockadoodledoos, quite appropriately mentioning a solid lump of dough, for all of his language here smacks of the kitchen, where he apparently wrote these things in a drunken stupor. Then, too, what a witty phrase, "to mix up a solid lump of dough"! And yet there are some who think this babbler is amusing! Let others judge what kinds of lumps Discussion mixes up; what is clear is that Luther mixes up such drugs as infect the minds of very many simple people. And just as that insipid joke about the lump of dough smacks of the gross spirit by which he is led, so too when he later calls my logical inference a "Leviathan, that is, an addition"—to make it seem that he knows Hebrew—he smacks of the spirit whose breath leads him to add many hyperboles to Holy Scripture that undermine its wholesome meaning. What does this "Leviathan" say? "Therefore free will has full power to do all things; therefore it can do them, itself being alone; therefore it can do it by its own power; therefore it does not need the help of the Spirit."[13] That Leviathan Luther added these words on his own, whereas my Discussion speaks quite differently. He thinks that if he repeats this lie hundreds of times, it will seem to be true, but he is quite wrong. Whoever repeats over and over again what is manifestly groundless does not make what he is saying seem less false but makes himself seem more shameless. For what was the point of that sophistical trifle "If I am willing, you will eat the good things of the earth" (Isa. 1:19), as if anyone could enjoy

12. Matt. 9:13 (Mark 2:17, Luke 5:32)
13. See n. 2, above.

the goods things of the land against God's will? This is nothing more
than a waste of time and paper.

This section confirms Luther's untrustworthiness. Here he repeats
what he has said so often elsewhere, that I attribute all power to free
will, and yet he himself cites these words of mine: "What was the
point of saying 'If you are willing, you will eat the good things of
the earth' if there is no freedom of the will?" Does someone who says
"if there is no freedom" attribute all power to the human will? And
a bit later: "What point is there in exhorting people to do something
if they are utterly unable to do it?"[14] Is this the language of someone
who attributes everything to our will? And yet, after Luther has cited
them, he adds: "What is the point of citing passages which prove
nothing, by themselves, and then adding the inference that they
attribute everything to free will?"

He adds insult to injury. For these passages have so far convinced
the church that free will has some power, and my inference does not
attribute all power to it. How often, to be sure, he blurts out that
throughout the whole discussion I separate grace from free will. And
yet here he reports these words of mine: "Zechariah demonstrates
the exercise of free will more clearly still and indicates the grace in
store for whoever exercises it."[15] Does someone who says grace is
in store for a person eliminate it? But to show how extraordinary
and glaring the shamelessness of the man is, I will quote some other
places from A Discussion. Having cited the testimony of Isaiah, I make
the following inference: "If the human will is in no sense free to do
good, or even (as some assert) is not free to do either good or evil,
what is the meaning of the words, 'if you are willing' and 'if you are
not willing?'" And a bit later: "Here too I do not see how we can
avoid attributing to [sinners] a will that is in some sense free to choose
good." The same point is made by the simile of the person tied up
with ropes, who is in no sense free. A little later I make the following
inference: "And where are those who claim that man does nothing but
is only worked upon by operating grace?" And a little later: "But what
can you ascribe to someone who can do nothing, good or bad? To
those who have absolutely no control over their will?" And somewhat
later: "All this would have to be meaningless once it is accepted that
doing good or evil is a matter of necessity." And again: "If everything
happens by necessity." And soon afterwards: "Are not all of Christ's

14. The Enslaved Will, p. 74.
15. The Enslaved Will, p. 75.

splendid commandments emptied of meaning if nothing is attributed to human will?" Likewise: "When good and bad deeds are mentioned so frequently, as is reward, I fail to see how there can be any room for absolute necessity."[16]

I will not go on to cite more instances, lest I overburden the reader. Although the part of *A Discussion* that cites Scripture in favor of free will is full of such inferences, nevertheless Luther has the gall to accuse me of inferring that everything is attributed to the human will, to the exclusion of grace. My inferences propose that grace is in store for anyone who does his best;[17] they exclude the sheer necessity which Luther introduces; they attribute something to free will, but only a little. What room is there, then, for those mindless insults: Discussion proposes one thing, proves another; doesn't know what she is talking about; contradicts herself? I do not intend to rebut his insults. It is clear on the face of it what sort of rhetorician Luther is, how consistent he is, never forgetting himself, never changing, always insulting.

On the distinction between Law and gospel

Poor Discussion is charged with another crime. "In the passages she quotes, she does not distinguish between the expressions of the Law and those of the gospel; for she is so blind and ignorant that she does not see what is the Law and what is the gospel." In fact, there is nothing that Luther is not ashamed to make up. Where do I make the words of the gospel into the words of the Law? Is it because I cite some passages that seem to invite us to grace rather than command what is to be done? Well, so be it. Isn't it true that Discussion took it upon herself to show that the invitations, promises, and blandishments of God also prove that the human will is not entirely devoid of action? For example, let us take a text most representative of the gospel: "Come to me, all who labor and are burdened, and I will refresh you" (Matt. 11:28). If the human will does nothing, why does he say to it, "Come"? No one says to someone who is tied up, "Come to me, I will give you food," but either takes the food to him on his own initiative or else unties him first. I grant that the works of the Law are not commanded here but rather we are required to listen to the word, and that prepares us for the gift of faith.

Then again: "Repent; the kingdom of heaven is at hand" (Matt. 3:2). Here the kingdom of heaven is promised, but only to those who do

16. *A Discussion,* pp. 12–14.
17. See n. 10, above.

penance. If the human will does nothing to promote conversion, why does the gospel exhort it to do so? Penance would have to be given, not commanded. So too in Isaiah 45:20, 22, "Gather together and come," and to the same people he says, "Turn to me and you will be saved." What does "gather together" mean? What does "turn" mean? Leave your idols, gather together with the Jews into one and the same church, and you will be saved through faith. If someone says, "Rise up," he seems to be calling upon the will of someone lying down; if he says, "Shake off the dust," that is equivalent to saying "Abandon your filthy vices"; someone who says, "Loose your neck from its bonds" is calling for repentance. Then comes a sentence in keeping with the gospel: "You were sold without payment and you will be bought back without silver" (Isa. 52:2–3). Again, the command "If you are seeking, seek" is an expression of reproach to someone not seeking with his whole heart (Isa. 21:12). "Turn" and "come" are exhortations to a complete and serious change of living. Most of the promises in the gospel are such that they have a command or a condition attached to them. For example, "search out," seek," and "knock" are commands; "you will find," "you will receive," and "it will be opened to you" are promises.[18] "Whoever believes and has been baptized will be saved" (Mark 16:16); "you will be saved" is an evangelical expression, but it includes the condition "if you believe," and if that is not fulfilled the promise is empty. And so wouldn't the promises that call upon us to keep the commandments be superfluous, together with the commandments themselves, if the human will does nothing? Where, then, is the confusion between the expressions of the gospel and those of the Law?

But Luther mixes truth with falsehood. If Discussion had proposed to speak only of commandments and punishments, then Luther would at any rate have a bone to pick. But since she set out to handle commandments, promises, blandishments, exhortations, adjurations, expostulations, reproaches, threats, fears, rebukes, curses, what was his point in distinguishing the language of the Law from that of the gospel except to display his marvelous knowledge of theology? At this point, see once more how true to himself Luther always is. When I cited these words from Isaiah, "Turn to me and you will be saved," he says this expression belongs to the gospel (Isa. 45:22). Right afterward he teaches that Zechariah's words "Turn to me" contain the whole Law with all its commandments and his other words "I will turn to

18. Matt. 7:7, Luke 11:9.

you" epitomize the gospel. The same expression in Isaiah belongs to the gospel, but in Zechariah it not only belongs to the Law but embraces the whole Law (Zech. 1:3). I have shown that no passage was taken from Isaiah that did not contain some commandment and that therefore Luther has no grounds whatever to say that they are all words of consolation or promise except for the first passage. I have demonstrated that even if they incontrovertibly did belong to the gospel they still tend to prove free will. I pass over his cockadoodledoo about words of command and his claim that from them I infer that free will does not need grace; he croaks this lie so often that I am sick and tired of refuting it again and again.

He has such a vast fund of verbal abuse that to his previous insults such as "utter blindness," "solid lump," "Leviathan," he here adds "dozing off," before he finally touches on the arguments. "'You shall love the Lord your God, etc.' is the greatest commandment of all (Mark 12:30) and is cast in the imperative mood. But from it we cannot infer that free will has any power, nor can it be inferred from any other commandments." What if I deny Luther's assumption? He will cite the scholastic doctors at me. It is shameless of him to cite the scholastics at me, since he does not accept the authority of any doctor, whether scholastic or not. As it is, since he admits that the Scotists and the theologians of the *via moderna* have a different opinion from his, why does he attribute more authority to one group than to another? If he has the right to use whatever supports his cause, I have the right to embrace whatever supports mine.[19] At this juncture how does Luther prove his assertion? Does it follow from the fact that few do love God with their whole heart that therefore they cannot do it? But let us grant that mankind cannot perform what the words of the commandment say; then what sort of inference is it to say that since they cannot keep this commandment they cannot keep any at all? Many people who do not love God perfectly, or their neighbor as they ought, do abstain from murder. And this commandment, "You shall love," has a special character: for what is commanded not only always increases here but also is perfected in the pious after this life.

What, then, is the meaning of those hyperboles "with your whole heart, with your whole mind, with all your might"? That God should

---

19. The Enslaved Will, p. 76. Luther claimed that among the scholastic theologians only the Scotists and the *recentiores* (those of the *via moderna*) believed that a person could love God with his whole heart. Erasmus claims the right to cite the Scotists and the theologians of the *via moderna* to support his case, just as Luther cited the other scholastics on his behalf. See the Introduction, n. 52.

be loved beyond all things so that neither wife nor children nor death
nor life should be put before him. Moreover, the perfection of charity
is said to be complete not because it cannot receive any additions but
because it has reached a certain level of its own in accordance with
our weakness. And if someone does not keep a commandment fully,
he is not immediately said to break it, especially in those qualities that
increase gradually, among which faith and the love of God are to be
numbered. God puts up with the weak until they improve, and he
helps them while they improve. This is the rationale by which God
requires perfect charity, and we can do what he requires with the
help of his grace if we do our best.[20] Here too, then, free will plays its
part, as the commandment requires. Nor does it follow from the fact
that no observance of the Law is pleasing to God apart from faith and
charity that therefore someone who keeps the commandment violates
it if his faith and charity are imperfect.

Luther goes on frisking about, imagining that he has been
extraordinarily successful. He mocks sleepy-eyed Discussion when she
infers an endeavor of the human will from Zechariah's words "Turn
to me"—just as someone with a lantern might cry out to someone
wandering in the dark, "Turn your eyes in this direction." I am
reluctant to waste my time and that of the reader with such trifles. Still
it is worthwhile to show what a grave and serious leader the world has
to bring the gospel back to it. "And according to this new grammar,"
he says, "'to turn' means the same as 'to endeavor,'" as if the meaning
of "turn to me" were "endeavor to turn" and "I will turn to you"
meant "I will endeavor to turn to you," so that sometimes he attributes
an endeavor even to God, perhaps also ready to provide grace even
to his endeavors. For if 'turn to' means 'endeavor' in one place, why
not everywhere?"[21] Where is that new evangelical claque to applaud
such wit? Here we have the blasphemous and trashy buffoonery of
a man who boasts he has an evangelical spirit. Such insults land not
on Discussion but on Augustine, Jerome, Ambrose, Chrysostom, and
other Doctors of the church.

Who said that "turn to" means the same thing as "endeavor"? These
are the words of Discussion: "Zechariah indicates both the endeavor of
free will and the grace in store for the one who endeavors,"[22] meaning
that both can be inferred from his words. If someone says to a boy,

20. See n. 10, above.
21. *The Enslaved Will*, p. 77.
22. *A Discussion*, p. 13.

"You will turn out to be a learned man," what is he pointing out? Isn't it that the boy should study hard? Therefore "to turn out to be" means "to study." If someone says to his steward, "Fix it so that I can live more comfortably in the country," doesn't he mean that he wants him to build something? Therefore "to live comfortably" means "to build." For this is the way Luther reasons. If someone says to a person who is facing away, "Turn this way," he indicates something which is in the power of that person to do. But thus far Luther has merely indulged in tomfoolery; now he spews out his blasphemies:—"I will turn to you" means "I will endeavor to turn, etc."

But how does he prove this scurrilous bit of sophistry? "If "to turn" means "endeavor" anywhere, why not everywhere?"[23] I will give him tit for tat. If a person who is not of sound mind is said to be furious, why does it not mean the same thing when Scripture attributes fury to God? If someone who is angry has boiling blood around his heart, why do we not think the same thing applies to God when Scripture says God is angry? If a person who has compassion feels distress, why do we not attribute distress to God? Now even if I had quite definitely interpreted "turn to me" to mean "try to turn to me," it would be far more tolerable than Luther's gloss on it: "Keep all the commandments, none of which you can keep."[24] But these things should be numbered among the delights of reading Luther. He accuses me of saying in an unqualified way that the testimony of Jeremiah "if you separate the precious from the worthless" indicates the freedom to choose, as if I attribute complete freedom to the will apart from grace.[25] But Luther should have remembered here what is said in *A Discussion* hundreds of times. Why was it necessary to say the same thing over and over whenever I cite a text, as if I were talking to schoolboys, not theologians—to say nothing of Luther, who never forgets, who is never puzzled, whom nothing ever escapes?

But finally he says goodbye to this pointless stuff—to which, however, he is always returning—and he teaches us with heroic authority that the word "turn" is used in Holy Scripture in two ways. "As used in the legal sense it expresses an order or command that requires not merely an attempt but a completely changed way of living: 'Let everyone turn away from his evil ways,' 'Turn to the Lord.' For there it involves fulfilling all the commands." And

23. *The Enslaved Will*, p. 77.
24. Erasmus' summary of Luther's position.
25. Jer. 15:19; *The Enslaved Will*, p. 77.

what shows this to be so? "As is sufficiently clear," he says. "In its evangelical usage," he says, "it expresses consolation and God's promises, which demand nothing of us and are offered to us by God's grace." Luther teaches us the two uses of this word. The first one, which is hyperbolic, he proves thus: "This is sufficiently clear"—he ought to have added "that everything is demanded, though nothing can be observed." For what mortal ever said that turning to God means keeping all the commandments rather than the beginning of a holy life? But let it be enough for us that Luther said it. How does he confirm the second usage? Psalm 125: "When the Lord turned the captivity of Sion" (or, as he teaches us to say, Zion).[26] Likewise: "Turn, my soul, to your rest."[27] Is Luther making a serious point here? When the Lord says that he is turning, he declares his grace. Does anyone deny this? He ought to have proved that whenever the Lord says "turn," it is an evangelical usage. For he declared that everything cited from Isaiah is evangelical usage except for the first passage. But in the other passages, which he does not except, the expression "turning" and similar words occur. But who is the source of this distinction of his? Nobody but him. Therefore the distinction of the ancient, orthodox fathers is more probable: when God says "turn" something is required from mankind, namely, that it make itself available to the grace which is offered; when he says "I will turn to you" he is promising that grace is available. This applies to the text from Jeremiah: "If you turn, I will turn to you" (Jer. 15:19). Both kinds of turning are expressed here: one part signifies the action of the human will; the other, the assistance of grace. Having discussed these points so felicitously, in his ovation he admonishes the filthy sophists together with yawning Discussion to distinguish the usage of the Law from that of the gospel, but in doing so they must follow Luther's pointer, which cannot go wrong. But see the lengths to which he carries hyperbole: the expression "turn" requires that we obey all the commandments of the Law, but "I will turn" requires absolutely nothing from us, not even faith, I imagine (Zech. 1:3).

After this auspicious beginning he takes up the passage from Ezekiel 18:21-22: "I myself live, says the Lord; I do not wish the death of the

---

26. Pss. 125:1 and 13:7. Erasmus twits Luther for using the spelling "Zion" instead of the usual "Sion."

27. Ps. 114:7; see *The Enslaved Will*, p. 77, where Luther refers (inaccurately) to Ps. 22.

sinner, etc."[28] Notice, my dear reader, the impudence of the man. The words of mine that he cites read thus: "In this chapter the phrases 'he turned,' 'he did,' 'he performed' constantly recur, in both a good and a bad sense. And where are those who claim that man does nothing, but is only passive to the action of grace?"[29] This is what Discussion says. Now listen to Luther: "See, I beg you, the extraordinary chain of reasoning. She was supposed to prove the endeavor and the effort, and she proves the complete deed, with everything accomplished by free will. I ask you, where are the people now who require grace and the Spirit? For he prattles away, saying: Ezekiel says, 'If a wicked man turns away and does what is right and lawful, he will live'; therefore the wicked man immediately does so and can do so. Ezekiel expresses what should be done; Discussion understands it to mean that it is being done and has been done, once again teaching us by this new grammar that 'to owe' means the same as 'to have,' 'to be required' means 'to be performed,' 'to demand' the same as 'to pay.'"[30] This is literally what Luther says. After that can anyone be surprised that I did not reply to him point by point? What can you respond to such drunken nonsense, to such patent falsehood and malice? This genuine Leviathan added "immediately has been done" and "is immediately had" on his own, not only shamelessly but also mindlessly. I infer that it can be done, though only with the help of grace.

With similar shamelessness he added that the human will can do everything without grace, although this passage, which he thoughtlessly reports, excludes only the opinion of those who teach that mankind can do nothing at all for his good but is merely passive to the operation of grace. He does not realize this, even though Discussion mentioned Karlstadt by name. If someone who writes this way is sober, then I never saw a drunk. He is equally sober when he sets one side over against the other as if they were completely contradictory: "Where are those who deny that the human will can do anything but say it is merely passive" and "Where are those, I ask you, who insist on grace and the Holy Spirit?"—as if it could never happen that the powers of nature should act together with the action of grace. But he himself confesses, I think, that in all the actions of nature the first cause acts principally but together with secondary

---

28. Here Erasmus combines Ezekiel 18:3 and 32, but in *A Discussion*, (p. 14) he quotes Ezekiel 18:21–23; in both passages the sense is similar.

29. *A Discussion*, p. 14.

30. *The Enslaved Will*, p. 78.

causes.[31] Nor has anyone disproved the opinion of those who do not
distinguish miracles from the ordinary processes of nature except by
their rarity. But to overlook some miracles that were once performed
when the time was right but have now become very rare because of
the circumstances of our time, we see that in the activity of grace the
Spirit of Christ always joins his action with natural feeling and powers
so that what is done will not seem prodigious and repellent. For no
one seeks out monstrosities; on the contrary, everyone shuns and flees
from them, inclined as we are to whatever has a relationship to nature.
You will find that the action of the Spirit was almost always such in
the apostles and other holy men. Nor does Luther deny this. Why
then does he get mixed up with a different opinion? Once again he
cockadoodledoos here that we join Pelagius in proclaiming "What
can you impute to someone who can do nothing, whether good or
evil?"[32] If Pelagius had proclaimed nothing more than this, he would
have been orthodox. As it is, he is numbered among the heretics
because he separated the action of the human will from the action of
grace. But Luther flees from the Pelagian heresy in such a way that
he thoughtlessly jumps from the frying pan headlong into the fire,
though there is a quite safe passage between the two.

Once more unhappy Discussion stumbles against the same stone:
when she cites the evidence of Ezekiel 18, "I do not desire the death of
a sinner but rather that he turn and live," (Ezek. 18:23, 32)[33] she makes
expressions of consolation into words of the Law, for now that he has
got hold of this interpretative trick, he bears down with it endlessly. If
these are not the words of the Law, why did he teach earlier that the
word "turn" contains the whole Law with all its commandments? He
will reply that here it is to be taken according to the usage of the gospel.
This is simply a shameless fantasy of Luther, for he could not produce
any evidence for it from Holy Scripture. It is one thing for God to
promise that he will turn Sion, quite another if he exhorts the sinner to
be turned or to turn himself (for this expression is also found and better

31. See *A Discussion* nn. 23, 25–26. Even though the *concursus generalis* (God's
general causality) was accepted by all, the degree of efficacy attributed to the
primary cause, God, or to secondary causes was much debated and has a bearing
on the power of man's will in moral acts. Generally theologians of the *via antiqua*
(such as Aquinas) tended to place more emphasis on God's causality, whereas
those of the *via moderna* (such as Gabriel Biel) assigned more efficacy to secondary
causes. See Oberman, *Harvest* 48–50.

32. *A Discussion*, p. 14; *The Enslaved Will*, p. 78.

33. See *The Enslaved Will*, n. 94, and *A Discussion*, p. 14.

translates the Greek ἐπιτρέψητε). As for the text he adduces from the Psalms, "Turn, my soul, to your rest,"[34] it tends to work against him; for whenever a person exhorts himself to contemplate heavenly things, the action of the will accommodating itself to grace is implied. What, then, does "I do not desire the death" mean? If we accept Luther's interpretation, it is equivalent to "I am merciful, I am not angry, I do not want to punish, I do not want you to die, I want to forgive you, I want to spare you." If God is not angry at a sinner, very many scriptural texts are lying, as when Paul writes in Romans 1, "For the heavens reveal the anger of God towards all the wickedness and injustice of mankind," and in the next chapter, "You treasure up for yourselves wrath on the day of wrath," and soon after, "wrath, indignation, tribulation, and distress against the soul of every man who does evil."[35]

You have heard Luther's gloss; now listen to the true interpretation. "I do not desire the death of a sinner," that is, I do not want the sinner to persist in his vices, lest he should die. What, then, do you wish?" I want him to turn from his shameful deeds and to achieve eternal life." These words, he says, proclaim the kindness of God, which inclines to mercy. I quite agree. But by implication a person who perseveres in sin is threatened with wrath and death. To whom is life promised? To the sinner? By no means, but rather to someone who turns himself. Grace impels the mind of the sinner; if he neglects it, if he closes his eyes and ears, what can you do with someone who refuses to be saved? God offers the sinner life; he offers to forget his previous sins; but he offers it to a sinner who repents: "Stop being a sinner, and my anger will immediately be changed to mercy and death will be replaced by life." Otherwise, if God did not desire the death of a sinner in an unqualified way, why does he throw so many thousands of sinners into hell? "Who does not know that there are a great number of places in Scripture which testify that the extraordinary mercy of God is free, accessible, available, ready at hand?" I grant it, but it is so to those who repent. Therefore whatever consolation of that sort there is in Scripture summons us to grace, but in such a way that it nevertheless requires the sinner to change his former life. Hence it is certainly not unreasonable to infer from such texts, however much they pertain to the gospel, that free will does exist in the natural order of things—which is what Luther denies. Of this sort is the text he quotes from Exodus 20:6: "I will have mercy on many thousands."[36]

---

34. Ps. 114:7 (which Luther had inaccurately cited as Ps. 22).

35. Rom. 1:18, 2:5, 2:8–9.

36. *The Enslaved Will*, p. 79.

These words pertain to the gospel, I grant it. But they are followed by "on those who love me." Is this enough? No, he adds: "and keep my commandments." Luther cleverly keeps quiet about this addition as well as about what preceded: "I am a mighty and jealous God, punishing sons for the wickedness of their fathers, to the third and fourth generation" (Exod. 20:5–6). You see that promises are joined with fearful threats, and mercy is not promised to just anyone but, rather, to those who love God and keep his commandments. I have already spoken about what he quotes from Matthew 11:28: "Come to me all of you." Of the same sort is the text in Paul: "You who are asleep, get up and rise from the dead and Christ will shine upon you" (Eph. 5:14). "Get up" and "rise" are expressions of impelling grace; "Christ will shine upon you," of consolation and promises.

Since, however, all orthodox interpreters agree that the dead whom the Lord called back to life present us with a type of the sinner who repents and turns to holiness, I think it is not without mysterious meaning that the Lord never aroused anyone without first calling upon him, a practice which was not, however, followed by the apostles. In Luke 7:14 he said to the young man, "Young man, I say to you, arise." In Mark 5:41 he called upon the daughter of the president of the synagogue: "*Talitha cumi,*" that is, "Child, I say to you, arise." In this passage those skilled in Hebrew advise us that *cumi* is a doubly conjugated verb, as if you should say, "Raise yourself up."[37] Similarly, he also called out to the brother of Martha, "Lazarus, come out" (John 11:43). Hence Luther is wrong when he infers that the power of free will is not confirmed by the words of the Law or the words of the gospel, since I have made it clear that it is proved by both.

But what did my Discussion infer from the words "I do not desire the death of the sinner"? That a commandment is being given which is to be kept? Quite the contrary, Discussion reasoned as follows:

37. Erasmus seems to refer to the fact that Hebrew (and Aramaic) verbs have multiple conjugations. *Cumi* belongs to the *pi'el* conjugation, the fundamental idea of which is "to busy oneself eagerly with the action indicated by the stem." See Gesenius' *Hebrew Grammar,* ed. E. Kautzsch, trans. A. E. Cowley (Oxford, 1910), 141. (I am grateful to my colleague, Professor Bernard Asen for this information.) I have not been able to discover any written commentary on Mark 5:41 which refers to the conjugation of *cumi,* but Erasmus had friends and acquaintances (such as Reuchlin and Oecolampadius) who knew Hebrew. A search of the database of the entire *Patrologia Latina* does not reveal any remarks about the grammatical character of *cumi.*

"Does the Lord in his goodness lament for the death of his people when he himself caused them to die? If he does not desire our death, surely we must impute it to our will if we perish."[38] Luther deliberately overlooks these words and obscures the matter with much convoluted verbiage, presenting us with new laws which he fashions and refashions at his whim. "An expression of the Law is directed only at those who do not feel or recognize their sins. So too, an expression of grace comes only to those who feel their sins, are afflicted by them, and are tempted to despair."[39] We utterly reject those hyperbolic laws of his. Quite the contrary, the Law enlightens well-disposed people so that they do not fall into sin; and words of promise are very often spoken to a rebellious people who turn God's kindness to them into a license to sin. And the commandment "Love the Lord, your God etc."[40] does not indicate that we ought to perform something that we cannot do but rather admonishes us that God is to be preferred before all creatures and that we should always make progress in loving him—which is within the power of mankind, with the help of grace.

And so there is nothing left for Luther to do but to triumph, if we will only concede to him that "I do not desire the death of the sinner" means "I am not angry with the sinner, but I want him to turn," that is, "not observe any of the commandments, which cannot be observed, but merely accept grace and do whatever he wants." How, then, does he triumph? He reckons that no passage can be cited which teaches more clearly that free will, itself being alone, does nothing but get worse and worse unless God with such great gentleness offers it the mercy he has in store for it. What does Luther mean when he says "itself being alone"? Does anyone teach that free will can do anything effectively to reach justification apart from grace? When it adapts itself—or, if you prefer, makes itself available—to impelling grace, it is not alone. Then again, what does he mean when he says "get worse and worse"? His own teaching, on the other hand, is that free will is no more than an empty name and that it cannot do anything at all, whether for good or evil, that it does not act with grace or without it but is acted upon by God. In some places he attributes free will to mankind in lesser matters; in other places he denies that a person can pick up a straw from the ground by the force

38. *A Discussion,* p. 14.
39. *The Enslaved Will,* pp. 79–80.
40. Matt. 22:37 (Mark 12:30, Luke 10:27).

of free will.[41] Such is the consistency of the man who so often charges me with not sticking to the issue at hand.

But to pass over the rest of his empty babble, what does Luther mean when he says, "unless you believe God is so frivolous that he pours forth words of promise so copiously not because they are needed for our salvation but because he takes sheer delight in loquacity." What new sort of eloquence is this? Doesn't this clause seem to mean that the numerous passages in Scripture where God summons sinners to repentance contribute nothing to our salvation but that God was thus pleased to babble away out of frivolity and garrulity?[42] But if he had said "unless you do believe," perhaps his language might have seemed less absurd.[43] We do not believe this, my good man. Quite the contrary, we are fully persuaded that God achieves the same goal by threats and alarms together with blandishments and promises, that is, to overcome our hardness of heart and to lead us to amendment, except that according to the outcome of his overtures he is more likely to frighten the headstrong and haughty with threats and afflictions while he summons with blandishments those who tend to despair. If the haughty are converted he ceases to threaten; if the others draw back from despair he promises that grace is available to them if they receive him. But with this proviso: that the human will makes some contribution to the conversion of those who are admonished by threats or summoned by promises. Otherwise, why are some converted while others harden their hearts all the more?

The secret and revealed wills of God

Here Luther has discovered another piece of sophistry in order to exclude all action on the part of the human will: God's secret will in such matters is not to be inquired into but to be worshipped. Once

41. In his *Assertio,* article 36 (WA 7 146:4–8; CWE 76 pp. 304–5) Luther asserts that "no one has it within his control to intend anything, good or evil, but rather . . . all things occur by absolute necessity."

42. That is, since Luther claimed that God's commandments cannot be kept, they contribute nothing to salvation and thus constitute mere loquacity on God's part.

43. Luther's sentence can be epitomized as follows: God's promises show that free will is impotent unless you should believe (*credas*) that God was merely babbling. Erasmus seems to mean that the use of the subjunctive *credas* (you should believe, happen to believe, may believe) leaves open the possibility of thinking God is a babbler, whereas the indicative *credis* (you do believe) would have eliminated that possibility.

again he has an axe to cut through all knotty questions. I do not deny that in some matters God's will acts in such a way that we should adore rather than scrutinize his counsel; but here I am arguing from Scripture that there is something inherent in the human will which is of such great moment that one person, when he is touched by grace, turns to it and is saved, another person turns away and perishes. But if nothing is to be imputed to the human will, but only God's will matters, why does God complain so often in Scripture that he has not been listened to, neither when he commands nor when he coaxes, neither when he frightens nor when he flatters? How can he be so shameless as to cry out "Why will you die, O house of Israel?"[44] when their death occurs because of his secret will, which must be adored?

Here we are presented with the distinction between God as he is preached and God as he is in his own nature, to make it seem by novel language that Luther is introducing something never heard of up to now, whereas this very commonplace distinction can be used to answer the question how God does not wish the death of a sinner and yet wishes it: he does not wish it by his signified will[45] and he does wish it by his effective will; or he wishes and does not wish it conditionally, that is, he does not wish it if the person himself wishes to turn away from sin and he does wish it if the sinner does not wish to repent. But in fact we have already excluded this distinction between God preached and God not preached, for we are inferring what God's will is as it is expressed for us in Holy Scripture;[46] we adore that secret

44. Ezek. 18:31, 33:11.

45. Latin *voluntate signi*, God's revealed will for his creation; see Oberman, *Harvest* 476 and Peter Lombard, *Sententiae* I dist. 45.7–12 (PL 192 643–44).

46. The distinction between *deus praedicatus* (God as revealed and preached) and *deus absconditus* (God as hidden) is analogous to the distinction between God's *potentia ordinata* (ordained power) and his *potentia absoluta* (absolute, unlimited power). In agreement with the view of Aquinas, late medieval scholastics advanced the view that the ordinary course of nature is in accordance with God's ordained power, which God has conceded to nature as well as to men in the governance of their own affairs in keeping with the revealed divine laws of Scripture. Theologians also attributed an absolute power to God, which in the thirteenth-century view (including that of Aquinas) was regarded as what God by his absolute power might have done but chose not to do. In the fourteenth and fifteenth centuries it became for some theologians a power to intervene and change or halt the ordinary courses of nature and events, so that divine intervention and miracles were attributed to *potentia absoluta*. In the conclusion

will hidden in its darkness, we do not examine it. But since he croaks away at us so often about God preached and not preached, to keep from seeming to have made this gloss up out of his own head, he cites for us Paul in 2 Thessalonians 2:4, where he is speaking about the Antichrist: "He is lifted up above everything which is called god and which is worshipped." This newfangled exegete takes "what is called and what is worshipped" to mean "God preached." He did not repeat the words of Paul out of his own head, I agree, but he fabricated out of his own brain an interpretation that is both forced and inconsistent.

First of all, what ancient interpreter ever dreamed what Luther brings up? Did Jerome, did Ambrose or Chrysostom or Theophylact or Augustine or Bede or Thomas?[47] Theophylact takes the text to mean that the Antichrist will abolish the worship of idols so that he alone might be considered as god, noting also that the Antichrist will not say he is God but will strive by his deeds to be considered as god. But Luther scorns the interpretations of the ancient fathers. Therefore let us examine this new interpretation of his in the light of the language of Paul, whose words he deliberately does not report lest they immediately betray how shameless his interpretation is. First of all, he interprets "what is called and worshipped as God" as meaning God not as he is but as he has become known to us. I ask Luther whether someone who adores God can rightly be said to worship him. He will grant it, I think. But a little before he himself said that that secret will, that is, the divine nature as it is, should be adored with the deepest veneration, and here he explains the matter differently.[48] Quite the contrary, we worship most profoundly that ineffable, unknowable, and inscrutable nature of God. And lest Luther should seek to evade the difficulty here, the translation "what is worshipped" is σέβασμα in Greek, derived from σέβομαι, which means "I venerate religiously something which is full of majesty."

Moreover, since Luther here mentions the Corycian cavern, where the majesty of the deity overwhelms human knowledge,

---

of *The Shield-Bearer* 2, Erasmus suggests that Luther also held the highly unusual view that human souls were saved only by God's *potentia absoluta*.

47. None of these exegetes agree with Luther in applying 2 Thess. 2:4 to the distinction between God's revealed and his hidden will. All apply it to the Antichrist's claim to divine worship.

48. That is, Luther earlier said God's hidden will should be adored, but here he says that God's signified or preached will should be worshipped or adored.

the passage about it primarily concerns adoration.[49] Furthermore, phrases separated by Paul are joined together by Luther, who says "what is called and worshipped as God," whereas Paul's words are "over everything which is called God or which is worshipped." The Greek reads as follows: ἐπὶ πάντα λεγόμενον θεὸν ἢ σέβασμα that is, "above everyone who is called God or anything else worthy of religious veneration," so that we understand σέβασμα to mean the shrines or idols of the gentiles. For the phrase "what is called" refers separately to each element, to God and to the noun σέβασμα, which was paraphrased by the translator as "what is worshipped." Paul added "what is called" precisely to show both that those who are called gods are not gods and that what are called *sebasmata* are not *sebasmata*. For Paul never applies the name God to anyone except the true God; or if he applies it to others, he adds something to let us know he is speaking of those who are falsely held to be gods, as when he says "the god of this world" (2 Cor. 4:4) and 1 Corinthians 8:5, "for although there are those who are called gods," using the same word "called" to signify that here too he is speaking of false gods. Paul also uses the same word, σέβασμα, in Luke's Acts: "For as I went along looking at your statues, I also found an altar on which was written 'to the unknown god.'" What is translated as "statues" is σεβάσματα in the Greek, a word that includes temples and altars and shrines and sanctuaries and statues. And Luther explains the same word here as "God as he is worshipped."

But wait a minute, my dear reader, you have not yet heard all the trickery Luther employs in this interpretation. He craftily inverts the word order. Everyone knows that it makes a great deal of difference whether you say "This craftsman is much spoken of" or "This man is much spoken of as a craftsman," for the second expression implies he is said "to be," whereas the first does not. In the first phrase the person who is a craftsman is said to be famous; in the second someone is said to be a craftsman who may not be one. Now if Paul had put "god" and *sebasma* before the phrase "is called," the meaning would at any rate have been ambiguous.[50] As it is, since both nouns follow the verb, there can be no other meaning except that there are those who are called gods although they are not and that there are *sebasmata* that are called so although they are not. In brief, I have shown you

49. On the Corycian cavern, see *The Enslaved Will*, n. 97.

50. That is, if Paul had said "the god or the cult object that is spoken of," he might have implied that he was speaking of the true God or a genuine cult object.

how conscientiously, how knowledgeably, how trustworthily Luther treats Holy Scripture for us, scorning all exegetes, whether ancient or modern; I trust this will make it quite clear to everyone how much credit we should give him in other places.

In fact, there was no need for such a distinction concerning God's will, because both the signified will and the effective will wish the sinner, if he persists, to go to hell. This distinction would have been appropriate if someone had argued as follows: if whatever God wishes happens, why do not all sinners change their ways? By the signified will he wishes that all do so, but not by his effective will. He could make it happen if he willed it in an unqualified way. And so whenever Luther is hard pressed by arguments he will take refuge in that inscrutable will of God and will make him God not preached where we assert God preached. It is very difficult to fight with this man, who does not recognize the laws of anyone else and time and again prescribes so many unheard-of laws for us. He demands that we grant there is a certain inscrutable will of God. We do so. He wants it to be adored. We adore it. What follows from this? Therefore Luther's paradoxes are true. What paradoxes? That all of Scripture is full of commandments, threats, promises, and blandishments, but the minds of mankind are not moved by any of them except when God wishes to impart sanctifying grace individually to some of them; that the laws and threats only point out sin; that the promises and blandishments only point out that grace is available; that nevertheless, because the will of good and bad alike is in no way free, neither the conferral of grace nor the thrust of the Law does them any good unless God draws both groups to salvation by his will, which it is wrong to speak about. And yet guilt is imputed to those who can do nothing of themselves, just as if they could; and they are condemned without deserving it—as he later candidly confesses—so that God may not seem unjust; and those who have not deserved anything, indeed have not even tried to deserve anything, are given immortality. But nevertheless, at the same time God is said to be absolutely just, even though it is characteristic of justice to give rewards which are deserved. But here he has another paradox: that faith has entirely perished unless God seems to be absolutely unjust but is believed to be absolutely just. This is the person who charges that I turn an indefinite proposition into a universal! God commands what we cannot perform or wish to perform but are nevertheless bound to perform; and he imputes guilt to our will, which was corrupted not by us but by our first parents, and he imputes it also to the justified. But why does he blame us for what we cannot perform and he does not wish to change? Luther calls upon God not preached and is off the hook!

Cockadoodledooing once again, he charges that I have forgotten the question at issue and prove something other than what I proposed. When I am about to cite evidence from Scripture, I begin as follows: "In the hope that truth may everywhere prevail, shining forth, it may be, from this discussion of Scripture like fire from the percussion of flints. First of all, it cannot be denied that there are many passages in Holy Scripture which clearly seem to support the freedom of the human will; and on the other hand, some which seem to deny it completely. Yet it is certain that Scripture cannot contradict itself, since it all proceeds from the same Spirit. And so we shall first review those which confirm our opinion; then we shall attempt to explain those which seem to oppose it."[51] This is the opening of the argument from scriptural passages in *A Discussion*. Now if the passages did not clearly establish free will and did not clearly eliminate it, still I would have fulfilled my obligation in the argument. Thus in the arguments of "the preliminary opposition,"[52] as the scholastics say, theologians sometimes cite and draw conclusions from texts on either side, and in the end they settle the matter by balancing the scale of truth. Having cited one passage, I go right on to recount various opinions about free will. Some I reject, but in such a way as to make it clear that I have no quarrel with them; some I indicate are not to be rejected, but they are such that if one of them wins out, Luther's teaching is defeated. To these taken together I apply the evidence I bring forth from Scripture. I make no attempt to conceal the opinions with which I particularly have to disagree; against them taken together I hurl the weapons of debate. And what do I say in this place? These passages must all be pointless once you posit necessity either in good deeds or bad. When I say this am I attributing everything to free will or rather excluding the opinion of Wyclif, which Luther in the heat of the argument approves of in *Assertion*,[53] though it is inconsistent of him to do so? Therefore Discussion does not frequently "blunder on one string—or "strynge" as Luther's manuscript has it—but Luther all too frequently blunders in his heartstring.[54]

51. *A Discussion*, p. 6.

52. See n. 4, above.

53. *Assertio*, article 36 (CWE 76 306).

54. The wordplay cannot be captured in English. Erasmus means that in *De servo arbitrio* Luther quoted Horace (*Ars poetica* 355–56) as *eadem corda oberret* (blunders

Finally, skipping over a good deal, he takes up that text in
Deuteronomy 30:11–14: "The commandment that I lay upon you
this day is not beyond you, nor is it located far away, etc." Here this
Braggadocchio[55] triumphs, giving us a grammar lesson on the meaning
of "above," "below," "in front of," "behind," "on the right," and
"on the left." I said that these words signify a propensity to keeping
the commandments, arguing, not making any pronouncement; and
if I had done so, what danger would there be in that, since our Lord
himself says in the gospel, "My yoke is easy and my burden light"?
(Matt. 11:30) But Luther exclaims: "What need now for Christ?
What need now for the Holy Spirit? How foolish it was for Christ,
by shedding his blood, to purchase for us a Spirit we do not need,
so that we might become more ready to keep the commandments,
when we are already so by nature." And he babbles away about many
other things of this ilk, always separating grace from free will—for I
formerly begged leave to use this common expression—whereas in
so many places I have coupled grace with free will in order that the
human will might be effective. He pretends not to notice the phrase
added here by Discussion: "if none of this is in our power in any
way at all."[56] A person who says "in any way at all" is not attributing
everything to free will. What makes the commandment difficult? A
will that is lazy. What makes it easy? Grace and a well-disposed will.
He says that "above" here must not be referred to our power but
rather to a place, in accord with grammar, as even boys in grammar
school know. To be sure. Therefore what is above us is on the roof;
what is below us is in the wine cellar. Quite the contrary, even among
boys in grammar school, "above," "below," "far," "near" refer more
often to dignity or ability than to a spatial position.

When Ovid writes, "However crushed I am and fallen even lower
than you, than whom nothing could be lower,"[57] does he mean that
he was lying under the feet of the person, who was himself prostrate
under the feet of all persons? Again, when we say, "You are far from
him whom you are trying to imitate," is the person addressed standing
in a place far removed in distance from the other person? Likewise,
when a person says, "You are getting close to the truth," does he

on the same string), where *chorda* is the more correct spelling. Erasmus goes on to
use *corde* (heart), where *c* without *h* is the correct spelling.

55. Latin *miles gloriosus* (boastful soldier), the title of a play by Plautus.

56. *A Discussion*, p. 16.

57. Ovid, *Tristia* 5.8.1–2; Erasmus slightly adapts the quotation to his context.

mean that the distance is short? When you read in the gospel, "He is above everyone" (John 3:31), do you understand that Christ surpasses everyone in dignity or that he is located in the highest place? So much for the grammar Luther teaches us. But let us grant what is the case, that Moses is indeed using figurative language but nevertheless he does so to signify that the commandment is presented to them so as to be ready at hand, not far to seek. What is the thrust of what Moses says except to deprive the people of any excuse if they fail to observe what is commanded? That is the meaning which Paul also assigns to this text in Romans 10:6–9, if we are to believe Chrysostom and Theophylact.[58] And even if that were not what Moses meant, I would still have a debater's right to twist the words in my favor. For what is ready at hand is certainly easier to get than what must be sought elsewhere.

Now let us look at Luther's interpretation. "Moses," he says, "testifies that he has done his duty, has laid down a law in which there is nothing that anyone can observe, so that they would have no reason to remonstrate with Moses, who has done what he was ordered to do, but rather with God, who imposed such a harsh law on his people, a law which they were required to keep unless they preferred to perish; and yet the one who commanded that the law be kept knew that none of them could carry it out."[59] I imagine Moses was not unaware of this, since he dealt with the people in such lengthy speeches, binding them with so many solemn obligations and ceremonies, for no other reason than to deceive them and lure them into a pit, so that once they have fallen they may know that they cannot perform what is demanded of them. Luther elegantly makes it clear that Moses is excused, but he shamelessly adds that the people have no excuse, and he even more shamelessly invents a God who commands, demands, inculcates so many things that cannot be observed at all, frightening them all the while, threatening them, destroying them.

Meanwhile he re-echoes his dogma at us. But that is the very reason we are protesting against him! I have demonstrated that his proof from Paul's "Through the Law comes the knowledge of sin" is harsh, absurd, and incoherent. "In these words of Moses," he says, "where is there any mention of free will?" I did not say that it is mentioned but rather that the words clearly imply that the human will

---

58. Chrysostom, *Commentarius in epistolam ad Romanos* 17.2 (PG 60 566); Theophylact, *Expositio in epistolam ad Romanos* 10.4–9 (PG 124 475–78).

59. Erasmus here summarizes p. 85 of *The Enslaved Will*.

can do something, and that if it fails to do its part, it is condemned through its own fault, and that if it does its part with the help of grace it is saved. We have already heard that cockadoodledoo of his many times: that words of command, demanding, threatening, exhorting do not establish a deed or the power to do anything; but from such words, according to the common sense to which Luther earlier gave the final decision in interpreting Holy Scripture, we can infer some such power. We make the same reply to his quibble about subjunctive, optative, and imperative verbs, and about indicative verbs used in an imperative sense: they do not establish a deed or the power to do anything, but they do indicate some power, unless the person who issued the commands is either stupid or insane or tyrannical. As for the inscrutable will, just as I grant that it is sometimes relevant, so too I distinctly deny that it is relevant to these numerous commandments. I care nothing about asseverations; I require Scripture and arguments.

In this passage he sings his own praises. "Let Discussion now go on," he says, "and tell us how it can be that a single, private person sees what the leading figures of so many ages have not seen." What has he taught that is worthy of a triumph? "Above" and "below," "far" and "near" are adverbs of place. But he neglects to say that they are most frequently applied to dignity, likeness, or ability, and the Apostle uses them in that way. But if Luther does not want to depart in any way from the literal use of words, how did the people have the commandment in their mouths as Moses explained it? Rather it was in his mouth and in their ears. But how could it be in their hearts, since many opposed the Law? Paul interprets "in their hearts" to mean "by faith" and "in their mouths" to mean "by professing it" (Rom. 10:10). And these very words, "to have it in their mouths," "to have it in their hearts," however you interpret them, indicate figuratively that the people can readily observe them if they want to. Indeed, since grace was available, they understood what they were told, they remembered it, they recited it with their mouths, so that there was nothing left to do but to manifest it in their deeds. And here he never stops croaking away at us about the issue and the probable opinion and the full power of the human will apart from grace, not considering that anyone will read my *Discussion* and catch him out in his malicious lies. What can you do with a debater who repeats these things in each section, thrusts them in over and over, hammers away at them, so that out of very weariness we are put off from replying to them? God does not wish to seem cruel and unjust on the one hand and to be believed to be just and merciful on the other. Quite the contrary, he has revealed to us many indications of his supreme justice and clemency, so that when we have seen such evidence we may believe them in other matters where our intellect cannot attain to the counsels of divine providence.

Erasmus' Response to Luther's Presentation of His Case

Is mankind universally sinful and lacking free will?

After this he prepares a fresh triumph: Discussion lies prostrate, covered with stab wounds, pierced not only by the weapons of the enemy but also by all the weapons she hurled at the enemy, which have been thrown back into her vitals. And yet the victor brings up another battle line, but more for the sake of the triumph than of battle. For who would think it worthwhile to fight against a lifeless corpse? But he does not bring up the whole battle line. For there would be no end of it, since every single jot and tittle support his dogma. You recognize, my dear reader, the hyperbole! He brings up only Paul and the evangelist John, in whom he will demonstrate how well he could distort texts if he had wished to display his power in other parts of Scripture. But I do not know whether it is for me to reply to these arguments. For Discussion had undertaken primarily to oppose two opinions: according to one, free will in itself can do nothing except evil, and in a good work it is not active but merely passive; according to the other, which is Luther's, free will is a meaningless phrase and can do nothing, either for good or evil. I have often declared that I neither approve nor disapprove of the opinion of the scholastics that free will by its own power can merit justifying grace at least *de congruo*,[60] but I am more inclined to approve than to disapprove.

I defended the opinion of Augustine, who teaches that free will does exist in mankind but that, because of sin, it is ineffective in obtaining justifying grace without the help of grace.[61] But he posits will and striving in mankind, though he claims it is ineffective; he posits impelling grace, which does not yet justify, and hence he posits that a person can stand on a middle ground, a place of transition, as it were, where a person can be numbered neither among the wicked

---

60. See *A Discussion*, n. 20.

61. Erasmus had explained the four opinions he gives here, those of Augustine (together with Thomas Aquinas), the scholastics of the *via moderna*, Karlstadt, and Luther at greater length in *A Discussion*, pp. 7–11.

nor among the justified but rather lives within the hand of grace, so to speak, which softens up the material it works on.[62] For he says that to desire grace is a first move made by grace;[63] still, many desire grace but live in sin. Yet he attributes this much to free will: it can turn away from the grace offered to it; it can make itself available to grace; it can withdraw from the grace it has obtained, either by negligence if it does not recognize grace as a gift meant to earn interest, or by arrogance if it claims for itself what belongs to God. For in good works Augustine does not allow man to claim even the tiniest bit for himself, since even what free will can do is a gift of God. By "good" I think he means what makes a person blessed, for there are various kinds of goods. But he thinks a person's will is active and acted upon in a good work, that is, it cooperates with grace. Now if Luther is directing his battle line against those who teach that free will can attain to justifying grace merely by its natural powers, he can take it up with others, not with me.

But let us take a look at this battle line of his. "Paul," he says, "writing to the Romans, takes issue with free will in defense of grace."[64] I immediately showed that what he assumes is false. For Paul is doing something else there: clearly he wants to check the arrogance of the philosophers, who scorned the grace of God as if they were perfect. But if Luther, who has so often said that free will does not exist and that everything happens by absolute necessity, is trying here to make the point that free will is not adequate for salvation without grace, I certainly agree with him. For grace is not incompatible with free will: it helps a weak will and changes it from more or less free to even freer. But come now, what does Paul really say? "The wrath of God is revealed from heaven upon all wickedness and the unrighteousness of men, who hold the truth of God in unrighteousness."[65] Luther

62. The comparison seems to come from kneading dough.

63. An almost direct quotation from *De correptione et gratia* 1.2 (PL 44 917); but in that work Augustine also recommends his *De gratia et libero arbitrio*, and Erasmus' summary here of Augustine's teaching about free will could be drawn from many of his works.

64. *The Enslaved Will* p. 86.

65. Rom. 1:18. The presence or absence of a comma after "men" (in either Latin or English) is crucial: with it the following clause is non-restrictive (all men do hold the truth in unrighteousness—Luther's position); without it the clause is restrictive (only those men who hold it in unrighteousness—Erasmus' position). In his *Annotations on Romans* Erasmus says the clause applies only to pagan philosophers (CWE 56 p. 47).

claims that the language in this passage is general, or rather, universal; first, that it pertains to all mankind, and then that we should accept as fact that whatever either the gentiles or the Jews did without faith in Christ was wicked and damnable, though what follows in Paul makes it clear that this passage applies to the gentiles: "What may be known about God was revealed among them. For his invisible qualities, from the creation of the world, etc." (Rom. 1:19–20). But this point is not very important. In fact, I showed before that the crimes to which Paul is referring do not apply to all the gentiles, but that the human race in general is being accused, not individual persons,[66] and that most people are such, so that a few exceptions do not preclude a general statement—something that happens frequently in Scripture, as Origen, Ambrose, and Augustine teach, giving many examples.[67] Before long I will take up the other point.

At the same time he leaves no stone unturned in an attempt to make an indefinite proposition into a universal one. "In this passage," he states, "I say that in Paul the meaning is the same if you said 'upon all the wickedness of men' or if you said 'upon the wickedness of all men.' For Paul follows the Hebrew idiom almost always." So says Luther, but he is the only one who does. See where he looks for support—from a Hebrew idiom. Sometimes Latin speakers also say "man" for "every man," as when they say "man is a rational animal." But because neither we nor the Jews always do this, Luther's argument is weak. But imagine that Paul had said "all men." How does that make the proposition universal, since he limits it by what follows: "of those who hold the truth of God in unrighteousness"? Though this applies to philosophers who lead shameful lives, it does not apply to all pagans, many of whom simply went wrong because they did not know the truth that was known to the philosophers. He also looks for support in the Greek article. "The Greek," he says, "does not have 'of those who hold' but 'of men holding,' as if this were a modifier, as it were, applying to all men, just as we say 'our Father who art in heaven.'" This is what he says. If the Greek article distinguishes our heavenly Father from our earthly father, then here, too, "of men holding" distinguishes the philosophers who hold the known truth in their unrighteousness from those who do not hold it, according to

66. See *The Shield-Bearer* 2, CWE 77 488–92.

67. Cf. Origen *Commentarii in Matthaeum* 18 (PG 13 1157–82); Ambrose, *De spiritu sancto* 3 [13] (PL 16 712–17); Augustine, *De spiritu et littera* 12.19 (PL 44 211–12).

Origen's interpretation.[68] Where, then, is the universal statement? It is probable that many Jews were saved after Christ's death even though they did not expressly believe that Christ was God and man, born of the Virgin Mary, sitting at the right hand of the Father, because these teachings had not yet been preached. Whatever sort of faith they had was sufficient for the time being. What if among the gentiles there were also some whose faith God approved of? For there were some who believed that God is the supreme mind, eternal, omnipotent, beyond our understanding, greater and better than anything we can imagine, the creator and governor of all things, who rewards piety and takes vengeance on wickedness.

It does not matter what they called this mind—the world, nature, Jove or some other name—with the understanding that God's goodness has supplied what is lacking to their natural powers. I want this to be said, however, just for the sake of argument, even though St. Ambrose in his book *The Calling of the Gentiles* expresses the opinion more than once that the providence of God has never been lacking to any era, people, or person.[69] Actually, when it is said that the anger of God is revealed, it is not to show that before the gospel no one knew that God takes vengeance on evildoers, since the Apostle writes about the philosophers, "who, though they recognized the righteousness of God, etc." (Rom. 1:32), but rather to show that after grace had been offered to all, they would now appear inexcusable for scorning the great gift that was offered to them. But Luther's inference is absurd: anger is revealed; therefore no one knew he deserved vengeance. It is revealed by being preached very clearly throughout the world; it is revealed so that any excuse, whether ignorance or despair, is eliminated, whereas previously many did not know they were sinning, and some did not believe that God exists or that the soul survives apart from the body.

Now, supposing that these revelations apply to all who did not believe in the gospel, it does not immediately follow that what is most outstanding in mankind is wickedness. For even though we grant that moral virtues are not sufficient to gain evangelical justification without faith, people still were not doing wicked deeds when they honored their parents, loved their children and wives, supported the poor, sick, and afflicted—all of which many of them did out of no other motive than that they considered such deeds in themselves to

68. *Commentarii in epistolam ad Romanos* 1.16 (PG 14 861).

69. Pseudo-Ambrose, *De vocatione omnium gentium* 2.25, 2.29, 2.31 (PL 51 710, 715–19).

be worthy of a good man and because they wanted the same things to be done for them if they fell into similar circumstances. You would have found such persons more readily among the uneducated than among the philosophers, if we are to believe their satirists.[70] Now the highest mental power, by which they knew God and through which they perceived and desired what is honorable, was not wicked simply because many were corrupted by the desires of the flesh and fell into shameful practices. And they did not lack free will simply because they abused it. But let us concede the point Luther is so eager to win, that all, both Jews and gentiles, were wicked before they believed in the gospel—which is quite false—how does that impugn my opinion? Is it true that wherever there is sin, there is no free will, since Augustine does not deprive even the Pharaoh of free will?[71] But if Luther is trying to show that the power of free will is not sufficient for salvation without the assistance of grace, I quite agree with him, as I said. But before the grace of the gospel had been sufficiently preached, that vague faith in the Anointed One was sufficient for the Jews, though it was not sufficient once the light of the gospel flashed out. Perhaps such persons were also found among the gentiles. And from that arose a stumbling block to the Jews and the contempt of the gentiles (1 Cor. 1:23). Thus the dawning light of the gospel made those who were formerly justified no longer justified if they did not believe in the gospel. And that is what Paul means when he says, "The anger of God is revealed from heaven upon all wickedness" (Rom. 1:18).

And so the anger of God would have been revealed in this way even upon many Jews who are now in heaven if they had not believed the gospel when it was preached, even though it is probable they did not know many truths revealed by the gospel, such as the divine and human natures joined in one hypostasis,[72] the consubstantiality of the Son with the Father, the Holy Spirit as God proceeding from each of them, the virgin birth, the resurrection, the ascension, the sitting at the right hand of the Father, the body and the blood received in the eucharist, and the other sacraments of the church. Moreover, just as someone who is justified is not immediately said to lack all

---

70. Philosophers were especially attacked in Aristophanes' *The Clouds* and Lucian's *Auction of the Philosophers* and *The Fisherman*.

71. *De gratia et libero arbitrio* 23.45 (PL 44 911).

72. "Hypostasis" is a technical term in trinitarian theology, meaning "substance" or "person." Divinity and humanity (two natures) are united in one substance in Christ.

vices, so too those who are said to be not justified are not so called because there is nothing good about them but because they are subject to many and great sins. But Luther makes this inference: they lack someone to jûstify them; therefore the very best they have is wicked. He delights in such hyperboles. Now he also distorts the phrase "in their thoughts," which in Greek is διαλογισμοῖς (Rom. 1:21), a word that seems to apply to those who are reasoning about something.[73] For Paul does not condemn them because they reasoned badly about God, whose sempiternal godhead they fully understood, but because they were corrupted by their desires and did not worship the God they knew as they should have. Thus Seneca mocks the worship of the gods, but he still thinks it should be observed, not because it is pious but because it is commanded by the public laws.[74] Just because reason without grace is overthrown by the passions, it does not follow that there is no propensity for good. And at the same time Luther is inconsistent. Over and over he denied that there is any striving towards virtue, and he says it again here. Nevertheless, seemingly forgetting himself, he says here: "It is impossible that no one among the Jews and gentiles acted and strove with the full force of his free will." And it does not follow that because the striving was imperfect in the absence of grace therefore it was wicked.

Moreover, as for Paul's testimony, "All have turned aside,"[75] which Luther distorts so as to apply it to all Jews, I have shown that it cannot refer to individual persons but is spoken generally, because many were such before the gospel, as is clear from their persecution of Christ. Luther makes an exception of those who were in the Spirit. But there were also such persons among the Jews before the spreading of the gospel and perhaps even among the gentiles, since the law of Moses, which was not given to all, was not binding on all, and the gentiles were not required to have a strict faith in all the articles, such as was required of the Jews, and of Christians even more strictly. For Luther applies this passage in Paul to the whole race of mortals, whereas holy Doctors affirm that it is spoken specifically about the Jews, whom he reproaches with the words of the Law, lest they should think these

---

73. Luther had glossed the Greek word as *argutis disputationibus* (subtle disputations), whereas Erasmus takes it to mean simply "thoughts, reflections."

74. Seneca mocks superficial, external worship of the gods in *Epistulae morales* 95.47–49 and 115.5; *De beneficiis* 1.6.3; and *Quaestiones naturales* 4.6.1–3. He approves of prescribed public prayers in *De clementia* 1.19.7–8.

75. Rom. 3:12, citing Ps. 13:3.

accusations pertain to the gentiles. They give two reasons for thinking the words are addressed to the Jews: first, for reasons proper to their own case, Paul directs against the gentiles such charges as he here levels at the Jews, namely in chapter 1; second, because Paul adds, "But we know that whatever the Law says is said to those who are under the Law."[76]

"But," Luther will say, "if these charges apply to the Jews, they apply all the more to the gentiles living without the Law, without God." Does he therefore want to claim that all these accusations are directed against the whole human race, with no exceptions whatever? Let him tell us, then, what period God had in mind, before the Law or under the Law, before the preaching of the gospel or afterwards? Does he have all periods in mind when he says what is reported by Paul? But before the Law there were Abel, Enoch, Noah, Melchizedek, Job, to whom these words do not apply at all. Under the Law many were praised under the heading of justice, and Scripture testifies that they sought God with all their heart, like David himself in this text: "With all my heart I sought you; do not hold me back from your commandments" (Ps. 118:10). But perish the thought that we should apply these words to the whole church of Christ.[77] Jerome and other reputable exegetes think the prophecy in this psalm[78] should be referred to the time when the Lord suffered, when all turned away from him, so much so that even the prince of the apostles forswore him.[79] But in fact the harsh things said here do not apply to these people or to Nicodemus or to the other men and women who were disciples of the Lord. Indeed, this episode tells about the piety of the women who provided the aromatic ointments;[80] nor did all the Jews hurl blasphemies at Jesus, nor did all agree to the death of an innocent man—to say nothing, for the moment, about the Jews who lived far

---

76. Rom. 1:17 and 3:19; cf. Chrysostom *Commentarius in epistulam ad Romanos* 7.2 (PG 6 441–42); Augustine *De spiritu et littera* 26.44 (PL 44 227–28) and *Contra secundum Iuliani responsionem imperfectum opus* 2.175 (PL 45 1217); and Jerome, *Commentariorum in epistolam ad Ephesios libri tres* 1.22–23 (PL 26 463).

77. Not the words in the preceding sentence but Paul's condemnations in Rom. 1:18 and 3:10–18.

78. That is, Ps. 13:1–3, cited by Paul in Rom. 3:10–13.

79. Jerome, *Commentarii in Esaiam* 1.1.21 and 16.59.7–8 (CCSL 73 20:9–12 and 73A 682:25–28); Augustine, *Contra secundum Iuliani responsionem imperfectum opus* 2.175 (PL 45 1217).

80. John 19:39–40; Luke 23:55–24:1.

away, scattered throughout the world and ignorant of what was going on in Jerusalem.

And so, even if we grant that these charges should be applied to the Jews, they cannot refer to all of them because we read in the same psalm: "who devour my people like a morsel of bread" (Ps. 13:4). How is it fitting to call them the people of God if they are the object of such harsh reproaches as could never be leveled even at all the pagans? Add to that the fact that the opening of the psalm shows that they are not spoken against all mankind but only against the wicked. For the psalm begins thus: "The fool said in his heart, 'There is no God'" (Ps. 13:1). And then, in the sight of God, the number is changed and an indication of generality is added: "All have turned away; all alike have become worthless" (Ps. 13:3). Christ assailed the tyranny of Satan at the very time when Satan's reign in the world was at its zenith. But if even at that time this prophecy did not apply to all mortals, there was never a time when it could be spoken against everyone, as Luther interprets it. But if we follow the teaching of Ambrose and refer the general expression to one part of the whole race, so that those who lack the Spirit of God are said to turn aside,[81] Paul's evidence has no value here, since he is trying to show that all mortals have sinned and lack the glory of God, which was revealed through the grace of the gospel. Now since it is clear that this evidence has been woven together from various parts of Scripture, these verses, "Their throat is an open sepulchre, they use their tongues for treachery,"[82] are not spoken by God looking out at the sons of men, but by the prophet against the enemies of piety. And then it is clear from what follows that not everyone was so wicked: "And let all who hope in thee, Lord, rejoice (Ps. 15:12)." Then again, what follows, "The poison of asps is under their tongues,"[83] is spoken against the same wicked persons, but it is clear from what follows that it does not apply to everyone: "But nevertheless the just will confess your name" (Ps. 139:14).

The next little piece, "whose mouth is full of cursing," is taken from Psalm 9,[84] where it is in the singular, and in that place mention is made of the just, whose desire the Lord has heard.[85] The last verse, "There is no fear of the Lord before their eyes," is from the opening

---

81. Pseudo-Ambrose, *De vocatione omnium gentium* 1.9 (PL 51 66).

82. Ps. 13:3, drawn from Ps. 5:11 and quoted in Rom. 3:13.

83. Ps. 13:3, drawn from Ps. 139:4 and quoted in Rom. 3:13.

84. Ps. 13:3, drawn from Ps. 9 (10):7 and quoted in Rom. 3:14.

85. Ps. 9 (10):17.

of Psalm 35 and is singular in number: "The fool spoke to himself; there is no fear before his eyes."[86] And that this is not spoken about the whole human race is clear from another verse in the same psalm: "But the sons of men hope for shelter under your wings" (Ps. 35:8). The three verses in the middle are taken from Isaiah, chapter 59,[87] where God is reproaching the people for their malice, not because they were born such but because they departed from the Lord out of a corrupt will, and he is not expostulating with anyone but the Jews. But Jerome points out that the verses in the middle of Psalm 13, from "open sepulchre" to "there is not fear of God," are not in the Hebrew but were added by some zealous person from Paul's citation because he thought that what was woven together from other places had been left out of the psalm.[88] Although in this passage the Apostle weaves together evidence from various places, although twice he changes the number so that what was said against a single person he turns against everyone, still Luther makes a marvelous to-do because Discussion said that sometimes the passages quoted by Paul offer him more support than they do in their original context.[89] In fact, however, this was said in praise of the Apostle, who fights with scriptural weapons so knowledgeably and diligently.

But to return to the point, if this whole passage pertains to the whole human race, as Luther claims, what will we do with the many men commended by God's testimony, some of them even sanctified in the womb? Finally, what will we do with John the Baptist, who was a prophet before he was born?[90] If it applies only to those who were in the flesh and not yet reborn in the Spirit, how is it consistent with what follows, "that the whole world may be subject to God"? (Rom. 3:19). For it is clear that here "world" does not mean only those dedicated to the world but the whole race of mortals from the beginning of the world all the way to the end. Origen even wonders if the passage applies to the angels—so far is he from excluding any human being.[91]

86. Ps. 13:3, drawn from Ps. 35:2 and quoted in Rom. 3:18; it is the last verse in the passage from Paul under discussion.

87. Ps. 13:3 (from "their feet are swift" to "path of peace"), drawn from Isa. 59:7–8 and quoted in Rom. 3:15–17.

88. Jerome, *Commentarii in Esaiam* (on 59:7–8) (CCSL 73A 682:25–35)

89. See *A Discussion,* CWE 76, p. 54 and *The Enslaved Will,* p. 91.

90. Because he leapt in the womb when Mary greeted his mother, Elizabeth (Luke 1:41–44).

91. Origen, *Commentarii in epistolam ad Romanos* 3.6 (PG 14 93).

Then again, if it applies to everyone, does that text "the poison of asps is under their tongues" apply to children, and will those who are too young to talk be said to have a mouth full of cursing? And will those who cannot yet walk have "feet swift to shed blood"?[92] But why am I talking about children? Was there ever among the pagans a people so abominable that everything that Luther claims fits mankind, one and all, is applicable to all of them?

You will say: what is this discussion driving at? That either Scripture is lying or that Paul cites it in bad faith? Far from it. But rather I want to parry the weapon that Luther considers most reliable. This general language applies to all mankind with the exception of Christ alone or, if you wish, of the blessed Virgin, supposing that the mother and Son can be counted as one. I say this because some interpret "all the way to one"[93] as "all the way to Christ," so that we should take it that an exception is made for Christ.[94] But actually, in my judgment, the true meaning of the prophet is that "all the way to one" has the same force as if he had said "not even one" and that "not even one" is equivalent to "none"—though this phrase "all the way to one" is not added on to this psalm, which is either Psalm 13 or 52.[95] And so I believe that this language applies to everyone in the fashion that I explained earlier; in one way the truth of the general language is valid, even though there are a few to whom it does not apply; in another way, it is valid if the general expression does not refer to individual persons but to groups of individuals, so that we take it to mean that there is no nation under the heavens which is not mostly corrupted by such vices and others like them. By such a figure of speech we say that a whole city is infected if no part of it is free of the plague or if there are very few who are not infected. But if someone wants to press such language by the exact rules of dialectic, we will tell him that "the greatest justice is the greatest injury" and he will be forced to interpret many other passages by the same rule. When he is completely unable to do this, he will allow us willy nilly to interpret this passage—or at least some phrases in it—according to common sense. Let me add that this passage is not directed at anyone except those capable of such crimes, that is, not at infants but at adults.

92. Isa. 59:7; Rom. 3:13, 15.

93. Latin *usque ad unum,* usually translated "not even one."

94. Augustine, *Enarrationes in psalmos* 13.2 (CCSL 38 86:12–20).

95. Erasmus means that the phrase *usque ad unum* (all the way to one) was not added to the Hebrew of Psalms 13 and 52 (as some phrases from Romans 3 were added to Psalm 13) but were present in the original Hebrew.

Finally, the whole gamut of wrongdoing falls upon the whole human race, but each single feature of it does not apply to each individual. For example, if someone said that all the Ninevites were corrupted by various sorts of wrongdoing, such as adultery, poisoning, robbery, and murder,[96] he would not mean that each individual did these crimes but that many of them did. Therefore Luther is acting shamelessly when he twists the text to apply the worst of these crimes to individual persons. "All have sinned and lack the glory of God" (Rom. 3:23).

This is true, but "Everyone says in his heart, 'There is no God' and 'Everyone has poison under his tongue'[97] cannot be said about individuals, not even the gentiles. Moreover, when Paul says, "There is no one who does good,"[98] either it is said hyperbolically, or no one is said to do good because very few do so, or else let us take it to mean not just any good but that good for which we were created and which is rendered to the blessed, which can only be bestowed by him who alone is truly good. Now if Luther, wildly exaggerating with his hyperboles, proclaims that there is nothing even in the most excellent part of mankind, namely reason, except the profoundest ignorance of God, and in the part next to it, the will, nothing but the greatest hatred and contempt for God, he fails to notice that by wildly overemphasizing these crimes while he is intent on winning he makes Paul contradict himself in the very same passage. How can it be consistent for the Apostle to mean now[99] that those about whom he wrote earlier "upon all the unrighteousness of men, who hold the truth in unrighteousness," and again "those who recognize the justice of God which condemns those who do such things as worthy to die, yet they not only do them but also agree with those who are doing them," how can it be consistent that those same persons are in the grip of the deepest ignorance of truth, morality, and God? This concerns the recognition of morality.

Concerning the recognition of God he presents the case to them as follows: "because, though they recognized God, they did not glorify him as God."[100] He was so far from attributing to them extreme

96. In the book of Jonah, God sent the prophet to condemn the sinfulness of the inhabitants of Nineveh.

97. Ps. 13:1, 3; Rom. 3:13.

98. Rom. 3:12, citing Ps. 13:1.

99. That is, in Romans 3.

100. Rom. 1:18, 32, 21.

ignorance of God that he reproached them because from known things they understood the invisible nature of God, and his sempiternal power, and finally his very deity itself (Rom. 1:19–20). How far are these words of Paul from Lutherly hyperbole! But as for the will, in another place Paul speaks as follows, playing the role of a sinner: "To will is at hand for me, but I find no way to carry out the good"; likewise, "For since the gentiles, who do not have the Law, do by nature what belongs to the Law, etc."[101] In these words he attributes to them not only the wish to do good but the performance of it.[102] And soon afterwards he introduces a courtroom for the conscience, as its thoughts defend and accuse each other in turn. Such ideas are not consistent with a Lutherly exaggeration of total ignorance. Similarly, he exaggerates the text "All alike have become worthless": "that is, altogether worthless." "Worthless in relation to the innocence of the gospel" is not enough for him. Likewise he overemphasizes "There is no one who does good": "With all their power they can do no good at all, but rather everything that they know and do is pervaded by the utmost malice."[103]

Up to this point I have been responding on behalf of the gentiles. Now let us go on to the Jews, to whom these texts properly apply, as Paul testifies. "In their most excellent faculties there was the profoundest ignorance of God." Then what is meant by this text: "But if you are called a Jew, if you take consolation in the Law and glory in God and know his will and, instructed by the Law, you approve of what is fruitful, etc."? (Rom. 2:17–18) Does this sound like the most profound and total ignorance? And yet this is said about wicked Jews. It is reinforced by what follows: "You teach others, but you do not teach yourselves. You preach against theft, but you steal" (Rom. 2:21). The Apostle accuses both groups: the gentiles because they recognized God by their natural powers, but they did not glorify him as God; the Jews, because, although they were instructed by the Law to know what they should avoid or seek, they turned their thoughts elsewhere. For he could not have justly accused their will if he had not attributed knowledge to them. But since Luther completely deprives mankind of knowledge and will, he consistently professes that God both saves and damns persons who do not deserve their lot, whereas Paul says in the same passage, "God is not a respecter of persons" (Rom. 2:11).

---

101. Rom. 7:18, 2:14.

102. That is, they do some good but cannot carry it out perfectly.

103. See *The Enslaved Will*, pp. 92–93.

But if he saves some and damns others with no regard for their deserts and placing no importance on free will, how can it be that there is no distinction of persons with God?[104]

When Luther has undone these knots, then let him carry on all he wants, overemphasizing individual deeds with his supertragical exaggerations. For he spends several sections doing that. As it is, the more he exaggerates, the more the Apostle contradicts himself! When these points are recognized, it is clear to anyone on the face of it how banal are those supertragical thunderclaps of his: "Therefore Christ redeems only the lowest part of a man; the most excellent part is its own redeemer." If you look at these smokescreens from afar, you would think there is something to them; if you bring your gaze up closer, they are sheer tomfoolery. Didn't Discussion candidly profess that both the reason and the will of mankind are vitiated by the sin of Adam, and even more so by our own sins?[105] But to say that no good remains in either the reason or the will not only goes against common sense but is even a wicked thing to say, since Paul attributes so much good to pagan philosophers and vicious Jews.

But Luther cheats us with verbal fallacies: whenever I say "good," he takes it to mean only the good which makes us blessed; when I say "understand," he takes it to mean perfect knowledge; when I say "to will," he takes it to mean that it is effective for justification without grace. And at the same time he makes many outrageous inferences: "If the residual effort is good, then what he says about them being subject to sin is false." What is he saying? Though he teaches us that even the justified are subject to sin in any work whatsoever, indeed are subject to the reign of Satan, he is shocked if any effort for good can be said to be in a person who is not yet reborn. I take "good" not as absolutely good but as something that is at a stage leading towards the good, just as we say that soil is fertile not because it produces a large crop but because, if cultivated, it can produce something and even now gives some spontaneous signs of that fact, inviting, as it were, the diligence of the farmer.

He also reasons in this fashion: "Here Paul is totally intent on showing that grace is necessary for all men. If, however, they could initiate anything on their own, grace would not be necessary." If one wished to quibble about the word "initiate," even the gifts of

---

104. That is, God would be distinguishing one person from another by arbitrarily favoring one over the other.

105. *A Discussion* (CWE 76 pp. 23–24, 27).

nature well up out of grace; but I take this up elsewhere. Doesn't this enthymeme fly directly in the face of ordinary common sense: If a sick man has any sort of digestion at all, he doesn't need a physician? If a wounded man can limp along in some fashion or other, he doesn't need a surgeon? Or to bring the comparison closer to home: if only the left eye is ailing, there is no need for an eye salve because the right eye is healthy? Or if someone has a fever, he doesn't need a physician because he does not have dropsy, pleurisy, catarrh, gout, or any of the other innumerable diseases? If any part of a person is healthy or semi-healthy, a physician is useless; so too, if there is anything in a person that is not extremely evil, grace is useless. What could be more absurd than such exaggerations? Shame in an adolescent becomes moral uprightness in a grown man: it is not a perfect virtue, but still, it is a virtue rather than a vice, just as it is a quality that is a hopeful sign of full-fledged virtue. So too physicians more readily and easily treat a well-regulated body than one that is not. Health is lacking, but there are some vestiges of former health which, if they are activated by medication, can play their part in cooperating with the physician's skill and sometimes even overcome the disease without the efforts of a physician. In fact, of course, our comparison is defective in this respect: we were created without a physician, often we get well without a physician, but without God we have neither existence nor health.

Finally, since even the vestiges that reside in a person remain because of God's goodness, to diminish them so much, to put them down, to destroy them is equivalent to making light of God's kindness. The haughtiness of the Jews was enormous, and thus the glory of the gospel was endangered; therefore Paul opposes their wicked self-confidence forcefully, with every weapon available to him. But I think he would have argued differently if he saw that a conviction of the necessity of all things now throws some people into despair and makes others abandon themselves to all kinds of sin, thinking to themselves: "What is the point of refraining from evil deeds? If it is predetermined that I am damned, any effort I make is useless. If I am destined to be saved, there is no reason not to follow my every whim." Why should we attach any importance to Luther's proving that all men are subject to God, that they are useless and reprobate if left to their natural powers, since Luther holds that a person, however justified, does nothing but sin in every work he performs, even in his best deeds—so much so that he deserves hell, as far as he himself is concerned? But because he has not proved this from Scripture, as he promised to do, I will not agree with him, as I promised to do.

He rejects the sophists, who will perhaps have the audacity, even after such mighty thunderbolts from Scriptures, to say that reason and will, though they err and deviate in act, still have the potency to perceive and seek something by their own power.[106] He rejects this sophism for two reasons: first, by affirming here that "does not seek God" means the same as "cannot seek God"; and then by arguing that if it is not understood to mean this, Paul's argument would be pointless. Both these points he brings up are false. For it has been shown that mankind, by its natural powers, both knows God and understands what is right and wrong in most circumstances; and certainly if people do, then they can. Moreover I have made it clear that grace perfects the good of nature. But what does not exist cannot be perfected, and there is no helping, restoring, encouraging, or healing what has no existence. But the material upon which grace works is man's free will. And it is absolutely absurd to think that there is no room for grace if reason perceives something by its natural power or if the human will in some matters is somehow inclined towards the good. And what is imperfect is not necessarily wicked. When Pilate tried to save an innocent man, his will was not wicked, but it was imperfect, and for that reason he did not carry out what he wished.[107] So too a person is said not to understand God if he does not know God as he ought to, not because he knows nothing whatever about God. He is said not to do good if he does not do the good that is appropriate to a human being, not because he does no good at all. So too, a person is said to be unwise if he has no wisdom about matters that are worthy of a wise man, not because he has no wisdom at all; and a person is said to be ignorant of rhetoric if he cannot perform the duty of a rhetorician, not because he knows nothing whatever about that skill.

But to make an end of it, what is the point of all this? "That all men may be taught that they lack the glory of God."[108] That is conceded even by the scholastics, who attribute more to free will than Discussion. And so Luther has won his point. But what point? "That by his natural powers no person can know anything about God." Paul himself, however, rejects this opinion, showing that the gentiles lacked the glory of God for the very reason that they did not worship the God they knew. Even Luther attributes to them a knowledge of

---

106. *The Enslaved Will*, p. 93. Act and potency are scholastic categories derived from Aristotelian metaphysics.

107. Luke 23:4, 13–25.

108. Cf. Rom. 3:23.

God and morality, but claims they had it through the Law; and he attributes it even to wicked Jews. And he assigns to the grace of God the very fact that they learned through the Law what God is, what is right, and what is wrong. But the role played by the Law for the dense Jews was played for the intelligent Greeks by natural ability and created things, and nothing prevents us from calling these things God's grace, since Paul says: "God revealed it to them."[109] The Jews, being dense, looked for signs; the Greeks sought wisdom. Take a look here and tell me whether Luther does not manifestly contradict himself. He says the wicked Jews understood God and the outlines of morality; and so reason perceives something by its natural powers. He will say: "They saw it with the help of the Law." But if the gentiles in their laws punished the same crimes as the Jews, it follows that by their natural powers alone they saw what is right or wrong in many circumstances.

With similar verbal trickery he overemphasizes that text of Paul, "so that every mouth may be stopped and the whole world be accountable to God"[110] (Rom. 3:19). If Luther stresses the literal meaning of the words, even four-footed beasts and angels will be accountable to God, that is, guilty, for the Greek is "brought to trial." But if we accept the Apostle's hyperbole here, recognizing that he called "the whole human race" the "whole world" to make his language more forceful, why do we not recognize the same sort of hyperbole when he is recounting the crimes of mankind? And here Luther reasons as he did a little earlier: "If a person has any power left by which he can know or will anything by his nature, every human mouth is not stopped," as if a person who confesses to many crimes but did not offend in some way or other were not accountable to the judge (in fact, one crime alone makes the whole man subject to punishment) or as if a sick man were not accountable to a physician if there is any part of his body which is, I will not say healthy, but rather unaffected by disease. In fact, one affliction is enough to make the whole man accountable to the physician.

But what a neat trick he has here, where he quibbles that "every mouth" is not to be understood as the mouth of every man, but rather as constituting the whole of any person, as if the individual powers of a person each had its own mouth. But why would it be absurd for reason to say: "I see how much one should strive to be honorable and

109. Cf. Rom. 1:19–23.
110. *The Enslaved Will*, p. 94.

to avoid what is shameful, and you, O creator of nature, gave me the ability to see this. Complete your gift and add what is missing"? Is this understanding not accountable to God? It is accountable, first of all because its knowledge is imperfect, and second because it sees that it cannot attain to what it should strive for unless it is assisted by grace. But if we do not allow any part of a person to be not accountable to God, that is, not wicked and deserving of punishment, the same absurdity will recur in relation to the justified: if there is nothing good about them, why are they called just? If there is, then there will be something not accountable to God, that is, not wicked and deserving of punishment. If he should reply that this good is not due to the person but to the gift of God, I will say the same thing about the Jew who knows what is right from the Law and about the pagan who knows God from created things and through the power of his intelligence and by his own diligence and who sees what is honorable, at least in part. Here again I pass over his assumption that reason is totally sound, since my Discussion says the opposite. He always dwells in extremes and never acknowledges any middle ground: he claims that reason is either totally sound or totally wicked.

Can free will fulfill the Law?

I could here put an end to the argument, since the notion Luther introduces about the necessity of all things has been totally demolished, and I took issue mostly with that. For what remains, like much of his previous volume,[111] is aimed at the opinion of the scholastics and contends that free will does not have any power to do a good work, that is, one that merits grace, and Discussion never undertook to defend the scholastic opinion. But I will touch on some points in passing. He exaggerates that text of Paul, "By works of the Law all flesh will not be justified in his sight" (Rom. 3:20), which he takes to mean that every person, of whatever condition or status, has nothing but sheer wickedness even in the most excellent powers of his nature, since even the works of the Law are condemned. I pass over his most insipid interpretation here, taking "all flesh" to mean "a person devoid of the Spirit," since "all flesh" signifies "every person," according to idiomatic Hebrew.

Moreover, when he takes the works of the Law to include not only the ceremonial laws but even the commandments of the Decalogue,

---

111. Erasmus here presumably refers to *Assertio*, article 36, which is devoted to free will and necessity. Article 36 is the second-longest article in that work.

he is inconsistent with himself, since earlier he taught that no person could keep any commandment, and here he grants that all the works of the Law are performed by free will but that they do not confer justification. For what are the works of the Law if not keeping the commandments of the Law? And among them are believing in God, loving God and one's neighbor. And so if he had said that the whole Law cannot be kept through free will without grace, we would readily subscribe to his opinion. Or if he had said that the external works of the Law, such as, "Thou shalt not kill," "Thou shalt not steal," "Thou shalt not commit adultery" do not confer justification if charity is lacking, we would tolerate such language. As it is, who ever heard anyone affirm that all the works of the Law are damnable and make people wicked, and that it does not matter whether they have exercised themselves in the Law with the greatest zeal or with moderate zeal or with no zeal at all? Finally, although we grant that works do not confer justification, certainly they do not make a person wicked unless they spring from a perverse motive. And indeed, since among the Jews circumcision removed original sin, if works of the Law neither confer justification nor make a person wicked, what is the source of that supreme wickedness in the most excellent parts of mankind? If he says "from evil deeds," he agrees with me, but in that case the works of the Law are not performed. For the absence of primal innocence is not straightaway wickedness or injustice.

Here[112] once again poor Jerome becomes his whipping boy and is in danger of being taken out of heaven and thrown headlong into hell because he taught that this passage in Paul is to be understood as applying to the ceremonial laws,[113] as if Jerome were the primary source of this opinion and it were not in fact propounded by all the Greek fathers.[114] For Jerome is more truly the translator than the author

112. In this paragraph Erasmus is replying to *The Enslaved Will,* pp 95–96, Luther's important argument about the ceremonial character of works of the Law.

113. Pseudo-Jerome, *Commentarii in epistolam ad Romanos* (on Rom. 3:20) (PL 30 660); through an intermediary, Georgius Spalatinus, Luther had expressed to Erasmus his disagreement with Jerome's position on this point and Erasmus' support of it as early as December 11, 1516 (see Allen, *Ep.* 501).

114. In interpreting Romans 3:20, the text Luther and Erasmus are discussing here, the Greek Fathers do not in fact take "the works of the law" to mean the requirements of the ceremonial, Mosaic law. Origen in *Commentarii in epistolam ad Romanos* 3.6 (PG 14 938) takes the law to be the natural law in men's hearts, because Romans 3:19–20 refer to "the whole world" and "all flesh" and so must refer to the gentiles as well as the Jews. Chrysostom in *Commentarius in epistolam*

of his *Commentary on the Epistle to the Romans,* though even who did the translation is not certain. Luther is quite right to favor Augustine, who is such a pious and famous Doctor of the church, though even in this matter Luther is hardly consistent: first of all, he detests scholastic theology, which was generated by Augustine exactly as Minerva was from the brain of Jupiter; and then he impudently rages against Jerome, who was venerated by Augustine himself both for holiness and learning. As for the spirit in which he does this, let him look to it himself. But where is it that Augustine strongly disagrees? In Augustine's later dispute with Jerome, which he wrote when he was an old man, he does not dare to affirm anything but professes that the question is most difficult.[115] But in the commentary he wrote on the Epistle to the Galatians he denies that the works of the Law justify those persons who trust in them in such a way as to scorn the grace of God offered through the gospel.[116] That much could be said about St. Simeon (Luke 2:25–32) or David himself. For he would not have been justified by the works of the Law if the coming of Christ had occurred in his era and if he had scorned the grace of the gospel, which is more abundant and hence requires more perfect righteousness. That is the reason Paul did not say simply "will not be justified" but added "in the sight of him" in whose eyes even the stars are not pure (Job 25:5); soon afterwards he calls this the "righteousness of God" (Rom. 3:20–21). But these matters are beside the point.

---

ad Romanos 7.1 (PG 60 441–42) and Theophylact in *Expositio in epistolam ad Romanos* on 3:19–20 (PG 124 383–86) take "law" here to refer to the whole Old Testament (which includes precepts such as those of Isaiah as well as the ceremonial law). But Chrysostom and Theophylact, commenting on a very similar Pauline text (Gal. 2:16), do take "law" to mean the Mosaic ceremonial law; see Chrysostom *In epistolam ad Galatas commentarius* 2.6 (PG 61 643) and Theophylact *Commentarius in epistolam ad Galatas* 2.6 (PG 124 978).

115. Augustine, Ep. 82.18–20 (PL 33 283–85). Augustine and Jerome are not disputing specifically about Romans 3:20 but about Paul's rebuke of Peter for Judaizing (Gal. 2:11–20). But the issue of justification by works of the Law is the same. Jerome takes the more extreme position that it is wrong for Christians ever to perform the works of the Law, whereas Augustine holds the more moderate (and Erasmian) view that it is permissible for Christians to relinquish the works of the Law only gradually, recognizing, of course, that they are neither necessary nor effective for justification. Augustine implies that the question is difficult, though he never says so explicitly, and he asks Jerome to correct him if his opinion is wrong. See Ep. 82.13–16 and 33 (PL 33 280–82 and 290).

116. Augustine, *Expositio epistolae ad Galatas* 17–19 (PL 35 2115–17).

Once more, out of his hatred of Jerome, Luther denies that
ceremonial works were lethal after the death of Christ. If he is
talking about the Jews who lived in the early days of the dawning
gospel, what he says is true. For they were allowed to preserve their
ancient ceremonies so that the Law handed down by God might
not be rejected disrespectfully but might become obsolete gradually
and honorably, as long as they did not put any hope of salvation
in such ceremonies. But who ever heard that the apostles tolerated
the circumcision of the gentiles? For Timothy had only one Jewish
parent, and yet Paul did not allow him to be circumcised until he sent
him to Judaea.[117] But after the grace of the gospel flashed throughout
the world, the Jews themselves were not allowed to observe the
ceremonial laws, even if they did not place any hope of salvation in
them; this was not because such bodily works were good or bad in
themselves, but because they hindered the propagation of the gospel
by giving occasion of offence to the weak and support to wicked
Jews. Hence Chrysostom cries out more sharply against Christians
who fast in company with the Jews than he does against adulterers
and drunkards.[118] But Luther talks as if such ceremonies should be
considered indifferent, like such things as standing, sitting, eating,
and drinking, though even these actions are also deadly if they are
performed otherwise than they should be. Furthermore, as for what
Luther says, "It is agreeable with this that anyone may do those things
yet not be doing anything illicit," that was true at one time among
the Jews, but it is not true in an unqualified way. When Augustine
spoke as Luther now speaks, he was rebuked by Jerome and he gave
thanks for the rebuke.[119] But actually this comparison does not hold
up, for we eat and drink, we sleep and wake to fulfill natural needs,
we stand and walk for some useful purpose, but the observance of
the Jewish ceremonies serves no useful purpose at all. And if we wish
to heed some who speak with no impiety, a pious person, who does
everything for the glory of God, acts meritoriously even when he
eats, drinks, sleeps, and plays.

Nor is it relevant to the issue at hand that in the Old Law
ceremonies were required as strictly as the moral commandments of
the Decalogue. But if it is true, how does it happen that someone who
keeps the sabbath does not sin while someone who gives alms does

117. Acts 15:28–29, 16:1–3.

118. Chrysostom, *Adversus Iudaeos* 1.2 and 2.1–3 (PG 48 846–47 and 857–62).

119. Ep. 82.17 (PL 33 282–83).

sin? For this is what that fellow has taught us: that however justified a person may be he sins in his works, however good. And so he infers that Paul is speaking about all the works of the Law, which include, as I said, the love of God and of our neighbor (Mark 12:28–31); and if that does not justify a person, what is there that can do so? But Luther makes the following argument: "Since the part of the Law that prescribes ceremonies has been abrogated, they can no longer be called works of the Law, since that Law does not exist." Such perspicacity! I ask you, by what figure of speech do we call those deeds works of the Law except that at one time the Law was in effect? And at that time it *was being* abrogated rather than *had been* abrogated; and it was abrogated to the extent that no one was to believe those works necessary to salvation. So far as its utility was concerned, it was to be abrogated gradually and only by the Jews. Luther says, "He could have explicitly said, 'The Law is abrogated.'" What importance would it have had if the Apostle had said this, since the Lord himself explicitly abrogated the Law when he said, "Up until John, there were the Law and the prophets,"[120] which was certainly spoken to the Jews, not the gentiles. In fact, Paul eagerly proclaimed the same thing whenever he had the chance. But because of the invincible stubbornness of the Jews and in honor of the Law, which was handed down by God, some time was granted to it, just as, after the death of outstanding men who have deserved well of the commonwealth while they were alive, we carry them out to be buried with honor; we do not thrust them out of their houses.[121]

And whenever Paul fails to say that the ceremonies of the Law are to cease, he does not do so for the same reason that, when Peter preached Christ in Jerusalem and he himself preached Christ in Athens, they called him a man, making no mention of his divine nature.[122] For this seems to be the primary reason assigned by scriptural exegetes that the Law was gradually phased out. Otherwise, what honor was there in keeping a Law that did no good and offered a stumbling block to many persons? Or what affront would it have been to the Law if the apostles, after the arrival of the truth, had immediately preached that it consisted of shadows and types, to be read indeed, but not to be put into execution? Doesn't Paul teach quite explicitly that the Law has

---

120. Luke 16:16, interpreted to mark the end of Judaism (the Law) and the beginning of Christianity (the gospel).

121. Cf. Augustine, Ep. 82.16 (PL 33 282).

122. Acts 2:22–36, 17:31.

been abrogated when he calls it a "tutor" whose authority lasts only "until the time predetermined by the Father"?[123]

The same point had been foretold long ago by the prophets. But the Jews were not yet capable of accepting this prophecy; indeed Christ himself humored their hard-heartedness on many points, lest they should have any feasible cause to recoil from the gospel. In doing so he incidentally confutes Luther's paradoxical doctrine that there is no opportunity for faith unless God seems unjust, whereas in fact God wishes to be seen as supremely just, since in so many ways he deprived the wicked of any excuse, in order to keep even those who perish from being able to look on him as unjust. And so I have shown that this passage cannot be understood to apply to all works whatsoever, since they include the love of God and our neighbor; and no one should be accursed if he relies on such works of the Law. What laws, then, is Paul talking about? Certainly it is about the ceremonial laws and, if we think something more should be added, about external works.

For, since, as Luther agrees, Paul is making the same point when he writes to the Romans as when he writes to the Galatians, and his language is to be interpreted according to the subject matter, as Luther showed, it is clear that Paul is angry at the Galatians not because they had been commanded to abstain from theft, adultery, perjury, false witness, but because they had accepted circumcision and observed the new moon, the sabbath, and discrimination in foods according to Jewish ceremonies. And what is said earlier about Peter conforming to Jewish practices is not concerned with just any works but with the selection of food and other Jewish ceremonies.[124] And writing to the Romans, who themselves had also been coaxed into conformity with Judaism long ago, he mentions circumcision and works. But what works? Theft, adultery, sacrilege, blasphemy (Rom. 2:21–25). For those who do not do such things are for that very reason not justified. To be sure, without abstaining from them there is no justification, but justification does not result merely from abstaining. Accordingly, Moses declares those who do not abide by all the precepts of the Law to be accursed, because there is no salvation for those who violate the commandments of the Law (Deut. 27:26).

Paul, on the other hand, declares those who rely on the Law to be accursed (Gal. 3:18), namely those who glory in the Law in such a way that they nevertheless do not observe the principal commandments of

123. Gal. 3:24, 4:2.
124. Gal. 3:1–5, 2:11–12.

the Law, and even more those who clung stubbornly to it, even though it should have been abrogated insofar as it presents shadows and types. For Paul does not say "who keep the Law" but rather "who rely on the Law," that is, who depend on it totally, not acknowledging the grace of Christ but attributing justification to their own powers. Now, though we grant that a person can fulfill part of the Law by the power of free will, nevertheless he would sin if he attributed justification to his own powers, since he has those very powers as a gift from Christ. Furthermore, since the whole Law looks towards Christ, it would be futile for him to observe the Law—indeed he would not even observe it—if he ascribed to the works of the Law and his own natural powers the glory that is due to the mercy of Christ.

I do not deny that Paul sometimes divides a person into the flesh and the spirit, except that sometimes he adds a third part, the soul, which Luther always refuses to recognize. Certainly here Paul simply uses "flesh" to mean "a human being": "No flesh will be justified by the works of the Law" (Rom. 3:20). But he adds "in the sight of God" to distinguish pharisaic justification from that of the gospel. And then, as for the text Luther quotes from Galatians 3:2, "Did you receive the Spirit from the works of the Law or by hearing of the faith?" it is clear that the Apostle is speaking of ceremonial works, without which the Galatians received the gift of the Spirit. The same point applies to the texts "Now justification by God is revealed apart from the Law" and "We hold that a person is justified by faith apart from the works of the Law" (Rom. 3:21, 28). For Paul does not think that adulterers, murderers, and thieves are justified. But that is what would follow if he thought that justification is bestowed by faith entirely apart from the Law, though, of course, someone who performs of his own accord more than is required by the Law is said to be free from the Law, since by surpassing it voluntarily he is not constrained by it.

After this, Luther repeats the old hyperbole, "Through the Law comes recognition of sin" (Rom. 3:20), treating it as if human reason does not see anything at all, as if there is no striving for virtue by the human will, though in fact the laws of the gentiles punish the same deeds as the law of God and though the philosophers exhort people so ardently to be virtuous. Quite the contrary, the Law was laid down not because before it mankind perceived nothing, but rather so that they might discriminate more fully between what is just and what is unjust and so that the reproaches of the Law might keep them from taking a flattering view of their sins. But on this point I think enough has been said above. And once more Discussion is made into a laughingstock because she reports the opinion of Augustine or, indeed, of all the ancient fathers. I have already admitted that what free choice discerns and what the will seeks are imperfect, but I also profess that if we perform even that much, grace is ready to come to our aid.

He also distorts that text of Paul, "Why then the Law? It was laid down because of transgressions, until the issue should arrive, etc." (Gal. 3:19).[125] And here once again Jerome takes a beating because he interpreted it to mean "in order to repress transgressions."[126] How hatefully he fumes against a man whose memory has been held sacred by God's church for so many centuries! Why is Jerome said to be dreaming about this passage when he is following, or rather translating, so many Greek fathers? Why do not Chrysostom, Theophylact, and Ambrose also share in the beating, since they give the same interpretation?[127] Luther's interpretation is not entirely false, but see how hatefully he puts it forth: "Because of transgressions, not indeed to repress them, as Jerome dreams, but to increase transgressions." In Romans 5:20 Paul says that the Law was introduced so that sin might abound; he does not say "so that sin might be increased." For it is one thing to be exacerbated and made known; another, to be increased. Certainly such novel language should have been avoided. And this was not the principal aim of the Law, though it followed as a consequence of the Law, and God turned this outcome to the good. But if you consider the goal of the Law, it was laid down to illuminate the path of simple people, to check the wicked and violent with fear so that they would not sin with complete impunity; and, if they did not cease, they would immediately be condemned as sinners by the Law. And so the Law either turned over a well-intentioned person to the grace prepared for him, or caused a person to sin less grievously and for that reason made him more susceptible to the healing of the gospel or prevented a person from pretending he was not unjust, so that perhaps in this way he might take refuge in grace. I earlier refuted this argument: "I would not have been aware of covetousness if the Law had not said, 'You shall not covet.'" For Luther concludes from this that reason of itself in no way distinguishes what is sinful from what is not (Rom. 7:7); but in fact Paul here is not

---

125. *The Enslaved Will*, p. 99.

126. Jerome, *Commentarii in epistolam ad Galatas* 2.3.19–20 (PL 26 366).

127. Chrysostom, *In epistolam ad Galatas commentarius* 3.19 (PG 61 654); Theophylact *Commentarius in epistolam ad Galatas* 3.19 (PG 124 991); Ambrose, *Commentaria in epistolam ad Galatas* 3.19 (PL 17 356).

speaking in his own person but rather in that of someone who is quite ignorant and thinks that virtue and vice reside not in the mind but in outward deeds. Was Paul ignorant of what even the philosophers saw, that what is honorable and what is shameful consist in a mental condition, which is the only factor that renders a person either happy or unhappy? The rest of this section is merely bombast that I have already refuted more than once.

With the same sort of magniloquence he takes up what follows in Paul: "Now, however, God's justice is revealed apart from the Law; the Law and the prophets bear witness to it through faith in Jesus Christ for all and upon all who believe in him. For there is no distinction: for all have sinned and lack the glory of God; all are justified by his grace through the redemption which is in Christ Jesus, whom God set out as expiation through faith in his blood, etc." (Rom. 3:21–25).[128] "Here," he says, "Paul speaks in real thunderbolts." I grant it. But are they "against free will"? I deny it. Against those who trust in their own powers? I agree. "The Apostle distinguishes God's justification from that of the Law." If by "justification by the Law" Luther means "Pharisaic justification," I go along with him; but if he means "justification by the entire Law," I do not, since the Law also teaches faith and charity, which a person does not achieve merely by his natural powers but with the assistance of grace, which was not lacking in ages past to the Jews who lived under the Law. It was revealed when Christ came; it did not originate then. Rather it was set forth more clearly and spread throughout the world more widely and abundantly. And it was revealed apart from the Law, that is, both to the Jews who had not observed the Law and to the gentiles who did not know it. But the interpretation that Christian justification exists apart from the Law can be taken in three senses: either that moral works of the Law are not required in baptized persons—which is an unholy sense; or that neither the Jews nor the gentiles when they approach the gospel are required to give an accounting showing that they have kept the Law, provided they repent and believe, and this is a true sense; or that no one is required to observe those commands which had been imposed on the Galatians by the pseudoapostles, and this is the truest sense of all. For I have already shown that Paul is dealing with such works in that passage.

But Luther's interpretation—that those who had kept the commandments of the Law as best they could, not completely but

128. *The Enslaved Will*, p. 100.

nevertheless sincerely, were not at all more capable of accepting grace, or that the gentiles who had lived lawfully and moderately to the best of their ability under paganism were not at all more apt to accept grace—is very far from the truth as I see it. An example is the Ethiopian, who was so easily converted by Philip (Acts 8:26–40), and Paul, who was so suddenly changed into a different person (Acts 1:9–19); but we do not read that Herod or the Scribes and Pharisees were converted, even though they had seen so many miracles, even though they knew the Law by heart. But if morally good works render a person more capable of accepting grace, and if the observance of the Law by a Jew before the promulgation of the gospel made him more fit for the gospel—and Luther concedes that these works are performed by the power of free will—then he is wrong when he concludes that free will is of no account. Again, if he concedes that grace is not given to those unwilling to receive it—and by means of free will we can turn away from grace, and if we do not turn away from it, we make ourselves available to it—it is clear that here, too, free will has some function. And his interpretation is ridiculous when he says "apart from the Law, that is, apart from everything that free will can do." We grant that free will cannot arrive at God's justification by its own power without grace, but that does not mean free will does not exist. Finally, we are not arguing here what God can do but what he does by his ordained power[129] and what he shows us in Scripture that we can hope for.

You have heard one marvelous thunderbolt, but listen to one that is even more marvelous: "Paul says that God's justice avails in everyone and upon everyone who believes in Christ." Where the Apostle says "reveals" Luther changes it to "has force" so as to support his dogma better. God's justice was revealed to all. Why did it not avail for everyone? To be sure, it would have availed for everyone if there were no free will. Insofar as the offer of grace is concerned, there was no distinction between Jew and Greek; but insofar as the inclination or disinclination of the will is concerned, there was a very considerable difference. "But Paul," he says, "divides the whole human race into two groups, those who believe and those who do not; to believers he gave righteousness; to unbelievers he denied it. But free will is something different from faith." Why not? For the eye is not the same as light. "But Paul says that whatever is apart from faith is not justified in the sight of God. If not justified, then unjustified, and if it is unjustified, it has to be sinful" (Rom. 3:21–22). Lest someone

129. See nn. 45–46, above.

should object here by proposing some middle ground, he pronounces that with God there is no such thing but rather that whatever exists is either good or bad. But earlier he conceded that there are some intermediate things, such as he claims the ceremonies of the Mosaic law are, since they do not justify anyone or commend anyone to God, and yet whoever observes them does nothing that is forbidden. And he cannot wiggle out of it by saying that there he meant intermediate things in human affairs, since he is clearly dealing with things that either commend us to God or do not; read the conclusion of section 223.[130] But this argument has already been confuted, for just as there is such a thing as an unfinished and imperfect faith, so too there is an imperfect righteousness like that of the centurion Cornelius. For he received perfect faith from the teaching of Peter and righteousness from the sacrament and the Holy Spirit (Acts 10). Now imagine for me some pagan who never heard the mysteries of the faith (and it was through no fault of his own that he did not) but has his mind set on learning what is best and living blamelessly insofar as he can through the guidance of nature; I do not think that everything he does is sinful, whether it be loving his wife and bringing up his children in a wholesome way or contributing as much as he can to the common good. "But his good deeds do not confer evangelical justification." I grant it, but they do invite the kindness of God to add on his own what is lacking to the powers of nature.

Behold, another thunderbolt: "All have sinned and lack the glory of God" (Rom. 3:23), a text I discussed earlier.[131] Here Luther cries out: "I beg you, could he have said it any more clearly? Imagine someone who acts through free will; would he sin in that endeavor of his? If he does not sin, why does Paul not make an exception of him? Certainly when he says everyone, he makes an exception of no one in any place, at any time, in any work, in any endeavor. For if you make an exception of a person for any endeavor or effort, you make a liar out of Paul, etc."[132]—all of which Luther thunders out with great force but also with great effrontery. For there is no less effrontery if you say that all who lack the glory of God sin in all their actions and faculties than if you were to say that all who lack the help

---

130. At the end of the prefatory letter to *The Shield-Bearer* 1, Erasmus noted that he sometimes put in the margin the numbers of Luther's sections (see CWE 76 94 and n. 8 there). For this passage by Luther see *The Enslaved Will*, p. 96.

131. See p. 252.

132. *The Enslaved Will*, p. 101.

of a physician are ill in every part of their bodies. And here, in order to make the passage give more support to his dogma, they[133] make justification either active or passive and glory either active or passive; a Hebraism is summoned up and interprets "lacking the glory of God" to mean not having anything that has glory in the sight of God. If to have glory is to recognize the gift of God with joy, then free will has something in which it has glory in the sight of God. If to have glory is to attribute what one has to oneself, not even the righteous have anything in which to glory in the sight of God. As for his universal challenge for anyone to step forward if he can sincerely say about something that he has accomplished by the power of free will "I know this pleases God," I will bring forward those people who, for all their inclination to sin and their hatred of their diseased state of mind, nevertheless seek the grace of the Spirit by almsgiving and other pious endeavors; they can say, "I have high hopes that God will have mercy on me and lend aid to my efforts by his grace." For to favor, I think, means to be mindful of and to lend aid.

But Luther demands that the person pronounce with certainty that these things please God. And if he does not, Luther takes any doubt about the favor of God to be a sign of disbelief. I hardly know whether any justified person can pronounce with certainty that any particular deed of his is acceptable to God, although in general he believes with certainty that God will not fail his own. But if the confidence of the justified is joined with fear and trembling—and Luther granted this before, teaching that fear arises from necessity and confidence from uncertainty—we believe with certainty that a person is justified through faith and charity. But whether this person or that has the true gift of faith and charity, I do not think we can know with certainty unless God reveals it to someone through special inspiration, as happened to Paul, who said, "I know who it is in whom I have believed and I am certain, etc." (2 Tim. 1:12) But I know pious persons who were dissatisfied with themselves because in all their life they never felt the inner consolation of the Spirit and who persisted all the more intensely in prayer and good works in hopes that God would deign to bestow that grace. These, I suppose, Luther would condemn for disbelief. Since this is the case, Luther is wrong when he concludes that free will, since it lacks that glory, is continually guilty of the sin of disbelief, for all its powers, endeavors, and efforts.

---

133. The plural pronoun, where one would expect "he," seems to include Luther's followers.

Congruous and condign merit

He lets fly another thunderbolt: "justified by the free gift of his grace" (Rom. 3:24). Here he jumps for joy. "What is this free gift? What is the meaning of his grace? If there is merit, where is justification freely given as a gift? Where are the defenders of free will now?" Once more poor Discussion is indicted because she constantly argues thus: "If there is no freedom of choice, what room is there for merit? If there is no room for merit, what room is there for rewards?"[134] Up to this point, what Luther says is not entirely false, except that where Discussion says "if there is no freedom of choice" he quotes it here as "if there is no free choice," as if I meant that the choice is free in an unqualified way. And then, where Discussion claims that there is some kind of merit, but a kind that a person cannot attribute to himself, either because it is of the slightest importance when compared to grace or because the whole process has its origin in God, here he reports it as if I meant merit that had an equal claim on reward. But when he adds, "But to what is it to be attributed if someone is justified without merit?" that is nowhere to be found in *A Discussion,* but rather Luther added it out of his own supremely free choice, unless he would prefer to have his choice called the slave of him who is the father of lies.[135]

Quite the contrary, throughout the whole argument Discussion avoids saying this so that salvation may not be attributed to human merit but rather that all may be assigned to grace. Concerning the damned, she asks to whom their downfall should be attributed if there is no freedom of choice but everything happens by sheer necessity.[136] But if *meritum de congruo* is taken to mean a certain sort of human worthiness which God in his kindness accepts from the effort of our powers, however little it may be worth, and if we take *meritum de condigno* to refer to duties performed, in whatever way, with the assistance of grace, then justification given as a free gift and salvation given as free gift are not inconsistent with the term "merit." Imagine two poor men, one of whom is wild and uncontrollable even in his poverty, the other who is temperate and makes good use of whatever he can get. A king makes the one wealthy and leaves the other in his poverty. What he gave to the one he enriched he gave as a free gift, and he gave it to one worthy of it, though the person

---

134. *A Discussion,* CWE 76 p. 57.
135. Satan (see John 8:44).
136. *A Discussion,* p. 18.

had not merited it; and he had good reason not to give anything
to the other one. For a person is said to be worthy of a favor if he
accepts it eagerly, uses it well, keeps it in mind, and is grateful for it.
For this response is attributed to him as merit. But if what Luther
preaches is true, that there is no merit whatever, then there are many
falsehoods in Holy Scripture, since there the merits of the pious are
approved, and the wicked have thrown up to them what their evil
deeds have merited. For when Luther changes merits into promises,
that idea deserves laughter, not rebuttal. The servant in the gospel
who earned five talents owed all the profit to his master, who had
given him the principal to invest. There was a certain worthiness here
insofar as the principal was given to a person who the master knew
would use it well. He is commanded to enter into the joy of the lord
(Matt. 25:14–21). In this instance the reward is still gratuitous, even
though his worthiness is still approved of. For just as people are said to
bestow benefits on those who are worthy of them because they give
them to persons who are grateful and make good use of them, even
though the donor is not giving anything that has been merited, so too
God, who knows the worthiness of a person before the outcome is
apparent, gives grace to those worthy of it, and from the unworthy he
takes away even what he has given.

And this can be said even if someone is suddenly called to grace
from paganism and a very vicious way of life. As it is, in many persons
the worthiness precedes the gift, as it did in the centurion Cornelius.
Otherwise why are we told that his "prayers and almsdeeds rose up in
the sight of God"?[137] And so this kind of merit is not inconsistent with
the free giving of a gift. But in fact where did Discussion say that a
person arrives at salvation through his own effort? She said that there
is a certain natural effort or striving towards virtue or happiness, but
the effort is imperfect and ineffective apart from grace.[138] Luther also
distorts the point that God looks favorably on one person because of
his effort and scorns another person who makes no effort. Quite the
contrary, God on his part offers himself to everyone; but to the person
who makes himself available, God does not offer himself in vain; to
the person who turns away, grace is offered in vain. And Discussion
does not deny that God sometimes calls a person who makes no effort
and does not want to be called. For God calls people in various ways:
he called the Ethiopian, who had just returned from worshipping and

137. Acts 10:4; *A Discussion*, p. 21.
138. *A Discussion*, p. 22.

was reading Isaiah (Acts 8:27–39); he called Paul when he was raging and breathing out threats and destruction (Acts 9:1–2); some persons he gradually prepares for his Spirit.

But what inference is Luther making when he says this: "Do they not make God a respecter of works, merits, and persons?" (Rom. 2:11). As for merits and works, let Paul reply: he promises a prize to those who contend;[139] he promises that deeds will be rewarded, that is, according to what was done while in the body (2 Cor. 5:10). How can God be called a respecter of persons if he distinguishes the worthy from the unworthy? Quite the contrary, he would, rather, be a respecter of persons if he saved one person and threw another into hell with no regard to the merit of either one but only because it pleased him to do so. For if he considers everyone equally unrighteous, why should he draw some and not others except that he favors the one and not the other? Now Luther grants that sometimes the human will cooperates with grace. But if it is not absurd that the will should assist, as it were, cooperating grace, why should it be absurd for the human will to make itself available, leaning, as it were, on preparatory grace? These actions do not prevent the whole process from being a free gift. No one is saved without the assent of his will, and yet that does not mean we owe salvation to the will. For it does not follow from "without this you are not saved" that "through this you achieve salvation." He grants that it is not without us that God works in us. If our contribution were not there, we would not be saved. Nevertheless we owe salvation totally to grace. If we make no contribution, God works in us without us. But if there is something of our own which God would approve of, why cannot we contribute something by accepting grace, and just as on the one hand the will cooperates with justifying grace, so too on the other hand why should it not cooperate with the grace that prepares for justification? And what is meant by those who introduce *meritum de congruo?* That there is some work that invites God's kindness without any particular grace? Discussion never said so, and if she had there would be no danger in it. Much less did she say that any work performed apart from grace has the same effect as *meritum de condigno.*[140]

But in this whole debate Luther confuses his own opinions with those of others. If he intended to defend all the opinions attacked by Discussion, he should also have defended the opinion of Karlstadt; if he

---

139. 1 Cor. 9:24; Phil. 3:14.

140. On *meritum de congruo,* see *A Discussion,* n. 20.

meant to defend only his own opinion, he should have defended the necessity of all things and the total nonexistence of free will for either good or evil. If he wanted to refute the opinion of the scholastics, which Discussion did not undertake to defend, why does he harass her with so many insults, such as "Indeed Discussion is not wicked, but she speaks and acts only as a wicked person does." Now we are compared with the Pelagians in such a way as to come off as worse than they, in two respects: first, they simply asserted *meritum de condigno,* but we teach the same thing under false pretenses and with deceptive language, distinguishing *meritum de congruo* from *meritum de condigno;* second, we place far less value on God's grace than the Pelagians, since they attribute a great deal to the free will which merits grace but we attribute only a tiny bit, which nevertheless merits the same grace.[141] To respond briefly to this verbal sleight of hand: if Pelagius had said what I think the theologians mean, namely that the grace of God will not be lacking to anyone who does the best he can and that God in his kindness will attribute to him the very effort on his part to struggle towards inviting grace[142] as a sort of merit, he would not have been condemned; and if this distinction between *de condigno* and *de congruo* had been discovered at that time, perhaps he would have avoided condemnation, at least insofar as this article is concerned, if he had rejected only *meritum de condigno.*[143] So much for the first slander.

To the second I reply that we do not diminish the greatness of God's grace, but rather we emphasize the incomprehensible goodness of God, who takes in good part the tiny bit that human weakness is capable of and from his own store supplies what is lacking. We grant that the words "to be justified as a free gift" are quite clear and also the words "if from works, then there is no grace" and much else that we read in Paul. But those who attribute something to free will have a firm recollection of those very clear words. These words, however, were spoken against the Jews in favor of the gentiles, and they ought to be understood according to the subject matter, namely that those who come to the gospel are not given grace as if it were owing to the works of the Law, which the Jews tried to foist on the gentiles—for example, circumcision and the discrimination of food and days—or to any other good deeds. If it were so given, the Jews would not have

141. *The Enslaved Will,* p. 104.

142. Yet another term for particular or preparatory grace. See *A Discussion* n. 22.

143. If he had taught only *meritum de congruo:* that is, if he had not taught that man merits or earns grace (*meritum de condigno*).

been accepted, since they did not observe the most important part of the Law, nor would the gentiles, who had no good works and came to the gospel from idolatry and fornication. Thus whatever is given in the absence of those works without which the Jews assert grace is not given is said to be given as a free gift. Still, it does not follow that no one can perform any deeds which invite grace. Pretending not to see this, Luther is just beating the air.

By the same stroke, everything he heaps up in the next section is undermined; for when the columns are removed everything built on them collapses. And then he scoffs once more at all the Doctors of the church, who even in the clear light of Paul were so blind out of fear of not leaving any room for merit. Quite the contrary, out of pious reverence for Holy Scripture they did not dare to introduce the absolute necessity of all things, which was not approved even by the more sound philosophers, especially since they saw so much mention made in Holy Scripture of merits, rewards, payment for works, prizes, contests, and crowns. And so Luther is not more sharp sighted than they but simply more reckless.

The true relation of faith and works; final assessments of Paul

Nor does the example of Abraham undermine free will. For the Apostle brings it up in opposition to the Jews, who contended that none of the gentiles was to be admitted to the gospel without being circumcised and observing the rest of the ceremonial laws, as if they were the reason for salvation. But since Abraham, even when he was not circumcised—which was the sign of the Law—merited to be praised by God as justified because of his faith, Paul infers that the gentiles can also be justified by the same faith without circumcision. The Jews thought very highly of Abraham; in that patriarch they took much pride. Nor was there any more remarkable instance of fidelity: "Beyond hope he believed in hope" (Rom. 4:18), and he believed so firmly that he did not hesitate to sacrifice his only son Isaac when he was commanded to do so, though all his hope of posterity rested in Isaac. And so Paul brings up this instance to shut the mouths of the Jews and to give the gentiles confidence. And when Luther distorts what is said about the ceremonies of the Law and external works and applies it to all human actions, he does so in his usual shameless fashion. For the very fact that Abraham believed in God was a work, and this was not the first time Abraham began to believe in

God, but he provided for us at that time a manifest example of faith. And so what, then, is Paul's point? To show that the works of the patriarch were all displeasing to God until the time when his belief in God's promises was imputed to him as justification? Not at all, for he believed before that, and his works were pleasing to God. Rather Paul is showing that his trust was so pleasing to God that by means of it he merited to be designated as justified, and that by the judgment of God himself, even though he was uncircumcised and not recommended by the observance of the Mosaic law. I pass over the fact that Luther repeatedly sings his old tune that whatever is not righteous is worthy of wrath and damnation, not recognizing any middle ground or any righteousness that is moral or imperfect.

But to one who works, Paul says, "his reward is reckoned as due; to one who believes, faith is imputed as righteousness" (Rom. 4:4–5). Paul means a Jew who works, one who is confident in his faith and charity and performs the works of the Law as if they conferred salvation. But righteousness is imputed to an uncircumcised believer precisely because his sins have been freely forgiven. For faith does not bestow justification if charity is lacking, for faith is the first approach to justification. This is confirmed by the testimony of David: "Blessed is the man to whom the Lord does not impute sin,"[144] that is, whose sins are freely forgiven through faith. What follows makes this even clearer: "How, then, is it reckoned, to the circumcised or the uncircumcised? Not to the circumcised but to the uncircumcised" (Rom. 4:10). Does this not clearly show that Paul is dealing with the ceremonies of the Law or at least with external works, which can be performed on a human level without faith or charity? "But Paul distinguishes one who works from one who believes." True, but he distinguishes one who works like the Jews, without charity, trusting in bodily works, as too many Christians do even today, from someone who believes in a Christian way, namely with faith that works through love (Gal. 5:6). These points easily dispose of the grand disquisition Luther makes here. For haste is necessary if the volume is ever to come to an end.

Nothing new is added in the next section except assertions, as he boasts of some battle line or other made up of the soundest of arguments which he could deploy if he wanted to and all but threatens to write a continuous commentary on all of Paul, interpreting him as he does here. It would be just as easy to interpret Homer or Virgil in this way.

144. Rom. 4:8; Ps. 31:2.

The next section contains nothing but empty bombast and vigorous assertions and hyperbolical exaggerations which we have heard and rejected time and again, and hence we will not detain the reader by reciting and refuting them. He boasts that he has already won the victory, and if we will not admit that, he is ready to deploy all of Paul against us. And that would be well and good if anyone would permit him to interpret Scripture all by himself and as he sees fit, rejecting the opinions of all others. But unless I am deceived, just as Paul very vigorously opposed trusting in human works because he saw that to do so placed the glory of the gospel in jeopardy, so too, if he were to see today how very many, because of the denial of free will and the introduction of absolute necessity, either despair or live complacently, as if it made no difference whether a person did good or evil works as long as they are confident that God paid the price for mankind's sins and will grant eternal life to all who believe in him, if he saw this he would defend free will more vigorously and extol the power of nature still left in mankind, as he does when he reproaches the philosophers for their wickedness.

He proceeds to bear down on us with two words used by Paul, flesh and spirit. In Romans 8:9 Paul writes: "You are not in the flesh but in the Spirit, if only God's spirit dwells in you. But if someone does not have the Spirit of Christ, such a person does not belong to him."[145] From these words Luther infers that all who do not have the Spirit of Christ are in the flesh, and that those who do not belong to Christ belong to Satan. We grant this also, as Luther teaches elsewhere: all, however righteous, are simultaneously under the reign of the Spirit and that of Satan because even in them the flesh lusts against the Spirit and the Spirit against the flesh. But what follows eliminates free will: "Whoever is in the flesh cannot please God." And so does what precedes: "The wisdom of the flesh is death, but the wisdom of the Spirit is eternal life"; and "The wisdom of the flesh is not obedient to the Law of God, for it is unable to be so."[146] What if I reply that these texts apply to the Jews who gloried in the letter of the Law but lacked the Spirit? For that was the starting point of this disquisition, although Paul, as he usually does, seems to draw out the discussion at length, touching on points marginal to his main subject.

But what does Luther infer from them? That free will, because it is in the flesh, cannot attain to the Spirit by its own power? This

---

145. *The Enslaved Will,* p. 109.
146. Rom. 8:8, 6, 7.

I grant most willingly. That whatever it attempts is wicked? I have already shown that this inference is false. That it does nothing good? I have already made a distinction in the term "good." Nor would it be absurd if some malefactor should be said to be pleasing to God insofar as God judges him to be suitable for receiving grace. For if a king sees people fighting against him on behalf of their lords, however wicked they may be, with great force and fidelity, he nevertheless tries to win them over to himself, hoping that they will fight for him with similar fidelity and eagerness. Whether Paul sinned when he persecuted the church of God, I will not decide at the moment. The Law prescribed that if there were some prophet whose teachings differed from the Law, he was to be eliminated. He had not seen Christ teaching and performing miracles; he had not heard the apostles. But he had heard that a certain Jesus was somehow designing the destruction of the Law and that by unanimous consensus the priests, Scribes, Pharisees, elders, and the people had arrested him, charged him, convicted him, condemned him, and raised him up on the cross and that his surviving apostles were devising the same mischief. In his heart he was pious; in the persons and facts, he was wrong. But however greatly he sinned—and he admitted it himself—still, from his mistake, God judged that he would be a vigorous defender of the gospel, just as in a woman a miscarriage is not a good work of nature, but it gives promise of her fertility, and for an adolescent to blush is not a virtue, but still it bespeaks a temperament suited to virtue.

Luther rejects the interpretation of Origen that mankind is divided into three parts: the spirit, the soul, and the flesh.[147] But since it is clear that Paul does this, let Luther explain to us what that third part of a person is, since he himself insists on no more than two. Origen is dreaming because he does not prove his own interpretation, and Luther proves his points by adducing such violent interpretations! Is to assert the same as to prove? "A bad tree cannot produce good fruit" (Matt. 7:18). If the fruit is human works, Luther teaches that not even the works of the justified are good. And he takes good fruit to mean not just good in any sort of way but good in the manner of the gospel; and we grant that free will cannot perform such works without the assistance of grace. If bad men give good gifts to their children

---

147. Origen often explains that man consists of three parts: the spirit; the flesh; and, between them, the soul, which can join itself with the spirit above it or the flesh beneath it. See his *Commentarii in epistolam ad Romanos* 1.5, 1.18, 6.1, 9.24 (PG 14 850, 866, 1057, 1226).

(Matt. 7:11), are adulterers sinful when they provide for their children according to the law of nature and of God? And so, just as some are said to be good not because they are endowed with perfect virtue but because they have made some progress towards probity, so too in Luke 11:13 the Lord called his disciples bad not because they were extremely vicious but because they were not perfectly good. If he had meant they were bad and wicked, he would not have added: "How much more will your heavenly Father give from heaven a good spirit to those who seek him?" And what is the relevance here of that text "Everything that does not spring from faith is sin" (Rom. 14:23)? For there Paul is talking about those who eat flesh against their consciences. For a person sins if he does something which is not a sin but which he judges to be so because of the weakness of conscience. This evidence could have been cited more appropriately at another place.

Then again, as for his citation from Isaiah 10 (though it is 65), "I was found by those who were not seeking me; I appeared openly to those who did not ask about me," how does it impugn free will?[148] The Law promised Christ[149] to the Jews; rejected by them, grace went over to the gentiles, who did not expect it. This offers more support for free will: the Jews were rejected because in the blindness of their perverse desires they spurned the grace offered to them, and undoubtedly they did so through free will; the gentiles, because they erred through ignorance, eagerly accepted grace once the word was preached to them, their free will responding, as it were, to grace. Furthermore, so far as individual persons are concerned, there were some who sought the Lord, both among the Jews and among the gentiles, that is, some who lived in such a way as to be capable of the grace that would come. And so if Luther means that those who prepare themselves for grace are seeking the Lord, even the Jews who were living according to the Law were seeking the Lord. What is said here applies equally to all mankind, none of whom sought grace but accepted it when it was offered even though it had not been sought. Now the saying of the prophet has two parts, one of which applies to the disbelieving Jews, the other to the gentiles who submitted to the gospel. For when he says, "Lo, here I am, here I am, to a nation that did not invoke my name," it was said about the gentiles. What follows, "I stretched out

---

148. Here Luther has simply "that example in chapter 10, taken from Isaiah." (*The Enslaved Will*, p. 40). As Erasmus should have known (and perhaps did know) Luther meant chapter 10 of Romans (Rom. 10:20), where Paul quotes Isa. 65:1.

149. "Christ" is here equivalent to "the anointed one, the Messiah."

my hands all day to a disbelieving people," applies to Israel, according to Paul's explanation.[150]

It is true that few of the Scribes and Pharisees, few of the philosophers submitted to the gospel, because they claimed righteousness for themselves through their own powers. Free will was not to blame, but rather their wicked desires, which had darkened free will in them more than in others. Concerning Paul, I have already said that he was swept along by a pious heart; he labored under a straightforward mistake, which required no more than an admonition for him to put aside; Christ suddenly changed him from a wolf to a lamb. But he does not do that for everyone: he gradually allures many and shapes them for grace. The Scribes and priests were not mistaken in a similar way. Accordingly, when Luther says that for the Jews much is attributed to free will and for the gentiles there is nothing to be attributed to it, both his statements are hyperbolic. For even among the gentiles there were some who on a natural level did what the Law requires, who strove for righteousness and happiness; and among the Jews the densest ignorance was combined with perversity: seeing they did not see, hearing they did not hear.

The testimony of John the Evangelist: Is free will of "the world" and of "the flesh"?

After these points, Luther takes out of John that terrible word "world," which even all by itself is sufficient for the slaughter and annihilation of the entire cohort of free will.[151] There can be no doubt that in the gospels the word "world" sometimes signifies the whole area of the earth—hence the apostles are commanded "to go out into the whole world and preach the gospel to every creature" (Mark 16:15) and in this very passage as well, "He came into the world and the world was made by him" (John 1:10); sometimes it means persons who love perishable things more than heavenly things—"You are not of the world; I have chosen you out of the world" (John 15:19). But what do you think we should understand here by "world" when John says, "And the world did not recognize him"? (John 1:10) "The human race." Just so. Why should it be surprising if the light of nature does not comprehend that light which the angels can hardly comprehend: divine nature joined with human nature in one person;

---

150. Rom. 10:20–21; Isa. 65:1–2.

151. *The Enslaved Will*, pp. 11–12.

a person born of a virgin; three persons, one God; the whole race of mortals condemned for the sin of one person and redeemed by the death of one person? I grant that this light could not be attained by free will or by that world devoid of God's Spirit. But that does not immediately mean that free will sees nothing—which is Luther's ridiculous inference: "The world hates Christ; the whole world is in the power of the evil one; the world, that is, free will, is under the reign of Satan."

Ambrose gives a much more correct explanation in his book *The Calling of the Gentiles:* that this expression, namely, "the world," is a general expression including the whole human race made up of the good, the mediocre, and the bad, but in such a way as to consist mostly of the bad; and so, in the idiom of Scripture, what applies to the mass of mankind is said to be of the world.[152] For this reason there was in the tent of the ark a holy place called κοσμικόν that is, "worldwide," which accepted not only Jews and proselytes but any nation whatever.[153] And so when the world is said to be "in the power of the evil one" (1 John 5:19), it is to be understood that the mass of mankind is such. And "whatever is in the world is the lust of the flesh and the pride of the eyes and the pride of life" (1 John 2:16) because most mortals are such even today, and were even more so then. Thus Jesus came into the world which he had created and was not recognized by the world, not because no one did so but because few did. "He came unto his own," that is, to the nation of the Jews, "and was not recognized by his own" (John 1:11), not because no Jews believed but because few did, compared to the crowd of unbelievers. He chose his apostles from out of the world. If the whole world hated God, did all the apostles do so before they were called by Christ? They were simple minded, not wicked. They were ignorant of many things, but they did not hate Christ. Such were both Nathaniel and Nicodemus,[154] who would have been saved through the Law if Christ had not come. But he called his apostles from out of the indiscriminate, simple-minded mob, just as before he had separated the Jews from the

---

152. Pseudo-Ambrose, *De vocatione gentium* 3 (PL 17 1084).

153. Interpreting the phrase ἅγιον κοαμικόν—"cosmic sanctuary" (Heb. 9:1), Chrysostom says that the sanctuary is called "cosmic" because it is accessible to all the people; see his *Homiliae in epistolam ad Hebraeos* 15 (PG 63 117). Chrysostom explicitly lists Jews, proselytes, Greeks, and Nazarenes as having access. See Erasmus, *Paraphrase on Hebrews* (CWE 44 pp. 235 and 363, n. 3).

154. John 1:45–51, 3:1–15.

rest of the nations so as to make them his own special people, although among the gentiles there were some who were acceptable to God and among the Jews some who were wicked and among the apostles a Judas was discovered. You now have a good view of the word "world" well and truly worked over.

"He gave to whoever accepted him the power to become sons of God, to those who believe in his name, who are not born of blood nor of the will of the flesh nor of the will of man but rather of God" (John 1:12–13). Here Luther promises us a new and unheard-of interpretation. He takes "blood" to mean the Jews who claimed[155] to be the sons of the kingdom, because they boasted that they were descended from the prophets; he takes the will of the flesh to mean the zeal of the people who were trained in the Law and in works, namely the fleshly and those devoid of the Spirit; the will of man he takes to mean the zeal of everyone in general, whether under the Law or apart from the Law—the gentiles, for example, and people of any sort—so that this is the meaning: we do not become sons of God by birth or by an endeavor to keep the Law or by any other human endeavor but only by a birth in God. "If, therefore," he says, "they are neither born of the flesh nor trained in the Law nor prepared by any human discipline, but are reborn from God, it is obvious that free will has no force." And here once more he seeks help from the Hebrew, which takes "man" to mean any sort of person, just as it takes "flesh" to mean by contrast people without the Spirit; but "will" is taken to mean the highest human power, namely the principal element in free will.[156]

What marvelous insight, Luther! Interpret Scripture in this way and you will win! But what does he mean by that phrase "I think"?[157] Is that a proper expression for someone who denies that anything in Scripture is unclear to him and who professes to have the Spirit of Christ? But if he is not saying this sincerely and adds "I think" out of dissatisfaction even with himself and for the sake of modesty, where is the victory he claims for himself from the words of John? Moreover, where is the simplicity that he demanded from us, even though here

---

155. Basel 1527 and LB have *noluerint*, which must be wrong because Luther, who is being reported here, has *volebant*. The correct reading *voluerint* has been followed in the translation.

156. *The Enslaved Will*, p. 113.

157. Luther wrote: "I think that 'man' in this passage is taken from the Hebraic sense . . ." See *The Enslaved Will*, p. 113.

he hauls in so many figures of speech where there is no need for them whatever, simply because it was expedient in promoting the cause he has undertaken? Is it not crystal clear to anyone that John is here distinguishing between the spiritual birth by which we are born as the adopted sons of God from the fleshly birth by which we are born as human beings from other human beings according to the ordinary law of nature? Why is Luther not satisfied here with Augustine, who takes blood to mean the seed of a man and a woman—or if the word "seed" is not acceptable, the material out of which the fetus is formed, "flesh" being the woman, the "man" being the husband, and "will" the two embracing each other?[158]

Earlier Luther tortured us with this word "become," inferring from it that man's will does nothing in this rebirth, even though from these words holy and reputable Doctors, one of whom is Chrysostom, show that human free will does something in the rebirth itself and in preserving the honor of adoption.[159] For he asks why the Evangelist preferred to say "he gave them the power to become sons of God," rather, than "he made them become the sons of God." For that is how he should have spoken if we make no contribution to our rebirth, just as we make none to our birth. For it would be quite absurd for someone to say "I thank God who gave me the power to become a man rather than a horse" instead of "who made me a man rather than a horse." Chrysostom replies that the Evangelist preferred to speak in this way for three reasons: first, in order to make it clear, by naming the power given by God, that no one can be shut out from this honor unless we shut ourselves out but rather that it is given to all, from the lowest to the highest; second, to signify that this grace is not poured out on us randomly or without our effort but rather that "when we ourselves want it," he says, "then we seek for it, for it is in our power to become sons of God—that is, if we do not display a mind ready to receive it, divine grace will neither come to us nor work anything in us," and so everywhere Chrysostom sets forth a choice which is not subject to violence or force but completely voluntary and free; and finally, John speaks in this way because through baptism God generously bestows on us the forgiveness of all our sins, but for us to stand firm in our innocence and not slip back into our filthy ways, that is a matter of our virtue and effort. To keep Luther from immediately branding Chrysostom as sacrilegious here, I will go right on to show

---

158. Augustine, *In Ioannis evangelium tractatus* 124.2.14 (PL 35 1394–95).

159. Chrysostom, *In Ioannem homiliae* 10.2–3 (PG 59 76).

that what Chrysostom says is pious if we prefer to interpret what John means instead of weaving slanders out of his words. John could have said more briefly: ". . . who are not born from human coition but rather from God."

But by depicting the coition of man and woman, he suggests a similarity in spiritual rebirth. For properly speaking we are not born from God, since nothing is properly born from God except God, just as nothing is born from man except man. But when he mentions seed and the will of a man and a woman, he modestly suggests that in rebirth there is a sort of embrace between grace and free will and that, while grace is certainly superior, this spiritual conception does not occur without the assent of our will. Perhaps he also indicates that we do not become the sons of God suddenly, but first we are given the power which is offered to us by the message of grace; if we accept and embrace it in return, then the Spirit is poured out on us by which we cry out "Abba, Father" (Rom. 8:15). And that does not mean that a person can claim grace for himself, since he would not have had it if it had not been freely offered; but it is not given to those who are unwilling or turn away from it.

Then comes "Of his fullness we have all received and grace for grace" (John 1:16).[160] Here once more he brings in a new interpretation: "grace," not from any merit or effort but "'for the grace of Christ,' just as Paul writes in Romans 5:15: 'the grace of God and the gift in grace of the one man Jesus Christ.'" What is Paul dealing with in these words? What but the grace of the gospel offered to all through Christ our redeemer? No Christian denies this. For that "in" is here used to mean "through" is clear from what follows: "For if by the sin of one man death reigned through one man, much more will those who receive the abundance of grace and gifts and justification live and reign through the one man Jesus Christ" (Rom. 5:17). Here, then, Paul is not showing a new grace through which grace is conferred, but he is indicating the source of grace, from whom it flows, and the minister of grace, through whom it flowed to all mankind; that is why he also calls it an abundance, because through Christ it was poured out most lavishly upon all nations. Therefore John said "grace for grace," not to signify that there are two kinds of grace but that it is bestowed differently, just as Paul said "from faith to faith."[161]

160. *The Enslaved Will*, p. 113.
161. John 1:16; Rom. 1:17.

Under the Law, faith was in the promises; under the gospel, faith is in things manifested. So too under the Law grace was from Christ expected; under the gospel, from Christ manifested. The one was more sparing; the other, more abundant. And still we grant that this gift was given to us by God as a free gift through Christ, not because there was no one who did any good work but because in admitting someone to the gospel the merits of his previous life were not taken into account, provided that the offered gift was accepted with alacrity. And so whenever Paul uses the words "grace" and "freely given," he is not opposing free will insofar as it eagerly accepts the grace offered to it, but rather the haughtiness of the Jews, who relied on works and who thought grace superfluous. But when Luther says that Discussion agrees with the sophists in saying that we obtain the grace of God and are prepared to receive it through our own efforts, if not *de condigno* then at least *de congruo*,[162] he is using the figure which in Greek is called ψευδολογία [false reporting]. I recounted this opinion; I did not defend it. The rest of his ranting and raving, where he cries out that we deny Christ more wickedly than the Pelagians, has nothing to do with me since it arises from a passage falsely expounded.

At last he brings out Nicodemus to undermine free will.[163] If free will is flesh, wickedness, hatred of God, and whatever else, Nicodemus is hardly an appropriate example. For I think that he was in such a condition that it would have been necessary for him to be saved even if Christ had not come at that time. Nor is it surprising that he did not understand the hidden teaching of Christ by the power of free will, since only the prophets or those inspired by the spirit of prophecy understood it. But such knowledge was not required of the general run of Jews; and I hardly know whether the prophets understood particular points as clearly as Christ after his arrival explained them to his followers. Accordingly, when Luther mentions many points that the world could not attain to by its natural powers, he is saying what is quite true: he is preaching to the converted. But by such arguments he does not persuade us that a person through free will neither sees anything nor can make any effort under the encouragement of grace.

He weaves together another syllogism, one which by means of antithesis is very antithetical to us. "Christ," he says, "is called the way, the truth, and the life antithetically, that is, in contradistinction to their opposites. Accordingly, whatever is not Christ is error, is a

---

162. See *A Discussion,* n. 20.
163. On Nicodemus, see John 3:1–15, 7:39.

lie, is death" (John 14:6).[164] Unless we concede this, we make Christ superfluous, since he came to redeem mankind, who had a sound free will; we make him unjust, since he condemned the whole person, who was healthy in his most outstanding feature. I will require that Luther answer this question: Is dialectic a method—that is, a way—of discovering the truth? If he says no, the whole chorus of the universities will cry out against him. If he admits that it is, he either will admit that dialectic is Christ or he will concede that there is some way that is neither Christ nor error. Dialectic demonstrates as necessarily true that if something is a man it is also an animal and, on the other hand, that if it is not an animal, it is not a man. Mathematicians have most certain and demonstrable truths of which none is Christ and yet none is a lie. Concerning life it is pointless to dispute. Christ is the light. Does it follow that whatever is not Christ is darkness? In Luke 10 the Pharisee who tested the Lord asked what the greatest commandment was. How could he be praised by Christ for responding correctly if his response was false? And how did he discern the answer if he was totally in darkness?[165] Luther will say that it was revealed to him through the Law, not through free will. Very well, but how did he know that among so many commandments this is the greatest? Surely he perceived this through free will. What need for a long disquisition? If whatever is not Christ is darkness, why did Luther himself at the end of his volume approve of the scholastic distinction concerning the light of nature, grace, and glory?

I have already spoken about the philosophers, who according to Paul saw God's power and his sempiternal divinity by the light of nature (Rom. 1:19–20). And yet Christ was not in them, as he was not in the Pharisee skilled in the Law who tested Christ. But what point is there in speaking about the philosophers, since the wicked devils have such great powers of perception that they believe in such a way as to tremble? (James 2:19). And certainly they have no share in anything beyond nature. I refuted the rest of the argument earlier.[166] A person is not healthy simply because he is in some way not diseased. A physician is not superfluous simply because a person who has a fever does not have gout. And if free will has some power to welcome grace, that does not mean right away that he can give himself salvation. And a judge is not unjust if he condemns a parricide

---

164. *The Enslaved Will*, pp. 115–16.

165. Erasmus conflates Luke 10:25–28 and Matt. 22:34–36; cf. Mark 12:28–34.

166. See p. 199.

who had nonetheless not committed adultery. These are simply clouds of words. And the stars are not dark simply because the sun is the light of the world. Christ, who is never in error, is the only way to eternal happiness. He alone is the eternal truth, who can neither deceive nor be deceived.[167] He alone is the only way by which the whole man achieves immortality.

Luther seems to me to have appended these things to make the book longer with such flourishes, since he hardly ever knows when to take pen from paper. For it is amazing how he plays the fool here by talking nonsense. "Whoever believes in him will not be judged; whoever does not believe is already judged, because he does not believe in the name of the only-begotten Son of God" (John 3:18).[168] "If free will," he says, "is numbered among those who believe, it does not need Christ. If it is not, it is damned; if it is damned, it is therefore also wicked; if it is wicked, it can make no effort towards piety." I will not examine here what he said before, that even a person who does not deserve it is damned, just as a person who does not deserve it is saved. But if wickedness is a perverted attitude towards God, just as piety is a religious attitude towards him, what will he say about infants who die without being regenerated by baptism? Certainly they do not have a perverted attitude, and yet they are damned.[169]

But I do not wish to waste the reader's time with such subsidiary matters; in that passage John is not dealing with just any sort of disbelief but with belief in the Son of God. God did not blame free will for not being able to achieve that belief. For it is clear that there were many Jews who knew nothing of the Son of God, though they expected a certain messiah to redeem the Jewish nation, and that there were even more who knew nothing of the Holy Spirit. In these matters belief is now required of us, for we are sufficiently convinced about them by Scripture, preaching, miracles, and the consensus of the whole world. In other matters people believe many things through free will: that God exists, that he is eternal, having no beginning or end, that he is beyond measure, incomprehensible, in control of all things, completely without parts or admixture, omnipotent, that nothing is or

---

167. This formula derives from Augustine's *Enarrationes in psalmos* 88.2.6.45 (CCSL 39 1238).

168. *The Enslaved Will*, p. 117.

169. The opinion propounded by Augustine; see, for example, *De peccatorum meritis et remissione et de baptismo parvulorum* 1.16.21 (PL 44 120). But he was also uneasy about it; see Ep. 166.4.9–10 (PL 33 724–25).

can be greater or better than he. Are such points not part of our belief? The gentiles believed that God punishes the wicked and rewards the pious. So much human reason could arrive at, but without grace it could not arrive at the mysteries of Christian belief. Therefore reason discerns, reason believes, the will makes some progress towards the highest good, but without grace it does not achieve eternal salvation, whether under paganism or Judaism or Christianity. And so what free will does is not nothing, and grace is necessary.

Luther goes on: "'Every man is a liar,' says Scripture.[170] What does free will say? It says that Scripture is a liar. Indeed, man is not a liar in the best part of him, his reason and will, but only in his flesh and blood and marrow, so that everything that entitles him to be called 'man,' namely, his reason and will, is sound and holy." How much leisure he must have to fill pages with such rubbish! What is the meaning of "Every man is a liar"? That everything a man encompasses by his natural powers is a lie? The notion is quite insane. What then? Namely, this: only God cannot fail to keep his promises, but every man can fail because his will often changes and he often does not have the ability to live up to what he has undertaken to do. But when will Luther stop singing to us that old, shameless, lying tune of his—that we make the whole human reason and will healthy and holy? Time and again Discussion says the opposite. But he thinks he is very witty, sporting such trifles as "flesh, blood, and marrow." Splendid jests indeed to be written by a person who boasts he has the Spirit of Christ. But let us take leave of such buffoonery.

Once more he sings the same old song he has sung so often about John 3:27, "'A person cannot receive anything unless it has been given to him from heaven.' You see that the power of free will is laid low. When John says 'not anything,' he excludes everything."[171] If Luther presses us with the unqualified meaning of the words, we also grant that a person has nothing which he has not received from God. But here the Baptist is not speaking about just any sort of thing but about the authority to baptize and forgive sins. For when Jesus began to baptize and preach the kingdom of God, as John had formerly done, the disciples of John, feeling a certain human affection for their teacher and not having a proper understanding of Jesus, reported to John, saying, "Rabbi, the one who was with you on the other side of the Jordan, the one to whom you bore witness, see, he is baptizing and

170. Rom. 3:4; Ps. 115:11; *The Enslaved Will*, p. 117.
171. *The Enslaved Will*, p. 118.

everyone is coming to him" (John 3:26). So too the Jews grumbled against John: "Why, then, do you baptize if you are not the Christ or Elias or a prophet?" (John 1:25). And when they demanded to know by what authority Christ did these things, he shut them up with a question, asking them in turn whether the baptism of John was from heaven or from men (Matt. 21:23–25). And so, since they were convinced that John had the authority to preach and baptize handed down to him from heaven but had their doubts about Jesus' power, John showed that the authority of Christ was far superior to his own, since Christ was the bridegroom and master and had descended from the bosom of the Father, while he himself was no more than an ordinary servant, "unworthy to loosen the straps of his sandals" (John 1:27). And so Luther should remember what he taught us elsewhere, that language should be interpreted according to the point that is being made: that no one can receive the authority to baptize or forgive sins or to abrogate the Law or establish a new law or to lay down the dogmas of the faith and perform similar actions unless he has received it from God, and that this highest power was in Christ alone, in whose abundance everyone shares. John did not forgive sins, and he was not the founder of the kingdom of heaven but a herald only and a forerunner. And yet he did what he did with authority given from heaven. What does this have to do with the power of free will? Free will does not institute the sacraments of the church or establish articles of the faith or abrogate laws made by God—all of which were done by Christ, who was the only one who could do them.

And here once more he sets new limits to the discussion: "We are disputing," he says, "not about nature but about grace; we are not asking about how we are on earth but about how we are in heaven in the sight of God." What is this but melodramatic language signifying nothing? Isn't the heart of the question how important our natural powers are in accepting and retaining the grace of God? And hasn't Discussion always joined the action of free will with the working of grace? Luther ought to remember his own limits to the discussion, since at one time he taught us the absolute necessity of all things. And yet here he speaks as follows: "For we know that man has been established as lord over creatures lower than he, and in relation to them he has rights and free will, so that they obey him and do what he wills and thinks." I will not take up the point that here he turns free will into a right, though it is one thing to will, another to have a right. And then he connects the outcome with free will. But if he means what he says, horses, bears, lions, and elephants do not always do what

we want, and so even in this area free will is eliminated. "But we are
asking whether man has free will in relation to God, so that he obeys
and does what man wills, or rather, whether God has free will in
relation to man, so that he wills and does what God wills and cannot
do anything except what God wills and does." This is what he says.
Who does not know that by God's absolute power there is nothing he
cannot do and that mankind is totally subject to his will so that he can
change it from mankind into nothing? But according to his ordained
power, a person frequently does what God does not will, and in a
certain sense God is forced by man to do what he does not will.[172]
He does not will the death of a sinner (Ezek. 33:11), and yet when a
sinner scorns all measures and does not will to repent, God is forced
to destroy someone he willed to live. And God wills that all should
be saved (1 Tim. 2:4), and yet contrary to that will very many perish
through their own vice. Finally, in matters where God has bound
himself by giving us his word, he does what we will, as, for example, in
the sacraments of the church when a wicked minister turns the bread
and wine into his body and blood and does so in a sense against God's
will and desire. Now if Luther is talking about both good and evil
men, what is the meaning of those words "except what God wills and
does"? But plenty has been said about these matters elsewhere. Here
is his conclusion: man cannot do any of the sort of things Christ did,
forgiving sin through baptism, laying down new doctrines, abrogating
the Law, establishing a new testament, unless he has power given to
him from above; therefore free will does not exist!

There follows in the same section: "'He who is of the earth belongs
to the earth and he speaks of the earth; he who comes from heaven is
above everyone' (John 3:31). Free will does not come from heaven;
therefore it is earth and savors of nothing but the earthly. And he who
speaks of the earth speaks wicked things."[173] This is the way he distorts
Scripture! In fact, John is here talking about himself, showing how far
removed his teaching is from the heavenly teaching of Christ, who
alone came down from heaven. And so because of his lowly status he
calls himself earth and says that he speaks earthly things by comparison
with the sublime teachings that would be preached by Christ, who
came from the bosom of the Father. For the rest, did John speak
wicked things? I think not, but rather lowly things compared to the
teaching of Christ. And what Luther quotes from John 8:23 has no

---

172. On God's absolute and ordained power see n. 46, above.
173. *The Enslaved Will*, p. 118.

relevance here: "You are of the world; I am not of the world. You are from below, I am from above." To whom was Christ speaking here? To the wicked and stubborn Jews, concerning whom he testified: "You will die in your sins," and a little later, "I speak of what I have seen with my Father, and you do what you have seen with your father."[174] "But those to whom he was speaking," Luther says, "had free wills, and yet he says they are of the world." What's this I hear? Did Discussion say free will is from heaven, that is, that it savors of nothing except the heavenly? What he adds is just as crazy: "What news would it be if he said they are of the world according to their flesh and gross passions? Didn't the whole world already know that? Then what need was there to say that mankind is of the world in that element it shares with the brute beasts, since the beasts are also of the world in this respect?" I ask you, my dear reader, don't such statements seem like visions seen in a fever or in dreams? Who ever said that the human reason and will are totally healthy and holy?

He repeats that text from John, chapter 6:44: "No one comes to me unless my Father draws him."[175] Here Luther gives the same interpretation as the Manichaeans, as Chrysostom indicates;[176] for they used these words of the gospel to teach that mankind can do nothing at all on its own. But if Manichaeus understood the gospel of John better than the orthodox fathers, let us follow him and be called Manichaeans instead of Christians. In that passage the Lord uttered sublime teachings about himself, teachings beyond the capacity of the human intellect: "I am the living bread who has come down from heaven," and "Whoever sees the Son and believes in him has eternal life, and I will raise him up on the last day" (John 6:51, 40). These are not the words of a man, but rather they bear the stamp of divinity. But they saw a human body; they heard a human voice; they knew his humble parents and lowly relatives. So to the Jews this utterance of the Lord seemed not only incredible but also blasphemous and wicked, and not only to the mob but also to the disciples themselves, so much so that some of them abandoned their teacher (John 6:67). And so when the Jews grumbled, the Lord answered them: "No one comes to me unless the Father draws him" (John 6:66), that is, no one believes in the divinity of the Son unless it is revealed to him by the Father, for it is beyond human capacity. It is clear on the face of it that that is what John meant.

174. John 8:21 and 24, 38.
175. *The Enslaved Will*, p. 119.
176. Chrysostom, *In Ioannem homiliae* 46 (45).1 (PG 59 257–58).

Now see how Luther reasons: "Free will by its natural power cannot believe that a man born of man can be God born of God; therefore it sees nothing at all and cannot assent to these words unless it is drawn by heaven; therefore it cannot assent to any truth!" First, he grants us, I think, that the word "drawn" here refers not to violence but rather to inviting and alluring. And we grant that the belief by which we are cleansed of sin is a gift of God, and a free gift. But this gift is not given to anyone who does not want it. The gift is offered, however, to everyone. The reason why it is not accepted by everyone is the free human will. In the same passage we read: "Everything the Father gives me comes to me; and I will not cast away anyone who comes to me." And in another place, the Lord invites everyone, saying, "Come to me, all who are distressed and burdened."[177] If a person comes to Christ, what need is there for him to be drawn? If he is drawn, how can he be said to come? And so the language of Christ mingles heavenly grace with the human will, for a person is at once drawn by the invitation of heaven, and he comes through the effort of free will. This is what Chrysostom has to say: "But this does not eliminate our choice; rather it shows that divine assistance is necessary and that we do not come unwillingly but making every effort and struggling to do so."[178] These are the word spoken by that mouth of gold.[179] And Luther cannot stand that word "effort" in my writings. But here there is reason to fear that Chrysostom will come off no better than Jerome.

Luther rejects what Discussion cited from Augustine—that a person is drawn not as if he were tied to a chain but as a sheep is drawn when it is shown a branch. He says that what Augustine wrote applies only to the pious, who are already sheep and are led by the Spirit of God wherever God wills. This answer cannot be more expeditiously disposed of than by saying it is false. For in that passage Augustine is not talking about those justified by the Spirit of God but rather about those who need to be justified. Not everyone is a sheep of Christ and follows the Spirit, but there are sheep who have wandered off; there are those who live and die having a wolf for a shepherd. For these are the words of Augustine: "Are you not drawn? Pray that you may

177. John 6:37; Matt. 11:28.
178. For difficulties about Erasmus' citation from Chrysostom, see CWE 77 p. 696 n. 1555.
179. "Chrysostom" is an epithet meaning "golden mouthed."

be drawn."[180] If Luther attaches any importance to Augustine, who prays that he may be drawn, doesn't he see that Augustine is making an effort to accept belief which he has not yet accepted? The gift of a ruler does not cease to be gratuitous if someone strives to get it through the help of friends. And the Lord says: "Whoever comes to me, I will not shut him out."[181] The journey to Christ is by faith; but "faith comes from hearing" (Rom. 10:17). But not everyone who hears believes. For the outer word is spoken in vain unless grace draws from within, but no one is drawn by grace unless he makes himself available to it.

Luther strings together another syllogism. "John," he points out, "says: 'The Spirit will convict the world of sin, because they did not believe in me' (John 16:8–9). Here you see that not to believe in Christ is called a sin. But this sin surely does not reside in the skin or hair but in reason itself and in the will. But the whole world is convicted of disbelief, and that sin was unknown to the world until the Spirit revealed it by convicting the world. Free will is also in the world, together with its reason and will; therefore it is guilty and damned, however great it may be."[182] My lord! What an intricate argument we have here, what distortion of Scripture to reverse its meaning! For that passage does not deal with free will but rather with the inexcusable stubbornness of the Jews, who might have had some sort of pretext to justify their refusal to believe in Christ's divinity because the weakness of his human body kept them from perceiving it. But because, after the Spirit was sent forth, they saw even greater miracles performed by the apostles in the name of the crucified than he had performed when he was alive but nevertheless persisted in their disbelief, they had no pretext by which they could excuse their sin.

Furthermore, as to what Luther says about the whole world being guilty of the sin of disbelief and not even knowing it was a sin, I think their ignorance of the faith, which is what John is talking about here, was not considered blameworthy in the Jews before the preaching of the gospel, or even in the early days of the dawning gospel, when the apostles called Christ a just man chosen by God, remaining silent about his divine nature. Nor was belief in the mystery of the trinity required from mankind before it was divinely revealed by the coming

---

180. Augustine, *In Ioannis evangelium tractatus* 124 26.2.9 (CCSL 36 260).

181. John 6:37, Rom. 10:17.

182. *The Enslaved Will*, pp. 119–20.

of the Son of God. On that count, then, there was no guilt on the part of free will—which at that time, as Luther says, was in the world (although elsewhere he denies it exists in the real world); otherwise all the Jews, however righteous, would have been lost, except for a few to whom this mystery had perhaps been made known by a special revelation. But if he contends that free will cannot believe anything by its own natural power, he is clearly contradicting Paul. I think I have already said enough on this point. But let us also grant that it cannot merit the gift of faith by its own power; it certainly can make itself available to impelling grace or it can also turn away from it and do other things which we have already mentioned time after time. For free will does not generate grace, but it is renewed by grace operating in a person in such a way that the human will itself also acts together with it, both in taking hold of it and keeping it and acting with it, and likewise in rejecting, lessening, and losing it.

Luther adds a hyperbole: "In Holy Scripture Christ is always named as the antithesis of his opposites, so that wherever Christ is not, there are Satan, error, wickedness, darkness, sin, death, the wrath of God, hell, and what not. But since the whole of Scripture speaks about Christ, it is totally opposed to free will." But that is not putting it strongly enough. "Each jot and tiniest tittle," as he says, "lays free will low." O powerful hyperboles!—but nothing more than hyperboles. The nation of the Jews expected Christ, but most of them did not know what he would be like. For they expected a very strong king who would redeem the people of Israel from servitude to the gentiles and would transfer dominion over the whole world to the Jews. Yet this elementary and crude faith was sufficient for salvation. Consequently, it is probable that, before the Law, to believe in one God was sufficient for salvation. But if we require from the Jews of the early periods the same understanding of the Son as the church requires from us, we will require of them an understanding of the Holy Spirit as well. But if they are not blameworthy for not knowing the Holy Spirit, neither are the gentiles for not knowing the Son; from the created world they could somehow apprehend the nature of God, but they had no means of apprehending the Son of God. Therefore Luther's assumption that wherever Christ was unknown, there was Satan, wickedness, and death is false. We grant that at the present time there is no salvation apart from the knowledge of Christ, now that the light of the gospel flashes its ray throughout the whole world.

The kingdoms of Christ and of Satan: The conflict between spirit and flesh

We also profess that, as Luther says, there are two kingdoms, that of Christ and that of Satan,[183] from which Christ snatches his own through the assistance of grace. But we posit the kingdom of Christ in the perfect, the kingdom of Satan in the perverted, and in between are infants and weak Christians. That sudden rapture of his happened to some when the Spirit performed miracles and taught in various languages. But we come off well enough now if Christ grows gradually in us. Though we are perfectly willing to grant those two kingdoms and that rapture, still, because no one is seized against his will, free will is not totally eliminated.

Luther returns here to that Achillean argument from Romans 7:14–25 and Galatians 5:16–24 concerning the fight between the spirit and the flesh.[184] More than once he reproaches Discussion for leaving it untouched, as if Discussion had undertaken the task of responding to his *Assertion*, even though she specifically points out that she is concerned with absolute necessity. But in fact she does not leave it entirely untouched, if a person reads my Discussion. But let us see what this Achilles has to contribute. "Even in the righteous the flesh fights against the spirit and the spirit in turn against the flesh." And he will not allow us to take the flesh as referring only to the grosser passions, since among the works of the flesh Paul mentions heresy, idolatry, quarrels, strife (Gal. 5:20), which clearly spring from those highest powers—reason and will. And so this is how he argues: "If human nature is so bad that even in those who have been reborn in the spirit it does not strive towards the good but even fights against and opposes the good, how should it strive towards the good in those who have not been renewed but are in the old man and serve in bondage to Satan?" What point has Achilles won here? That in the reason and the will there are also wicked impulses and perverse judgments? Didn't Discussion frankly admit this? In fact, though, even these impulses have their origin in those grosser passions, which cause us to love what is seen more than what is unseen. For by the flesh I do not mean only debauchery and lust, although in one place Jerome interprets it so.[185] Greed is a gross matter; often enough it gives rise to envy. Lust

---

183. *The Enslaved Will*, p. 120.

184. *The Enslaved Will*, pp. 120–21.

185. Jerome, *Commentarii in epistolam ad Galatas* 3.6.19–21 (PL 26 413–15).

is a gross affair; it frequently gives rise to deadly anger. Debauchery is a gross business; not infrequently it leads to slander. And so it is true that in the reason and will of wicked persons these detestable vices reign. But in what parts of a person do these fruits reign: "charity, joy, peace, patience," and so forth?[186] Isn't it in the same parts? "They reign," he will say, "but by the gift of the Holy Spirit; but those reign from the viciousness of nature."

Accordingly, since nature is common to all, there reigns in everyone without exception "fornication, impurity, lewdness, lust, slavery to idols, poisonings, aggression, strife, jealousy, anger, quarreling, dissension, factions, envy, murder, drunkenness, reveling, and similar vices."[187] These drives are not felt by all who have been reborn in Christ, as they would if they had their source in nature, which is common to all; rather for the most part they arise from a vicious education, from free will turning to what is worse, rather than from nature. But if you look at nature in and of itself, then just as it has an inclination to vice, so too it contains seeds of great virtue. But if the flesh wars also in the pious, then every single one of them ought to have all these urges. Though we grant that they come off from the battle victorious, what shall we say about the perfect? We grant that no mortal in this life has made such progress that he feels not the slightest itching of sinful emotion, but I certainly think there are many who do not feel any urge to commit murder or to poison someone. Why, then, does Paul mention these things? Because he is writing to persons many of whom were weak and not yet cleansed of the habits of their former lives, as was also true of the Corinthians. He urges them to make progress in Christian living and also, just as they had departed from the beliefs of the pagans, to withdraw from their morals, which he summarizes here, not because many of them committed such sins but because their Christianity was weak, so that the habits of their former life tempted them to vices only recently abandoned. Accordingly, the vices that Paul lists here do not apply so much to human nature as to minds depraved by vicious living; in them the flesh longs for the horrible vices reported by the Apostle.

But if free will is condemned so thoroughly because it has within itself an inclination to such vices, let it be praised because it has the seeds of virtue and an inborn horror of such vices, which cannot be shaken off by a habit of sinning, no more than humanity itself

---

186. Erasmus is referring to the twelve gifts of the Holy Spirit (Gal. 5:22–23).

187. Gal. 5:20–21; Erasmus is imagining how Luther would reply.

can be shaken off. The Pelagians denied that there is such a thing as original sin, and their opinion was rightly condemned.[188] But those who place such enormous emphasis on original sin come close to the far more dangerous error of Manichaeus,[189] and they give an opportunity to the flagrantly vicious to excuse their sins and blame them on nature. Among the pagans there is also a battle between reason and the emotions, which Paul calls the flesh. But if heresies, envy, and such sins are in the reason and will, as Luther teaches, the highest part of the mind is in a conflict with itself, while the will is balanced, as it were, between them, inclining now to one side, now to the other. So too in those faculties there is both spirit and flesh. For here "spirit" does not signify the Holy Spirit, but a human mind prepared by the gift of the Spirit to struggle against the flesh. And just as those who lack the Spirit often conquer by free will the passion which tempts them to sin—as, for example, many who lack grace are addicted to prostitutes but still win out over anger which tempts them to commit murder, not out of fear of God or of punishment but only out of a natural horror of such a nefarious crime—so too those who are led by the Spirit conquer such passions much more easily by their free will, which somehow works together with the Spirit.

Hence this passage does more to support free will than to eliminate it. But Luther's exaggeration of the power of the flesh even in the pious, just as it comes close to the error of the Manichaeans, so too it diverges from what Paul says shortly thereafter: "But those who belong to Christ have crucified their flesh, together with its vices and passions" (Gal. 5:24). Certainly those who have the Spirit of Christ belong to Christ. How, then, does flesh do battle if it is crucified and dead, together with its vices and passions? I say this not because I am unaware that in holy persons there is a continual mortification of the flesh as long as they reside in the dwelling of our earthly body but rather in order to refute Luther's exaggerations, which attribute too much to the flesh and Satan, just as they overemphasize original sin, to avoid attributing anything to free will. So much for this passage in the Epistle to the Galatians.

Chapter 7:14–25 of Romans, however, is a long and difficult discussion. I will preface my remarks on it by noting that there Paul

---

188. See *A Discussion,* n. 15.

189. Manichaeism was a dualistic, necessitarian system which placed the principles of good and evil in conflicting equality. Early in his life Augustine was attracted to it, but he later rejected it vigorously.

is not talking about himself but in his own person speaks of someone who has been conquered by his passions and is enslaved to sin. For when the Apostle made these statements he was not dead by means of the Law, nor was the commandment devised to put him to death, since he observed the Law very fully, nor was he sold into slavery to sin, nor did he do the evil he did not want to do, nor was he so unhappy that he wanted to be freed from this mortal body, which forced him to do what he did not want to do; rather, he took this role upon himself as a teacher, so that he could show that no one can be free from sin except by the grace of the gospel. I am not unaware, however, of how mightily St. Augustine struggles, in the first book he addressed to Boniface, to make this whole passage fit Paul; but he distorts much of it so radically that the more zealously he tries to persuade me the less I agree with him.[190] Another prefatory remark: almost all the ancient fathers do not interpret this passage as referring to original sin, but rather to a habit of sinning that corrupts both human reason and will. Or if they apply some text in it to original sin, certainly they apply most of the passage to vicious habits.[191]

With this in mind, let us see how this passage undermines free will. Certainly the sinner, who both lacks the Spirit of God and has been sold into slavery to sin—for that is the character Paul takes upon himself, so as to give less offence to the Jews—does not do the good which he wills but the evil which he hates. How does he will the good? Because he delights in the Law and assents to it, perceiving through his natural judgment that it is just and good. For the Law says: "You shall not steal, you shall not bear false witness against your neighbor, you shall not commit adultery" (Exod. 20:14–16). The sinner sees that what is commanded by the Law is just, being aware that it is unjust to do to another what he would not wish to be done to him, and by a certain natural inclination he is driven to what is good, but overcome by passion he does what according to natural reason he does not will but rather hates and detests. The fact that his conscience protests against the sin he commits is evidence that the Law is good. But if a sinner who has not yet become inhuman should do something right, he feels a certain mental pleasure, and this also

---

190. Augustine, *Contra duas epistulas Pelagianorum* (addressed to Pope Boniface I) 1.8.14–1.11.24 (CSEL 60 435–44). In *Annotations on Romans* 7:25 Erasmus reacts in the same way to Augustine's interpretation and argues for Origen's view that Paul here speaks under the persona of someone else (CWE 56 195–98).

191. Cf. Augustine, *Annotations on Romans,* on 7:14–25 (CWE 56 192–98).

argues that the Law is good. But when Paul adds "according to the inner man" (Rom. 7:22), that cannot be taken to refer to the Spirit, since Paul is playing the role of someone who has not yet received the Spirit. Rather by "the inner man" he designates natural reason, to which the will is joined, though the will can turn either way. For what he here calls the inner man he shortly calls the mind: "I see another law in my members fighting against the law of my mind," and a bit later: "As one and the same person I serve the law of God in my mind, but in my flesh I serve the law of sin" (Rom. 7:25). He says this about a Jew who is fleshly and lacks the Spirit of God. When he says, then, "Now it is not I who do that deed but the sin that resides in me" (Rom. 7:20), what does he mean by "it is not I who do that deed"? It is not I insofar as I am a human being possessing reason. For it is characteristic of a human being to live by the commands of reason; of brutes, to be led by emotional drives.

What does he mean by "the sin which resides in me"? Clearly the habit of sin that has somehow become a second nature and has fixed its seat in the mind so that it scorns reason and drags the will along willy-nilly; for the will assents when it listens to reason, and when it gives itself over to passions it does not assent. This is what the Apostle means by "To will is ready at hand, but I find no way to carry it out" (Rom. 7:18). Even a person corrupted by a habit of sin is sometimes horrified by his baseness and is goaded towards virtue by his reason; but his will, depraved by familiarity with sin, is overcome, and the person does what he does not will and abstains from what he does will. And this is "the law in my members, fighting against the law of my mind." Sin has acquired a right by the habit of sinning. But this right springs not so much from nature as from depraved morals. Otherwise, when Paul says "Now it is not I who do this deed but the sin that resides in me," if you apply that to nature, the language will smack of the Manichaeans' opinion, and nothing could be more detestable than that. And so this whole passage supports the opinion of Discussion, who attributes to mankind the seeds of what is right and a natural pressure to do what is virtuous, though that instinct is ineffective apart from grace.

That Paul is here speaking in the persona of someone else is clear from what follows, where he speaks once more in his own person: "Now, therefore, there is no damnation for those who are in Christ Jesus, who do not walk according to the flesh. For the law of the Spirit of life has freed me from the law of sin and death" (Rom. 8:1–2). But if "there is no damnation for those who are in Christ," what grounds can Luther have for saying that every righteous person sins mortally in his works, however good they may be, and that Satan reigns in the righteous under the reign of the Spirit because of the flesh, which he interprets as meaning the vitiated nature of mankind? And since "those who belong to Christ," as I said, "have crucified their flesh, together with its vices and passions" (Gal. 5:24), should this dead flesh still have so much power that in the deeds which the Spirit works in the righteous it commingles sin deserving of hell? I am very much opposed to this overemphasis on original sin, mitigating as it does the sins of mankind and agreeing with the teachings of the Manichaeans. Manichaeus teaches that only a single part of a person is irreparably vitiated, namely, the flesh. Luther makes the whole person vitiated, so that not even the Spirit performs a good work in him. But the ancient fathers interpreted this passage and ones like it, where Paul discusses the death that is transmitted to all because of the sin of one person, as referring to the sin by which we imitate Adam,[192] and it seems to me that all the elements fit this meaning better, since Luther's twisted meaning is not even self-consistent. But if he scorns Chrysostom, Ambrose, and the person whose commentaries on all of Paul's epistles have come down to us under the name of Jerome—whoever's they are, they are learned[193]—let him imagine that I proposed this interpretation from the context itself. His Achilles has been repelled and free will defended—which is what he demanded.

Now Luther gives two reasons why he does not wish to have the gift of a free will that can endeavor to do something towards salvation: first, because he could not hold up amid so many assaults of demons and dangers; second, because he would always have a restless conscience, always in doubt whether any work he performed was pleasing to God.[194] As it is, since God has placed salvation outside the power of free will and taken it to himself, and since God promised he would save Luther not by Luther's efforts or progress but by his own mercy and grace, Luther lives in confidence and certitude because the one who promised is trustworthy and also so powerful that no force of demons or adversities can snatch from Christ what he has claimed

192. Augustine, *Annotations on Romans,* 5:12 (CWE 56 139–61); see also Erasmus' paraphrase of the same text (CWE 42, p. 34 and 147 notes 12, 14–15).

193. See Erasmus' *Annotations on Romans,* on 7:14–25 (CWE 56 192–98, especially 195 n. 4 and 198 n. 17) and his paraphrase of the same passage (CWE 42 43–45 and 159 n. 8).

194. *The Enslaved Will,* p. 121.

for himself. "No one," he says, "will snatch them from me, because the Father, who gave them to me, is more powerful than anyone" (John 10:28–29). Thus it happens that at least some are saved, whereas all would perish if the matter depended on the power of free will. As it is, they are confident because, even if they sin, Christ will not blame them for their offenses but will either pardon them or correct them. This is pretty much the opinion of Luther, who adds that he is talking about what he learned from long experience. Whatever was the former condition of his conscience, whatever it is now, it is his business to see to it; it is not my part to examine it. But we are not inquiring here about what he judges to be more advantageous to himself but rather what is the will of God; and it could happen that a person might be free from worry about his conscience and still not be very safe. But in fact, who can be sure about his conscience when it is uncertain whether he is numbered among those God selected to be saved even though they do not deserve it? For even if he is certain about grace, he is not certain about whether God will take grace away. But he does take it away, as Luther himself taught, not from those who have offended but from whomever he wishes, so that it is not in man's power either to reject or retain grace.

Now if God had promised eternal life to those who believe in him and had added nothing further, a person could flatter himself by believing he has a suitable faith; whether anyone can know that for sure, I do not know. As it is, since good works are required so often and since Paul says, concerning evil works, "Whoever does such things will not possess the kingdom of God" (Gal. 5:21), I am afraid that those who believe in God's promises in this way might be deceiving themselves. God is merciful; he forgives sins, but he does so only for the repentant, for those who counterbalance their malefactions with good deeds. But if it makes no difference what our works are like as long as we have some sort of faith, why was it said that "giving alms extinguishes sin as water does fire"? (Ecclus. 3:30). Why do we say in the Lord's Prayer, "Forgive us our offences as we forgive those who offend against us"? (Matt. 6:12). David sings to the Lord not only of his mercy but also of his judgment. What does Luther mean when he says that a person is unequal to demons and to dangers if he tries to do anything through free will? Has anyone ever taught that a person can hold up against the assaults of wicked spirits defended only by free will? But they add grace to free will, which is inadequate in itself. "One demon is stronger than all mankind put together." But a demon is not allowed to do whatever he likes, not even against the wicked. And God, who aids and strengthens free will, is stronger all by himself than all the demons put together. If Luther should say, "What need is there for free will, since grace is sufficient?" it was for our own good, it was God's pleasure that we have it, just as I showed in Discussion,[195] and I will say something more about this at the conclusion of this volume.

God's justice and mercy seen through nature, grace, and glory

After this Luther makes a long digression on a commonplace theme, declaring that man is nothing compared to God, and he complains that "though we grant, as nature teaches, that human power, strength, wisdom, knowledge, substance, and everything we have is absolutely nothing by comparison with God's power, strength, wisdom, knowledge, substance, still we are so perverse as to assail only God's justice and judgment and claim so much for our judgment as to want to comprehend, judge, and evaluate God's judgment,"[196] and so on with other disquisitions on this point that in my opinion have nothing to do with the matter. For if he is talking about God himself, some have discussed his substance, as the theologians do. Some have lifted up their faces against God's strength, and do so even now, like the person of whom Paul says, "He lifts himself up above every object of worship and all that is called god" (2 Thess. 2:4), but the pious also discuss the same points. Thus the wicked grumble against the judgment and justice of God, but the pious discuss the same things insofar as it is right to do so. And just as it is not impious to investigate the power, wisdom, and goodness of God from created things and Holy Scripture, so too it is not wicked to investigate the justice of God from the same sources; and those who do so do not place their judgment above God's judgment, just as they do not place their wisdom above his. We grant that he is incomprehensible in every respect, except insofar as he has willed to become known to us. And, to twit Luther's inconsistency in passing, even though he has said so often that all the power of free will is mere blindness and the most profound darkness, still he grants here that a great deal of knowledge about God is grasped by our natural powers and human reason. Why should we not investigate God's justice using Holy Scripture, since

195. See *A Discussion*, p. 7.
196. *The Enslaved Will*, pp. 122–23.

he himself in the prophets so often challenges his people to pass judgment, as if he were prepared to risk that they could show him to be in some ways too little mindful of what is fair and just? But I have said something about this matter before.[197]

Luther goes on to declare that even in external affairs the world is governed by God in such a way that human reason is forced either to believe that there is no God or to believe that he is unjust or unaware of human conditions, as evidence he quotes the jesting verse of the lover: "I am often tempted to think there are no gods."[198] He quotes the well known proverb: "The worse someone is, the luckier he is."[199] He brings in Epicurus and Pliny, who thought that there is no divine providence but that everything happens by chance.[200] He brings in Aristotle, who said that the highest being is happy in contemplating only itself and would be miserable if it saw so much injustice and suffering.[201] He brings in Job, together with the prophets, who were tempted to doubt the justice of God. But what is the point of all this? To show that God's justice is nowhere apparent but must only be taken on faith? How do we believe that God exists? Isn't it through faith? And yet the gentiles also perceived from created things that God exists, and they said he is the best and the greatest. Someone cannot be the best if he is unjust. Faith does not preclude all natural knowledge but rather perfects it. But if they perceived God's justice, telling of how confessions are extracted in the underworld, where the pious are rewarded and the wicked tormented, why will Luther not allow that persons who have the Spirit from heaven should speak of God's justice? I do not know how Demosthenes felt.[202] What Cicero felt is apparent from that fragment of the letter he wrote to Octavius when he was apparently determined to die, threatening that he would go to the most holy souls of the Brutuses, the Decii, and the Catos and

197. See CWE 77 505.

198. Ovid, *Amores* 3.9.36

199. *Proverbia sententiaeque Latinitatis medii aevii,* ed. Hans Walther, 6 vols (Göttingen, 1963), nr. 25698b.

200. Pliny, *Naturalis historia* 2.5.14–27. For Epicurus' views about the gods, see Diogenes Laertius, *Vitae philosophorum* 10.81, 97, 122–24; and Lucretius, *De rerum natura* 1.44–49; 2.1058–63; 2.1090–1104; 5.110–234.

201. Aristotle, *Metaphysics* 12.9.

202. Demosthenes committed suicide by taking poison when the Greek revolt against Macedon failed; see Plutarch's *Lives, Demosthenes* 29–30.

report to them the sufferings of the republic.[203] He knew, therefore, that the souls of the good survive death and he contemplated that he would journey to the rest they enjoy. And Socrates, when he was about to die from drinking hemlock, did not complain about the injustice of the gods, but he congratulated himself that at the behest of God he would journey to Aristides, Phocion, and the other most praiseworthy men who were leading a happy life after being released from their bodies.[204] And Cato of Utica, when he saw that the victory would fall to Julius Caesar, did not condemn the gods for injustice, but he said that in the affairs of the gods there is an impenetrable darkness.[205] We say the same thing whenever we cannot make out why God does something that seems to us to be unjust.

But if we think that this whole discussion is resolved simply because we are convinced that though the wicked flourish here in bodily comforts they lose their souls, and that there is life after this life in which no good deed remains unrewarded and no evil deed unpunished, both of these points were known to the gentiles. The Stoics proclaimed that anyone who lacks the habit[206] of virtue is miserable even though he prospers to the height of human capacity in power, wealth, ancestral masks, beauty, age, health, strength, intelligence, eloquence and that, on the other hand, a wise man, even though overwhelmed by every sort of misfortune and bodily disaster, is nevertheless happy. Though it is clear that this is true, nevertheless Luther says it cannot be grasped by human reason. What then? Am I making the gentiles equal to Christians? By no means. But what only a few understood or rather thought to be true is now most firmly grasped through faith by children, the uneducated, and mere women, so much so that they would sooner face death than have this belief of theirs torn from them. It is not relevant to the present discussion to deal with the case of Aristotle; nevertheless Aristotle did not deny

---

203. Pseudo-Cicero to Octavianus in *The Correspondence of M. Tullius Cicero* ed. Robert Y. Tyrrell and Louis C. Purser, 7 vols (London and Dublin 1899–1918) 6.290. Cicero was brutally murdered at the command of Caesar and Anthony; see Plutarch's *Lives, Cicero* 47–48.

204. Cf. Plato, *Apology* 40c5–41c5. Socrates does not mention Aristides or Phocion.

205. The closest I can come to this is a speech placed in the mouth of Cato by Seneca (*Epistulae morales* 71.14–16), in which he emphasized the composure of the gods and our ignorance of the flux and reflux of human affairs.

206. *The Shield-Bearer* 1, n. 250.

that the gods abstain from governing the world so as not to grow miserable from seeing so much injustice and suffering, but he also thought that, once the governance of the world had been set up, there was no need for them to be concerned about it. And yet, because he reasoned that nothing could be happy if it had nothing to do, he concluded that they are happy in contemplating themselves.[207] We say the same thing about the true God, who is nonetheless happy as he knows, provides for, and governs all things.

Now just as if he had persuaded us that God's justice cannot be grasped in any way, neither by the pagans through their natural powers nor by the pious through the gift of grace, he presents us with a scholastic distinction of which, contrary to his usual manner, he approves, placing before our eyes the three lights of nature, grace, and glory.[208] "According to the first light it is incomprehensible how a good person is afflicted and an evil person thrives." I have shown that this is not incomprehensible, since the Stoics deny that happiness depends on such matters and the poets also teach that after this life rewards and punishments are laid up for the pious and the wicked. But how God saves someone who does not deserve it and damns someone who does not deserve it—which is certainly true in the case of unbaptized infants—I do not think can be understood satisfactorily by natural reason, since, if we are to believe Luther, not even the leading teachers of the church up till now have been able to understand why God damns an adult who does not deserve it; I leave infants out of the question because I think it is best to leave them to the judgment of God. But if this is easily perceived by the light of grace, either all the Doctors in the past have lacked this light or they held something different from what they wrote.

If that is conceded, then they deceived the people entrusted to them. I do not think that even in the light of glory it will be clear that God casts someone who does not deserve it into eternal fire. Once more, let Luther look to his consistency: earlier he said that free will, however great it may be, is nothing but absolute darkness; here he grants to it a light by which it perceives something without knowing or loving Christ. If he should say "only about human matters, nothing about the divine," I have already shown that much can be perceived by the light of nature both about the divine and about virtue. But how will we see by the light of glory that God punishes

207. See n. 201, above.
208. *The Enslaved Will*, p. 122.

the undeserving—which we certainly cannot perceive by the light of grace—since the light of Scripture teaches that no one perishes except willingly and by his own fault and since the impious, on their way to destruction, are reproached because they refused to hear the one who was calling to them, because they rejected salvation?[209] However great the light of glory may be, it does not conflict with the light of Scripture.

On Luther's epilogue

All that remains is the epilogue of this Lutherly disputation,[210] the first article of which is this: "For if we believe," he says, "it is true that God foreknows and preordains all things and that his foreknowledge and predestination cannot be either mistaken or hindered, free will has no existence." To this I have replied that free will is no more hindered by the foreknowledge of God than it is by the knowledge or foreknowledge of men. I have shown that not even the will of God takes away free will, since those things which depend on the mutable human will are willed by him contingently, so that his foreknowledge cannot be mistaken (since he foresees whatever way the human will will turn, to one side or the other) and his will is not hindered (since if a person turns to one alternative through free will, God would have willed the very choice which the person made). God permits, however, rather than wills, evil deeds, and I have already distinguished his signified will from his conditional will.[211]

The second article is this: "If we believe that Satan is the prince of this world lying in ambush and battling with all his might against the kingdom of Christ, so that he will not release men unless he is forced to do so by the divine power of the Spirit, it once more becomes clear that there can be no free will." To this I have replied that Luther enormously exaggerates the power of Satan and the wickedness of the flesh. And yet we frankly admit that a human sinner cannot free himself from the tyranny of Satan by his natural powers without the assistance of grace, but it does not follow from this that mankind has no free will. For we do not take "free" to mean the ability to do whatever one wishes by his own power.

The third is this: "If we believe that original sin has undone us to such a degree that even in those who are led by the Spirit it is always

209. Cf. Matt. 25:41–46.
210. *The Enslaved Will*, pp. 125–26.
211. See n. 46, above.

busy making trouble for us by struggling against the good, it is clear that in a person devoid of the Spirit there is nothing left that can turn towards the good, but only towards evil." To this I have replied that even we do not teach that free will by its own power can effectively turn from evil towards the good except with the assistance of grace, but rather that even in evil persons there is a certain inborn horror of baseness and a tendency or an inclination towards virtue, in accord with the highest powers of the mind, which have been corrupted but not extinguished in mankind, and that those powers can do something by making themselves available to grace, whether operating or cooperating grace, and by not turning away from grace.[212]

The fourth is this: "If the Jews, who pursued righteousness with all their might, fell headlong into unrighteousness, and the gentiles, who pursued wickedness, obtained righteousness unexpectedly and as a free gift, it is likewise clear from the fact itself and from experience that a person without grace can will nothing but evil." To this I replied that here righteousness does not mean the righteousness that corresponds to innocence and is opposed to vice, but rather the righteousness of the Jews, which consisted in observing the ceremonies and performing external works. In the pursuit of this righteousness the carnal Jews were tied to the letter and did not obtain true spiritual righteousness, which was revealed by the gospel; and the gentiles, who were set apart from the observance of the Law (that is, did not pursue the righteousness of the Jews), obtained true righteousness by conforming to the gospel, which promised them remission of their sins as a free gift. A gift is not given to someone who does not want to have it. And a gift does not cease being gratuitous if, when by free will someone makes himself available to the offered gift, God, who is merciful to all, judges him worthy to receive it because, when he is invited by grace to accept it, he complies and does not turn away. If we take "good" to mean what makes a person blessed, we grant that free will is not sufficient by itself either to seek or to obtain it, since whoever truly wills that good already has what he wills. But we posit that there are certain good deeds that do not justify but prepare for justification and are conducive to the retention and augmentation of righteousness. In such deeds, according to some, free will plays some part. Others prefer to think that even in such deeds there is preparatory grace and also some faith, although it is imperfect and not adequate to the justification of the Spirit. But God in his goodness will not allow any mortal to lack this grace.

212. See CWE 77 p. 585–94.

The fifth is this: "If we believe that Christ redeemed mankind by his own blood, we are forced to grant that the whole man was lost; otherwise we make Christ either superfluous or the redeemer of the lowest faculties. Therefore free will does not exist." I responded to this by showing that no part of a person is totally sound but that nevertheless in the highest faculties of the mind there remains a certain knowledge of virtue and a pressure and inclination towards what is right, but because of the tyranny of sin these vestiges are unequal to the task of achieving the grace of the gospel. But when Luther bases his argument on this, as if I considered all human faculties to be healthy and sound, he has no better grounds for concluding that Christ would be superfluous or a redeemer of the lowest faculties than if someone should say that for him a physician is superfluous because his intestines are healthy, though he suffers from ailments in his head and stomach, or that he has no need of a barber because he can see shadowy figures through the rheum in his eyes.[213]

Finally, Luther gives the tragedy a comic ending. You would say the fellow is speaking with brotherly love and is concerned about the salvation of his neighbor. I am addressed as "my dear Erasmus." He beseeches me in the name of Christ to take up a better cause. I am proclaimed to be endowed by God with many great gifts, which are also most noble, with various talents but especially intelligence, learning, and eloquence. He demeans himself so as to profess that he is nothing, except that he ventures to boast that he is a Christian. I am praised to the high heavens because out of all his opponents I am the only one who took up the principal matter, the only one who went for the jugular. For this reason he offers me thanks from the bottom of his heart and is angry with those who troubled him with irrelevant questions and with others who now boast of having new spirits and new revelations; he thinks that if they had followed my example, the Christian world would have more peace and concord. What could be calmer and more loving than this language? But how does it match earlier parts of the work, where I am painted in different colors? Here he attributes too much to me; there he strips everything from me; he is never balanced or even consistent.

It would have been better if he had moderated his style throughout the whole dispute and in doing so had been consistent. In that way

---

213. Erasmus is thinking of barber-surgeons. According to Celsus, *De medicina* (6.6.1E–F, 6.6.16A–C, 6.6.35) certain kinds of ophthalmia which produce rheum are to be treated by bloodletting. Cf. Erasmus, *Adages* 1.6.70.

he would have gained credibility and would have shown himself as a model of the Christian debater. But if he wished to correct an erring friend, all his witticisms, jeers and insults, mocks and moues, could have alienated even someone who was attentive and willing to be taught; they served only to make a knotty problem even more involved, and they deprived him of most of his credibility. It is surprising that he thanks me from the bottom of his heart because of all his opponents I am the only one who argued this point, since among others John Fisher, bishop of Rochester, published a volume in which he defended free will against Luther's *Assertion,*[214] and I know that he is not unaware of it. He should rather have thanked me on the grounds that of all his opponents I am the only one who handled the matter without contempt for anyone and with unfailing politeness, and that feature, at least, he should have imitated. As it is, while others treated him roughly, he spews out all his bile on me, thinking he can put me to flight with savage language; later—and at the advice of his friends, I suspect—he goes against the grain by tempering his style. In fact, if he was as concerned about the peace and concord of the Christian people as he makes out he was, he would not have treated many points, and he would have played out the whole script quite differently. But if he had handled the matter in a genuine Christian spirit and had come to the aid of failing piety with appropriate moderation, he could not have put me off either with praise—whether sincere or feigned, to me they are certainly odious—or with insults and mocks and moues.

And if I cannot handle the matter any more skillfully than I did in *Discussion,* he begs me to be content with my gift and to go on busying myself about promoting language and good writing, which up to now I have done with great praise and profit. On those grounds he himself also respects and reveres me and confesses that he owes not a little to my labors. If he thought I was unequal to the task I had undertaken, why did he reply to me rather than to others? As for his pretext of my authority, I have shown how silly that argument is. He says it is not surprising if God instructs Moses through Jethro or Paul through Ananias.[215] Such remarkable modesty! But this tune differs strikingly from what preceded it. As for me, even from the time of my childhood I would not be reluctant to learn what it is necessary to know. But did Jethro instruct Moses or Ananias Paul in the same

214. See *The Shield-Bearer* 1, n. 41.
215. Exod. 18:13–27; Acts 9:10–19.

fashion as Luther here teaches Erasmus? Even a grammar-school teacher would not instruct a child in an elementary class with such insolence. As for his wish that God would make me as superior to him in this matter as I am in all others, indeed I would not wish to be superior in error. Certainly up to this point Luther has not convinced me of the point he has tried with all his might to make me accept; so far is he from doing so, that now I attribute somewhat more to free will than I did before.

And because Luther wrote to some friend, "Let Erasmus learn about Christ and say farewell to human wisdom; no one understands these things unless he has the Spirit of God,"[216] I alluded to this in the conclusion of *A Discussion,* where I reply: "If I have not yet understood what Christ is, certainly up to now I have been far off target. But I would very much like to know what spirit so many Doctors and Christians had."[217] To this he responds by saying, "I think you yourself see what that implies," meaning that it is extraordinarily shameless of me to think that up till now I have known Christ, that is, have been a Christian. For that is all I meant, and I make no claim to arcane knowledge of Christ but only to a knowledge of him that is sufficient for salvation. But when he adds, "But all will not be mistaken just because you or I are mistaken," I do not understand very well what he means. If he is in doubt about whether he is mistaken, why does he speak a little later as follows: "I have not discussed, but I have asserted and I do assert, and I do not want anyone to have the right to pass judgment, but I urge everyone to submit"? But he will deny that this remark was made out of modesty, not sincerely. But how can he set me apart from everyone, since if I am mistaken, I am mistaken with everyone? It would have been more fitting for him to say: "You have not escaped error simply because you are in error together with the Doctors of the church and the people of Christ."

He adds these words: "God is preached as marvelous in his saints, so that we may consider as saints those who are far removed from sanctity." This is the eulogy he bestows on all the Doctors of the church and all the nations of Christendom from the time of the apostles up to the present age—except for Manichaeus and Wyclif. What he adds is quite true: "And it is not hard to imagine that, since you are human, you have not correctly understood or examined with sufficient care the Scriptures or the sayings of the fathers according to

216. See *The Enslaved Will,* p. 126 and CWE 76 p. 88, n. 404.
217. *A Discussion,* p. 30.

which you think you have hit the bull's-eye." But the same words could be turned back on him: What are those sayings of the fathers, since he himself grants that all the Doctors of the church assert free will except Wyclif? Unless, perhaps, he is suggesting that they meant something different from what they said.

But how does he gather that I am careless and ignorant? Because I profess that I am discussing, not asserting. "No one writes this way," he says, "if he sees deeply into the matter and understands it correctly." Quite the contrary, we see that no one asserts more vehemently than someone who knows very little about the matter. I did assert that free will exists; what it does and to what extent it acts, I said that I discuss, because the opinions of the orthodox vary. If I had said "most certain assertion" instead of *A Discussion,* if my parting sentence had been "I have not discussed but rather I have asserted and I do assert, and I do not want anyone to have the right to judge but rather I urge everyone to submit," would that have made my opinion the tiniest bit more certain? Finally, he prays for me that the Lord, whose case this is, will enlighten me and make me a vessel of his honor and glory. Yes indeed, even a tiny, tiny vessel, if it is too much to be an itsy-bitsy vessel.[218] For I would prefer, I would certainly prefer to be a fragile little Samian saltcellar in the house of God than a large iron barrel in a family which is not recognized by the Lord. And at the same time as this pious fellow wishes these things for me, he makes me blind and a contemptible and shameful vessel,[219] and together with me he includes the universal church, hardly thinking what I in turn could pray for him if I delighted in such trickery.

Erasmus' Conclusions

The terms of the controversy and their history

Up till now I have responded, not without considerable tedium, to Luther's disputation, or rather brawl. Now let us touch a bit on the heart of the matter and quickly come to the end of the volume.[220]

218. Luther uses the diminutive *vasculum* (perhaps because Erasmus was known to have a fondness for diminutives—he liked small details, not great brush strokes); Erasmus goes him one better by coining a comic diminutive of his diminutive, *vascululum.*

219. Cf. Rom. 2:21 and 2 Tim. 2:20–21.

220. On Erasmus' presentation of his own views in *The Shield-Bearer* 2, see CWE 76, Introduction, xcvi–civ.

And so, first, to take up the case of the expression itself, we grant that the Greek word τὸ αὐτεξούσιον is a lofty expression, as is the Latin *liberum arbitrium* ["free choice" or "free will"], which came to us straight from the schools of the philosophers in the early years of the church; the philosophers attributed a great deal to human reason because they were ignorant of grace. But because we who have been instructed in Holy Scripture rightly attribute the most to grace, the loftiness of the name does not quite correspond to the thing it signifies. To be sure, we must also grant that neither the Greek nor the Latin for it can be found anywhere in the canonical books. But if someone wanted to call the term into question as a strange expression, that should have been done in the early years of the church. As it is, since these terms were used by those who were nearest to the apostles in time or had even seen the apostles, and since by common consent throughout the ages up to our own times they have been accepted by the leaders of the church with no depreciation of grace, it is foreign to Christian moderation to make a melodramatic fuss over them now, especially since so many terms that are not found in Holy Scripture have been accepted to the point that it is heretical to refuse to acknowledge them, such as "consubstantial," "the perpetual virginity of Mary," and "three persons, one essence."

But the words "fate" and "necessity" have always been looked upon with disfavor by the more judicious philosophers, and with even more disfavor by Christians. For the two words have the same meaning; what the Greeks call ἀνάγκη the Latins frequently translate as *fatum*. No other feature of Manichaeism was more execrable than its devising of two principles: it made one part of man irrevocably evil, the other part necessarily good, and thus introduced a double necessity into the one person. This was the reason that Julian, who revived the Pelagian dogma,[221] charged that Augustine agreed with Manichaeus by exaggerating original sin and thus diminishing free will and attributing everything to grace. But in his books addressed to Boniface, Augustine energetically rejected this charge as false.[222] I do not see how Luther can do so, however, since he takes the

---

221. Julian was a Pelagian attacked by Augustine, who accused him of using his attack against Augustine's doctrine to convict the holy Fathers of Manichaeism; see Augustine, *Contra secundam Iuliani responsionem imperfectum opus* 1.2 (PL 45 1051).

222. Augustine, *Contra duas epistolas Pelagianorum* (addressed to Pope Boniface I) 1.2.4–1.4.8 (CSEL 60 425:11–429:20).

entire person as flesh, even with respect to his primary faculties and makes Satan reign in the flesh even after the infusion of the Spirit, since he overemphasizes original sin and the vitiated nature of man, and since he denies that man is in any way capable of accepting or rejecting grace, but is simply acted upon by God as a saw is acted upon by a carpenter. And so you see he has gone wrong here in two ways: first, even though all novelty is a stumbling block, they[223] not only do everything they can to eliminate terms that are fully accepted but they also try hard to bring back terms that are novel and long-since totally rejected, paying no attention to the objections of Paul, who ordered Timothy to avoid or to reject profane verbal novelties (1 Tim. 6:20). If it is pious to reject such words when they appear, it is wicked to bring them back after they have been long-since totally rejected. They cannot put up with the term "free will," which derives from the philosophers but was also accepted by the most ancient orthodox teachers. And he favors the term "fate" or "necessity"! What is their source? The casters of horoscopes. Who uses them? Pagan poets, but all the orthodox have always disapproved of them.

So much for the terms. Now let us consider the matter itself. Before this argument about grace and free will became very bitter, the orthodox attributed a little more to human powers than they did afterwards. Augustine was once one of their number: he attributed faith and good will to our natural powers; for the former attribution he apologizes, and he recants the second after the emergence of Pelagius. But if you consider how little is left to free will by this man and those who follow him—Bernard, and whoever wrote the two books on *The Calling of the Gentiles* which go under the name of Ambrose, and likewise whoever wrote the books of *Hypognosticon* which go under the name of Augustine—you will grant that they assert the term "free will" rather than approve of the thing.[224] For

223. Apparently Erasmus switches to the plural here because he includes Wyclif and Karlstadt along with Luther.

224. Augustine *De gratia et libero arbitrio* 1.1–3.5 (PL 44 881–5); these three chapters are devoted to defending free will, but the remaining twenty-one chapters defend grace. Pseudo-Ambrose in *De vocatione omnium gentium* defends free will in chapters 7 and 8 of book 1 (PL 51 653–7), but in most of the other chapters and particularly in the last eleven chapters of book 1 (15–25 PL 51 668–86) and in some of the chapters of book 2 he emphasizes the unfathomable mysteries of the workings of grace. The Pseudo-Augustine *Hypognosticon* (PL 45 1611–64) is predominantly anti-Pelagian and hence places most emphasis on grace rather than

St. Bernard, who seems to have drawn whatever he has to say on this
subject from the books of St. Augustine, even though he tries hard
to avoid seeming to do so by deliberately making up new terms,
defines it as follows: the free condition of the mind on its own.[225]
When you hear this you think he has a very grand notion of free
will. So too he defines the will as follows: "The will is a rational
movement presiding over sensation and appetite." He attributes so
much to it that he adds reason to it only as a handmaiden, as it were.
And at the same time he denies that there can be any necessity where
there is a will, adding that where necessity reigns neither good nor
evil can be attributed to anyone.[226]

This, then, is the splendid prelude. But when he gets down to
it and divides man's activity into three parts—nature, counsel, and
pleasure—meaning by counsel an effective assent to grace when it
is offered, there he attributes nothing at all to human power, just
as Augustine does not. By pleasure he means the consummation
of human happiness, which frees us not only from sin but from all
suffering. And so he posits three freedoms: natural freedom, freedom
of counsel, and freedom of pleasure, for he seems to have delighted
in such novel words. In the latter two he attributes nothing to man,
for they are liberations rather than freedoms, and God effects them
in us with no contribution from us. I am talking about the origin of
justifying grace—in which they insist man does nothing, although
after the inception of grace the human will acts together with it—and
about the happiness of the next life.[227] There remains natural freedom,

free will. Since all three works are primarily anti-Pelagian (especially the first and
the third) it is hardly surprising that they place much more emphasis on grace
than on free will.

225. Bernard of Clairvaux, *Tractatus de gratia et libero arbitrio* in *Sancti Bernardi
opera,* ed. J. Leclerc and H. M. Rochais, 8 vols. (Rome, 1957–77), III 167:13,
30, tractatus 1.2 and 2.3. An English translation may be found in *Treatises III: On
Grace and Free Choice . . .* translated by Daniel O'Donovan with an introduction
by Bernard McGinn, *The Works of Bernard of Clairvaux 7,* Cistercian Fathers Series
19 (Kalamazoo, MI, 1977), 55.

226. *Tractatus* 2.3–5 in *Opera omnia* III 168:1–169:15 / *On Grace and Free Choice*
in *Treatises* III in 58–9.

227. That is, about freedom of counsel (granted by God's free gift of justifying
grace) and freedom of pleasure (granted by grace in the next life). Discussing
another set of three—thinking the good, consenting to it, and carrying it out—
Bernard's Latin may be translated: "If, then, God works these three things in us,
namely, thinking, willing, and accomplishing the good, the first he does without

which he attributed to man subject to sin as the same sort of freedom he attributed to the wicked spirits: they are able to will neither good nor evil but only to will.[228] Augustine seems to have meant the same thing when he attributed free will also to Pharaoh, because Pharaoh willingly did what he did, even though he had no freedom to do good.[229] And he says several times that the human will is always free but not always good.[230] At any rate the freedom that they attribute to vitiated nature is certainly a wretched thing, hardly worthy of that splendid word. And then Bernard's subtle point that the will cannot be forced because if it is forced it ceases to be a will, that seems to me—and I say it with all respect for such a great man—to be almost sophistical and of no use in solving this problem.[231] And it seems unlikely that the earliest theologians, such as Irenaeus, Tertullian, Origen, and Hilary, who attribute free will to mankind, meant by it what Augustine and Bernard did.[232] It is also irrelevant that some attribute free will to wicked men and damned spirits insofar as they can do one thing or another, not that they can do or choose what is good.[233] But in fact there is even controversy among the scholastics

---

us; the second, with us; and the third, through us. . . . There can be no doubt, therefore, that the beginning of our salvation rests with God, and is enacted neither through us nor with us. The consent and the work, however, though not originating from us, nevertheless are not without us." See *Tractatus* 14.46 in *Opera omnia* III 199:9–11, 15–18 / *On Grace and Free Choice* in *Treatises* III 105–6. Erasmus says "they insist" because he is referring to the position held not only by Bernard but by Augustine and his followers.

228. Bernard uses *natura* (nature), *consilium* (counsel), and *complacitum* (pleasure) in the special senses explained by Erasmus: the natural freedom to will (though not to will what is salvifically good), the freedom to choose what eliminates sin (what is salvifically good), and the freedom to carry out the choice so as to attain true pleasure here or (most completely) in heaven. Of these the last two depend solely on grace, and the first, man shares with the condemned angels. See Bernard, *Tractatus* 4.11–12, 8.24–7, 9.30–1 in *Opera omnia* III 173:19–175:17, 183:16–185:21 / *On Grace and Free Choice* in *Treatises III* 66–68, 181–83, 85.7.

229. Augustine, *De gratia et libero arbitrio* 23.45 (PL 44 911).

230. Ibid., 15.31 (PL 44 899), for example.

231. *Tractatus* 2.4 in *Opera omnia* III 168.10–17/ *On Grace and Free Choice* (*Treatises III* 58).

232. An idea confirmed by Pelikan in *The Christian Tradition*, vol.1, 279–84.

233. Bernard, for example, makes this point in *Tractatus* 9.30–31 in *Opera omnia* II 187:8–188 (*Treatises* III 85–87).

about whether God can force the will of the demons, even with violent coercion.[234]

But to get to the point without beating about the bush, this much Luther has on his side: no one who has not been reborn can will anything good by means of free will; and from this there follows a certain kind of necessity, which Luther calls necessity of immutability, but it can also be posited in the good angels and in God, since God cannot change his nature and the good angels cannot degenerate into evildoers. But from the start Luther should have refrained from using this execrable word instead of inciting uprisings and then having to bring forth a novel distinction about necessity. But in fact on this point Luther adds on his own that, just as a person who sins cannot turn to the good by his own power, so too someone reborn in the Spirit cannot turn to evil unless grace is arbitrarily withdrawn, and he denies that this can happen because someone deserves it, just as grace is offered to a person without his deserving it. They[235] also grant that in cases where there is no will, there is also neither sin nor merit, no more than in brute beasts, who have only a natural appetite because they lack reason, without which there is no will. In fact, however, some attribute reason also to brute animals, but a reason below that of mankind; and in mankind there remains the sensitive appetite, which is sometimes called will and is in fact a sort of will. However that may be, there is little difference between the natural appetite that we have in common with brute animals and a will that is inborn in everyone but is so wrenched towards evil that it cannot turn in any way towards the good.

The Pelagians taught that original sin was not transmitted to the descendants of Adam but only death, which in itself is not evil and which Pliny even says was given to mankind by the gods as a great

234. Peter Lombard says that both the good and bad angels have free will, even though the good cannot turn to what is evil and the devils cannot turn to what is good. Thomas Aquinas analyzes the point in greater detail. But Gabriel Biel takes up specifically the point about coercion of the devil's will, setting out to prove on the one hand that the choice of the will, both of the good and the bad [angels], is free from coercion, but that in a special sense the fixing takes away their free will insofar as concerns acts immediately caused by God, but not as concerns other acts undertaken by the will. Hence, as concerns the acts of beatification the good [angels] are not free. So too the bad are not free as concerns the act in which their essential misery consists. See Gabriel Biel, *Epitome et Collectorium ex Occamo circa Quatuor Sententiarum Libros* (Tübingen 1501; repr. Frankfurt am Main 1965), sigs ee5–5v.

235. That is, presumably, Luther, Wyclif, and Karlstadt.

benefaction, so much so that Ambrose also wrote *The Goodness of Death*.[236] Luther rightly disagrees with this opinion, but he goes wrong in that he enormously overemphasizes original sin, rebounding from Pelagius so as almost to run into Manichaeus. For when he leaves in human nature no seeds of virtue and no inclination towards what is good but rather makes human nature totally flesh, that is, wicked passions, does he not present it as so evil that grace does not so much recreate nature as create a new nature? He derives this distortion from the fact that the transition from vice to piety is said to be a rebirth and a resurrection, as if it were a change from not being to being and from death to life, because Paul calls someone who is reborn a new creation (2 Cor. 5:17). Luther pays little attention to the fact that all this is said figuratively according to idiomatic Hebrew speech and that it signifies an extraordinary change in a person, just as we say that a person has come to life if he is recalled from the depths of despair to good prospects and we say that someone has become another person if there is an enormous change in his behavior. Thus exegetes teach that the blind man in the gospel, whose sight Christ restored, signifies human nature, not because it sees nothing on its own, but because it is overwhelmed with dense darkness, and sees very little compared with what is revealed by the light of grace.[237] The same human nature is signified by the woman who was bent double, by Peter's mother-in-law when she had a fever, by the dead daughter of the president of a synagogue, by the paralyzed man.[238]

But there is a great difference between disabled or sick and deceased. Nor is it necessary that in figures of speech (and Scripture is full of them) the similarity hold in all respects. On one point, clearly, the exegetes agree: free will has been wounded by sin, not destroyed; disabled, not amputated; it is sickly, not dead; blear eyed, not blind; bent over, not laid low, so that it is damped down, not put out. And yet in the course of an argument they sometimes act as if they were insisting that it is quite extinguished insofar as the knowledge and execution of good is concerned—which is what Luther constantly and strenuously asserts, or rather he simply denies there is any such thing as free will at all. Whoever wrote the book *Hypognosticon* teaches

236. Pliny, *Naturalis historiae* 2.5.27; Ambrose, *De bono mortis* (PL 14 539–67).

237. Mark 8:22–26, 10:46–52; John 9:1–12. Augustine, Gregory, Bede, the *Glossa ordinaria*, and Thomas Aquinas all make this point.

238. Luke 13:11–13; Matt. 8:14–15; Mark 5:22–43; Matt. 9:2–7. Gregory, Jerome, Hilary, Bede, and the *Glossa ordinaria* all make this point.

that it is deprived of the benefit of being able to choose but that the name and the rationale remain.[239] By "rationale" I think he means a mental notion of something that was once part of created nature and can exist again in nature when it is restored. But if the will is not properly said to be free unless it can turn to good or evil by its own power, there seems to be no freedom in corrupt nature, and according to this rationale free will is indeed nothing more than a name with no reality.[240]

Grace and the process of conversion

The ancient fathers also agree in professing that the human will, once it is freed by the Spirit, cooperates with grace, so that Paul says: "We are co-helpers with God" (1 Cor. 3:9). And on these grounds they establish a fountain of merit, because by willing we assist, as it were, the grace acting in us. But since every process has three parts— a beginning, a growth, and a fulfillment—in the beginning and the fulfillment they attribute nothing, as I said, to the human will but rather they assign everything to the grace that draws and perfects. In the middle, between the grace that draws towards justification and that which fulfils in glory, there they attribute something to free will both for good and for evil, namely, in that once it is freed by means of grace it cooperates with operating grace or it withdraws itself from it.[241] But if grace does not remain except insofar as we will it to do so, and if a person can dismiss grace by means of free will—and if he does this he deserves hell and if he does not he deserves eternal life—I do not see any reason why the same cannot be said about justifying grace, which Augustine calls operating grace. If the whole work is ascribed to grace but it is nevertheless carried out by a person who acts together with the action of grace, and at the same time no injury is done to grace, why should it be absurd to say that in a similar way human free will strives for operating grace? The Pelagians also agree with the orthodox in professing that grace cooperates with free will. But Augustine will not tolerate it when they say a person's

239. Pseudo-Augustine, *Hypognosticon* 3.4 (PL 45 1623): "Through sin, therefore, mankind's free choice lost any possible good but kept its name and rationale."

240. "A name with no reality" (*titulus sine re*) is Luther's phrase in *Assertio*, article 36 (WA 7 146:6; CWE 76 p. 306).

241. On the three parts of the process, see *A Discussion* (CWE 76 p. 67). Bernard of Clairvaux makes this triple division in his *De gratia et libero arbitrio* 14.49; see *Treatises III*. On operating and cooperating grace see *A Discussion*, n. 22.

good intentions are aided by grace, as if the onset of grace depended on man and a person's good intentions preceded grace, so that the assent whereby a person makes himself available to operating grace merits justifying grace.[242] And therefore Augustine will allow God to be called not the helper of good intentions but their bestower.[243] And that is the reason for his basic principle: God does many good things in man that man does not do; but man does many things that God does not do.[244] By these words he means that God makes our will good with no help from us. In order to untie this knotty problem, he introduces a third kind of grace, namely, preparatory grace, which he seems to distinguish from operating and cooperating grace.[245] By this device he avoids attributing anything to human choice in the reception of justifying grace.

But even if we concede that the grace of God is given only to those willing to accept it and that preparatory grace is a gift of God, it will be necessary to have another preparatory grace to prepare us for the preparatory grace, and another one to prepare us for that one, and so on to infinity, until we come to the gift of nature. But since the theologians profess that there is only one grace, which is called by various names according to its various effects, they could also have made up other names for grace. Hence it seems simpler to say that our disabled natural powers are always helped by the assistance of grace, whatever kind of grace it may be. What the Pelagians meant I do not know. I can only go by Augustine's quotations from the books of Julian, which, in my opinion, might have been held to be true if they were favorably interpreted. A large part of this argument seems to have arisen from words rather than from the matter itself, and such verbal battles, if there is any admixture of human competitiveness, can easily turn into brawling.

When we speak of merit, we do not automatically mean the kind that excludes grace, as is the case in ordinary transactions, where, once

---

242. For example, *De dono perseverantiae* 21.54 (PL 45 1026–27); *De praedestinatione sanctorum* 3.7 (PL 44 964–65); see McSorley, *Luther: Right or Wrong?* 73–76.

243. *Contra duos epistolas Pelagianorum* 3.4.13 (PL 44 597).

244. Erasmus misremembered the second clause. Augustine has: "Therefore God does many good things in man which man does not do: but man does none which God does not make him capable of doing." See *Contra duas epistolas Pelagianorum* 2.21 (PL 44 586).

245. See Pseudo-Augustine, *Hypognosticon* 3.4.5 and 3.13.29 (PL 45 1624, 1635–36).

a craftsman has got a just wage for his work, no favor[246] is owed on either side (though in the obligations of friendship, even after a good deed has been amply repaid, a mutual debt of favor remains in full). Such are the works and such are the merits which, the apostle Paul writes, are inconsistent with grace. But we speak of the sort of merit which excludes the unworthy. The more precious God's grace is, the more it should be embraced when it is offered and the more it should be preserved when it has been offered. Therefore just as we say that someone is unworthy of favor if he neglects it when it is offered or does not preserve it once he possesses it but rather misuses it, so too, in a sense, a person is worthy of God's gift if he accepts it eagerly when it is offered and, once it has been accepted, takes the greatest care not to lose it. Oftentimes gratitude alone makes people worthy of generosity, and ingratitude, on the other hand, makes them unworthy. Thus someone who teaches gratis i.e., without charge, communicates his learning much more willingly and eagerly if his students are eager and attentive than if they are listless and malcontent. And yet the teaching does not lose the character of a free gift, simply because a person with natural talent and eagerness to learn is judged worthy of an education, unlike another who lacks those qualities. And just as no human being confers a benefit on someone unwilling to have it, so too no one would bestow a benefit on someone who he knows would abuse it shamefully. And among human beings a person is said to bestow a benefit on someone unworthy of it if he gives it to someone who refuses to accept it or does not accept it appropriately. Then, too, people consider a person unworthy of what he has received if he did not acknowledge the generosity of the giver or used the gift inappropriately or neglected it. Nor is he said to be unworthy because he did not deserve the benefit but because he did not acknowledge it. For not having deserved it is common to the worthy and the unworthy. But someone who is said to be unworthy is so for two reasons: both because he did not deserve it and because he did not receive it and keep it as he ought to have done. And someone who is said to be worthy is not designated as such because the benefit was owed to him because of his merits—otherwise it would be repaying a debt, not conferring a benefit—but because he is unworthy in one way only, that is, because he has not merited it; but in another way he is worthy in the eyes of the giver, who wishes to exercise his generosity freely indeed, but also correctly, that is, to confer a benefit,

---

246. Latin, *gratiam*.

not waste it. For nothing is more wasted, as the proverb rightly says, than what is given to the ungrateful,[247] and according to Publilius he who bestows a benefit on someone worthy of it receives a benefit by giving it.[248] And someone is said to be worthy of greater generosity if he has received lesser gifts gratefully and used them well. Nor does such worthiness keep the benefit from being a free gift and wholly owed to the generous giver; it merely excludes unworthiness. Nor does it change the benefit into a wage owed for work but rather it keeps the benefit from being given to someone who does not want it or is ungrateful for it and would misuse it.

For among human beings it must be supposed that someone who does not accept it as he ought would not use it well. We should imagine the same thing happens with God's grace. He is, of course, a benefactor by nature, "giving richly to all" (Rom. 10:12), and he is not depleted by his generosity and has no need of favors in return; but still he does not will to bestow his generosity on those who scorn it or are ungrateful or abuse it. For what is given either because it has been earned by past merit or in hope of a profit is not a benefit but is, rather, in the one case payment of a debt and in the other doing business rather than exercising generosity; so too it is not beneficence but extravagance—indeed it is not a good deed but rather a crime—to give something that will injure the person who receives it. Moreover, just as a person is rightly said to be stripped of grace if he abuses it, so too he is rightly said to receive an increase of grace if he has used God's gift well. And the expression "merit" does not imply a debt or a wage but rather excludes the unworthiness of the person who receives or possesses something.

In this way those in the gospel who made excuses when they were invited to the banquet are said to be unworthy of it.[249] What then? Were the blind and the lame and the paupers on the street corner worthy? Not at all, and perhaps even somewhat less so than the others if we are speaking of merit that deserves a reward. But they are said to be worthy because they gratefully embraced a gift freely given. And to embrace is to assent and to assent is the beginning of human happiness. But the servant in Matthew who industriously invested the

---

247. Cf. *Perit quod facis ingrate* (What you do for an ungrateful person is wasted), in Henry T. Riley, *A Dictionary of Latin and Greek Quotations, Proverbs, Maxims, and Mottos, Classical and Mediaeval* (London, 1876), 329.

248. Publilius Syrus, *Sententiae* 65.

249. Matt. 22:2–8; Luke 14:16–24.

talent entrusted to him was enriched with the profit and was put in charge of greater resources—that is, of ten cities, according to Luke;[250] and nevertheless he owed everything to the free generosity of his master. On the other hand, the servant who buried the single talent he had received was deprived of it, and what was taken away from the lazy servant was added to the gains of the industrious one. But the lazy one was cast into outer darkness: if he was punished thus after he returned the talent to his master just as he had received it, how would he have suffered if he had squandered it irresponsibly? "To those who have it shall be given and they shall abound; but from those who do not have, even what they have shall be taken away."[251] For someone is said not to have if he has a benefit in such a way that he does not have it, that is, if he either ascribes the favor to his own merit or uses it otherwise than he ought. In this case, then, what is called worthiness in someone who receives and uses something well is what I think the theologians call congruous merit.[252] That expression, if it is rightly understood, is not inconsistent with the term "grace," just as the term "wage" or even "obligation" is not inconsistent with grace, especially if you take it as springing from God's promise. The promise is freely given, and whatever springs from that source is a free gift; but it is not congruous that such a great grace should be bestowed on those who reject it or increased for those who misuse it.

Therefore, just as there is a merit that implies a wage, so there are works that imply a debt and that are diametrically opposed to grace, such as the works of the Jews that Paul is dealing with in Romans 3:20: "All flesh will not be justified by the works of the Law." And likewise Galatians 2:16: "knowing that a person is not justified by the works of the Law except through faith in Jesus Christ." It is frivolous for a certain exegete to split hairs by stressing the word "except," since it is patent that here it means no more than "but only."[253] Nor is there any danger that good works will seem to be excluded by faith, since in that passage Paul is speaking about the works of the Jews, which were performed without faith and charity; truly good works, however, have faith as their source because it works through love.[254]

250. Matt. 25:14–30; Luke 19:11–27.

251. Matt. 25:24–30; here Erasmus followed his emended translation from the Greek in *Novum testamentum* (LB VI 130E–132A).

252. See *A Discussion,* n. 20.

253. Erasmus makes the same point in his *Novum testamentum* (LB VI 811 n. 24).

254. Cf. Gal. 5:6.

Paul is speaking of the works of the Jews in Romans 4: "But to him who works a wage is assigned not according to grace but as something owed."[255] And the Apostle says this not as a general truth but in the context of the arrogant belief of the Jews, who thought that eternal life was owed to them in return for their external works, in just the same way as wages are owed to a carpenter when he has finished a piece of work, and if he were not paid he would have the right to sue for the debt.

So too in Corinthians: "If because of works, then not by grace; if by grace, then not because of works."[256] But in Romans 2:7 he is dealing with a different sort of works: "But eternal life to those who pursue glory and honor and immortality through patience in doing good works." Likewise in 2 Corinthians 5:10: "So that each may receive what is due him according to his behavior when he was in his body, whether good or evil." This sort of works does not conflict with grace, but rather is attributed to faith which works through love (Gal. 5:6), because faith is the original source from which everything pours forth that makes us truly pleasing to God, and faith is a free gift of God, but yet it is not given to the unworthy, though it is given to the undeserving. Moreover, since all things are present to God, just as he is rightly said to take grace away from those who abuse his gifts, so too he is rightly said not to give grace to those who he knows would abuse it to their own detriment. And thus it comes about that it is not only not unjust but even merciful for him not to give his grace at all to some or to take it away after it has been bestowed. We could say as much about how the gifts of the Spirit are variously distributed, some receiving more, others less. For just as it is right and just for a human being to take away a benefit from someone who uses it badly after he has received it, so too it is right and just for God not to impart his grace to those who he knows will abuse it, with no less certainty than a human being knows that another human being has not used a gift well. At this point, if someone objects that God ought not to confer his grace on someone who will abuse it, we can reply that God offers his grace to many who are unworthy so as to give an example to the good and to throw fear into the wicked and to make it manifest to everyone that those who perish do so through their own

---

255. Rom. 4:4. The Froben edition (Basel 1527) and LB read 2 instead of 4. Either Erasmus or the typesetter cited the wrong chapter.

256. Erasmus or the typesetter erred here: the text cited is not from Corinthians but is Romans 11:6.

vices, since grace will not fail anyone unless he fails himself—I am
speaking only of adults.[257] And so we have removed the scruple that
tormented Augustine, who was so worried that if a person assented to
preparatory grace, he might seem to merit justifying grace.[258]

Another scruple ought to be removed, the one that made him
afraid that the onset of grace might seem to arise from free will.
He professes that the Pelagians proclaimed an anathema upon those
who thought that grace was given according to merit.[259] If the
Pelagians genuinely proclaimed that, there can be little doubt that
they meant merits to which a corresponding reward is owed. One
point in Julian's writings Augustine will not tolerate: that a person's
good intentions are aided by grace. From this he infers that a person
has good intentions without grace but that they are feeble and are
assisted when grace is joined with them. If you grant this it seems
that grace springs from man, whereas in man there is nothing good
except what arises from grace.[260] But in my judgment Augustine
would have had no need to be afraid about this point if he had made
distinctions in the term "good," as I have done for the terms "merit"
and "wages." For just as there are various gradations of grace, so too
there are various gradations of goodness or righteousness. Augustine
himself invented many names for grace, according to the gradations
of their effects, distinguishing sufficient from proficient, operating
from cooperating, and then again operating from preparatory. I
hardly know whether impelling grace differs from preparatory grace
in that preparatory grace moves the will and sometimes impelling
grace does not.

Now there can be many gradations of preparatory or impelling
grace, just as God transforms a person in various ways and step by step,
in the same way as nature forms a person step by step and a physician
restores a person step by step. And so, whenever a person assents to
the operating grace that confers righteousness, the onset of grace does not

257. Erasmus means that since infants are not morally responsible, they cannot fail
themselves. He makes the reservation because Augustine often uses the salvation
of children, who cannot earn grace through the use of free will, to refute the
Pelagians.

258. *De diversis quaestionibus ad Simplicianum libri duo* 1.2 (PL 40 110–27), *De
praedestinatione sanctorum* 3.7–4.8 (PL 44 964–67), *De dono perseverantiae* 21.54
(PL 45 1026–27).

259. *De gratia et libero arbitrio* 5.10–6.15 (PL 44 887–91).

260. Augustine, *Contra duas epistolas Pelagianorum* 18.36–24.42 (PL 44 567–71).

come from the person but rather from preparatory or impelling grace, which comes first, using some occasion to incite a person to take thought so as to be displeased with himself and want to be better. The ways in which God does this are innumerable: sometimes by means of a faithful wife, servant, or friend, he calls an unfaithful husband, master, or friend; sometimes he gets the same effect by sickness, bereavement, or inflicting some other calamity; sometimes he does it by the ministry of the word; at other times, by miracles, apparitions, or dreams; and often he hunts down a person from ambush, as it were, and saves him through what pleases him most, as, for example, uxorious men through their wives, and he snared St. Hubert as he was hunting,[261] and he captures avid students through writings; some he draws by the secret whistling of the Spirit.

And good intentions are not automatically said to be good in the sense that they confer beatitude, for whoever has truly good intentions has been justified by grace. But here we use "good" in the sense of something that approaches some resemblance to goodness and withdraws from evil to some extent—unless, perhaps, we like that opinion of the Stoics, who make all sins equal, teaching that a person is suddenly either completely good or completely evil. But even if, according to some rational scheme, this were true, nevertheless, because such discourse is abhorrent to common sense and foreign to the usual way of thinking in Scripture, it is to be rejected.[262] The Stoics provide the simile of a man who has fallen into water, and they say that it makes no difference whether he is many feet from the surface or two inches away from it if in any case he dies by drowning. Augustine preferred a comparison drawn from light and darkness. For there is no little difference between someone who lives in total darkness, so that he cannot make out anything at all, and someone who makes out something through the darkness, although with uncertainty, by a light which shines far off, however dim it may be, and someone who sees everything clearly by a light that shines nearby. By the same stages, I think, a person proceeds from bright light to total darkness.

261. St. Hubert was hunting a stag on Good Friday when everyone else was going to church. In a clearing the stag turned and displayed a cross between its horns. A voice from the stag said, "Unless you turn to the Lord, Hubert, you shall fall into hell." Hubert was converted and later became bishop of Maastricht. His feast day is November 3. See *Butler's Lives of the Saints,* ed. and rev. by Herbert Thurston, S. J., and Donald Attwater, 4 vols (New York, 1956) IV 247–48.

262. For an effort to discern Stoic elements in Luther, see Marjorie O'Rourke Boyle, "Stoic Luther," *Archiv für Reformationsgeschichte* 73 (1982) 69–93.

Both of these processes are exemplified by the tunnel dug through a mountain for the road from Baia to Naples.[263] When you enter it you have light for a while because of the height of the vault, but before long the light gradually disappears, until finally you come into impenetrable darkness, such as is said to be found in hell. That ordeal would be unbearable if it lasted very long. But a little further on a dim light appears. The light comes through a shaft drilled through the ridge of the mountain above, and it is dim and doubtful. It is quickly left behind and you return to profound blackness. When you have gone a little further something like a tiny little star appears in the distance. As you get closer to it, the light becomes more ample and bright, until you can see everything very clearly. What does not correspond in this comparison is that in it we move towards the light, whereas the light of grace moves towards us instead, as the sun gradually disperses the darkness of night by coming to us. And the correspondence would be better if there were a light that moved towards us as we in turn move closer to it, as grace draws near to those who draw near to it. And so, just as a person does not immediately have full vision when he sees by the doubtful light of early dawn, so too a person upon whom some light of grace has breathed its glow is not immediately good, although he is far removed from the profound darkness in which he could not make out anything at all. And yet if he does not turn his eyes away from that light but focuses upon it as much as he can, he is worthy of being shown more light.

But because this change in a person is spoken of as a rebirth, we should also discuss the elements in this simile. What is fastened to the womb is not a person right away: the mass is formed by nature and grows in the manner of plants and mushrooms; then it also has sensation; finally when the fetus has been fully fashioned by the craftsmanship of nature, it comes out. It looks like a living creature, but considerable time will pass before the rational soul emerges. But nevertheless, by such stages a complete human being is produced. And what makes it a human being is not infused unless the matter is prepared beforehand. For pedagogical purposes, let us imagine that first there is the feminine fluid, shortly thereafter a thickened

263. A tunnel through the promontory of Posilipo between the Bay of Naples and the bay of Baia, possibly constructed by Marcus Agrippa in 27 BC, is 2,244 feet long, 21 feet wide, and in some places as much as 70 feet high; it forms the so-called Grotto of Posilipo; see *Encyclopedia Britannica,* 9th ed., 24 vols (New York: 1878–1888), XVII 188. Erasmus visited Naples and the tunnel in April 1509; see Ep. 756:17–21. Cf. *Adages* 5.2.20.

mass, then a plant, then an animal, then a human being but one that is immature and imperfect, and finally a true human being. And in the same way as we are born, so are we reborn. I always make an exception for the absolute power of God, who can suddenly transform whomever he wishes; I am speaking about what usually happens.[264]

Furthermore, since sin is said to be a disease and Christ is called the physician, let us analyze this simile also. Many are the stages the physician must traverse to achieve the health of an ailing patient. He opens the veins lest the immediate danger of death should overwhelm the sick person, he prescribes his diet, he uses medication to purge the body, a little later he uses other means to purge it,[265] always accommodating his skill to the powers of nature—which, using its inborn power to fight against the hostile disease and eagerly striving for health, collaborates, as it were, with the physician's skill, and his skill in turn assists this natural power; finally, when nature has regained its strength the physician builds up the patient with strengthening medication until he is completely well. And just as sick people have a certain natural power that abhors sickness and longs for health (which cannot, however, be achieved in severe cases without the effort of a physician), and a patient will not be helped unless he makes himself available to the physician but will grow worse instead, and just as man has an inborn power to see but has it in vain if light is not available (and even light itself is useless if he turns away or closes his eyes), and he will not see what he should unless he focuses his eyes on it as he should, so too grace eggs on nature step by step when it is darkling and sickly until it arrives at that gift which makes us blessed, at least so far as this life is concerned. For to be blessed is to be free of sin and endowed with righteousness.

But just as there is a goodness, or rather goodnesses, which, properly speaking, are not so but rather movements, as it were, towards that sufficient grace that the moderns call "the grace which makes pleasing,"[266] so too there are also levels of justification, which gradually form a person and lead him to true justification, but nevertheless in them a person can claim nothing for himself. For imagine, if you will, someone who has acquired a fear of hell and divine judgment because of the sudden death of friends; he is not yet justified, but nevertheless

---

264. See nn. 45–46, above.

265. Presumably a clyster, or enema.

266. This is the same as justifying grace.

"the fear of the Lord is" at least some "beginning of wisdom."[267] To what does he owe his horror? To nature? Not at all, you will say, but to impelling grace. If he embraces impelling grace by means of free will, it is fitting[268] that God in his goodness should add more abundant grace; but if he turns away and rejects the gift, whatever it may be, it is by the vicious action of his own will that he perseveres in wickedness. Now if he is shaken by this fear so as to sin less grievously and more timidly, no longer reveling in the worst vices, he has made some progress towards justification. And then if he stops sinning, he comes even closer. If he busily engages in pious works with the same zeal he devoted to the service of his vices, he has true justification. But yet God is not so cantankerous that if someone rejects grace once, he immediately leaves him to his own devices.

Quite the contrary; until a person dies, God never ceases to use all manner of circumstances to offer occasions to repent. I make an exception of those who, because of their extraordinary malice, are handed over to their own reprobate understanding (Rom. 1:28). Therefore, what Augustine says is true: a person's good intentions are not aided by grace but given by grace, if he is referring, as I think he is, to the good will by which a person is justified.[269] But just as there is in man a natural inclination to vice that Satan continually exploits to tempt him to sin, so too there is in man a natural desire for virtue, though it is imperfect. The impelling grace of God stimulates this desire in thousands of ways to lead it to justification, egging on a person's latent, feeble impulse. If someone calls this natural inclination towards virtue and piety a good intention, there is nothing absurd, as far as I can see, in saying so. But we owe this very intention to the grace which arouses and assists it and which will finally perfect it if we do not neglect the grace. Certainly I do not see here any reason to fear that grace would not be grace, since this natural pressure would be feeble without grace, and to assent to preparatory grace does not merit justifying grace but only excludes a person's unworthiness, just as a sick person is no less beholden to a physician because at the urging of the doctor he submitted himself to his treatment, but by doing so

---

267. Ps. 110:10; Ecclus. 1:16.

268. Latin *congruit*; Erasmus is alluding to *meritum de congruo*. See *A Discussion*, n. 20.

269. Erasmus is somewhat imprecise here: Augustine assigns to grace not only the good will by which we are justified but also the initial good intentions which are inspired by impelling or preparatory grace, although they do not produce justification but only lead up to it.

he avoids being unworthy of having the physician undertake his cure; and if someone is saved by the advice of a friend, he professes that he owes his life to him, even though the friend's advice would have been useless if he had not willed to follow it, and it was within his power to neglect the advice. Now if you wish to give the name impelling grace to the particular occasions by which a sinner is admonished to repent, I do not have much against it. And yet in these also the will is not entirely inactive, since we lend our ears and give our assent to the occasion which admonishes us, and we certainly do this by our natural power; I am not talking about the assent which gives justification but that which somehow prepares for it.

Augustine's stance on the human will

Now let us grant that such natural movements of our minds, imperfect as they are without grace, spring from our natural power. Will this pose any risk to God's grace? I do not think so. How is that? Because whatever good remains in us and everything that we can do and are is itself a gift of God. Therefore, any motion away from vice and any progress we make towards virtue has its origin in grace, not in us. This is so in spite of the tune Augustine is always singing: "What do you have that you have not received?" And: "If you have received it, why do you boast as if you had not received it?"[270] The same tune could be sung to someone boasting about riches, beauty, strength, famous ancestry, good health, mental dexterity, or success. And then if someone looks down on a woman, self-satisfied because he was born a male, couldn't those same words be thrown up to him, "What do you have that you have not received?" And so this saying of Paul does not exclude free will but rather represses the arrogance of a man who does not acknowledge that whatever he is and whatever good he has, if he has any at all, was given to him by God as a gift. The same point is made in 2 Corinthians 3:5, through a distinction between the phrases "by ourselves" and "from ourselves": "We are not capable," he says, "of thinking of anything by ourselves as if from ourselves, but rather all our capacity comes from God." Even what we can do by our natural powers springs from us in such a way that it nevertheless comes from God, the fountain from which all things flow.

---

270. 1 Cor. 4:7, a favorite proof-text of Augustine, who cites it at least thirty-one times in his anti-Pelagian works. See especially *De praedestinatione sanctorum* 5.9–10 (PL 44 967–68) and *De correptione et gratia* 6.9–10 and 7.12 (PL 44 920–23).

Time after time Augustine chants the phrase "The will is prepared
by the Lord," but yet I have not yet discovered the place in Scripture
from which he took it.[271] But, unless I am mistaken, he also quotes
a text from Proverbs 16:1: "Man's part is to prepare his soul,"[272] of
which I have spoken elsewhere.[273] From these two texts it follows that
the will is simultaneously prepared both by God and man; and just as
man's will and grace act together in a good work, in the same way they
work together in the acquisition of grace, not because man acts in any
way so as to create grace, but because he presents himself as capable
of grace in proportion to his own ability. Now even though the word
"prepare" here means nothing different from "help," Augustine shies
away from the word "help" but embraces the word "prepare"; and
he does not accept the word "helper" but does accept "bestower," as
if someone who helps a feeble will to be truly good, so that whoever
has it is blessed, does not bestow a good will. But Augustine, as I
have said, means a sufficient or perfect will, And the other writer[274]
was talking about a good but imperfect intention, which would be
rendered sufficient by the assistance of God's grace. And imperfect
knowledge and imperfect will can have many gradations, since our
faith and the will through which we are justified are not perfect in this
life, and yet it is called a good will.

The virtues of the pagans and of the
Old Testament Jews

But if someone should say that a person not yet reborn in the Spirit
has no faith or knowledge of what pertains to piety, no good will, no
righteousness, no virtue (no matter how imperfect), he is proposing
something more paradoxical than all the paradoxes of the Stoics, since
in the histories of the pagans we read of some examples of virtues

271. In his anti-Pelagian writings Augustine cites this text at least twenty-eight
times. See, for example, *Contra duas epistolas Pelagianorum* 1.18.36, 2.9.20, 4.6.13,
4.9.26 PL 44 567, 585, 618, 628. It is cited in each of the six books of *Contra secundam
Iuliani responsionem imperfectum opus* (PL 45 1050–1607). Augustine was following
the Septuagint version of Prov. 8:35 ἑτοιμάζεται θέλησις παρὰ Κυγίου.

272. Prov. 16:1; see, for example, *Contra duas epistolas Pelagianorum* 2.9.19–20 (PL
44 585–86).

273. *A Discussion* (CWE 76 p. 63 and CWE 77 pp. 601–2).

274. That is, Augustine's Pelagian opponent, though at *Contra duas epistolas
Pelagianorum* 3.4.13 (PL 44 597), where Augustine makes this distinction, he refers
to the Pelagians in general.

such that they sometimes rightly put us Christians to shame, and in the books of the philosophers we find precepts so similar to those in the volumes of the prophets that some have tried to teach that they were taken from there. From such sources there arose among them certain good deeds which I grant did not merit or generate justifying grace but nevertheless rendered the mind more capable of receiving grace, as long as hypocrisy or reprobate perceptions did not get in the way; this is analogous to what the philosophers also say, that certain accidental forms make matter more capable of receiving the principal form.[275]

But if someone wants to ascribe also to grace whatever the gentiles either knew or performed, I have no objection as long as it is conceded that human free will got that far with the help of grace; if they had continued to progress in such knowledge and deeds, they would have attained eternal salvation through the same grace. For although Jerome in *To Ctesiphon* seems to think that everyone to whom the law of Moses was not available perished,[276] nevertheless I find more probable the opinion of the person—whoever he was—who wrote *The Calling of the Gentiles:* that divine providence is not lacking in any era or to any kind of people.[277] Thus, before the law of Moses was handed down, it is clear that many were holy under the law of nature. But since the law of Moses was handed down to only one people and there was no command to preach it throughout the whole world like the gospel but only to the posterity of that nation—although they did not turn away converts—it is binding only on those to whom it was handed down or on those who professed it of their own accord. And indeed the Pharisees are reproached in the gospel because they

275. For example, the "accident" of proper quantitative extension in the fetus makes it more capable of receiving the substantial form of the soul. For the Aristotelian terminology (substance, accident, matter, form) see Simon Blackburn *The Oxford Dictionary of Philosophy* (Oxford and New York, 1994) 4, 142, 234, 366.

276. Jerome, *Epistola 133, Ad Ctesiphontem adversus Pelagium* 9 (PL 22 1157); as an extreme example of charges that seemingly could be brought against God for injustices in the Old Testament, Jerome mentions that a roommate of his, Porphyrius, raised the objection that everyone who did not have access to the law of Moses was damned. Jerome does not himself endorse the idea (or specifically reject it). Augustine discusses the problem in Ep. 102, *Sex Quaestiones contra paganos* 2 (PL 33 373–76).

277. Pseudo-Ambrose, *De vocatione omnium gentium* 19, 25, 29, 31, 33 (PL 51 706, 710–11, 715–18).

travelled over land and sea to make a single convert who would be doubly damned to hell.[278]

Therefore, just as the law of nature did not justify but prepared for justification, so too, although the law of Moses did not confer perfect righteousness, it nevertheless prepared for it, in this way, if no other, that by fear it restrained the Jews from sinking into extreme wickedness. For a person whose wrongdoing is tempered by fear is more curable than someone who has thrown off all fear of God and shame before men, glorying and reveling in the worst vices. This, I think, is what Paul meant when he said he had labored more than all the rest (1 Cor. 15:10). For the Law had prepared the Jews for Christ, although it did not confer justification. For they already knew that there is one God, that the gods of the pagans were demons hostile to mankind, that there is no salvation except from God; the knowledge of these points and others like them made them more capable of receiving the gospel. But Paul had undertaken the harder task of instructing the gentiles, some of whom believed that there is no God, others that the gods are not concerned with the affairs of mortals; others had an extremely low opinion of the gods, thinking they are as they are portrayed in mythology; many thought that nothing was left of a person after the funeral pyre. And yet he found some among them who had sinned less grievously, that is, whose minds were less perverted, and the same thing happened among the Jews. Perversion, however, springs not from nature but from free will. For it is one thing to be perverted; another, to be mistaken. It is one thing to lack justification; another, to be wicked.

But Luther so exaggerates the corruption of nature that he puts it on a par with the malice of Satan, whereas Scripture says: "God made the nations of the earth curable, and there is no deadly poison in them and no reign of hell on the earth. For justice is everlasting and immortal," but injustice brings with it death. "And the wicked have summoned it by their words and deeds" (Wisdom 1:14–16). Moreover, that the author is here speaking not about original sin but about sin chosen by the will is clear from what follows: "For the wicked say to themselves, thinking to themselves wrongly, etc." (Wisdom 2:1). Accordingly, just as we grant that human nature was corrupted by the sin of our first parents, so too it is clear that it has within it not inconsiderable seeds of virtue and piety. But if we make mankind totally wicked simply because they were born so, let us

278. Cf. Matt. 23:15.

make the same mankind totally pious because a seed plot of piety is inherent in them. In fact, the reason that more turn to vice than to virtue is not so much a corrupt nature as degenerate education, bad companionship; a further reason is that the enticements and rewards of vices are ready at hand, whereas virtue is a very difficult and burdensome undertaking, and its enticements are not immediately obvious. That is the reason many are more inclined to evil deeds. Now just as we grant that sin was known more fully through the law of Moses, so too it cannot be denied that the laws of the gentiles, most of which preceded Moses, punish many of the same crimes as are punished by the law of Moses. And so the law of nature also shows there is sin, and this knowledge generates a horror of sin. That this is true is clear from what the pagan poets write about the torments of conscience and the avenging Furies.[279] But if the law of Moses has enough force to make us seek refuge, after we know our sins, by imploring God's help, what is there to keep the law of nature from impelling us to do the same, according to its own small measure? And if prayer prepares us for God's grace—as Luther also concedes—why should we be any less prepared for it by morally good works, among which, I think, prayer is included?

I do not care for these Stoic notions that whatever is done apart from grace is equally damnable, so that the tolerance of Socrates is no less grievous an offence in the sight of God than the cruelty of Nero. Granted that whatever is done without the gift of faith and charity and is not referred to God is not truly good, still, whatever does not conflict with faith and charity and makes an approach to them, as it were, can be called good in some sense. At the same time, imagine, if you will, gradations of faith and of charity which have not yet attained effective faith, which is only given by God. Imagine, if you will, a pagan philosopher who knows that there is one mind that created and governs all things, than which nothing better or greater can exist and from which all good flows forth, that rewards good deeds, that he acknowledges should be worshipped with purity of heart; but he tolerates the commonly accepted ceremonies, partly because he despairs of being able to bring the uncultivated crowd to believe anything else, partly because he believes it is to the advantage of the people to be restrained by such a religion until something better emerges, and in the meantime he admonishes those whom he

---

279. See, for example, Aeschylus' *Eumenides*; Euripides' *Medea*; Procne and Myrrha in Ovid's *Metamorphoses* 6.600–4, 10.319–55; and Dido in Virgil's *Aeneid* 4.24–27.

thinks can be taught; he exerts himself to fulfill as well as he can his duties to his country, his parents, wife, and children, ignoring the ill will stirred up by virtue and hoping to be rewarded by that mind for his good deeds. That some of the pagans had such an attitude is testified by their own books. What then? Shall we say that such a person, when he is conducting himself extremely well, sins quite as much as if he got rid of his wife with poison and prostituted his children? At all events I think that such a person does not lack faith entirely and that his works do not stir up God's wrath but rather that he renders himself capable of receiving God's goodness and makes himself suited to it.

Augustine and congruous merit

Let us bring forward Augustine when he was not yet a Christian, but stood at the crossroads deliberating into which sect it would be most proper for him to be initiated. For he was a Manichaean not because he approved of that heresy but so that he would not seem to belong to no sect at all. He had his doubts about Christ, but his attitude was to join whichever sect he discovered to be best. To determine that, he listened to Ambrose, read Paul's epistles, discussed beatitude with his friends, prayed, gave alms, stayed away from the profane theaters, was horrified by disgraceful deeds, had a single concubine to whom he was conjugally faithful—which in a pagan was not considered to be an offense. While he was striving, as it were, for the Lord's grace by such deeds as these, shall we say that he stirred up God's wrath as much as if he had killed his mother with poison? How absurd! But if such morally good works, or whatever you want to call them, prepare a person for God's grace or if, as the scholastics say, they earn it by *meritum de congruo,* what is absurd about this opinion?[280] And if Augustine, through the power of free will, could listen to the sermons of Ambrose, read holy books, make contributions to the poor, make time for prayers and meditations, converse with pious men, and ask them to pray to the Lord for his salvation, what reason is there to hiss so vehemently at the opinion of the scholastics, according to which a person merits justifying grace *de congruo* through morally good works? We are frightened of verbal shadows, when in reality there is no absurdity. If someone should say that through such deeds a person can in some sense be prepared for grace, they would put up with it, I think; as it is, even though

---

280. See *A Discussion,* n. 20.

the same thing is meant by someone who says "grace is merited *de congruo*," they are offended.

What I have set forth about Augustine could also be said about someone quite taken up with many vices but who is nevertheless dissatisfied with himself and desirous of being endowed with a better attitude. For I have heard some people saying, "Would that God would give me faith! Would that he would endow me with an upright will!" and I knew their faith was not sincere and their life was disreputable. I replied to them, "It is your part not merely to wish mildly for God's gift, but also to strive for it." "By what means?" they said. "Read holy books, go to holy sermons, pray frequently, give money to the poor, ask pious men to pray for your salvation, little by little withdraw from vices as much as you can; if you do these things which are under your control, God's grace will not be wanting to you." And I think I gave pious advice. Whoever wishes for a holy will does not entirely lack it; and whoever wishes for the gift of faith does not entirely lack faith, but rather he wants his imperfect qualities to be perfected through the assistance of grace. Nor does it make much difference whether you say that these works are performed through free will or that they are done with the continual inspiration of particular grace, which advances but does not perfect.

But in fact it is more plausible to profess that they are not devoid of the grace of God, who gradually advances the minuscule human power which is inadequate by itself. For you owe no less to someone who gave you at one stroke the capital to do business for a long time than you do to someone who bestows on you every day what is sufficient for that day. Moreover, someone is giving every day if he has it in his power to snatch away what he gave. For in this process the free gift of grace is not turned into an obligation, but rather the manner of giving is changed. And in this way grace is not given according to merit—a view detested even by the Pelagians—but care is taken to avoid seeming to give it to the unworthy. By the unworthy I do not mean those who have not merited God's gift, but those who refuse and turn away from it. Moreover, there is no reason to fear that grace might seem to have its origin in natural power, since even that natural good, as I have often said, is a free gift of God, greater in some, smaller in others. Nor does a person automatically have something of his own to boast about, unless he wants to claim for himself what he has from another. And if there is so much danger of boasting, a person can also preen himself on the special gift of God, since what pious people have taught is true, that even in the midst of virtues vainglory lays its ambush. Finally, there is a risk that even what can be done by natural power might be snatched away, if it is used otherwise than it should be. Hence, just as we thank God for good bodily health and other benefits, it is fitting that we should thank him for these gifts, praying that by his inspiration he will perfect what is imperfect. And because in a certain sense someone gives every day if he does not snatch away what he is able to snatch away, there is good reason for us always to be importunate with God, either by thanking him for what we have received or praying that he will preserve and augment what he has generously deigned to bestow on us. This sort of merit, then, does not block grace but causes a person to receive grace more fittingly and generously.

I go over and over these points to show that a large part of this controversy among the ancient fathers had its origins in and was exacerbated by expressions not taken in a proper way. Jerome is outraged with Ctesiphon—although his anger seems to be a pretence—because he had written that a person could be saved if he wanted to be, but with the assistance of grace. Jerome himself says: "To will and to run are mine, but this very thing of mine, without the continual help of God, is not mine."[281] The language is different; the meaning is the same. Finally, to handle this whole subject of the ways in which God's grace works in mankind leads to many profound issues which it is not necessary to examine with great thoroughness. It is clear that whatever we have derives entirely from the generosity of God. But to determine how he dispenses his munificent gifts to us—though it may be the subject of pious speculation—I certainly do not think it is necessary. And yet no other subject appeals so much to Augustine. I have shown that the opinion of the scholastics, which, among those views which have not been rejected, allows most to free will, is not all that different from the opinion of Augustine, except that they differ in words rather than in meaning. Whenever the ancient fathers mention merit, they mean that sort of merit which excludes grace, as when someone is motivated by great services performed for him to return the favor and would be ungrateful if he did not, or if someone pays a hired workman the wages due to his efforts. But a benefit is rightly withheld from anyone who neglects it, refuses it when it is offered, uses it badly after he has received it, or is ungrateful to the one who gave it to him. On the other hand, a person somehow merits if he

281. *Epistola 133, Ad Ctesiphontem adversus Pelagium* 8 (PL 22 1160, PL 22 1154).

accepts it readily, acknowledges the greatness of the benefit, uses it skillfully, is mindful of it, and proclaims it. For to have given or extended thanks to God, who does not need to exchange favors with anyone, is to have returned his favor.[282] Similarly, since there are many types of righteousness and of good will and faith, and because the ancient fathers did not distinguish them with sufficient clarity, they did not always seem to have paid sufficient attention to what others said, and they were not very consistent themselves, so that, if you carefully compare and examine the individual parts of a disputation, you will notice that they sometimes say the same things as their opponents and that they do not always agree among themselves when they are dealing with the same issue—as, for example, it seems to Jerome absurd to say that God crowns his own good works, which he has performed in us,[283] whereas in Augustine no opinion is more commonly repeated;[284] sometimes in the same disquisition one part may not agree very well with another because they have not distinguished their terminology clearly enough.

But none of them is so hostile to free will that he does not attribute something to it. "Just as Adam, who was created upright, was able to persevere in the good through free will, he fell because he chose not to stand. If he had willed to do so, it would have been his merit, not his guilt." These are the words of Augustine in his book *Reproof and Grace,* chapter 11.[285] He could have held out if he had willed to do so, because God gave him assistance through which he could have persistently clung to whatever good he willed and without which he was unable to do so. But because he did not will to hold out, certainly the fault is his, just as the merit would have been his if he had willed to hold out. So too a person freed by grace can remain in the state of grace if he wills to do so, and if he perseveres, he merits; if he does not will to do so, he is guilty of a sin. Here, at any rate, merit and guilt are ascribed to free will. For I do not think it

282. In Latin, *Nam Deo, qui nullius eget mutua gratia, egisse gratias aut habuisse retulisse est.* The sentence is difficult to put into English because in Latin *gratia* can mean grace, thanks, or favor.

283. *Epistola 133, Ad Ctesiphontem adversus Pelagium* 5–6 (PL 22 1154).

284. For example, *De gratia et libero arbitrio* 6.15 (PL 44 890–91).

285. Erasmus paraphrases the first three sentences of Augustine's *De correptione et gratia* 11.32 (PL 44 935). The Froben edition (Basel 1527) reads 2 instead of the correct 11 (which appears as xi in LB). The typesetter of the 1527 edition may have read 11 as the roman numeral II.

is relevant to the issue to investigate whether Adam's natural gifts were supplemented with grace, without which he could not have persevered, and whether his natural gifts would have sufficed against all temptations, since he was immediately conquered by Satan's first assault. It is enough to hold that Adam in paradise was as he is described in Holy Scripture, even if we do not reply to all the curious questions always being asked.[286] Free will, then, as Augustine says, sufficed to do evil but had too little strength to do good unless it was assisted by an all-powerful good.[287] He sets "had too little strength" in contrast with "sufficed." And when he mentions the all-powerful good, he implies a certain human good that is feeble and needs the assistance of grace.

But what is that good except what a person can achieve by his natural power?—not that he immediately becomes blessed but that he is more prepared for the grace of God. A person who understands much through human reason and believes certain truths about God, who has drunk in a love of wisdom from the books of the philosophers, who has striven for a habit of virtue according to his own small measure, is somewhat more capable than a crude soldier who has lived in a profound state of ignorance and the grossest vice and who never gave a thought to God. And so does a person have what he has not received? Not at all. But it does not follow that since he did not receive it as a gift but as a legacy, therefore he did not receive it.[288] Likewise it does not follow that since he did not receive it in one way, therefore he did not receive it in any way. But if I wanted to indulge in sophistry, I could point out that it is not even true that free will suffices to do evil. For it would not suffice if it were deprived of the general motion of the first cause. Therefore, it receives the very power it has to will evil and commit sins. Since, then, there is inherent in mankind

286. For example, Peter Lombard in *Sententiae* II dist. 29 asks whether man before he sinned needed operating and cooperating grace and whether he had virtues before the fall (PL 192 719). Since the scholastic theologians usually wrote commentaries on this work, the questions about Adam's prelapsarian state multiplied. For example, Thomas Aquinas, commenting on *Sententiae* II dist. 29, asks whether man in a state of innocence needed grace; whether he had it; if he had it, whether the grace of the human race would have been greater than it is if he had persisted in innocence and whether human acts would have been more effective and meritorious.

287. Augustine, *De correptione et gratia* 11.31 (PL 44 935).

288. That is, the reader of philosophical books owes his wisdom to the past; it is a legacy, not a gift of God's grace.

a certain inborn power that seeks virtue, even though it has been disabled by sin, this faculty is stirred up by various circumstances, one of which is the Law, which uses rewards to encourage right conduct and punishments to deter from wrongdoing and thus makes a person aware of his sin and dissatisfied with himself, even if the sin is secret, and on the other hand makes him rejoice if he is not in violation of the Law. But if the law of nature partly does what the law of God does and a certain beginning of good is attributed to this law when it makes sins known, it is not absurd to attribute this partial and incipient good to free will.

Then again, if, once the gradations of grace have been distinguished, someone wants to give the name grace to every occasion that invites us to a better life, I will allow it, as long as it is also allowed to call our natural powers a grace. What example can you give of a person so brutalized by vice that if you ask him seriously whether he wants to be free from vice and dear to God, he will reply that he does not want to? And as Seneca writes, a large part of goodness is the will to be good.[289] The further that will leaves imperfection behind, the closer a person is to grace. But if we grant that some will to goodness, however minuscule, springs from nature, it is not impious to say that a person's good intention, which is impotent in itself, is helped by the access of grace. Augustine grants that texts from 2 Paralipomenon 15[:2], "The Lord is with you if you are with him" and "if you seek him, you will find him; but if you abandon him, he will abandon you," make it clear that free will exists, both for good and for bad. But he disagrees with his adversaries in that they say that our merit consists in our being with God and that the grace by which God in turn is also with us comes according to this merit; they say likewise that our merit consists in seeking him and that the grace of finding him is given according to this merit. There is a similar text in 1 Paralipomenon 28:9: "If you seek him, he will be found by you; and if you send him away, he will reject you forever."

Augustine grants that from this text also free will is rightly inferred, but he will not put up with those who posit human merit here: "If you seek him expecting a reward, he will be found by you." This controversy seems to me to spring from words rather than facts. For if someone who is commanded to seek the Lord does not scorn impelling grace and accommodates his power to it, in

289. *Epistulae morales* 34.3.

some sense he makes himself worthy of more abundant grace, and it is not absurd to call this "merit," not because it equals the benefit and turns grace into wages that are owed, but because it excludes unworthiness. But Augustine takes "merit" to mean wages. For he makes it clear that that is what he means when he says: "And they work in every way as hard as they can to show that God's grace is given according to our merits, that is, that grace is not grace."[290] For there is a kind of merit which excludes grace and demands wages that are owed, like those of a workman who can sue you in court if you do not pay him his wages. If you pay him, no favor[291] is owed on either side. According to this sense of the word, I think, they had pronounced an anathema against those who said that God's grace is given according to human merits.

But while Augustine shudders too much at the notion that the beginning of grace should be attributed to free will, he does indeed grant that free will is consistent with God's commandments, as when John says, "My dearest brothers, let us love one another." But he denies that this does any good unless the one who commands adds a certain amount of love, so that when free will has been admonished by the commandment it seeks the gift of God.[292] And so he seems to say that, besides the grace which impels through the commandment, the will needs a certain imperfect grace, which is infused by God, so that when this has been received the will seeks justifying grace, because John added in that passage, "Love is from God." But thus we go around in circles! For if someone has imperfect grace, he is not yet justified. How then will he seek justifying grace, since free will is not yet liberated? It does not follow automatically that justifying charity does not come from God, even if we grant that a person can have a certain kind of charity towards God through his natural power. Augustine says in his book *Reproof and Grace,* addressed to Valentinian, "To long for the assistance of grace is the beginning of grace."[293] But if we concede that even in vicious persons there is a certain longing for grace based on natural perceptions, once more there is a danger that the beginning of grace springs from free will; and that would be a

---

290. Augustine discusses both texts in *De gratia et libero arbitrio* 5.11 (PL 44 888).

291. Latin *gratiam.*

292. 1 John 4:7; Augustine *De gratia et libero arbitrio* 18.37 (PL 44 903–4).

293. *De correptione et gratia* 1.2 (PL 44 917).

quite abominable idea, if whatever free will can do is not poured forth by God as a gift.

But if in those gradations by which we gradually leave a vicious habit behind and approach justification someone wants to add particular grace, I consider this a pious opinion. But I do not consider it compatible with Christian tranquility to whip up melodramatic uproars over these tiny points. Maybe it would be better for everyone, according to Paul's saying, to have room, up to a point, to indulge in his own insights.[294] When he struggles against the Pelagians to protect grace, Augustine attributes so little to free will as to grant it something in name more than in fact. Then again, when he locks horns with those who said that infants were not damned by the sin contracted from our first parents, he says that infants who died without baptism must burn in eternal fire.[295] Later theologians tempered both opinions, attributing somewhat more to free will than he did, and distinguishing congruous merit from condign merit, acquired faith from infused faith, a perfect will from an imperfect one,[296] and likewise mitigating the condemnation of infants by distinguishing the pain of loss from pain of the senses.[297] And Jean Gerson[298] does not seem to despair entirely of the salvation of infants if parents of extraordinary piety earnestly appeal to the kindness of God.[299]

---

294. Rom. 14:5; "up to a point" (Latin *hactenus*) seems to mean "up to the point where the church promulgates an official pronouncement."

295. *Contra secundam Iuliani responsionem imperfectum opus* 2.117, 3.199 (PL 45 1191, 1333); *Contra Iulianum* 5.11 (PL 44 809).

296. Erasmus has in mind the late scholastic teaching about congruous merit.

297. Peter Lombard, *Sententiae* II dist. 33.5 (PL 192 730); Thomas Aquinas, *Scriptum super libros Sententiarum* II dist. 33 q 2 aa 1–2. The pain of loss is the deprivation of the joys of heaven; this is suffered by unbaptized infants in limbo. The pain of the senses is inflicted on sinners in hell.

298. Jean Gerson (1363–1429) was a leading scholastic theologian who became the Chancellor of the University of Paris. A moderate reformer and a renowned preacher, he wrote important works on the Great Schism and on mystical theology.

299. *Sermo de nativitate gloriosae Virginis Mariae consideratio* 2. Gerson's Latin may be translated: "Therefore pregnant women and also their husbands, on their own and through others, ought to diligently pour forth their prayers to God and to the guardian angels on behalf of the child in the womb. They ought to fly to the refuge of the other saints, both men and women, so that the unborn infant, if it should happen to die before reaching the grace of the waters of baptism, might mercifully be consecrated by the high priest, our Lord Jesus, with an

Now what theologians think too restrained in Augustine's opinion
about free will, Luther thinks excessive; he introduces the term "a
necessity"—which Augustine constantly refrained from using—and
he does not even grant free will the power to withdraw from grace,
a power Augustine does not deny to it.

anticipatory baptism of the Holy Spirit. For who knows whether God hears,
indeed who cannot devoutly hope that he will never scorn the prayers of the
humble who place their hope in him? But, short of a revelation, there is not, I
think, any certainty about it." See Jean Gerson, *Opera omnia* ed. Louis Ellies du
Pin, 5 vols. (Antwerp 1786) III 1350.

BIBLIOGRAPHY and ABBREVIATIONS

Abbreviations used in this work

Adages   Erasmus' *Adages, Collected Works of Erasmus* [CWE], vols. 31–36. Toronto: University of Toronto Press, 1982–2006.

Allen   *Opus epistolarum Des. Erasmi Roterodami.* Edited by P. S. Allen, H. M. Allen, and H. W. Garrod. 11 vols. and index. Oxford: Oxford University Press, 1906–1958.

ASD   *Opera omnia Desiderii Erasmi Roterodami.* Amsterdam, 1969–

CCSL   *Corpus christianorum, series Latina.* Turnhout, 1952–.

CSEL   *Corpus scriptum ecclesiasticorum Latinum.* Vienna, 1866–.

CWE   *Collected Works of Erasmus.* Toronto: University of Toronto Press, 1974–.

LB   Erasmus, *Opera omnia.* Edited by Jean Leclerc. 10 vols. Leiden, 1703–1706. Reprinted Hildesheim: Georg Olms, 1961–1962.

LW   *Luther's Works.* Edited by Jaroslav Pelikan, Helmut T. Lehmann, et al. 55 vols. Philadelphia: Fortress Press, 1958–1986.

PG   *Patrologiae cursus completus . . .series Graeca.* Edited by. J.-P. Migne. 162 vols. Paris, 1857–1912.

PL   *Patrologiae cursus completus . . . series Latina.* Edited by. J.-P Migne. 221 vols. Paris, 1844–1902.

WA   *Martin Luthers Werke, Kritische Gesamtausgabe.* Weimar, 1883–.

Bibliography

Augustijn, Cornelius. "Erasmus as Apologist: The *Hyperaspistes II,*" *Erasmus of Rotterdam Society Yearbook* 21 (2001): 1–13.

———. *Erasmus: His Life, Works, and Influence.* translated by J. C. Grayson. Toronto: University of Toronto Press, 1991.

Bejczy, István. *Erasmus and the Middle Ages.* Leiden: Brill, 2001.

Bentley, Jerry H. "Erasmus, Jean Leclerc, and the Principle of the Harder Reading." *Renaissance Quarterly* 31 (1978): 309–21.

Bietenholz, Peter B. and Thomas B. Deutscher, eds., *Contemporaries of Erasmus: a Biographical Register of the Renaissance and Reformation*. 3 vols. Toronto: University of Toronto Press, 1985–1987.

Brecht, Martin. *Martin Luther*. Translated by James Schaaf. 3 vols. Philadelphia: Fortress Press, 1985–1983.

Copenhaver, Brian P. "Valla Our Contemporary: Philosophy and Philology." *Journal of the History of Ideas* 66 (2005): 507–25.

Coppens, J. ed. *Scrinium Erasmianum*. 2 vols. Leiden: Brill, 1969.

Emser, Jerome. *A German Translation of* Hyperaspistes 1. Leipzig: M. Lotter, 1526.

Erasmus. "An Examination concerning the Faith." Edited by Craig R. Thompson. In CWE 39, *Colloquies*, 419-47.

———. *Compendium Vitae Erasmi*. In CWE 4, 404–6.

———. *Praise of Folly*. Translated by Clarence H. Miller. New Haven: Yale University Press, 2003.

Gleason, John B. *John Colet*. Berkeley: University of California Press, 1989.

Godin, André. *Erasme lecteur d'Origène*. Geneva: Droz, l982.

Gordon, Bruce. *The Swiss Revolution*. Manchester, UK: Manchester University Press, 2002.

Halkin, L. E. *Erasmus ex Erasmo: Érasme, éditeur de sa correspondence*. Aubel, Belgium: P. M. Gason, 1983.

Hendrix, Scott H. *Luther and the Papacy*. Philadelphia: Fortress Press, 1981.

Ijsewijn, Josef. "Erasmus ex Poeta Theologus." In Coppens, *Scrinum Erasmianum*, 2:375–89.

Janz, Denis, ed. *The Westminster Handbook to Martin Luther*. Louisville, KY: Westminster John Knox Press, 2010.

Kaminsky, Howard. *A History of the Hussite Revolution*. Berkeley: University of California Press, 1967.

Kolb, Robert. *Martin Luther: Confessor of the Faith*. Oxford: Oxford University Press, 2010.

Kroker, Greta Grace. *Erasmus in the Footsteps of Paul: A Pauline Theologian*. Toronto, 2011.

Luther, Martin. *Ausgewählte Werke*. Edited by H. H. Borcherdt and Georg Merz. Supplementary series, vol. 1 *Dass der frei Wille nichts sei*, translated by Bruno Jordahn, annotated by Hans Joachim Iwand and Bruno Jordahn. Munich: C. Kaiser, l954.

————— *The Bondage of the Will*. Edited and translated by Philip S. Watson. In LW 33.

Luthers Werke in Auswahl. Vol. 3 (Schriften von 1524 bis 1528). Edited by Otto Clemen, 5th (revised) edition. Berlin: de Bruyter, 1959.

MacCulloch, Diarmaid. *The Reformation*. New York: Viking, 2004.

McConica, James. "Erasmus and the Grammar of Consent." In J. Coppens, ed., *Scrinium Erasmianum*, 2:77–99. Leiden: Brill, 1969.

McSorley, Harry J. *Luther: Right or Wrong? An Ecumenical-Theological Study of Luther's Major Work, The Bondage of the Will*. New York: Newman Press, 1969.

Oakley, Francis. *The Conciliarist Tradition*. Oxford: Oxford University Press, 2003.

Oberman, Heiko A. *The Dawn of the Reformation*. Grand Rapids, MI: W. B. Eerdmans, 1992.

—————. *The Harvest of Medieval Theology*. Cambridge, MA: Harvard University Press, 1962.

—————. *Luther: Man between God and the Devil*. New Haven, CT: Yale University Press, 1989.

Otto, August. *Die Sprichwörter und sprichwörterlichen Redensarten der Römer*. Reprinted Hildesheim: Georg Olms, 1988.

Panaccio, Claude. *Ockham on Concepts*. Aldershot, UK: Ashgate, 2004.

Payne, John B., Albert Rabil Jr., and Warren S. Smith Jr. "The *Paraphrases* of Erasmus: Origin and Character." In CWE 42, xi–xix.

Rummel, Erika. *Erasmus and his Catholic Critics*. 2 vols. Nieukoop: De Graaf, 1989.

Roetzel, Calvin. *The Letters of Paul: Conversations in Context*. 4th ed. Louisville, KY: Westminster John Knox Press, 2009.

Scheel, Otto, tr. and ed. *Luthers Werke*, Ergänzungsband 2. Berlin: C. A. Schwetschke und Sohn, 1905, pp. 214–550.

Seidel-Menchi, Silvana. *Erasmus in Italia, 1520–1580*. Turin: Bollati Boringhieri, 1987.

Stadtwald, Kurt W. *Roman Popes and German Patriots: Antipapalism in the Politics of the German Humanist Movement*. Geneva: Droz, 1996.

Stevenson, Burton, ed. *Macmillan Book of Proverbs, Sayings, and Famous Phrases*. New York: Macmillan, 1948.

Stump, Eleanore. "Augustine on Free Will." In *The Cambridge Companion to Augustine*. Edited by Eleanor Stump and Norman Kretzman, 129–48. Cambridge, UK: Cambridge University Press, 2001.

Tracy, James. *Europe's Reformations, 1450–1650.* 2nd ed. Lanham, MD: Rowman & Littlefield, 2002.

———. *Erasmus of the Low Countries.* Berkeley: University of California Press, 1996.

———. "Erasmus and the Arians: Remarks on the *Consensus Ecclesiae.*" *Catholic Historical Review* 67 (1981): 1–10.

Trigg, Joseph. *Origen.* New York: Routledge, 1998.

Trinkaus, Charles. Introduction to CWE 76. Toronto: University of Toronto Press, 1999.

Valla's *De Libero Arbitrio Dialogus (A Dialogue on Free Will),* trans. Charles Trinkaus, in *The Renaissance Philosophy of Man,* ed. Ernst Cassirer, Paul Oscar Kristeller, and John Herman Randall (Chicago, 1948), 173–4.

Wander, Karl Friedrich Wilhelm. *Deutsches Sprichwörter-lexikon: ein Hausschatz für das deutsche Volk.* 5 vols. Leipzig, 1867-1880. Reprinted by Scientia Verlag: Aalen, 1963.

Watson. See Luther, *The Bondage of the Will.*

Wengert, Timothy J. *Human Freedom, Christian Righteousness: Philip Melanchthon's Exegetical Dispute with Erasmus of Rotterdam.* New York: Oxford University Press, 1998.

Wetzel, James, "Predestination, Pelagianism, and Foreknowledge." In *The Cambridge Companion to Augustine.* Edited by Eleanore Stump and Norman Kretzmann, 49–59. Cambridge, UK: Cambridge University Press, 2001.

INDEX

Abel, 43, 253

Abraham, 51, 105–7, 112, 279

Absolute power of God, 7n16, 294, 331

Achilles, 28, 120, 299, 304

Adam, x, 68, 107–8, 122, 211–12, 259, 288, 304, 320, 341–42

Aldine press, 12

Alexander of Hales, 2

Alexander the Great, 158

Ambrose, St., 1, 230, 240, 249–50, 254, 270, 285, 304, 317, 321, 338

Ananias, 125, 313

Andrew, St., 105

Antichrist, 81

Apollo, 174

Apostles' Creed, xvi, 156

Aquinas. *See* Thomas Aquinas.

Arians, xxiv n82, xxvi, 43, 54, 139, 160, 168, 201

Aristodes, 308

Aristotle, x, xi, 28n74, 47n40, 53, 123, 123, 133n15, 212n250, 307-8

Arnobius, 1

Asaph, 123

Athens, 267

Augsburg, xix

Augustine, St., xiv, xviii, xx, xxiii, xxvi–xxviii, 1, 8, 11n31, 12, 15n40, 21, 22n61, 23n63, 32, 36, 51, 61–62, 84n103, 95, 119, 136–37, 145, 148, 161, 164, 167, 170, 173, 176, 177–78, 190–1, 197–98, 200, 202, 204, 206, 208–11, 213, 220, 230, 240, 247–49, 251, 264–66, 270, 287, 291nn167–169, 296–97, 302,

316–19, 321n237, 322–23, 328–29, 332–34, 338, 340–43, 345–46

Baal, 35, 131

Baer, Ludwig, xxii n74

Balaam, 222

Baptism, 291, 294, 345n299

Basil, St., 1

Bede, Venerable, 240, 321nn237–38

Bernard of Clarvaux, St., xxvii, 36, 159, 198, 206, 317–19, 322n241

Biel, Gabriel, 320n234

Bolanus, 209

Boniface, Pope, 316

Boniface, Tribune and Count, 302

Brunfels, Otto, 135n22

Brutus, 307

Bugenhagen, Johann, xxii n71, 154, 163

Cacus, 176

Cain, 43, 69

Cajetan, Thomas, xix

Calvin, xxi n67

Cambrai, xi

Capito, Wolfgang Faber, 150

Carthage, 177

Capreolus, 2

Cato of Utica, 307–8

Cato (Dionysius), 40n23

charity, 20, 44–45, 141–42, 183, 274, 280, 326, 337

Charles V, Emperor, xxi–xxii

Charybdis, 29, 104

Chrysippus, 191

Chrysostom, John St., 1, 230, 240, 245, 264n114, 266, 270, 287–88, 295–96, 304

church (hidden or revealed), 32,
    41–44
Cicero, 44, 124, 133n14, 140, 307
circumcision, 264, 268, 278, 280
Colet, John, xi

Collège de Montagu, xi
condign. *See* meritum.
congruous. *See* meritum.
Constance, Council of, xx, 169n116,
    179
Cornelius, 213, 273, 276
Corycian caverns, 81, 149, 240
Counciliarism, xix-n60
Councils of the Church, xxiii, xxvi, 2,
    28, 32, 43, 56, 127, 134, 139,
    152, 156, 171
Ctesiphon, 340
Cyprian, St., 1, 170
Cyril, St., 1

David, 124, 146, 253, 265, 280, 305
Decalogue, 96, 263, 266
definition of free will, 6
demons, 26, 38, 40, 46, 53, 121,
    136, 170, 191, 305–6, 320n234
Demosthenes, 124, 149, 307
devils. *See* demons.
Diet of Worms, xxi
Dionysius, tyrant of Sicily, 27
Doctors of the Church, xxvi, 30–31,
    127, 137, 152, 160, 166, 171,
    185–86, 230, 252, 287, 314–15
Dominic, St., 4
Donatists, 170, 180-81
Durandus, 2

Echo, 211
Eck, Johann, xx
Emser, Jerome, 157n85, 175n136
Enoch, 253
Epicurus, xxv, 123n137, 136, 143,
    165, 307
Erfurt University, xvii
Esau, 43

Ethiopean, 272, 276
Eucharist, xx n65, 172, 183, 188,
    251

Faber, Johann, 41, 182
faith, 17, 20, 28, 44–45, 102, 142,
    149, 153, 155, 183, 199, 210,
    274, 280, 305, 326–27, 337
fathers of the church, xxiii, xxvii,
    33–34, 39–41, 50, 141, 169–
    70, 172–73, 264, 304
fetus, development of, 330–31
Fisher, John, St., 140, 313
flesh, 41, 45, 53, 92, 97, 109, 112,
    223, 263, 268, 281–82, 286,
    299, 301, 304, 326
Frederick the Wise, xvii, xx n62, xxi
Francis, St., 4
Furies, 337

Gabriel Biel, 2, 7
Gamaliel, 6
gentiles (Greeks), xxiv, xxvii, 35,
    87–91, 110–11, 125, 249, 251,
    258, 261–63, 266, 271–72,
    278, 283–84, 286, 288, 290,
    308–9, 311, 335, 337
Gerson, Jean, 345
Gideon, 67
Giles of Rome, 2 glory, 101–2, 122–
    24, 149, 273–74, 309
God's will, revealed (ordained) and
    secret (absolute), 80–82, 238–
    39, 294
grace, kinds of, 8n22, 198, 212, 237,
    247–48, 277–78, 311, 318,
    322–23, 326, 328, 331–33,
    335, 338–39, 343–44
Greeks. *See* gentiles.
Gregory, St., 2n3, 136, 321nn237–38

habit, 212, 222
Hebrew, 69, 87, 101–2, 224–25,
    236, 249, 255, 263, 274,
    285–86

Hector, 28
Henry VIII, King of England, xxii, 221
Herman, Nicolaus of Altdorf,
    157n85
Herod, 146, 272
Hilary, St., 1, 211, 319, 321n238
Homer, 218, 280
Horace, 28n63, 36n11, 136n26,
    209n243, 221
Hubert, St., 329
Hutten, Ulrich von, 143n5
Huss, Jan xx, 43, 52–53, 158,
    177–78
hyperbole, 28, 222, 224, 229, 257–
    58, 262, 298

incarnation, 149, 251, 295
indulgences, xviii, 126
Inquisition, 43
Irenaeus, 319
Ishmael, 43
Isaac, 43, 157

Jacob, 43, 157
Jerome, St., xiii, xxvi, 1, 41, 95–96,
    99n111, 137–38, 148, 161,
    163, 211, 224, 230, 240,
    253, 264–66, 270, 299, 304,
    321n238, 335, 340–41
Jerusalem, 254
Jethro, 126, 313
Jews, xxiv, xxvii, 38, 49, 54, 87–91,
    111–12, 136, 160, 199, 249,
    251–52, 258–60, 261, 263, 266,
    268, 272, 278–79, 283–86, 291,
    293, 295, 297–98, 302, 311
Job, 124, 233, 307
John Damascene, St., 1
John St., the Evangelist, 109, 111,
    117–18, 292–93
John the Baptist, 49, 113–14, 118,
    293
Jonas, Justus, 157, 182, 192n186
Joseph of Arimathea, 42
Judaea, 266

Judaism, xiv
Judas, 286
Julian (a Pelagian), 316, 323, 328
Jupiter, 265
justification (sanctification), xix–xx,
    20–21, 26, 29, 35, 48, 99–100,
    102, 104–7, 212–13, 237, 248,
    251, 259, 264, 268, 271–74,
    280, 311, 318, 322–23,
    329,331, 333–36, 338, 345
Judgment of God, 123
Juvenal, 145n55

Karlstadt, 11n32, 16n44, 46n37,
    183, 205, 207, 210, 233, 277

law (Old Testament), xxvi, 14, 48,
    70–71, 74–75, 77, 79–80,
    85, 87, 89, 91, 93, 95–101,
    104, 107, 110–11, 113, 144,
    146–47, 187, 193, 218, 222–23,
    225, 227, 234, 237, 245, 246,
    251–53, 258, 262–71, 273,
    278–79, 281, 283, 286, 289—90,
    298, 302, 311, 326, 335–37, 343
law (secular), 48, 145
Lawrence, St., 185
Lazarus, 236
Leipzig, xx
Leo X, Pope, xvi
Leviathan, 76, 225, 229, 233
lights of nature, grace, and glory,
    124–25, 149
Lombard, Peter, 133n17, 191,
    320n234, 342n286
Lord's Prayer, 305
Louvain University, xv
Lucian of Samosata, xxv, 57, 143,
    165,184–85
Luciferians, 173
Lycurgus, 21

Manichaeism, 2, 173, 177, 29, 181,
    295, 301, 303–4, 314, 316,
    321, 338

Martha, 236
Mary, the perpetual virginity of, 131,
    155–56, 185, 316
Melanchthon, Philip, xxii, 41n25,
    134–35, 141n44, 143n50,
    154, 163
Melchizedek, 253
meritum condignum (condign merit),
    8n20, 103–4, 114, 275–78,
    289, 345
meritum congruum (congruous
    merit), 8n20, 103–4, 114, 205,
    212, 275–78, 289, 324–26,
    338–39, 344–45
Messiah, 63, 147
Midianites, 67
Minerva, 265
Montanus, 166
More, Thomas, St., xv, xxvii
Moses, 12, 15, 47, 49, 63–64, 72, 74,
    83, 85, 97, 125, 144, 146, 245,
    252, 280, 313, 335–37

Nathaniel, 285
nature, grace, and glory, 309–10
natural influence, 9, 10n26
necessity, xxv, 2, 14–15, 16–20,
    18–20, 24, 58, 61, 107, 187,
    205, 263, 274, 281, 299
Nero, 337
New Testament, xiii, xxviii
Ninevites, 257
Nicodemus, 6, 114, 285, 289
Noah, 253
Nominalists, xvii

Octavius, 307
Oecolampadius, Johannes, 41n25,
    150, 154, 163, 167
ordained power of God, 7n16, 294
Origen, xii, xiii, xiv, 1, 110, 178, 282
original sin, 59n69, 108, 209,
    211-12, 215, 249–50, 255,
    264n114, 288, 301–2, 310,
    317, 320, 336, 345

Ovid, 38n18, 123n135, 132n12, 307

Pandora, 192
Papacy. See Popes.
Papists, 150
Pelagians, xv, xviii, xxiii, 7, 11,
    20–21, 29, 59, 67, 72, 104,
    114, 139, 194, 198, 204–5,
    207, 210, 234, 289, 301,
    316–17, 320–23, 345
Pelicanus, Conrad, 30n77
Peter, St., 162, 321
Pharaoh, 206, 251, 273, 319
Pharisees, 4, 52, 162, 225, 268, 272,
    282, 284, 290, 335
Philip, 272
Phocion, 308
Pierre d'Ailly, 7n17
Pilate, Pontius, 63, 156
Plato, xii, 1n2, 37, 132nn12–13
Pliny the Younger, 37n15, 123,
    159n92, 307
Plutarch, 33n4
Pomponius Mela, 81n97
Pontitianus, 197
Popes, xxvi, 2, 28, 32, 38, 43, 45–46,
    50, 64, 52, 56, 127, 134, 140,
    152, 156, 158, 171, 179, 187,
    204
Posilipo, tunnel of, 330
predestination, xxi
Proteus, 40, 59, 135, 165, 168, 176,
    208
Publilius Syrus, 325
purgatory, xix n57, 28, 126

Quintilian, 53, 84n104, 131n9,
    149n67

reason 62, 65–66, 70, 85, 92–93,
    111, 117, 120, 124, 199, 211,
    215, 292, 299–301, 306
Reformation, ix
Renaissance, ix

Sabbath, 266
Saducees, 51, 157
Satan, xxii, 28, 46, 53–55, 61, 68-
    69, 73–74, 93, 95, 109, 112,
    115–16, 120, 125–26, 159,
    166, 179–81, 188, 207, 222,
    254, 259, 298–99, 301, 304,
    310, 317, 332, 336, 342
scholastics, xxv, 41, 47–48, 61, 72,
    76, 91, 114, 130n8, 133, 143,
    150, 165, 195, 229, 243, 261,
    263, 278, 309, 319, 338, 340
Schwärmer, 46n37
Scotus, John Duns, Blessed, xi, xvii
    n51, xxiv, 2, 7, 29, 76, 205,
    210, 229
Scripture, Holy xxv–xxvi, 1, 3, 5, 14,
    16, 30-39, 45, 47–51, 55–57,
    64, 79, 86, 91, 116, 127–28,
    131, 133–34, 141–45, 147–52,
    154–55, 162, 166, 170, 216,
    219, 224, 231, 234–35, 238,
    242–43, 246, 254, 260, 272,
    276, 279, 281, 285–86, 291–
    92, 297–98, 306, 310, 316,
    321, 329, 336
Scylla, 29, 104
Semi-Pelagianism, 205n230
Seneca, 252, 343
Septuagint, 334n271
Simeon, St., 265
skepticism, xxiii, xxv, 45, 142–43, 165
Socrates, 308, 337
sophists. See scholastics.
Spalatin, George, xv
Spirit, Holy, xxii, xxiv–xxv, 3, 4,
    5, 6, 15, 17, 23–24, 32–37,
    34–37, 43, 45, 54, 68, 70, 83,
    97, 109, 112, 115, 119–20,
    125, 128–30, 136, 138–39,
    141, 147, 149, 164, 166–67,
    172, 187, 193, 196, 204, 212,
    233–34, 243, 251, 255, 261,
    263, 273–74, 281, 286, 291,
    296–99, 301, 303–4, 310, 314,
    320, 322, 327, 334
Staupitz, Johann, xvii
Stephen, 52
stoics, 36, 308–9, 329, 332, 334, 337
Syrtes, 173

Tarquin, 174
Terence, 194n195
Tertullian, 1, 20, 165–66
Theophylact, 1, 240, 245, 264n114,
    270
Thomas Aquinas, St., xvii n51, 2,
    11n31, 149n66, 172, 175n139,
    204, 209, 212n250, 215, 219,
    240, 321n237, 342n286
Timothy, 152, 317
Trinity, 285, 297
Turks, 38
Titus, 50, 152
Tyndale, William, xv

Valla, Lorenzo, ix, 2, 25n26, 32, 177
Vertumnus, 40, 135
Vestal Virgins, 41
Virgil, x, 32, 42n27, 111n123, 133,
    176n141, 194n192, 280
virginity, 137
Vitrier, Jean, xii
William of Ockham, 7
Wittenberg, xvii, xxii n71, 152
world, 112, 255, 284, 295
Worms, Edict of, xxi
Wyclif, John, xx, xxiii, xxvi, 2, 11n33,
    32, 61, 150, 169n116, 177–78,
    206, 315

Zwingli, Huldrych, xxi n67, xxvi,
    41n25, 150, 163